Jonathan Gawne

Spearheading D-Day

AMERICAN Special Units OF THE NORMANDY INVASION

Back in the United States, sailors at the Office of Naval Intelligence in Boston study the announcements of the landings in Normandy.
(Courtesy Niles Laughner)

Histoire & Collections

Spearheading D-Day
table of contents

Introduction

You may be asking yourself why the world needs another book on the invasion of Normandy. I often wondered that myself, but the more I read about D-Day the more I realized that a great many things have been left undocumented. Even worse, too many authors have assumed that erroneous information found in other books was true. Most of the existing books on D-Day deal with the overall plan for the landing and what actually happened. This is a book that tries to tell the story of what was planned from the soldiers' and sailors' points of view.

The seed for this book was planted in June 1969 when my father first took me to Utah Beach. He did not take part in the D-Day landings, but came ashore on Utah Beach on the 4th of July as a platoon leader in the 8th Infantry Division. I didn't know it at the time, but the school report I later wrote on D–Day was just a start in my quest to figure out what really happened.

Joe Geary of the 6th Naval Beach Battalion shamed me into writing this book. In 1992 the U.S. Navy commissioned a missile ship named the *U.S.S. Normandy*. Veterans of Army units that landed on the beaches were honored guests at the event. By this time I thought I knew just about all there was to know about the invasion: Joe showed me how wrong I was. The Navy had ignored their own men from the Beach Battalions at the ceremony. Joe Geary heard about the christening and came anyway. He stood off to the side holding a hand lettered sign mentioning his unit. He asked me, "*Do you know what the Beach Battalions did on D-Day ?* " My response was "*No, but I'll find out.*"

What followed was a hunt for information no one else had looked for. It resulted in an article about the Beach Battalions that was published in *Militaria Magazine*. Other authors have since copied that information for their own books, but at least the "fighting sons of beaches" now have a toe hold in history. Sadly, Joe Geary died a few days after receiving the first copy of the article. He was never able to tell me if I did a good job or not, but somehow I bet he's at least pleased his unit is no longer unknown.

I then continued my hunt for obscure units or facts on the landings. There are too many to put in just one book. The list of units that played a part in Overlord is endless. They range from Navy weather ships that provided the reports used to determine when D-Day should be, to the men who manned the radios sending false messages as part of Operation Fortitude. The invasion was a massive team effort and to those that I do not mention I beg forgiveness and understanding. But I do hope you will learn that it was not just the 1st, 4th, and 29th Divisions storming ashore by themselves.

You will note that this book does not include airborne units. There are already entire volumes written about the men who came in by parachute and glider. They are the focus of intense study and for the most part their tale has been told. The same holds true for the myriad "special forces:" the OSS, SOE, and SAS. They have never lacked for fame and also have their own books. I have chosen to deal primarily with the seaborne assault and the units that took part in it.

This book can only be considered an introduction to the subject. An entire volume could be written on each unit and the story would still not come close to being complete. My editor and I have done our best in trimming the massive amount of material I

This cartoon was used for the title page on the Navy Communications Annex for Overlord. The stack of paperwork the poor sailor carries is an understatement to the total amount that was actually generated.

have accumulated. In no way do we consider this the final word on the invasion. I have tried to provide a framework for others to build upon, and hope that future historians will be able to examine these units in greater detail.

I have based this book on the original orders for Overlord, after-action reports, unit histories, and interviews with veterans. I have not always taken the veterans at face value: I have always attempted to double check and confirm their facts with multiple sources. I too would have a hard time remembering something if I went through a war, then waited 50 years before someone asked "*What did you paint on your helmet?*" I am amazed the veterans proved as good sources as they did.

The Orders and Annexes for Overlord are massive. There are also a number of revisions and corrections that were issued as D–Day grew closer. This paperwork is scattered through a number of different files, so

great care must be taken to ensure that the records being used are the last ones issued before 6 June. A number of things were changed in the weeks beforehand, and previous researchers have been led astray by relying on an earlier document. The Omaha Beach landing diagram shown in most books is based on the 11 May 1944 orders. This was slightly changed in the 28 May 1944 orders, but most researchers seem to have missed that. I can only assume that a few minor points were altered on a unit basis too late to be recorded on paper.

I tried to keep my use of secondary sources to a minimum, as I quickly learned that many of them repeat the errors of their predecessors. Some myths die hard. To anyone else contemplating a book on Normandy, or any other battle for that matter, you must rely primarily on original source material.

To simplify matters in writing about different military organizations I have adopted the system of using the company letter and next higher numbered organization, or battalion number and organization. A/116 stands for Company A, 116th Regiment. 3/16 would indicate the 3rd Battalion of the 16th Regiment. B/743 would mean Company B, 743rd Tank Bn. This shorthand is not correct for the time period, but helps to clarify the text.

Unless otherwise indicated, photographs are from the Army, Navy, Marine Corps, and Coast Guard collections stored at the National Archives. Some of the color shots are still frames taken from U.S. Coast Guard movies made during the invasion. These films are also to be found in the National Archives.

This book opened up a number of questions that I hope will someday be answered. The landings at Utah Beach have never been properly documented and there seems to be some controversy as to what actually happened. The same holds true for the reorganization of the naval shore organization with the arrival of the NOIC. The red/purple smoke question is quite deserving of further study in itself. The actual power of the storm of 20 June in relation with other storms on the Normandy coast needs further investigation.

More information continues to crop up. Just as this book was due at the printer's I was able to confirm that medics in the 29th Division were actually ordered not to paint red crosses on their helmets. The origin of this order is thought to be the Division Commander, but I have not yet been able to prove this.

No matter how hard one tries to be complete, the story continues to grow. I hope that future D-Day historians will attempt to focus on new areas of study, because there is still an enormous amount of information that has not yet found its way into print.

Jonathan Gawne

Chapter 1. Before the Storm

The Assault
Training Center

"The Mission of this school is to prepare you for an assault on the French Coast"

THE development of the techniques and units used in the Normandy landings can be traced back to various military bases in the United States. Little Creek, Virginia trained Navy crews in handling small boats; Camp Edwards on Cape Cod was home to the Army Amphibious Forces; and Fort Pierce, Florida was the training ground for many special amphibious units.

Troops were given basic instruction in amphibious warfare while in the United States, but it was expected that more detailed training was to be provided overseas in the theater of operation. An Invasion Training Center was organized in the Mediterranean, but not everything that worked in those warm quiet waters would work on the stormy coast of Normandy. The Army needed a place somewhere in England to prepare for the invasion of France.

The job of setting up the Assault Training Center was given to Lt. Col. Paul Thompson. Thompson

(Computer graphics by Morgan Gillard. © Histoire & Collections 1998)

THE ASSAULT TRAINING CENTER

- DUKW crews training area
- Regimental landing exercise
- Impact range
- LCVP boarding point
- Billeting aera
- Individual training and demolition experiments

was an engineer officer who had graduated from West Point in 1929. From 1937 to 1939 Thompson had been assigned as assistant military attaché in Berlin. This gave him ample time to study the tactics and operations of German military engineers and their fortifications. He wrote a series of landmark studies on German engineering tactics used in the invasions of Poland and France. His writings, later collected and published in the book *Engineers in Battle*, were instrumental in helping the American military prepare for war with Germany.

In early 1943 Thompson was sent to England and given the task of organizing the Assault Training Center. The ATC was to have two main jobs: to test and develop methods of landing in France, and to train up to and including regimental sized units in those methods. This American ATC would be similar to the British amphibious school at Inveraray. Certain tactics and information were shared between the two schools, but there were some differences in how the two nations planned to operate.

Thompson chose the British Commando facility at Woolacombe Beach in Devon as the site for his ATC. In June 1943 he set up his headquarters in the Woolacombe Beach Hotel and started constructing the facilities he would need. The nearby harbors of Appledore and Instow were used by the naval forces supporting the ATC. The 112th Engineer Bn. set to work clearing British mines that had been laid on the beaches in the 1940 invasion scare. Then the engineers set about building roads, troop quarters, and the infrastructure needed to run a military base. Although Thompson had requested that the civilian population be moved from the area, his request was

Above.

Officers observe an attempt to land troops at night. These were not as successful as daylight landings, and ATC doctrine focused on landing at first light to provide a full day for the men to capture the beach and set up defenses against a counter-attack. The Dodge weapons carrier with the loudspeaker used to direct the landing has the bumper markings: "ASLT TRG CTR."

Right.

DUKWs of the 453rd Amphibious truck company prepare for an exercise at Woolacombe Beach in October 1943. The men standing by the "Beach Office" are a mixture of soldiers and sailors; both Army and Navy uniforms were a common sight at the ATC. The rope bumpers on the DUKWs cushioned the shock when pulling up alongside a ship. The wooden triangular markers were used to steer the DUKWs in to the proper landing zone.

refused. A few shells did go astray during training maneuvers, but it had been decided that the local population did not pose a hindrance to ATC training efforts.

The ATC would eventually require a support staff of 96 officers and 1,935 men. The assault school at the ATC would require an additional 125 officers and 2,600 enlisted men for instructors and demonstration troops. Many of the men used for demonstration purposes came from the 156th Infantry Regiment. This unit had been an element of the Louisiana National Guard before the war. Due to the French background of Louisiana, most of the men from the 156th spoke French. Later on the men from the 156th would be chosen for their linguistic ability to help fight the black marketeers operating around Paris.

Right.
Getting vehicles and equipment to the shoreline was not always enough. These men from an antitank company have gotten their WC-63 and 57mm antitank gun stuck in the sand at Woolacombe Beach. The ATC was also concerned with different ways to get vehicles across the beach once they had landed. It was considered vital that traffic flow quickly across the invasion beach, to prevent any congestion.

This 2nd lieutenant has been observing the progress of the construction of the Assault Training Center. He wears the standard wool uniform underneath his M1941 field jacket. His brown service shoes are well polished, but his M-1938 canvas leggings have started to fade from repeated immersion in the salt water. He wears a khaki trench coat as protection from the offshore winds. His garrison cap is the dark chocolate brown color worn only by officers. On his cap is the gold and black piping worn by all Army officers regardless of their branch of service. The metal insignia indicating his branch is on his left collar; not visible in this photo. He carries standard M3 6x30 binoculars in the M17 brown leather issue case.
(Reconstruction)

Above.
The ATC collected information from similar institutions such as the Invasion Training Center in the Mediterranean. Here men of the ITC test whether a 250 pound bomb will detonate German mines buried in the sand nearby. What they found was that the closer mines would detonate, but those further away would become unstable with the explosion and pose a great hazard to men attempting to disarm them later on.

Many of the U.S. Navy sailors manning the ATC landing craft were billeted in the *U.S.S. President Warfield*. This ship had been a passenger ferry operating between Baltimore and Norfolk before the war. It had been refitted and sent to England early in 1942. The *Warfield* was moored in the Taw River where it quartered 60 officers and 700 men. When the ATC closed, the ship would be used as a command and control ship off the Normandy coast. After the war the *Warfield* would be refurbished one last time to carry Jewish refugees to the emerging state of Israel.

The entire region around Woolacombe Beach was used to some extent for the ATC. In practice landings the troops would board their landing craft at the southern end of Saunton Sands from a promitory called Crow Point. Army DUKWs would sometimes be used to tow the landing craft out to sea. Most of the demolition experiments and individual training were conducted on Saunton Sands. The rocky area at Baggy Point was used to train men on landing in rough terrain. Croyde Bay was generally used for the training of DUKW crews. The beaches on Woolacombe Sands were used for the larger scale regimental landing exercises. Morte Point was used as the impact range for artillery and air-to-ground fire. Most of the visiting troops would stay in tent cities placed inland, with the majority in tents in the billeting area just behind Woolacombe.

The American engineers constructed dummy landing craft on shore to teach men how to embark and disembark from the various models. These dummy craft proved useful in working out how to fit the most men and equipment into the small craft. Also constructed were "assault training lanes" where troops could land and work their way inland through

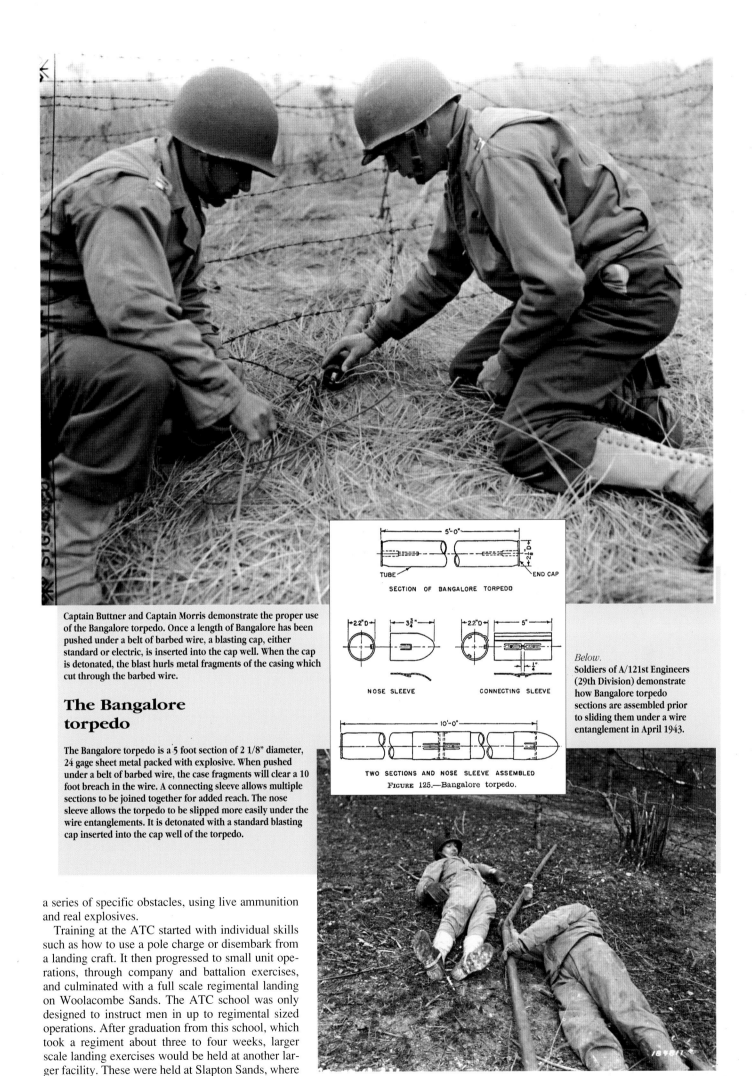

Captain Buttner and Captain Morris demonstrate the proper use of the Bangalore torpedo. Once a length of Bangalore has been pushed under a belt of barbed wire, a blasting cap, either standard or electric, is inserted into the cap well. When the cap is detonated, the blast hurls metal fragments of the casing which cut through the barbed wire.

The Bangalore torpedo

The Bangalore torpedo is a 5 foot section of 2 1/8" diameter, 24 gage sheet metal packed with explosive. When pushed under a belt of barbed wire, the case fragments will clear a 10 foot breach in the wire. A connecting sleeve allows multiple sections to be joined together for added reach. The nose sleeve allows the torpedo to be slipped more easily under the wire entanglements. It is detonated with a standard blasting cap inserted into the cap well of the torpedo.

Below.
Soldiers of A/121st Engineers (29th Division) demonstrate how Bangalore torpedo sections are assembled prior to sliding them under a wire entanglement in April 1943.

SECTION OF BANGALORE TORPEDO

NOSE SLEEVE   CONNECTING SLEEVE

TWO SECTIONS AND NOSE SLEEVE ASSEMBLED
FIGURE 125.—Bangalore torpedo.

a series of specific obstacles, using live ammunition and real explosives.

Training at the ATC started with individual skills such as how to use a pole charge or disembark from a landing craft. It then progressed to small unit operations, through company and battalion exercises, and culminated with a full scale regimental landing on Woolacombe Sands. The ATC school was only designed to instruct men in up to regimental sized operations. After graduation from this school, which took a regiment about three to four weeks, larger scale landing exercises would be held at another larger facility. These were held at Slapton Sands, where

the local population had been evacuated to allow the military to fire live ammunition and not have to worry about damaging civilian property.

The larger exercises held at Slapton Sands helped to improve the plans for D-Day. The most notable incident at Slapton took place during Operation Tiger. On the night of 27 April 1944, an LST convoy heading for a practice landing at Slapton Sands was attacked by German E-boats. Due to poor communication there was no armed escort for the landing craft and two LSTs were sunk and a third badly damaged.

Above.
Colonel Paul Thompson is shown here on an inspection of the Assault Training Center with Lt. General Jacob Devers in October 1943. Colonel Thompson is in the back seat and has an unusually large colonel's eagle painted on his helmet. The following jeep has bumper markings to the 156th infantry regiment - a unit that provided many of the ATC school troops.

Below.
This assault boat team is probably waiting to board a landing craft for a trial landing at the ATC. Visible in the photo are men carrying pole charges and Bangalore torpedoes. The tripod of an M1919A4 light machine gun is being carried by one man, while others around him have boxes of machine gun ammunition. This boat team must be one that substituted the light machine gun for a BAR and bazooka team.

General Charles Gerhardt (Commander of the 29th Infantry Division) discusses an amphibious exercise with General Omar Bradley, commander of the 1st Army. Gerhardt insisted his men should always wear their chin straps fastened just as he does in this photo. General Huebner, commander of the 1st Infantry Division, looks on from behind.

197 sailors and 441 soldiers (mainly from the 1st Engineer Special Brigade) were killed.

Many years later the popular press would discover the Operation Tiger disaster, however it has always been mentioned in official reports and was only kept secret during the war years. The Tiger disaster convinced the Allies they had to send their bombers to strike the German E-boat pens in France. Enough damage was done to the E-boat squadrons to severely cripple the E-boat threat to the D-Day convoys.

Experimentation

The primary task of the ATC was to develop and design the means of successfully landing in Normandy. The "Special Doctrine Board" was set up at the ATC to work out the best way of landing in France. Lessons learned in other theaters of operation were studied, experimental equipment was examined, and different techniques tested. Although information from the Pacific was provided to the ATC, the lessons learned during the small island invasions were not always thought applicable to a major invasion of France. Intelligence sources kept the ATC staff informed of the improvements spotted in Hitler's "Atlantic Wall." Any new fortification or obstacle photographed was examined in detail to find the best way of overcoming it during the invasion.

Information on the Atlantic Wall was gathered in many different ways. Small groups from the British Combined Operations Pilotage Parties (COPP) landed on French beaches at night to gather sand samples and inspect fortifications and obstacles. Aerial photographs were meticulously inspected for any new fortification or obstacle. One of the more interesting means of obtaining information was to parachute a basket of homing pigeons onto the farms near the beaches. French farmers would find the baskets when they went out to work in the morning. Inside they would find instructions and supplies for caring for the pigeons, how to secure a message to the pigeon's leg, and a list of questions the Allies wanted answers to. These ranged from what new constructions were going on in the area, to how was

Top left.

Training at Woolacombe Beach included the use of the 12 pound pole charge as seen here. The head of the charge swivelled to allow it to be placed flush against a vertical surface. Twin lines of primacord ran down the 8 foot pole to two M1 fuse igniters.

Left.

The pole charge is a 12 pound pack charge fixed to the end of an 8 foot pole. It is designed specifically to be shoved into a pillbox opening. Like the pack charge, it was constructed by the individual demo teams on a unit level. There were two igniters at the base of the pole, leading to a short fuze. The blasting caps were near the bottom of the pole and two lines of primacord (an explosive filled cord) ran up to the main explosive. The twin igniter assemblies were to prevent misfires.
(Computer graphics by C. Camilotte, © Histoire & Collections 1998)

Above.
September 1943, this soldier is running through a barbed wire entanglement with a pole charge during a demolition exercise. Note the white engineer tape on the ground marking a safe lane through a minefield.

Top right and opposite.
The 8 foot pole on a pole charge could be used to shove the explosive into the opening of a pillbox. It was designed to swivel so that the charge could be propped up flat against a vertical surface. These two photos illustrate the different force the charge had when placed both flat, and at an angle, to a concrete wall.

Below.
The M1 pull fuze lighter used on the primacord lines of the pole charge.

DEMOLITION CHARGES
The pole charge

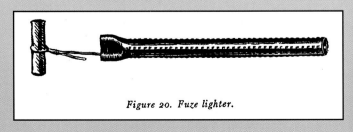

Figure 20. Fuze lighter.

Above and right.
The M1 flamethrower used two different tanks of pressurized gas which were filled from larger tanks. One tank, of compressed nitrogen (above), was carried on the back of the flamethrower and provided the thrust to shoot the fuel approximately 20-40 yards. A second smaller tank of hydrogen (right) was attached to the firing wand. The hydrogen was used for the small flame in the firing wand that ignited the fuel.

Inset.
Detail of the flamethrower firing wand gas burner assembly.

the morale of the local German troops.

Lt. Col. Thompson commanded the ATC from 2 April 1943 until early March 1944. For the first month he and his staff studied all available information on the French coastline to determine what kind of defenses they would be going up against. They decided that the Germans would use no more than one platoon per 2,000 to 2,500 yards of beach. The Germans would therefore have to use a number of machine guns, emplaced in fortifications, to compensate for their weak numbers. Everything the ATC tried was based on the assumption of a small number of defenders with multiple automatic weapons in strong positions.

ATC experiments tried different ways to land tanks and vehicles, different organizations of the landing teams, different types of equipment and explosives, and different timetables for landing units. Anything that could give the Allies the edge in bringing the American Army safely ashore and keeping it there was tested, evaluated, and tested again.

To provide covering fire during the initial landing

(Continued on page 18)

This view of a flamethrower team practicing at the Assault Training Center shows how the assistant operator is needed to open the valve at the rear of the weapon. In the landing, the assistant would carry the operator's carbine, his own rifle, and a 5 gallon jerrycan of thickened fuel as a refill.

Below.
The M1A1 flamethrower was the model used by the assault troops at Normandy. Thickened gasoline was carried in the two main tanks. Pressure from a tank of nitrogen forced the fuel through the firing wand. In this wand a spark lit a small flame of hydrogen gas. As the fuel was propelled out of the firing wand it caught fire. Total firing time was less than 10 seconds before the flamethrower needed to be refilled.

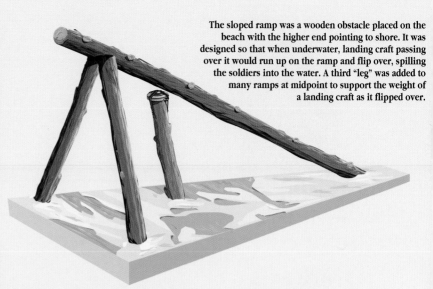

The sloped ramp was a wooden obstacle placed on the beach with the higher end pointing to shore. It was designed so that when underwater, landing craft passing over it would run up on the ramp and flip over, spilling the soldiers into the water. A third "leg" was added to many ramps at midpoint to support the weight of a landing craft as it flipped over.

The engineers based at the Assault Training Center were kept in constant use building and repairing beach obstacles and other training structures. Often they would construct an obstacle on one day, see it blown up later on, and return to build it again the next day. This soldier, from an Engineer General Service Regiment based nearby, has been brought in to provide additional manpower for the construction projects. He wears a warm uniform to protect himself from the cold offshore breezes. A heavy mackinaw and scarf are worn over the standard wool shirt and trousers. Rubber overshoes protect his boots and leggings when working near the sea. The constant use of explosives required the helmet liner to be worn as protection against flying debris.
(Reconstruction)

Below.
These mock-ups of the element "C" obstacle were made of wood due to the scarcity of metal in England. Steel models were constructed to determine the exact explosive charges needed to destroy them, but the men did their initial practice on wooden models. At right can be seen a few steel pyramid obstacles.

German

The hedgehog was composed of three metal beams welded together. This obstacle could rip a hole in the side or bottom of a landing craft, but was also developed to block landing craft and stop them in the killing zone of the German beach defenses. Many of the hedgehogs were held firm in concrete footings so they could not be easily pushed aside. After the invasion these steel beams were scavenged by the Americans and used to construct hedgerow cutting devices on the front of tanks.

Above.
 Models and other training aids were used to develop amphibious doctrine and teach it to the students attending the school. This model shows placement of beach obstacles, fortifications, and a possible plan for the landing craft.

each Obstacles

actual placement of obstacles, see on pages 136-137)

Angled stakes, made of either wood or concrete, were placed pointing out to sea. They would punch a hole into the hull of any boat running into them. Roughly every third stake had a land mine secured to the top. Due to a shortage of waterproofed mines, the Germans were forced to use regular land mines, which deteriorated swiftly in the harsh salt water environment.

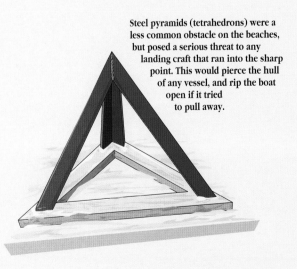

Steel pyramids (tetrahedrons) were a less common obstacle on the beaches, but posed a serious threat to any landing craft that ran into the sharp point. This would pierce the hull of any vessel, and rip the boat open if it tried to pull away.

Previous page, bottom.
The Element "C" was sometimes known as a Belgian gate. This was a large metal structure placed in the outer band of obstacles. The three vertical prongs were designed to rip the bottom out of larger landing craft. This obstacle was designed to be heavy so that it could resist the action of the tide, as well as not be pushed aside by a larger landing craft such as an LST or LCI. Element "C"s were also found on shore used as temporary roadblocks.

(Computer drawings by Christophe Camilotte after the author's documentation, © Histoire & Collections 1998)

Right.
This ATC training aid is a mock-up of the side of a transport ship. The troops are climbing up the rear of it, but when they get to the top they will climb down a cargo net (just visible at top) to practice disembarking from a ship. This was no easy task when carrying a full load of equipment.

operations 105mm howitzers were chained to the deck of an LCT. As the landing craft moved to the shore, one man called out the slowly decreasing range to the artillery crew. However, trials showed that M-7 self-propelled howitzers had slightly better accuracy in this manner of firing, and an additional advantage of being able to drive right off the landing craft into action.

One of the biggest questions revolved around the use of smoke screens during the landings. After extensive trials the ATC concluded that smoke screens caused as much confusion to the assaulting troops as to the defenders. Smoke screens in

One of the lessons learned from the North African landings in 1942 was that sand jammed weapons carried ashore through the surf. To protect the guns in future landings, the Army developed clear plastic bags, in various sizes, made from a material called Pliofilm. At some point in the middle of 1944 these bags were made in a dark green color, although there is no evidence that any of the dark green bags were used in Normandy.

Normandy would be limited to protecting ships at sea from the German shore batteries and to hide the beach in case of German air raids. The prohibition of smoke screens would become a curious footnote for the Omaha landings. When rockets set fire to the

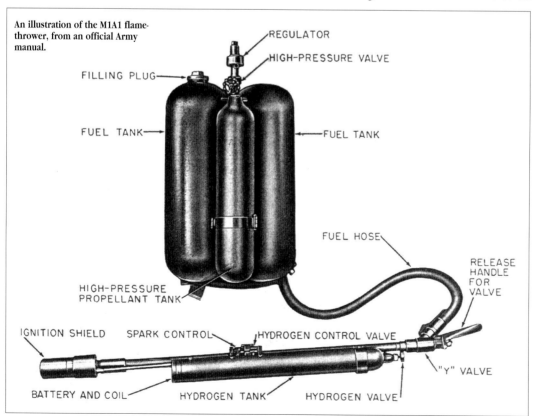

An illustration of the M1A1 flame-thrower, from an official Army manual.

REGULATOR
HIGH-PRESSURE VALVE
FILLING PLUG
FUEL TANK
FUEL TANK
HIGH-PRESSURE PROPELLANT TANK
FUEL HOSE
RELEASE HANDLE FOR VALVE
IGNITION SHIELD
SPARK CONTROL
HYDROGEN CONTROL VALVE
"Y" VALVE
BATTERY AND COIL
HYDROGEN TANK
HYDROGEN VALVE

The *U.S.S. President Warfield*

Many of the sailors manning the landing craft at the ATC were housed in the *U.S.S. President Warfield*. The *Warfield*, shown here with some of the ATC landing craft moored at right, had a fascinating history. Originally a vehicle and passenger ferry in Chesapeake Bay, she was sold to the British in 1942. It was later claimed that she was part of a convoy to England that served as a diversion from the Allied ships heading to invade North Africa in Operation "Torch." However, there is no evidence to back this claim up and it appears to have been created by an overenthusiastic Navy Public Relations Officer.

When the imminent Normandy invasion finally made the ATC redundant, the *Warfield* was transferred back to the U.S. Navy on 20 May 1944. After refitting she was sent to the coast of Normandy where she operated as a control ship for the traffic headed to, and from, France. The *Warfield* was anchored alongside the British ship *Centurion* that served as one of the breakwater ships in the artificial harbor. The core of her crew was made up from men from the *U.S.S. Milwaukee*, and the rest was built up with men from craft lost during D-Day. While anchored off Normandy she provided a place for a few lucky men out of combat to take a break in clean sheets. As one of the few Navy ships that let enlisted men sleep in staterooms with bathtubs, the *Warfield* was nicknamed the "Statler" after the famous hotel chain.

On 12 November 1944 the Normandy beaches closed down and the *Warfield* once again left for refitting in England. Starting in February 1945 she made roughly 15 trips up the Seine River bringing thousands of soldiers inland from the port of Le Havre. Carrying an average of 800 men per trip, she brought troops upriver to the forward staging area at Duclair and the cigarette camps. In July 1945 the *Warfield* was sent back to the United States where she was decommissioned on 13 Sept 1945 and put into mothballs. Later, she was purchased by a Jewish group who claimed they were going to use it as a river boat in China. Under great secrecy, the *Warfield* sailed back to Europe, picked up a load of 4,550 Jewish refugees and attempted to bring them to a new home in Palestine. The Jewish crew then renamed the *Warfield* the *Exodus 1947*. The British Navy attempted to stop the *Warfield,* and at one point a British destroyer rammed her. The treatment of the *Warfield* is considered one of the causes of the insurrection that finally drove the British out of Palestine and allowed the Jewish State of Israel to be formed. It had been planned to make the *Warfield* a floating museum of the 1947 Exodus, but in 1952 the ship caught fire and sank near Haifa. Remains of her hull are still there, and in honor of the 50th anniversary of the Jewish Exodus Israel issued a stamp commemorating this historic ship.

grass on the bluffs behind the beach, it produced an unplanned for smoke screen that allowed many troops in the area to get ashore unharmed.

The Boat Team

There had been many ideas for the best way to organize the infantry for an amphibious landing. Some favored creating special assault divisions, highly trained and organized for just this function. After much study it was decided that the best method would be to reorganize only one of the three regiments in an infantry division for the assault.

Right.
One of the failed experiments performed at the ATC was the construction of piers out of sandbags. The sandbag piers proved useless when the tides washed them away. The development of the artificial Mulberry harbors made them unnecessary.

Left.
The two bazooka teams of the assault boat team cover the advance of the wire cutter section as they scale the dunes. At Woolacombe it was found that the bazooka was not only a good antitank weapon, but extremely useful in knocking out bunkers. Each bazooka team carried 20 rounds total in the landing.

Below.
The bazooka, invented in 1942, essentially put the shaped charge warhead of an antitank rifle grenade onto a rocket. The name "Bazooka" came from a strangely shaped musical instrument developed by the American comedian Bob Burns. Later in the war a second model which broke down into two shorter pieces was adopted, but on D-Day this M1A1 model was what the troops carried ashore.

Bottom.
This bazooka range gave soldiers practice firing rockets into small pillbox openings. The left side of the target has been cut back in preparation for a new casting of concrete. By the time the new left side has hardened, the right side will need to be replaced.

Once ashore, this assault regiment would change back into standard infantry regiment configuration as soon as possible.

One of the concerns was that landing craft in an invasion might become scattered or sunk during the operation. Therefore, it was important that each landing craft should carry a mixture of men and equipment to provide each team with the tools it needed to breach the German fortifications. Thus the idea of an Infantry Assault Team, also referred to as an Assault Boat Team, was born.

In September 1943 trials on the best composition for the boat team started. The primary factor in the organization of the boat team was the capacity of the landing craft. The American LCVP generally carried 30 fully equipped men, so the boat teams were set at a maximum of 30 men. The three standard rifle companies (6 officers, 198 enlisted men) in an infantry battalion were reorganized into six boat teams of 30 men each. The heavy weapons company of the battalion was reorganized into 5 support boat teams and one command support boat team. The exact composition of the boat teams changed frequently as the ATC experimented and perfected the best possible mix of men and weapons. ATC developments were

DEMOLITION CHARGES
The pack charge

The pack charge is a 16 pound explosive device composed of 32 half pound blocks of TNT. The charge is detonated with an M1 pull igniter. At the ATC, assault demolition men were trained to construct their own pack and pole charges; these items were not issued pre-made. Due to the yellow label of the TNT blocks, it was recommended that the charge be camouflaged by carrying it in a burlap bag (sand bag). Photographs show men at the ATC with smaller 10-12 pound pack charges, but the last pre-invasion document regarding these charges suggested the use of 12 pound pole and 16 pound pack charges.

Below.
This soldier has placed a 10 pound charge of TNT on a concrete obstacle to test the damage the explosive will do. He is inserting an electrically fired detonator cap into one of the TNT blocks. This charge is basically the same as the pack charge used by the assault troops, but without a carry handle.

Inset.
A 1/2 pound block of TNT as used in assault demolition charges.

Computer graphics by C. Camilotte, © Histoire & Collections 1998)

always put forth as suggestions rather than a definitive set of instructions. It was always left up to the unit commander to decide what was best for his men. This led to a number of minor differences in the composition and tactics of the assault regiments.

The ATC planners decided that the best weapon for dealing with pillboxes was the high velocity gun of a Sherman tank. The tank gun could fire at the opening of a pillbox while the assault team made its way close enough to use the flamethrowers and demolition charges. Ideally each assault team should have landed with its own tank as fire support, but heavy armored vehicles made the smaller landing

Below.

Four 105mm howitzers are chained to the deck of this LCT to provide supporting fire during a landing. Once the LCT had landed, it was quite an effort to unchain the guns, then get them behind the trucks to be towed off onto the beach. In the D-Day landing self-propelled M-7 Priests were used in this role instead of towed howitzers.

craft unstable. The ATC staff found so many problems with using tanks in small landing craft that they preferred the main assault force to be a heavily armed infantry team. The British could not understand why the Americans refused the offer of their special armored vehicles for the invasion. Given the experiences of the ATC, and the terrain behind the American beaches (high bluffs behind Omaha and flooded ground behind Utah), it was probably for the best that the Americans chose to go with a concept they knew would work.

Another of the organizations explored by the ATC was at the battalion level. It was assumed that an

Above.
Troops from the 29th Division, including some of the Military Police Platoon, move from an LST onto a Rhino Ferry during an exercise at Slapton Sands. The ATC was only large enough for landings up to regimental size. Divisional scale assaults were conducted further south at the Slapton training area.
The bumper markings of the jeep on the left appear to be from the 165th Signal Photo Company. It was not uncommon for photographers to retouch their photos with the bumper markings of their own unit so that they would be assured credit for the shot.

invasion would be performed by a Regimental Combat Team (RCT). This was an infantry regiment that was rounded out into a combined arms team with various attached units. Each RCT would have its own armor, artillery, engineer, and medical support reporting directly to the regimental commander.

Each RCT was broken down into three Battalion Landing Teams (BLT). Each BLT was also a self-contained unit with all the elements needed for a successful attack. The plans called for one BLT to land per beach sector. A beach sector was a stretch of beach roughly 2,000 yards wide, which was broken down into subsectors known by a color (i.e. Easy Red beach and Easy Green beach).

The 116th Infantry Regiment went through the first course at the ATC in September 1943. By the following March there had been enough changes in the program that the 116th returned then for a refresher course. Infantry regiments from the 1st, 4th, 28th and 29th Divisions were trained at the ATC. In the 1st Division only the 16th Infantry Regiment went through ATC training. It was thought that the other two follow-up regiments (18th and 26th) did not need the special training after their combat experience in Africa and Italy.

Many other types of units received amphibious training as well. 15 Antiaircraft Bns, the 2nd and 5th Ranger Bns, and elements of the Engineer Special Brigades. A selection of 2,000 men from every part of the 101st Airborne Division were given the basics in amphibious operations. In the event that the division had to make a landing, it was hoped that having

(Continued on page 32)

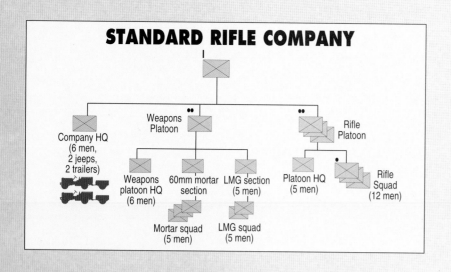

STANDARD RIFLE COMPANY

Company HQ
(6 men,
2 jeeps,
2 trailers)

Weapons
Platoon

Weapons
platoon HQ
(6 men)

60mm mortar
section

LMG section
(5 men)

Mortar squad
(5 men)

LMG squad
(5 men)

Rifle
Platoon

Platoon HQ
(5 men)

Rifle
Squad
(12 men)

RIFLE SQUAD

Squad leader (Staff Sergeant)

Assistant squad leader (Sergeant)

BAR TEAM

BAR Gunner

Assistant Gunner

8 Riflemen

Members of an Engineer Special Brigade disembark from an LCI during a training exercise. The two ramps on the bow make this vessel easy to identify. Although LCIs could carry a complete infantry company to shore in one trip, it was felt unwise to land such a tempting target until all direct enemy fire on the beach had been suppressed.

Left.
An Ordnance Corps inspector, wearing an armband marked "ORD" inspects the waterproofing job done by the crew of this Sherman tank. Of special interest is what appears to be some type of waterproof fabric pasted around the gun mantle and muzzle, as well as around various other openings. This technique does not appear in other D-Day photographs, which may indicate that this is an experiment to determine the best method of waterproofing a tank.

Below.
Special waterproofing kits were provided for armored vehicles. The M7 Priest self -propelled gun was open topped, and so needed a higher wall of sheet metal to prevent water from spilling into the crew compartment. The M-4 Sherman tank could be submerged in seven feet of water if all openings were sealed and the two vents were installed. The M-10 tank destroyer and M-7 Priest's rear deck design meant they needed only one air intake vent.

Left.
Tanks needed to cover up the large air vents on their rear decks. This was done by adding large sheet metal vents for air intake and exhaust. These vents, officially called "fording stacks," not only provided air flow to the engine, but were sealed to prevent water from seeping into the engine compartment. Once on shore the tank crew could pull the attachment pins and these vents would fall away.

Waterproofing was the responsibility of the unit mechanics and drivers. They were trained at a special school operated by the Ordnance Corps. It was far cheaper to spend a few hours carefully sealing all openings, than have to pay for an entire new vehicle. These men have installed the air intake tube attached to the windshield and have sealed the engine of this truck with waterproofing compound.

Below.
The M8 gun carriage was a Stuart light tank equipped with a short 75mm howitzer in the turret. Until a port was captured to assure dry landings, every vehicle destined for France had to be waterproofed so it could travel to shore from a depth of at least three feet.

Waterproofing the vehicles

Left.
This 105mm howitzer has been thoroughly waterproofed for its landing on Omaha beach. It is a gun from the 32nd Field Artillery, and has the battle names "Troina" and "Oran" painted on the gun shield. The yellow rectangle, also painted on the shield, appears in the center of the white star of other 1st Division vehicles and may be a tactical symbol for the unit. The crew has encased the breechblock and other major components in a waterproof material of asbestos paste. All of this must be stripped away on the far shore before the gun will be ready to fire. The man on the gun has a painted 1st Division insignia on his helmet.

Below.
Here a waterproofed jeep is tested at one of the waterproofing schools in England. The large tube on the right side of the windshield is the air intake for the carburettor. A smaller tube was used to prevent a vacuum from building in the crankcase. As long as the jeep was running, there was enough pressure in the exhaust system so an exhaust tube was not needed.

Below.
This jeep engine has been properly waterproofed. It is not surprising that unless the asbestos based waterproofing compound is removed in the dewaterproofing procedure the engine would eventually overheat. All vehicle drivers were warned of the consequences of not removing the waterproofing compound as soon as possible on the far shore.

Embarkation

This MP is from the 1st Division Military Police Platoon. The yellow band on his helmet indicates he is from a divisional MP unit. A Springfield grenade launcher has been clamped to a thin metal tube on the windshield. This tube was part of the waterproofing system and vented the crankcase. The rifle is encased in a clear plastic bag to keep it dry in the landing. When each vehicle was waterproofed, a check list was attached to it with locations for inspectors to initial. This check list was double sided with an American flag on the front and instructions for dewaterproofing on the rear. This is the small American flag seen on the windshield of most vehicles.

29ers, their patches blocked out by the censor, receive their issue of matches prior to D-Day. Writing names on uniforms, such as "Johnny" seen here, was not common in WW2, but did happen. In the 29th Division some NCOs made replacements mark their names on their uniforms like this, to help everyone learn their names faster. Note the horizontal white bar on the back of the helmet indicating an NCO.

Opposite page.
Convoys heading to the embarkation points were very tightly scheduled, although it was not uncommon for the men to get ready to move out, then have to wait long hours until it was their turn. Military Police worked long hours under the direction of the Transportation Corps to make sure that everyone got to their correct destination. As the soldiers said, it was a case of "hurry up and wait."

Above.
Each man in the invasion was issued with a week's worth of PX rations. On the hood of this jeep is a sample of some of the different PX rations used by the Army: toothbrushes, shaving cream, cigarettes, candy bars, razor blades and pipe tobacco.

Right.
For roughly two weeks before the troops boarded their ships the men were held in secure marshalling areas. Many were small camps strung out along the side of a road, and called "sausage camps" due to their sausage-like appearance when drawn on maps. Here the men made their final preparations and waited for the order to move to the ships. To prevent aircraft from counting the troops in each camp, areas such as mess lines were covered by canvas. The censor has blocked out some, but not all of the 29th Division insignia worn by these men.

a few men trained in amphibious techniques would be helpful. This would later come in handy when some of the glider infantry of the 101st were brought ashore in landing craft.

Lt. Col. Thompson left the ATC in March 1944 to assume command of the 6th Engineer Special Brigade. One of his first actions at the 6th ESB was to send his quartermaster and DUKW units to be trained at the ATC. Many of the officers and men from the ATC were transferred to various elements of the invasion force, where their extensive understanding of amphibious assaults could be put to use. The ATC was finally disbanded on 26 May 1944. The time for planning and training was at an end.

Above.

This well-known photograph shows a group of 1st Division GIs waiting to sail to Normandy. The divisional insignia has been painted on most of their helmets and some of them (though not all) wear the shoulder patch. Everyone wears the standard wool trousers with the M41 field jacket or winter combat jacket. Behind these men are some of the cranes that would be used by the engineers to unload the supplies that would follow the initial assault. The lone black soldier at right wears HBT fatigues. He is not a member of the 1st Division, but either from the 320th Barrage Balloon Bn, or from one of the support elements of the 5th Engineer Special Brigade. Visible underneath the soldier sitting in the front row (with his trouser legs rolled up) is a dark OD object with light colored trim. This appears to be an assault jacket. It is interesting to note that their boots have turned almost black from the anti-gas dubbing.

Opposite page.

There is a wealth of small details in this photo taken in England just before the invasion. Troops can be seen from the 1st Division, Armored Forces, and Engineer Special Brigades. Rolled up camouflage nets with interwoven burlap strips are visible on most of the vehicles. A piece of wood has been used to stop the rattle of the gasoline can on the jeep nicknamed "Blondie." Various types of sticks, some cut right from the tree, are used to hold up the waterproofing tubes. The soldier at the very front has used adhesive tape to secure his M-1936 suspenders.

Right.
The unit markings of all vehicles were to be removed from the bumpers for security reasons. To speed up the progress of the convoys, cards were placed on the front of the vehicles identifying what convoy and what ship they were bound for. As an added security precaution, the ship information did not specify the actual number of the craft, but a reference number assigned by the Army. This method allowed the Navy to change vessels if one suddenly became unavailable due to engine trouble or other problems.

Below.
The M4 high speed tractor was used primarily to tow the 90mm antiaircraft gun, the 155mm howitzer, and the 280mm and 8 inch guns. Although called a high speed tractor, its top speed was about 30 mph. The three horizontal stripes seen on the front are a code used to indicate the battery or company a piece of equipment was assigned to. A five digit number (seen above the bars) was given to every company sized unit. Specific colors were used for the bars based on the final two digits of the unit code. This allowed troops to recognize their company equipment without giving away unit information.

Above.
 Once at their final destination, troops frequently had to wait a while until it was their turn to board the ship. When time permitted, vehicles were covered by camouflage nets per regulations. Although most of the German Air Force had been driven from the sky, the Allies were still worried about fast reconnaissance aircraft getting over the embarkation ports and photographing the preparations.

Right.
These soldiers have already reached the port, and receive a last hot meal before boarding the craft that will carry them to France. Many of the smaller landing craft did not have mess facilities for the troops and the men were issued K-rations for the trip across the Channel.

A group of medics from an Engineer Special Brigade board an LCT for the trip across the Channel. Some have attached extra life belts to their stretchers so they would float to shore if jettisoned in the water. Although these men carry stretchers and wear aidman's pouches, they curiously do not wear red cross armbands.

Previous page, top.
This half-track is armed with quad .50 caliber machine guns. It has been given the nickname "Brass City" probably due to the large amount of fired brass shells the vehicle fills with when firing. A faint camouflage pattern can be seen painted on the side of it. This is unusual as most American vehicles were painted only in the standard olive drab. Every spare inch of space seems to be filled with extra supplies and crew possessions.

Above.
Another view of the same group of LCTs shows more quad .50 M16 half-tracks. These half-tracks were designed as

antiaircraft defense, but they were also very effective weapons when used against ground targets. Soldiers are settling down for their ride to Normandy. Most of the men are putting on and adjusting their inflatable life belts. The two soldiers in the center foreground have camouflage painted helmets. There seems to be a mix of both the standard M41 field jacket and the winter combat jacket with the knit collar and cuffs. This jacket was warmer, more durable, and a highly sought after item.

Below.
This jeep is driven onto an LCT by a member of the First Division, whose shoulder insignia is visible. A yellow tactical marking has been painted on the vehicle's left side. Another shot in the same series shows a jeep with an Engineer Special Brigade medical unit boarding the same ship.

Above.
Hardened beaches, known as "hards", were constructed to expedite the boarding of the landing craft. The appearance of the concrete squares also earned them the nickname "chocolate bars" or "chocolate squares." Here a truck carrying a light aircraft backs into LST-391 at a British port. These planes were reassembled in France, and provided observation for artillery units.

Left.
An officer stands on the rampway directing vehicles as they are loaded onto an LCT. A white line has been painted down the center of the craft to assist the drivers as they back onto the vessel. Two M-7 self propelled guns are already on board. Driving a tracked vehicle in reverse into such a tight area was not an easy task.

Above.
LCT(5)s, with superstructure placed in the center of the craft, are loaded at a "hard" on the English coast. According to the loading lists for Overlord, the LCT-199 was scheduled to land at H+120 minutes with elements of the 197th AAA Bn, and the 5th Engineer Special Brigade, on Easy Red beach. The LCT-195 was scheduled to land at the same time with the same mix of troops at Fox Green beach.

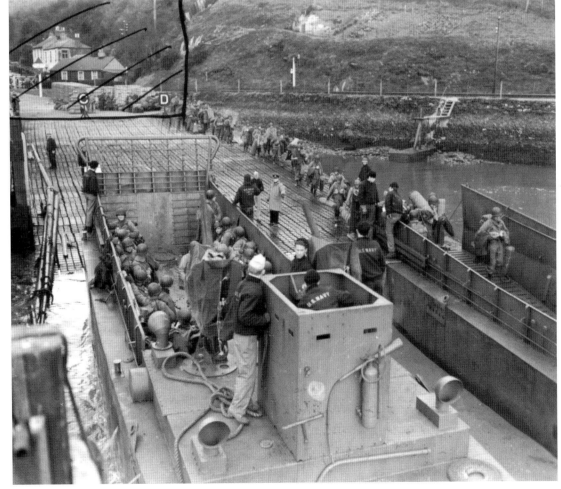

Right.
It was considered dangerous to sail a fully loaded LCM across the rough Channel, so troops were carried over in a larger ship, then transferred to the LCMs on the morning of D-Day. These troops are using the LCM to bring them out to their transport from a "hard" somewhere in England. The censor has indicated the coastline was not to be shown. This photo provides a good view of the armored position for the LCM coxswain.

Chapter 2.
"Lower all landing craft"

The role of the U.S. Navy

THE U.S. Navy played a vital role in the Normandy landings. Obviously, the Navy was instrumental in getting the troops and equipment from America to England, and then across the Channel to the Normandy Beach. The Navy was involved in almost every aspect of Overlord, from providing fire support to the airborne divisions, to developing loading diagrams for the landing craft.

Task Force 122, under Rear Admiral Alan G. Kirk, was in charge of the naval aspects of the invasion. TF 122 was broken down into smaller elements. Those most concerned with the American sector were Force "O", "U" and "B." Force "O" was bound for Omaha Beach, loaded from the area between the ports of Portsmouth and Poole, and commanded by Rear Admiral J.L. Hall from his flagship the *U.S.S. Ancon*. Force "O" was further broken down by landing waves into Forces "O-1," "O-2" and "O-3." Force "U," commanded by Admiral Moon on board the *U.S.S. Bayfield*, was loaded from the area between Plymouth and Torcross, and was bound for Utah Beach.

Force "B" was known as the "follow-up force." It was commanded by Commodore C.D. Edgar and contained the troops scheduled to come in after the

Task Force 122 - Admiral Kirk- Control Force
Task Force 124 - Rear Admiral Hall- Assault Force "O"
Task Force 125 - Rear Admiral Moon- Assault Force "U"
Task Force 126 - Commodore Edgar- Follow up Force "B"
Task Force 127 - Rear Admiral Wilkes- Service
                Force of TF 122
Task Force 128 - Captain Clark- Mulberry Harbor

Right.
The *U.S.S. Texas*, BB-35, was one of the oldest ships to participate in the Normandy Invasion. On D-Day her task was to shell Pointe du Hoc with her big guns, and fire at the emplacements in the Vierville-sur-Mer area with her smaller guns. Once the Shore Fire Control Parties were on shore, the Texas was in direct support of the 3rd Battalion, 116th Infantry.

Opposite page, top left.
Rear-admiral Hall was the commander of Force "O," which was tasked with carrying the 1st and 29th Divisions to shore and providing naval fire support.

Opposite page, top right.
This German shore battery, one of the emplacements making up the Saint-Marcouf battery (northwest of Utah), is an example of what the battleships were trying to knock out on D-Day. A direct hit was needed, even for a 16 inch shell, to penetrate the reinforced concrete walls. Visible in this photo are places where smaller shells have just knocked off some of the concrete. Some photographs show pillboxes with foot sized depressions in the concrete. These were constructed by the German engineers as a place to put soil and grow vegetation for camouflage, not locations where shells hit.

"Thank God for the US Navy"

This quote is often attributed to the Vth Corps commander, Major General Leonard Gerow. It was, in fact, originated by Colonel B.B. Talley who was a Vth Corps observer watching Omaha Beach from a landing craft. He sent this message to his commander, General Gerow. Gerow passed it up to General Bradley, and it has always been assumed that Gerow originated it.

> "*I do not expect to be repulsed on any beach*"
> Rear Admiral
> J.L. Hall

assault units had gained a toe hold in France. These ships were loaded at the ports of Fowey and Falmouth and were not scheduled to arrive off Omaha Beach until late afternoon on D-Day. Forces "G," "S," and "J" were destined for the Commonwealth beaches. The fourth major American force was the Gunfire Support Group under Admiral Morton L. Deyo. These heavily armed ships had the furthest to travel and left Belfast, North Ireland on 3 June. At roughly the same time, 250 British and American navy minesweepers set out to clear a path through the German minefields. The minesweepers took their bearings from a series of underwater acoustic buoys that had been carefully positioned in the Channel a week before.

Above.
Men of a chemical weapons unit bring their 4.2 inch mortars and ammo carts aboard LCVPs from AP-33, the *U.S.S. Bayfield*. The *Bayfield* was the command ship for the Utah landings. These men may be from the 87th Chemical Bn. that landed at Utah. They wear M-1936 musette bags and the standard lightweight gas masks.

Below.
This front view of an LCVP shows how small the space was for a thirty-man boat team. The British LCA was slightly narrower to accommodate the extra armor. The wooden crate on which the officer stands serves no known official purpose. The troops carry the assault gas mask and an extra blanket stuck in their packs.

Opposite page.
What appears to be the same men as in the previous photo climb from the LCVP to an LCI. According to the jacket of one sailor this is LCI539. One of the soldiers facing the camera has a 1st Division insignia painted on his helmet.

A detailed time schedule organized all vessels into convoys depending upon the speed, and the slowest were to sail first.

Following the minesweepers, the slower convoys of Force "U" set out on the afternoon of 3 June. At this time the original date for D-Day of 5 June was still in effect. Convoy U-2A, consisting of 37 LCTs, 50 LCMs, and 23 other small craft, set off on the afternoon of 3 June as planned. But weather reports demanded that the date of invasion be pushed back to 6 June and an order was sent out to all convoys to return to port. Convoy U-2A finally got back on the evening of 4 June, but found that there were no berths available for the small craft. Most of these small craft were forced to stay at sea until the morning of 5 June when they set out again for the Normandy coast. When these boats unloaded at Utah Beach they had been at sea for 3 nights and 2 days in rough waters. The men on board were tired, cramped and seasick. Other convoys suffered a similar fate. It was the slower craft, the LCMs and LCTs, that due to their small size suffered the worst effects of the rough Channel waters.

All convoys were to make their way from England to Point "Z." Around point "Z" was a 5 mile area

Above.
This helmet was worn by an LCVP crewman at Normandy. It has the gray band painted around the shell, and the liner has been totally painted in this color. This band was to quickly identify naval personnel on the beaches. On the front of the liner, and also at the rear of the shell, the sailor has painted his first name. Possibly as a joke he has scratched a pirate's skull and crossbones into the front of both the shell and liner.

Right.
Two LCSs in the foreground, with an LCVP, and a LCT(6) in the background. The Landing Craft Support was a small motorboat designed to guide the assault waves to the beach and provide supporting fire. They were armed with a twin .50 caliber machine gun, two .30 caliber machine guns, and twelve 5-inch rocket projectors.

Left.
With a crew of three and a range of about 100 miles, the LCVP (Landing Craft Vehicle, Personnel) was capable of carrying up to 36 men or a 3-ton vehicle. But it was prone to swamp in rough waters. This was generally the first landing craft to hit the shore. It was carried on a larger transport ship then lowered into the water for the final run to the beach. The coxswain, visible behind the helm wheel, steered from a rather exposed position.

swept clear of mines called Piccadilly Circus. From this area each convoy formed up with others heading to the same beach and followed a sea lane clear of mines to a carefully marked area off the appropriate beach. A minesweeper laid the last marker buoy off Omaha Beach just after midnight on 6 June.

At approximately 0200 hrs on the morning of D–Day the transport ships entered their assigned area and anchored 11 miles out to sea. They were so far offshore because this was the maximum range of the 155mm guns emplaced at Pointe du Hoc. The battleships anchored 11,000 yards offshore, and the smaller destroyers were only 5,000 yards offshore. At approximately 0400 the landing craft would be lowered and the assault troops would be loaded into them. The small boats would form into circles awaiting the order to move to the beach. At 0430 the

A Navy Chief Petty Officer painted his helmet with the insignia of his rank, Chief Machinist's Mate, so that he could be quickly identified in times of crisis. The gray band indicates he was a sailor in the invasion. This type of Navy rank marking was generally a personal preference, depending on if the Skipper accepted the idea or not.

first landing craft waves were directed to the line of departure by a group of subchasers.

The line of departure, 4,000 yards off the shore, was marked by small patrol craft. This line was where all elements of the landing wave were organized for the final run to the beach. Landing craft waves circled here until given the signal to head for the beach. LCGs formed up on the flanks of the assault waves. LCCs were given charge of shepherding the waves into the correct beaches. Five minutes before the first wave was to head for shore, the control craft turned on a light. Five minutes later this light would go out, and that would signal the first wave to cross the line of departure and head to shore.

The sea lanes that had been cleared of mines were narrow. The gunfire support ships were anchored in place so they would not accidentally move into a mined area. This gave them a stable platform to fire from, but also made them an easier target for the German artillery to hit. Just after 0500 German coastal guns opened up on the Allied ships and the

THE ALLIED NAVAL GUNFIRE SUPPORT ON D-DAY			
	UK	US	French/Dutch
Battleships	3	3	0
Monitors	2	0	0
Cruisers	17	2	3
Destroyers	37	31	5
Gunboats	0	0	2

fire was returned by a few vessels. At 0530 the bombardment group started their planned fire on the German emplacements. This plan called for specific German targets to be hit by the naval guns. The *U.S.S. Texas* shelled Pointe du Hoc with her 14" guns and used her 5" guns on the fortifications around Vierville.

The first assault waves were still making their way to the beach when the naval guns started to fire over their heads. By now the sun had risen and the shore was in clear view. At 0600 the Air Force added to the show when 450 B-24s were to drop 1,285 tons of explosives on Omaha Beach. The fear of dropping these bombs short of the target and onto the landing craft caused the drop to be delayed for a few seconds. This caused the bombs to fall inland by as much as 3 miles. On Utah Beach 276 B-26 bombers were more accurate and dropped 4,400 bombs on the beach emplacements. This destroyed important German equipment and made the Utah landings easier for the assault troops.

While the landing craft were making their way to shore, a number of different weapons were firing on the beach defenses. 32 Sherman tanks fired at the shore over the bow of their LCTs. 37 self-propelled M-7 Priests shelled the coast with their 105mm howitzers on the way in. At 2,000 yards out the M–7s ceased fire, as they could no longer depress the guns enough to fire over the front ramp of their LCT.

The most impressive display was the LCT(R)s. At 3,500 yards off the beach they formed into a line 100 yards apart. When these craft got to the correct posi-

General Charles Gerhardt, commander of the 29th Infantry Division, moves from the destroyer escort *U.S.S Maloy* (DE-791) to an LCS (Landing Craft Support) for his trip to Omaha Beach. The LCS was equipped with machine guns, rocket launchers (visible at left) and smoke pots (seen on the stern) to provide cover if needed. The job of the LCS was to guide the landing craft to shore, then provide covering fire.

tion they each fired off 1,064 5"-rockets. To hit the beach area these rockets needed to be fired when the LCT(R) was exactly the right distance from shore. Different sources claim different distances for these craft, but it appears to be roughly 3,000 yards. Most of the rockets were fired too soon and landed in the surf, causing little damage. The men of G/16 reported seeing thousands of dead fish in the water killed by the rockets. One LCT(R) reportedly did hit the area surrounding the E-3 exit. In any case, it appears that some of the rockets may have landed on shore and set fire to the grass.

When the landing craft were near to the beach the control craft was to fire a black smoke rocket which signalled all naval fire to shift from the beaches to targets off to the flank or further inland. All this shelling caused a cloud of dust and smoke that obscured some of the landmarks on the beaches and may have contributed to many of the landing craft coming in at the wrong spot.

But all this fire did little to the defenses on the beaches. The Navy had asked for more ships, or more time for the bombardment group, but the request was denied. The American planners had specifically asked to delay H-hour by two hours so the beach defenses could be pounded, but General Montgomery denied the request on the grounds that he did not want the assaults on the five different beaches staggered over time.

For the rest of the day the Navy continued to provide fire support directed either by spotter planes overhead, or Shore Fire Control Parties that landed

Right.
This aerial view of an LCT(6) shows two M7 Priests with trailers, two half-tracks, and a jeep. Clearly visible is the rear opening of the LCT(6) which allowed two LCTs to join together back to back to form a pontoon bridge. The LCT(6) could also use this rear opening to take on vehicles from an LST while at sea.

Below.
Aerial view of an empty LCT(6). The LCT(6) was similar in size to the LCT(5), but the superstructure was moved to the sides, making room for a small opening in the stern of the craft. LCT crews felt that living conditions were slightly better aboard the more modern LCT(6) than the older LCT (5).

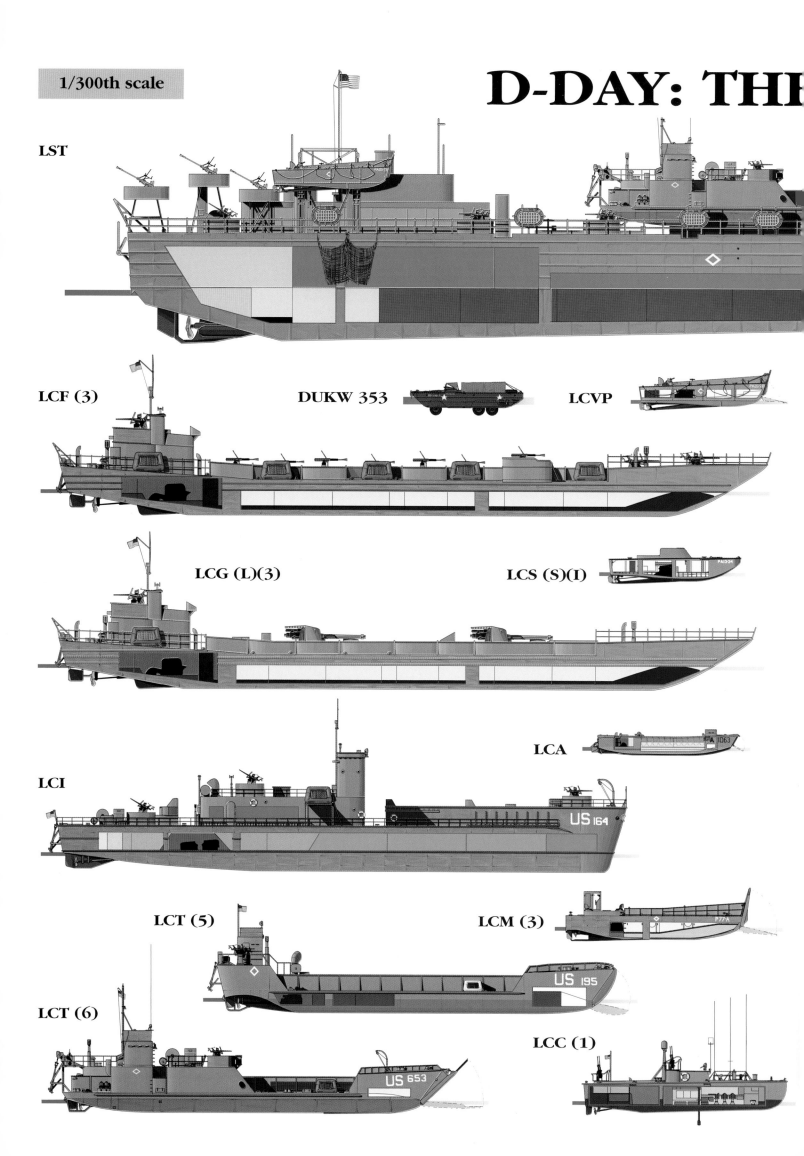

D-DAY: THE

LST

LCF (3)

DUKW 353

LCVP

LCG (L)(3)

LCS (S)(I)

LCA

LCI

US 164

LCT (5)

LCM (3)

US 195

LCT (6)

LCC (1)

US 653

LANDING CRAFT

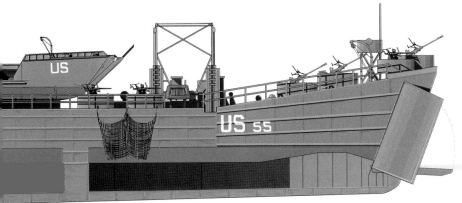

US

US SS

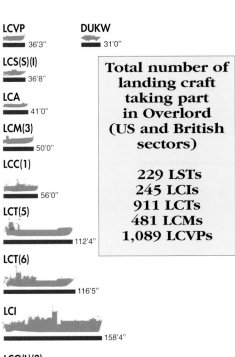

LCVP	36'3"	DUKW 31'0"
LCS(S)(I)	36'8"	
LCA	41'0"	
LCM(3)	50'0"	
LCC(1)	56'0"	
LCT(5)	112'4"	
LCT(6)	116'5"	
LCI	158'4"	
LCG(L)(3)	192'0"	
LCF(3)	195'9"	
LST	328'0"	

Total number of landing craft taking part in Overlord (US and British sectors)

229 LSTs
245 LCIs
911 LCTs
481 LCMs
1,089 LCVPs

LCS (S)(I)

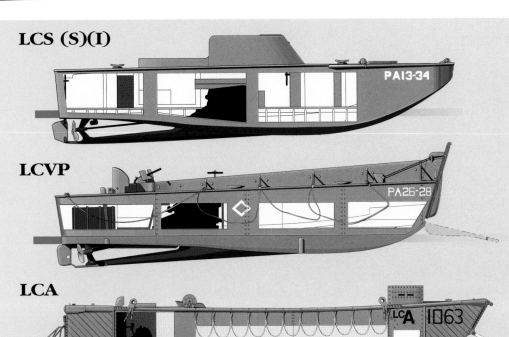

PA13-34

LCVP

PA26-28

LCA

LCA 1063

LCM (3)

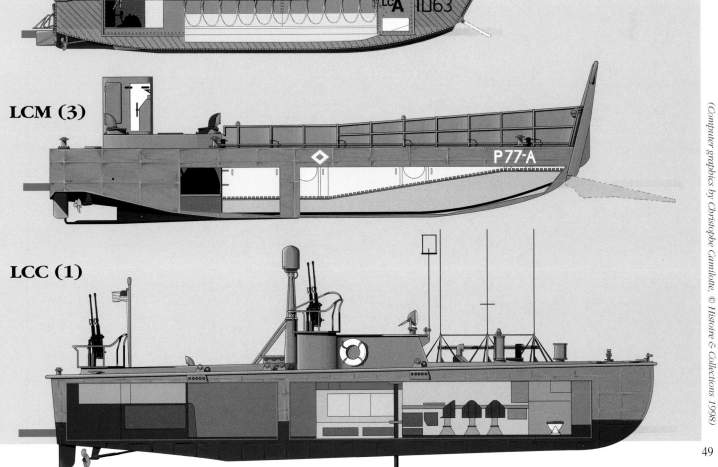

P77-A

LCC (1)

1/100th scale

(Computer graphics by Christophe Camilotte, © Histoire & Collections 1998)

49

with the troops. In the morning hours the destroyers were particularly helpful in moving into shallow water and firing at targets of opportunity. The shallower water was supposedly clear of sea mines, so the destroyers were allowed to maneuver outside the assigned fire support lanes. Many soldiers on Omaha give the credit for their success to the destroyers that risked running aground to provide close fire support against German emplacements.

At Utah beach one of the primary control craft was sunk, and another delayed in crossing the Channel. The remaining control craft attempted to coordinate the landing, but the resulting confusion, coupled with a strong current, pulled the landing craft to the left of the planned beach. It was decided to shift the invasion beaches to where the troops were actually landing, and the plans proceeded with few problems.

At Omaha Beach the confusion caused by powerful German defenses, too few gaps in the beach obstacles, and a strong current pulling to the left caused many of the landing craft to land in the wrong location.

Top, right and bottom.
An LCT was launched from an LST by flooding the ballast tanks on one side of the LST and sliding the smaller craft over the edge. This launch takes place in Plymouth Harbor in February 1944.

The Landing Craft

A surprising fact about Overlord was that the factor limiting the number of men that could be landed was the availability of landing craft. The Pacific Theater, with its emphasis on naval operations, needed as many landing craft as it could get. Every new batch of landing craft had to be carefully divided between the European and Pacific theaters. The original Overlord plan called for a simultaneous landing in the south of France, but this had to be postponed until August due to a shortage of landing craft.

Particularly in short supply were the larger LSTs (Landing Ship, Tank - by Navy terminology a ship was at least 200 feet long, anything shorter was called a craft). The shortage became even greater after three LSTs were sunk or damaged during Operation Tiger.

There were many different types of small craft that played an important role in the invasion. Of particular interest are those designed to land on the

beaches. Battleships and destroyers are large enough to warrant mention in many books, but the smaller craft tend to get lumped together or forgotten outright.

It is important to keep in mind that each class of landing craft had different variations. There were at least four different basic models of LCTs used at Normandy, not counting the variations with different weapons or equipment. Therefore, the correct version or type of a craft must be known before any specific information about it can be assumed. As a rule of thumb, the larger the craft, the more versions of it were built during the war.

Landing Craft, Vehicle, Personnel & Landing Craft, Assault

The first landing craft to hit the beaches were the smallest. These were the LCVPs (Landing Craft, Vehicle, Personnel). They could carry roughly 30 men or a small vehicle such as a jeep. LCVPs were armed with two .30 caliber machine guns and manned by a crew of three sailors (the coxswain and

Although taken in the Mediterranean, this photo illustrates a typical LCT crew in standard Navy working uniform. The sailors wear dungarees and chambray shirts, while the Ensign wears the officer's working uniform of cotton khaki shirt and trousers. Note the amphibious forces non-regulation insignia painted next to the LCT number. The one-piece HBT coveralls were not a standard Navy uniform, but issued as an outer gas-protective garment.

two machine gunners). Some LCVPs carried a fourth crewman who could be a signalman or boat wave commander. The plywood hulled LCVPs were carried on larger ships to the invasion area, then lowered into the water on davits. They were an open air boat with no amenities for the crew and designed to be used for only short periods of time before returning to their parent ship.

British transport ships had a different version of the LCVP which they called the LCA (landing craft, assault). The LCA was longer, but narrower than the LCVP. More importantly, it had more armor plating which made the craft ride lower in the water. This caused many problems on 6 June, when the rough seas sloshed into the heavily laden LCAs and some swamped. A few of the American assault units – Rangers, 1/116th, and elements of the 16th Infantry – were transported to Normandy on British ships and were landed in British crewed LCAs.

One important thing to keep in mind was that most of the ships taking part in the invasion carried a few LCVPs on board. If that ship did not have any troops

on board to bring to shore, such as the command ship *U.S.S. Ancon*, those LCVPs would be used to carry men from other transport ships. LCVPs were assigned where they were needed, not just to carry troops from their own parent ship.

After bringing their load to shore, the small craft (LCVP and LCA) were to return to their parent ship for new orders. It could be 4-6 hours before the first wave LCVPs were able to return to their ship for refuelling or food. In many cases they would only make only one trip into the beach on 6 June. Once the German guns on the beaches were destroyed, it became more practical to land men and equipment in larger craft. The LCVPs were advantageous because they provided a small target when the Germans still commanded the beach, but later on it was easier to land a fully organized infantry company on an LCI.

After the initial landing, many of the LCVPs went back to their ships and were hauled aboard. Others were assigned to LCVP flotillas and given specific orders such as bringing important men or material from ship to shore. Some of the LCVPs were left on their own in these flotillas when their parent ship returned to England for another load of men. These orphaned LCVPs were kept in constant use running errands up and down the beach. Each morning they would receive their assignment from the flotilla officer. They might be sent anywhere on the entire invasion front.

If they could not get back to their regular area by nightfall, they would pull up on whatever beach they

Top.
The central superstructure of the LCT(5) is clearly visible behind this load of jeeps. The drivers wear impregnated HBTs over their regular field jackets. Sticking up from the jeeps are supports for the waterproofing tubes: a thick tube for air intake, and a thin one to vent the crankcase.

Right.
Once the load of vehicles had disembarked from the LCTs, casualties would be brought on board for the trip out to a hospital ship or specially designated medical LST. It was important to keep the flow of casualties moving off the beach, because the Germans frequently tried to bomb the landing beaches. They knew that the beaches were the bottleneck that everything had to flow through and any bombs dropped in the area would have a chance of hitting something.

were near. The crews slept on stretchers and pulled a canvas top over the boat at night for cover.

The crewmen normally lived on K-rations, but if they were in the right area they could get a hot meal from a most unlikely source. Some of the merchant ships sunk to form the Gooseberry breakwater were being used as antiaircraft gun platforms. Their decks and cabins were out of the water and they were still able to operate their galleys to provide a hot meal to the gun crews or anyone who tied up alongside.

The hardest job these LCVP crews had to perform was burial detail. About 3 weeks after the invasion a number of bodies began to float up to the surface. Every effort was made to provide a proper land burial for casualties, but these bodies were too water-logged to stand the trip ashore. The LCVPs would tow the corpses to a hospital ship, where they would be identified and sewn into a canvas shroud. A 50

This coxswain of an LCVP steers his craft from an exposed position, so he wears Navy rubberized foul weather gear to protect himself against the spray. The anti-gas goggles on his helmet will come in handy if the sea gets rough. He has painted "USN" in white letters on the front and back of his outer uniform according to last minute orders issued to Navy personnel. He has also painted a gray stripe on his helmet so he will be easily identified as a sailor. Unlike the LCVP passengers who wear an inflatable life belt, the boat crews were issued a gray kapok life vest that provided greater buoyancy. An Army lightweight gas mask is carried in case the Germans attempt to repel the invasion with chemical weapons. A pair of work gloves are important to protect his hands during the cold of the early morning hours. *(Reconstruction)*

Above and right.
The LCT(R) was a British modified LCT with 1,064 rocket launching racks mounted onto a false deck. The five inch rockets were fired in 24 salvos and would cover an area 750 yards x 160 yards. Once the rockets had been fired, the racks and false decking could be removed and the craft used as a standard LCT.

Below.
The bow of an LCT is jammed with vehicles from an antitank unit. Following the three jeeps placed at the front are three 1 1/2 ton trucks towing 57mm antitank guns. These trucks contain a wide variety of equipment, including: ammunition crates, a bazooka (far left), Bangalore torpedoes (center), and round cans of additional waterproofing compound. Although the trucks may seem half empty, this space was needed to carry the rest of the gun crew.

Above.
Side view of LCT-515 dried out on Utah Beach,
LCT-528 is behind it.

Left.
The stern shots of beached LCT-515 provide a good
view of the LCT(6). At left is the stern anchor winch.
The stern anchor was a feature used in most landing
craft: it was dropped as the craft moved to shore,
then a powerful winch helped drag the craft off the
beach back into deeper water.

Below.
Front view of LCT-528 on Utah Beach. Depending on
the slope of the beach, ramp extensions were
sometimes needed to assist vehicles boarding, or
disembarking from, landing craft.

pound block of concrete would be tied to each body, and the LCVP crew would be given the sad task of bringing the bodies a few hundred yards away, then dropping them back into the ocean.

Landing Craft, Mechanized

The next larger craft was the LCM. LCMs could be either carried on ship davits, or towed across the Channel. Due to the danger of swamping in rough seas, most LCMs were towed across the Channel and not loaded with troops until the morning of D-Day. LCMs can be readily identified by their unique perforated bow ramp.

There were a few different sizes of LCMs. The early LCM(1) had been designed to carry a 14 ton light tank or truck ashore. As tanks grew larger and heavier, the LCM(3) was developed with a longer hull and greater buoyancy which allowed a 30 ton tank to be carried. An additional six foot section was added to the LCM(3) amidships. This extra section on the now designated LCM(6) did not decrease performance, and provided greater freeboard when carrying a Sherman tank. The British had their own versions of the LCM.

Both the LCM (3) and (6) had a crew of 4 men and were armed with two .50 caliber machine guns. Like the LCVP, the LCM was not designed for the crew to live aboard and it remained dependent upon a parent ship over long periods of time. The most important role played by LCMs on D-Day was transporting the engineer teams assigned to demolish the beach obstacles.

Landing Craft, Tank

The LCT was an ocean-going vessel designed to land more than one tank or vehicle on a beach. This was the smallest craft that had been built with space for the crew (1 officer, 12 men) below deck. The two main versions of the LCT used in Normandy were the LCT(5) and LCT(6). The LCT (6) was a newer model which moved the deckhouse from the rear of

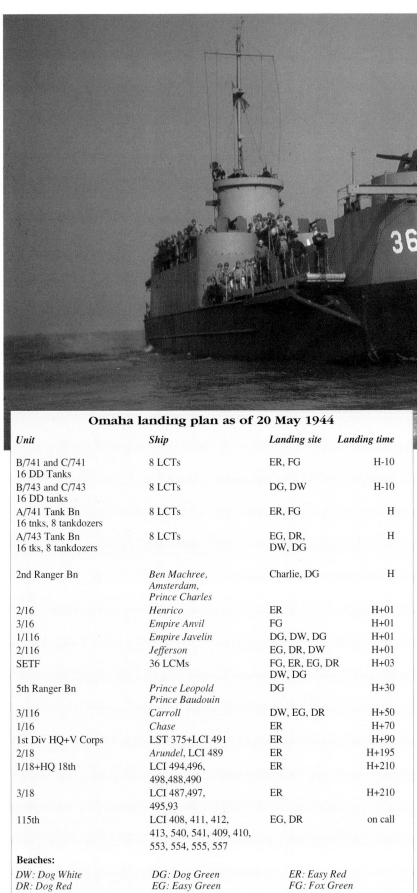

The LCI (Landing Craft, Infantry) had berths for 188 men below decks. It allowed an entire infantry company to land as a single unit without having to split the men up between different landing craft. It was armed with four 20mm guns, and while the passengers may not always have had a comfortable ride, at least they had a chance to stay warm and dry (but crowded) before hitting the shore.

Omaha landing plan as of 20 May 1944

Unit	Ship	Landing site	Landing time
B/741 and C/741 16 DD Tanks	8 LCTs	ER, FG	H-10
B/743 and C/743 16 DD tanks	8 LCTs	DG, DW	H-10
A/741 Tank Bn 16 tnks, 8 tankdozers	8 LCTs	ER, FG	H
A/743 Tank Bn 16 tks, 8 tankdozers	8 LCTs	EG, DR, DW, DG	H
2nd Ranger Bn	Ben Machree, Amsterdam, Prince Charles	Charlie, DG	H
2/16	Henrico	ER	H+01
3/16	Empire Anvil	FG	H+01
1/116	Empire Javelin	DG, DW, DG	H+01
2/116	Jefferson	EG, DR, DW	H+01
SETF	36 LCMs	FG, ER, EG, DR DW, DG	H+03
5th Ranger Bn	Prince Leopold Prince Baudouin	DG	H+30
3/116	Carroll	DW, EG, DR	H+50
1/16	Chase	ER	H+70
1st Div HQ+V Corps	LST 375+LCI 491	ER	H+90
2/18	Arundel, LCI 489	ER	H+195
1/18+HQ 18th	LCI 494,496, 498,488,490	ER	H+210
3/18	LCI 487,497, 495,93	ER	H+210
115th	LCI 408, 411, 412, 413, 540, 541, 409, 410, 553, 554, 555, 557	EG, DR	on call

Beaches:

DW: Dog White	*DG: Dog Green*	*ER: Easy Red*
DR: Dog Red	*EG: Easy Green*	*FG: Fox Green*

the craft to the side, allowing for a vehicle opening at the stern and better quarters for the crew. The LCT(6) could join stern to stern with another and form a floating causeway to allow vehicles to move across them to shore. The rear opening could also be used to allow vehicles to move from an LST onto an LCT while still at sea. The rear opening did not have a ramp, but vehicles at the correct height could drive right on board.

Above right.

There was space below deck on LCIs for the men they carried, but it was very cramped. Officially, troops were only to be on board an LCI for up to 48 hours. There was really no space available for them other than to stay in their bunks, and try not to get seasick.

Although considered an ocean-going craft, LCTs were generally carried to the theater of operations on board the larger LST. Each LCT could be broken down into three sections and an LST could carry five of these sections, or one assembled LCT, on her deck. A complete LCT was launched from an LST by flooding the ballast tanks on one side of the LST and sliding the smaller craft over the edge. When sections were shipped on an LST, a crane lifted them off and a crew bolted and welded the three sections together. During the Normandy operation most LCTs made their Channel crossing on D-Day towing an LCM behind them.

The British used a variant of the LCT called the LCT(A). This was an LCT(5) with some additional armor added to the craft. The LCT(A)s were given the job of bringing ashore the tankdozers of the groups assigned to clear beach obstacles, as well as the non-amphibious tanks of the 70th, 741st and 743rd Tank Bns.

LCVPs load up with troops in England prior to a practice landing. The coxswain at his steering wheel and the round machine gunner's positions are visible at far right. The machine guns have not been mounted to protect them against unnecessary exposure to salt water. On the side of the craft can be seen a stream of water being pumped out by the bilge pumps. On D-Day these pumps were overworked and had to be supplemented by troops bailing with their helmets. Notice how the crewman at far left uses the side of the craft to move up and check that the ramp is secure.

Landing Craft Tank, Rocket

The LCT(R) was a special modification of a British LCT. 1,064 5"-rocket launchers filled the deck space. The rockets were fired at a fixed 45° angle and launched when the craft was at the proper range to the target. They timed their approach so that the first assault wave was roughly 300 yards off shore when they fired. A full salvo would saturate an area 750 x 160 yards with 7 lb explosive charges. LCT(R)s needed to travel at flank speed when launching their rockets. The backwards force caused by the rocket engines would actually slow and reverse the LCT, momentarily throwing off the aim.

Landing Craft, Gun

The LCG was another British variation built on the LCT. Two 4.7 inch naval guns were mounted onto a false deck. These guns were manned by British Royal Marines. It was thought that Marines might be better suited to provide close-in ground support fire than sailors trained for naval gunnery. Their purpose was to provide gun support to the initial landing waves. It was believed that an LCG in close to shore would have a better chance of spotting, and engaging, a hidden German emplacement. If needed, the LCG could beach itself to become a stationary gun emplacement.

Four LCGs supported the Utah landings and five supported the troops at Omaha. Their orders were to *"move in as close to the beaches as navigational positions permit delivering neutralizing fire on beach defenses."*

Prior to H-hour their primary targets were concrete pillboxes on the beach. After H-Hour they were not to fire on beach targets unless specifically ordered to by the Commander, Gunfire Support Craft. They would fire on targets of opportunity only in emergencies, and if the craft commander could clearly recognize that Allied troops were not within 1,000 yards of the target.

Landing Craft, Flak

The LCF (also built on an LCT hull) provided floating antiaircraft protection. Their orders were to *"patrol initially around the transport area and boat lanes so as to provide maximum antiaircraft protection to ships and craft. Then move in on flanks to protect boat lanes and beaches as directed by the Commander of Gun Fire Support Craft."* Armament averaged four 2-pounders and eight 20mm guns.

Landing Craft, Infantry

The LCI looked more like a conventional ship because it did not have a ramp in the bow. These were shallow draft craft designed to carry 200 men for up to 48 hours. There were bunks below decks for the troops, but the quarters were tight. The men were landed on the beach by means of two narrow ramps carried at either side of the bow. Like most landing craft, the LCI was to drop a stern anchor as it went into the beach, ramming ashore at full speed to push up on the sand as far as it could go. When the troops left the craft, the loss in weight would allow the LCI to winch itself back out to deep water.

The LCI was used to bring in complete companies of the second infantry regiments to land in each sector. It was thought that these craft would make too good a target to bring to shore in earlier waves when the Germans still had 88s able to fire on incoming ships. However, not all such weapons had been destroyed by the time the first LCIs landed. At Omaha, a few LCIs were destroyed by artillery fire, while others ran into mines placed in the beach obstacles.

This photo of LST-325 dried out on the beach provides a good example of the size of an LST. The rear anchor of the 325 is clearly visible. In the background can be seen the LST 388. Unloading ships by drying them out was slower than using the Loebnitz Pier, but was a practical way to keep the flow of supplies moving across the Channel.

Along with the standard LCI built by the Americans were a number of civilian ships that had been converted to the LSI class. These were generally used by the British Navy although some, such as the *Princess Maud* [an LSI (H) - for hand hoisted davits] carried American troops in the invasion. The British LSI(L)(Large) was the equivalent of the American attack transport ships. These were the '*Empire*' class ships that landed some of the American assault troops.

Landing Ship Tank

Called "Large Slow Targets" by their crews, the LSTs were the most important of all ships because

Above.

LSTs chosen to serve as hospital ships waited until they were filled with casualties before returning to England. This meant not only filling the stretchers on the bulkheads, but the floor of the tank deck as well.

Left.

Some of the LSTs sent to Normandy were specially equipped as hospital ships. Brackets, such as shown here, were mounted in the bulkheads to support stretchers. Extra medical staff, including Army doctors and technicians, were placed aboard before the ship left for Normandy and could handle most of the immediate medical needs of the wounded. One casualty has a helmet painted from the Provisional Engineer Special Brigade hanging from his stretcher.

The Landing Ship Tank (LST) was the largest of the vessels that could land vehicles and men right onto the beaches. Here can be seen the massive steel bow doors that open up to let the ramp down. The LSTs were the most important ships used in the war. Considered ocean-going ships that could travel the world under their own power, they were armed with one 40 mm gun (seen over the bow) and six 20mm guns.

they could carry 2,000 tons of men and equipment right up to the beach and unload them through the bow doors. LSTs also carried from 2 to 6 LCVPs that could be used as additional landing craft for the first waves. LSTs were true ocean-going ships with a range of 6,000 miles. Below deck accommodations were provided for the 100-man crew. Some limited room existed below for passengers, but many of the troops chose to stay with their vehicles for the crossing.

Heavier vehicles such as tanks were carried on the LST tank deck, and lighter vehicles under 10 tons could be carried on the top main deck. A large elevator was used to move vehicles up and down from the top deck. Orders were issued for all vehicles with antiaircraft weapons to be carried on the top deck to provide extra firepower in case of air attack. Every available space on an LST was packed with men and vehicles to the point where some trailers were unhooked and placed sideways to gain a few additional feet of room. Scale models were built of the LST decks and types of vehicles, and different loading combinations tested with these models to find the best way of filling the ship.

LSTs could be unloaded in a number of ways. The Normandy tides generally prohibited them from unloading through the bow doors onto the beach while afloat. One popular method was partially unloading an LST onto a Rhino Ferry for the trip to the shore. This was time consuming, but was a safe and reliable way to get men and equipment to the beach. Many LSTs towed a Rhino Ferry behind them on their first trip across the Channel. On later trips the LSTs towed some of the different elements to be used in the artificial harbors.

Plans called for a pier to be built as part of the Mulberry artificial harbor that the LSTs could pull up to and let the vehicles drive off onto. For the few days that this pier was in operation it worked well. After the storm destroyed the Mulberry harbor and pier, the LSTs were unloaded by a technique called "drying out." Once the beaches were out of the range of German artillery, LSTs were brought in at high tide and anchored. When the tide went out their cargo could drive off the bow ramp onto the beach and head inland. The down side to this technique was that the LST had to wait another 12 hours until the next high tide to re-float and back off the shore.

During the first few days of the invasion most LSTs left to pick up another load in England as soon as they were unloaded. A few were designated as hospital ships and remained off the Normandy coast. These LSTs had brackets welded into the bulkheads on the tank deck to hold stretchers and the ships received extra medical staff and supplies. Wounded men were brought from the frontline to the beach, where they were transported out to these medical LSTs. Doctors on board were equipped to perform many operations, and a number of lives were saved by not having to wait until the men got back to England. The ships stayed off the coast until they were filled with wounded, then they carried the casualties back to hospitals in England.

Landing Craft, Support and Landing Craft, Control

There were two small craft that, although referred to as landing craft, were never intended to land on the beach. The LCC was a navigational boat designed to mark the line of departure and to perform preliminary hydrographic surveys. The crew of 14 men not only manned three .50 caliber machine guns, but operated a sophisticated radio room containing radar,

This sailor could be from any of the vessels anchored off the Normandy coast in the early hours of D-Day. He wears an N-1 alpaca lined jacket against the morning chill. Underneath this jacket he wears the standard Navy working uniform of light blue chambray shirt and blue denim trousers. Anyone venturing out on deck was required to wear a helmet as protection against falling antiaircraft fragments. Like many sailors, he has painted his olive drab issued helmet in Navy gray.
(Reconstruction)

UNITS CARRIED ON *U.S.S CARROLL* ON D-DAY

Unit	men	vehicles	beach	landing time
121st Eng C Bn.	147	-	Dog Green	H+40
D/81 Chem Weapons Bn.	90	-	Dog Red	H+40
K/116	185	-	Dog Green	H+50
I/116 and 111th FA F.O.	208	-	Dog Red	H+50
L/116	203	-	Dog Green	H+50
M/116, Det NSFCP, det 3/116, det 743rd Tk Bn. det D/81st Chem Bn.	279	-	Dog Red	H+57
Hq & Hq Co 116th and 29th Div. attachments	25	-	Dog Red	H+60
Hq & Hq Co 116, 3/116 Det 5th Ranger, Det 1st Div and Vth Corps	124	15	Dog White	H+215
Det 29th Div, 2/116,1st Arty	73	14	Dog Red	H+215
Total	**1,414**			

underwater sound equipment, and radio direction finders.

The Landing Craft Support was a small 36 foot wooden motorboat designed to guide the assault waves to the beach and provide close supporting fire. They were armed with a twin .50 caliber machine gun, two .30 caliber machine guns, and twelve 5-inch rocket projectors. The LCS would herd the initial waves of LCVPs to the correct beach, and attempt to suppress any emplacement nearby.

Attack Transports (APA)

Vehicles needed to be carried on LSTs and LCTs, but the majority of the men were transported across the Channel in larger ships. The U.S. Navy officially designated transport ships that carried their own LCVPs and LCMs as "APAs" (Attack Transports). A standard troop transport designed only to carry men from one port to another was classed as an "AP." Before 1943 all transports were classed as AP. During that year those that were able to transport troops from port to shore were reclassified as APAs.

Above.
The *U.S.S. Charles Carroll* APA-28 carried the 3rd battalion of the 116th Infantry to Normandy. It is shown here in 1942 while serving as AP-58 (standard transport). In 1943 APs with the ability to land troops in an amphibious assault were redesignated as APAs, and the *Carroll* became APA28.

Left.
Waiting to leave for Normandy on board the *U.S.S. Henrico*, two men pass the time in their cramped bunks. These men (S/Sgt. Albert Rafin and Pfc. Matthew Plis) may be from the 2nd Battalion of the 16th Infantry Regiment, the unit the *Henrico* carried to Normandy.

A typical APA was the *U.S.S Bayfield* (APA-33). This ship was 492 feet long and carried 18 LCVPs, 4 LCMs and a few small command and control craft. APAs such as this carried anywhere from 1,200 to 1,400 men. Generally they carried an infantry battalion, along with various detachments scheduled to land with that battalion.

Getting the men and equipment into the smaller craft was handled differently by the various transports. The standard American method was to put all heavy equipment (flamethrowers, bazookas, mortars, etc) in the LCVPs, lower the craft into the water, and have the troops climb down nets or rope ladders. This was quite hazardous as the small LCVPs rose and fell with each swell. If a man lost his grip on the wet rope net he could fall between the ship and craft and be crushed (or his heavy pack and rifle would pull him under the water). The British had designed their ships with stronger davits to allow rail loading. This allowed them to load the troops into the LCAs at the railing, then lower the boats into the water. The American davit design was supposedly not strong enough to lower a fully loaded LCVP safely.

Some American transports realized how difficult it would be for the men to get into the LCVPs in the rough sea and rail loaded their boats against regulations. Some Army officers insisted their men be rail loaded no matter what the danger. The margin of safety proved enough and there were no accidents. On the *Empire Javelin* the men boarded the craft by sliding down special canvas chutes, called helter-skelters by the British Navy.

Uniforms of the U.S. Navy

During the invasion the Navy working uniform was the most commonly worn. For enlisted men this was dungarees and a light blue chambray shirt. The officer's working uniform was a cotton khaki shirt and trousers. Once in the combat area the men were required to wear a helmet instead of the traditional white sailor's hat. Unlike the Army troops who wore

Above.
An alternate method to unload an LST was to marry an LCT (6) to the bow of an LST. Vehicles could then be driven off the LST ramp right onto the rear of an LCT(6) which, due to its shallower draft, could bring the vehicles right to the shore. The jeep shown here is from the 4th Infantry Division headquarters. A Rhino Ferry could be used in place of the LCT(6).

Below.
The view as the LCT pulls away from the LST 282 with a full load.

Above.
The view forward as an LCT makes its way to shore.

Right.
Men of the 16th Infantry Regiment climb aboard the *U.S.S Henrico* for a boat drill during exercise Fabius. Unlike the typical rope nets, the *Henrico* uses a chain ladder with wooden rungs. Boarding the boats in the calm waters of Weymouth harbor was much easier than trying to climb down the ladders in rough seas.

an inflatable life belt, sailors were issued a dark gray kapok life vest. When the weather was colder they could wear either a dark blue lined jacket that resembles the Army tanker's jacket, or the newer gray-green colored N-1 jacket lined with alpaca.

One of the fears the Navy commanders had was that trigger-happy soldiers would see sailors in their unfamiliar uniforms on the beach, mistake them for Germans and shoot them. To prevent this an order went out just before the landing for all sailors who might end up on the beach to paint "USN" on the front and back of their uniforms in large, white letters. The men who should have done this were main-

Main Transport Ships at Omaha and primary unit carried

LSI(L) *H.M.S. Empire Javelin*	1/116th Inf.
APA-30 *U.S.S. Thomas Jefferson*	2/116th Inf.
APA-28 *U.S.S. Charles Carroll*	3/116th Inf.
APA-26 *U.S.S. Samuel Chase*	1/16th Inf.
APA-45 *U.S.S. Henrico*	2/16th Inf.
LSI(L) *H.M.S. Empire Anvil*	3/16th Inf.
AP-76 *Anne Arundel*	2/18 Inf.
AP-67 *Dorothea Dix*	mixed
AP-77 *Thurston*	mixed
LSI (s) *H.M.S. Prince Charles*	2nd Rangers
H.M.S. Ben Machree	2nd Rangers
H.M.S. Amsterdam	2nd Rangers
H.M.S. Princess Maud	SETF
H.M.S. Prince Leopold	5th Rangers
H.M.S. Prince Baudouin	5th Rangers

Transports For Utah

APA-33 *U.S.S. Bayfield*	
APA-13 *U.S.S. Joseph T. Dickman*	
HMS Empire Gauntlet	
APA-5 *U.S.S. Barnett*	

Prelude to Utah Beach, the Iles de Saint-Marcouf

Three miles off Utah Beach is a cluster of small islands called the Iles de Saint-Marcouf. The largest of these island, Ile du Large (630 x 335 yards wide), had the remains of a 19th century fortress on it as well as a lighthouse. Aerial reconnaissance had indicated the Germans were working on the island and the Allies were afraid that they were installing coastal artillery guns. If heavy artillery had been emplaced on these islands they would have been perfectly positioned to cause a great deal of damage to the ships of Force "U." If the Germans had only a small observation team on the island they could have directed the coastal guns on the mainland with great accuracy.

A detachment of troops from the 4th and 24th Cavalry Squadrons, under the command of Lt. Col. Dunn, were assigned the job of landing on the islands and destroying any guns positioned there. The cavalrymen had no real training in amphibious operations, so Scout and Raider officer Lt(jg) John Tripson was assigned to train them. Taking part in the operation was a detachment from the 4th Cavalry Squadron Headquarters, Troop A from the 4th Cavalry Squadron, and troop B from the 24th Cavalry Squadron.

The force of 6 officers and 118 men crossed the Channel in the *H.M.S. Empire Gauntlet*. The small ship PC 484 carried the detachment headquarters and resupplies of ammo for the men. LCS-12 was used to carry 2 scouts from each troop and their rubber rafts to shore, as well as provide supporting fire. The destroyer *U.S.S. Bates* was assigned for heavier gun support should the need arise. The landing plan called for the scouts to slip ashore in their rubber boats, then the remainder of the men were to board four LCAs from the *Empire Gauntlet*. Two waves were planned to bring the entire force ashore. Each LCA carried five seven-man rubber rafts in case the LCA could not find an appropriate landing spot.

The troops landed without any problem. What they found was that the Germans had not been setting up gun emplacements, but had mined and booby trapped the islands. The small force of 124 cavalrymen took casualties (3 officers and 2 enlisted men were killed) from the mines before they realized there were no Germans there. By the end of the day the tiny force had suffered 19 men killed or wounded from the mines. After the islands had been captured, the cavalrymen were to wait until relieved by a detachment from the 535th AAA Bn. One LCA remained at the island to serve as a shuttle to the mainland. When relieved, the cavalrymen of the Marcouf assault force were sent to guard VII Corps headquarters.

ly the small boat crews, beach battalions and NCDUs. Photos show some, but not all Navy personnel painted these letters. There is no explanation for why some did and others did not.

The same orders called for Navy personnel to paint a 2" band of gray on their helmets. These bands are seen on the helmets of small boat crews, beach battalions and NCDUs, but not on the crews of larger ships. Many sailors on the larger ships had already painted their helmets completely gray. The gray band, with letters *USN* in some cases, was to show the man was a sailor with duties on the beach. They were not to be moved off the beach by MPs or ordered into combat.

Helmets were mandatory in the invasion area because of the danger posed by antiaircraft fire. What is often forgotten is that everything fired into the air eventually comes back to earth. When the ships off the invasion beaches fired their antiaircraft guns, small fragments of metal and spent bullets rained down for miles around. It was a standing order for anyone above deck on any ship in a combat area to wear a helmet.

The small boat crews wore a wide variety of uniforms. Most had their dungarees or officer's khakis as a first layer, then wore impregnated Army HBT fatigues over that. They also carried gas masks. Some had the Army assault masks and others the standard Navy mask. Personal preference might add one of the warmer Navy jackets or the rubberized foul weather gear.

The boat crews left in the beach area, while their parent ship returned to England, had little space for extra clothing. They wore whatever they could scavenge from the beach, Army supplies, or beg from the larger ships. One LCVP crewman recalled getting his first change of clothing from a British ship, and so wore British Army hobnailed boots for the next few weeks.

Officers wore their rank insignia on their shirt collars, but most sailors did not wear any distinguishing marks on their uniforms. They wore their ratings (naval rank and specialty) only on their dress uniforms. Many had painted their names, ship name, or ratings on their jackets so they could easily be identified. Some painted their ratings and names on their helmets, but this seems to have been a matter of personal or group preference on each ship.

This Navy officer can be identified as a Commander by the gold oak leaves on the collar of his khaki working uniform. As the commander of an LCI flotilla, he will be stationed on board one of his LCIs scheduled to land on the beach. He has been issued with gas impregnated HBT fatigues. Over this he wears an N-1 jacket. Once his vessel gets across the Channel, he will replace his officer's visor cap with a steel helmet and strap on a pistol. Naval authorities were concerned that German soldiers might actually try and attempt to board the landing craft when they came into the beach. On D-Day all landing craft officers would carry a .45 as protection against this unlikely, but possible, threat. *(Reconstruction)*

The Bombardment Group

Combat ships were assigned to fire on German defenses as part of the Bombardment Group. Their orders were, at H-40 minutes or as soon as visibility permitted, to deliver counter-battery destructive and neutralizing fires on beach defenses. After H-hour they were to deliver fires called for by assigned Shore Fire Control Parties (SFCP) or spotter aircraft. The ships were only to fire at targets specified by the SFCP unless it was clear that there was no danger to Allied troops. Targets further inland could be directed by the high performance observation aircraft.

The Fire Support Groups (FSG) for Omaha (Force "O") and Utah (Force "U") were similar in structure. Each was divided into six different types of ships. Fire Support Groups 1 and 2 were provided with detailed locations of German shore batteries beforehand. Each ship had its own specific targets to strike unless they were directed to fire on other, more important, targets. In theory the heavier ships were to fire at the German shore batteries or targets further inland. The smaller destroyers, with their lighter

Above.
Once the landing craft were lowered and filled, each wave would form into circle in a holding pattern until given the order to head to the beach. These LCVPs circle during one of the practice invasions at Slapton Sands.

Left.
This group of soldiers getting ready to land in an LCT have crowded to the front for a view of Utah Beach. Generally, only vehicles and their crews were carried in LCTs. After the initial landings, they were sometimes used to shuttle men from larger transport ships to the shore.

Opposite page, top.
This is the view out a porthole as an LCI comes into Omaha beach. It is unknown what date this photo was taken on, but was probably a few days after the landing.

Opposite page, bottom.
LCI-81 is shown sinking off Omaha Beach. Coming to its aid are a Coast Guard rescue cutter, and a few passing LCVPs. The shoreline is obscured by smoke and haze, showing how some of the coxswains might have had a hard time spotting landmarks on shore.

guns, were to target German emplacements on the coast.

Support Group 3 was composed of destroyers. They were directed to patrol as part of the screen around the main body of ships until contacted by SFCPs or required to take up gunfire tasks.

Fire Support Group 4 was composed of subgroups 41, 42, 43, and 44. FSG 41 was the control group for all vessels in FSG4. FSG 42 was composed of LCG(L)s (with 4.7 inch guns). The LCGs would provide supporting fire on the coast at ranges closer than the larger ships. LCGs 424, 426 and 449 would support the 29th Division landings, LCGs 687 and 811 would support the 1st Division landings. They were specifically to target concrete pillboxes on the beach that were holding up the men on shore. Each ship had from 120-150 rounds for their 4.7 inch gun. The crews of these guns were Royal Marines. It was thought that Marines would have a better grasp of

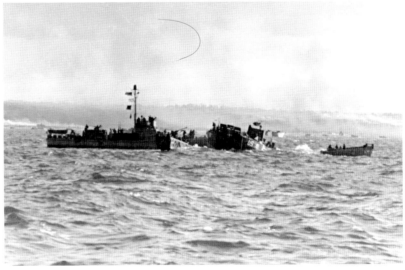

Above.
These casualties are being carried to a hospital ship by an LCVP. Paratrooper jump uniforms and boots are visible. The man being tended to at center clutches a German helmet to his chest, and rests his head on a pillow of camouflaged parachute material. It seems he is not about to give up what may be his only souvenir of the war. The LCVP crew all have USN painted on their uniforms and grey bands on their helmets.

Below.
Landing craft crewmen enjoy a warm meal of British self-heating soup cans. All men have "USN" painted on their uniforms and grey bands around their helmets. The central figure wears the rubberized foul weather jacket with leggings, while the man on the left wears a standard Army field jacket. Although difficult to see, the coxswain at right wears a gas detection brassard on his left arm.

Fire Support Groups for Force "O"

● Fire Support Group 1
Texas, Glasgow, destroyer group 1
These ships were assigned targets in the 29th Division sector of the beach.

● Fire Support Group 2
Arkansas, Georges Leygues, Montcalm, destroyer group 2
These ships were assigned targets in the 1st Division sector of the beach.

● Fire Support Group 3
destroyers *Baldwin, Franklin, Thompson, Harding.*

close support of land actions than a strictly naval crew.

FSG 43 was the LCT(R)s (rocket launching craft). They were to take up position in a line abreast so they could fire on the beach when the first wave was 300 yards offshore. This FSG was composed of LCT(R)s 366, 423, 447, 450, 473, 482, 452, 464 and 483. After firing, these craft were to return to the transport area and reload their rocket launchers. They were to be ready to fire again by H+210 minutes upon orders from the Gunfire Support Commander. On D-Day it seems that the majority of their rockets fell short into the surf. They reloaded and were ready to fire a second time, but by then the troops were far enough inland that it was not safe for them to launch their second volley.

FSG 44 was composed of British LCT(A)s carrying standard Sherman tanks of the 741st and 743rd

A salvo of five inch rockets is fired from a LCT(R). Unfortunately on D-Day, most rockets were launched out of range, landing in the water instead of destroying land mines and obstacles on the beach.

Tank Battalions. These tanks were issued 150 extra rounds of ammunition to start firing at 3,000 yards out (about H-15) all the way to the beach. The tank crews were told to fire at pillboxes, fortified houses, or other beach defenses that were holding up the assault. Each LCT(A) carried two standard Sherman tanks, and a tankdozer that was attached to the Special Engineer Task Force: the unit assigned to clear the beach obstacles.

FSG 45 was composed of the LCF flak boats that were to keep a careful watch on the skies in case the Luftwaffe made an appearance. They were initially to protect the transport area, but as the invasion progressed they were to disperse so as to provide maximum protection to the entire offshore area.

FSG 5 was composed of LCTs carrying M7 Priests of the 58th and 62nd Armored Field Artillery Battalions. In the orders these boats were referred to as LCT(HE)s, in reference to the high explosive rounds the M7's 105mm gun fired. Following 200 yards astern of the LCRs, these guns were to shell the beaches and surrounding terrain from 8,000 yards, starting at H-30, until the first waves landed and moved inland. The M7s were scheduled to land at H+90 when it was hoped the beach and exits would be clear. Extra ammunition was stored in the LCTs so the M7s could land with a full load of ammo.

Below.

These men wear an assortment of Navy and Army uniforms while they lounge on a pile of rations. The man at right wears a gas detection brassard on his left arm, and the short brimmed Army mechanic's cap. The sailor at left wears the gas protection eyeshields on his painted helmet. These were commonly used for protection against the spray.

FSG 6 was composed of subgroups 61 and 62. These LCS(S)s (Landing craft, support) were to accompany LCTs carrying DD tanks to the beach, lead the DD tanks to the proper beach, and approach as close as possible while providing support fire until H+1 hr. They were authorized to furnish close supporting and counter-battery fires on the beach where the ship's officer clearly recognized that his own forces would not be endangered by them.

Both FSG 61 and 62 (as the subgroups were known) were each composed of 12 LCS(S). FSG 61,

The first LCIs at Omaha Beach were not scheduled to land until H+70. According to Ellis Peatie, the engineering officer for the LCI 520, his was the first LCI to land troops at Omaha. The LCI 520 was not slated to land until much later in the day, and was used by Captain Lorenzo Sabin, commander of the Close Gunfire Support Group, as his headquarters. Captain Sabin had the LCI 520 move close to the beach to observe the results of his LCT(R)s and LCGs. When he saw that the German emplacements were still operational he ordered the skipper of the 520 to immediately land the vessel in order to get as many men on shore as quickly as possible. It is estimated that the LCI 520 touched down on Omaha at roughly H+35, and was able to unload and retract from the beach without being hit.

supporting the 1st Division landings, had 1 LSC from the *U.S.S Chase*; 1 from the *U.S.S Henrico*; 4 from the LST 374; 3 from the LST 376; and 3 from the LST 6. FSG 62, supporting the 29th Division, had 1 LSC from the *U.S.S Carroll*; 1 from the *U.S.S Jefferson*; 3 from LST 315; 3 from LST 310; 3 from LST 317; and 1 from LST 375.

This was the support the Navy would provide to the Omaha landings. The troops at Utah had fire support groups involving similar vessels, tanks from the 70th Tank Bn, and M7s from the 65th Armored Field Artillery Bn.

The Coast Guard

The U.S. Coast Guard has traditionally been involved with patrolling American waters to prevent smuggling and provide assistance to ships in distress. As early as 1799 a law was enacted that allowed the U.S. Navy to use Coast Guard ships and personnel in times of war. In November 1941 an executive order transferred the Coast Guard to the Navy for the duration of the war. Until 1 January 1946 the Coast Guard was, in effect, a part of the Navy. Navy and Coast

Force "O" Gunfire Support Ships
(not counting the smaller 40 and 20mm guns)
12 destroyers with 5" guns
U.S.S Augusta - nine 8" guns, eight 5"
U.S.S Arkansas - twelve 12", ten 3"
U.S.S Texas - ten 14", six 5" ten 3"
H.M.S. Glasgow - twelve 6" eight 4"
Georges Leygues and *Montcalm*- nine 6" eight 3.5"

Force "U" Gunfire Support Ships
(Larger than Force "O" as there were more coastal batteries in the Utah area)
H.M.S. Hawkins - seven 7.5", four 4"
H.M.S. Enterprise - five 6"
U.S.S Nevada - ten 14", sixteen 5"
U.S.S Quincy - nine 8", twelve 5"
U.S.S Tuscaloosa - nine 8", eight 5"
H.M.S. Black Prince - five 6"
H.M.S. Erebus - two 15", six 4"
Plus eight attached destroyers to provide beach support while these ships fired at the coastal guns.

Right.
A Coast Guard coxswain hit by machine gun fire is transferred to a larger ship where he will receive medical attention. Members of his crew have painted their uniforms and helmets with "USCG" instead of USN. The passengers on the LCVP are members of an Engineer Special Brigade MP unit.

Below.
Later in the invasion, specially marked hospital boats were used to carry casualties out to hospital ships. For the first few days, regular landing craft were used to carry men ashore and bring casualties back with them on their return trip.

Guard uniforms are essentially the same, with only a small embroidered shield on the sleeve of the dress uniform to indicate Coast Guard.

Most of the Coast Guard missions in WW2 were similar to its peacetime duties. Guardsmen patrolled beaches, kept ports and harbors secure, rescued sur- vivors from shipwrecks, and prevented smugglers (or spies) from entering the United States. The rapid expansion of both the Navy and the Army (which had its own ships in the Transportation Corps and Mine Planter Service) caused a shortage of trained seamen and ship officers. Experienced Coast

Right and bottom.
This M1 helmet was worn at Normandy by a Coast Guard Lieutenant. The two bars stand for rank and the shield for the Coast Guard emblem.

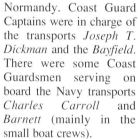

Guardsmen were assigned as crewmen on both Army and Navy vessels as needed. During WW2 351 Navy and 288 Army vessels were manned by Coast Guardsmen.

The Coast Guard had more experience with small boats and shallow water so they were naturally assigned to landing craft. Ten large attack transports (APAs) and twelve small transports (APs), and nine Auxiliary Attack Transports were manned by Guardsmen. These ships carried their own smaller landing craft which needed Coast Guard skills. Ten out of the 76 LSTs crewed by the Coast Guard took part in the Normandy invasion, along with 24 out of the 28 Coast Guard manned LCI(L)s. Four of the Coast Guard LSTs were assigned to the British Sector. Four of the Coast Guard LCI(L)s (85, 91, 92, 93) were lost during the landings. They were the only Coast Guard manned LCIs lost during the entire war.

There were 97 vessels manned by the Coast Guard at

Normandy. Coast Guard Captains were in charge of the transports *Joseph T. Dickman* and the *Bayfield*. There were some Coast Guardsmen serving on board the Navy transports *Charles Carroll* and *Barnett* (mainly in the small boat crews).

Coast Guard Rescue Flotilla One was formed specifically for the Normandy operation. It consisted of sixty 83-foot cutters (USCG-1 through USCG-60). They were given the task of rescuing men stranded in the water. The cutters were provided with special hoisting and lifesaving equipment and the crews given intense medical training. Thirty were assigned to the British beaches, and thirty to the American sector. During the initial landing only five cutters were to follow the landing craft into the beaches. The rest were to stay with the transports, as that was thought to be where they would be needed most.

Above.
These crewmen on Coast Guard Rescue Cutter 6 have painted the skull and crossbones on their helmets. This does not appear to have been a common practice, and it may be that only this one ship used this marking. This pirate insignia is particularly humorous as the Coast Guard's traditional job was to prevent pirate activity.

Once the rescue cutters saw the damage the German shore defenses were doing to the smaller boats closer to shore, they moved in and eventually pulled 1,438 men from the water. On 20 June most of these rescue craft were assigned to the Dispatch Boat Service to carry important documents and personnel to and from England. CG-27 and CG-47 sank in the storm of 20 June, but these were the only losses to the rescue flotilla.

The Coast Guard played an important role at Normandy. Not only did they provide experienced crews for the landing craft and transports, but they saved the lives of many men adrift in the water.

Squadron VCS-7

The larger ships normally carried seaplanes for observation craft. These planes were slow and they would be easy targets for any German land based antiaircraft fire. A number of Navy floatplanes had been shot down by the Germans during the invasion of Sicily. Eventually, Shore Fire Control Parties would land and be able to direct the naval gunfire onto their targets. Until these small groups of men got to shore and made their way to the front lines, the Navy needed aircraft to observe and direct its fire against the German shore batteries.

The Air Spotting Pool was officially known as No. 34 Tactical Reconnaissance Wing and was composed of four British Navy Squadrons (808, 885, 886, 897), five R.A.F. Squadrons (2, 26, 63, 144, 268), and U.S. Navy Squadron VCS-7. VCS-7 was formed specifically for the first day of the invasion. Training for these groups started in February 1944.

Above.
Lt. Commander William Denton, Jr. was the commander of Navy Squadron VCS-7. He wears a mixture of U.S. Navy and British flight gear. Denton and his men flew high performance aircraft to observe and direct the gunnery of the fire support ships.

Left.
Lt. Alexander Smith, a pilot from the *U.S.S. Augusta*, stands in front of a jeep with the marking "N.A.F. 419" (Naval Air Force?). He wears his U.S. Navy G-1 flight jacket over the naval aviator's dress green uniform.

Right.
Lt. Francis Cayhill, a pilot from the *U.S.S. Augusta*, is helped into his parachute harness by one of the American sailors assigned to serve as ground crew for VCS-7. These sailors were given special training to service the British aircraft and get them back into action over Normandy in a minimum of time.

Below.
Lt. Robert Callard temporarily traded in his slow Navy seaplane for a fast British Spitfire. Navy seaplanes were quickly shot down by German land based antiaircraft fire at Sicily, forcing the Allies to use faster planes to direct naval gunfire.

Bottom.
Three U.S. Navy pilots discuss their mission to observe and direct naval support fire at Normandy. Behind them the censor has covered up the marking "U.S. Navy VCS-7."

British pilots were given a crash course in directing naval gunfire, and 17 U.S. Navy pilots of the slow Kingfisher and Seagull seaplanes were taught to fly the high performance Spitfire and Mustang. VCS-7 was commanded by Lt. Commander William Denton of the U.S. Navy.

Starting at dawn, two aircraft were to be over the beaches at all time. One plane would observe for the ships, while the other flew as the wingman and provided protection against German fighters. The range from their airfield at Lee-on-Solent allowed each flight to stay on target for only 45 minutes. This meant that for total coverage one flight had to be on its way to Normandy, a second flight on station, while a third was returning to England for refuelling.

Starting at sunrise (H-40 minutes) and running until H+50 minutes, six groups were to be on station over the beaches. From H+50 to H+140 only three groups would be available. From H+140 to H+185 the number would go back to six and then for the rest of the day remain at only three. The Air Spotting Pool flew over 400 sorties on D-Day, observing 135 "shoots" by the Navy guns. Six aircraft in the Air Spotting Pool were shot down by German flak on D–Day.

Not only did American pilots fly the Spitfires, but American naval ground crews performed maintenance on them. Shortly after the invasion the U.S. Navy Spitfire Squadron VCS-7 was disbanded, making it one of, if not the, shortest-lived squadron in naval history. After assisting the naval bombardment of Cherbourg, VCS-7 returned its Spitfires Mk V to the RAF on 29 June.

Scouts, Raiders, and Beach Jumpers

One of the misunderstood units of World War Two is the Amphibious Scouts and Raiders. Very little has been written about this elite unit, whose job was to scout proposed landing beaches and mark them for the first waves of assaulting troops. Their role in the Normandy landings is not commonly known.

The Amphibious Scout and Raider school opened at Ft. Pierce, Florida in January 1943. Technically it was a joint Army-Navy program, but the Scout and Raider program tends to be thought of as more of a Navy operation. Some of the instructors were former staff of the Army Amphibious Training Center at Camp Johnson in Carrabelle, Florida (which had closed down just prior to the opening of the Scout and Raider school).

The Scout and Raider Army classes taught men from the Recon Troop and Engineer Bn. of infantry

divisions the rudiments of scouting invasion beaches in a condensed one month course. The 4th, 28th, 31st, 45th, and 77th Infantry Divisions sent men to this school. The Navy course was a two month program that stressed tough physical training. This included radio and visual signalling, small weapons training, small boat seamanship, and engine repair skills.

Scouts and Raiders were trained to infiltrate enemy held beaches at night and survey them as possible invasion sites. They used small rubber boats and Folboats (a small kayak-like craft) to sneak into shore undetected. In May 1943 an extra month was added to Scout and Raider school primarily for demolitions training. The final exercise of the Scout and Raider students was to infiltrate a nearby military base whose guards had been put on alert. To their credit, the Scouts and Raiders were always successful.

Scouts and Raiders were considered experts in amphibious operations, and thus some of their men were assigned as staff advisors around the world instead of being given missions to land on enemy beaches. In December 1943 a handful of Scout and Raider officers and men were assigned to Rear Admiral Kirk's Task Force 122 for the Normandy invasion.

Two of these officers were Lieutenants Phil Bucklew and Grant Anderson. After attending the British Escape and Evasion school, they participated in reconnaissance landings on French beaches in

training in recognizing landmarks on the shore would get the first waves to the right place, where other men would begin marking the landing sectors.

Some of the Scouts and Raiders would use the 56 foot LCC to get the waves of landing craft organized at the line of departure. The rest of the Raiders would use the 36 foot LCS(2) (Landing Craft Support Mk 2) to guide these waves to the shore. The LCS was armed with a twin .50 caliber machine gun, two .30 caliber machine guns, and 12 five-inch rocket projectors. These weapons were to be used to provide covering fire for the first waves to hit the beach. Neither of these vessels was constructed to land on the beach and although called "landing craft" neither had a bow ramp like more conventional landing craft.

Heading to Omaha Beach Lt. Phil Bucklew felt that the water was too rough to launch the amphibious DD tanks of the 741st Tank Bn. He advised that the tanks would swamp unless they were brought right in to the shore. His advice was ignored and most of the 741st DD swimming tanks were swamped in the high seas and went to the bottom.

conjunction with the British COPPs (Combined Operations Pilotage Parties). They helped map off-shore currents, beach gradients, and gathered sand samples to ensure that the chosen beaches could support the weight of armored vehicles. Other Scout and Raider men trained on beach obstacle demolitions with the NCDUs at Woolacombe Beach.

The primary job the Scouts and Raiders were given at Normandy was to help guide the assault waves into the proper beaches. Scout and Raider officers captained nine LCCs (Landing Craft Control). Some of these men were veterans of the Sicily landing. Although the Scouts and Raiders had been trained to land on the beaches first, marking them for the following assault troops, the decision was to use them to guide the first few boat waves to the proper beaches. It was hoped that their special

Members of the Scouts and Raiders detachment train at Fort Pierce, Florida in different sized rubber assault boats.

Off Utah Beach a Scout and Raider officer, Lt. Robert Halperin, was to guide the first landing craft waves into the beaches. At the line of departure he realized that one of the two Patrol Craft (PC-1217) marking this line had capsized and the assault waves were drifting south. He did his best to keep the boat waves compact so they would at least land together in one place. Once on shore his crew fired their rockets and machine guns to provide covering fire as the troops stormed up the beach. He then pulled a number of casualties out of the ocean, including some paratroopers from the 101st Airborne Division who had been dropped into the ocean by mistake.

After D-Day the Scouts and Raiders were used for

Left.
This class for Beach Jumpers is instructing them in the use of wire recording equipment. Magnetic tape had not yet been invented, so reels of magnetized wire, as well as standard records, were used to play deceptive sounds to trick the enemy into thinking a landing was taking place.
It was the intention of Douglas Fairbanks Jr. to use the same sort of special effects as Hollywood used in film making. His connections with the movie industry helped to design some of the devices that allowed a group of small boats to simulate an entire invasion fleet.

all manner of miscellaneous related jobs. They picked up survivors struggling in the water, surveyed beaches and ports, and prepared charts for the artificial Mulberry harbor. Although they had been given extensive training in getting assault troops to the proper beaches, they were not allowed to use all their skills to make sure the assault troops landed in the correct place. Had these men been properly used, by allowing them to land on the beaches before daybreak and properly mark them, the invasion may not have been as chaotic as it was.

The Navy Beach Jumpers were another elite force of the U.S. Navy, but one that was not used at Normandy. Beach Jumpers were the idea of film actor Douglas Fairbanks Jr. who wanted to form a unit trained to deceive the enemy as to where a landing was taking place. These units used sound recordings to simulate a fleet anchoring offshore, or other special devices to convince the defenders that an entire fleet was about about to land, when there were only a handful of small boats involved. They were quite skilled in deceiving enemy radio and radar stations.

The Beach Jumpers were used in the Mediterranean to divert German attention from actual landing beaches, but they were not used at Normandy. Lt.Commander Douglas Fairbanks, Jr. did consult with the Overlord planners, but as far as is known took no part in any actions on D-Day. This was probably because the British already had special units for deceiving the Germans and were already working on a grand scheme of deception for the second front, known as Operation Bodyguard. The Beach Jumpers did take part in many of the Mediterranean landings and played a major role in the invasion of Southern France. They also served in the Pacific.

Above.
Scouts and Raiders were trained to fire these 5" rockets from racks on each side of their LSC. Set at a 45 degree angle, these rockets needed to be fired at exactly the right range from the target. They were aimed by pointing the boat at the target and firing them when at the correct distance.

Right.
The LCS (Landing Craft Support) was one of the principal boats used by the Scouts and Raiders. This model was armed with twin .50 caliber machine guns in front, three .30 caliber machine guns, rocket launching racks at each side, and racks for smoke pots at the stern. At Normandy, Scout and Raider crews used these boats to guide the initial waves to the correct landing beaches under the direction of the Landing Craft Control.

Chapter 3 The Assault troops

THE first troops to land on the enemy beaches in Normandy were to be infantrymen from specially trained assault regiments. There was a group of officers in the U.S. Army who felt there should be specially trained elite assault divisions to spearhead such invasions.

This faction was overruled by the more popular belief that elite units grouped the best men in one place and lowered the effectiveness of the rest of the Army. It was felt that given the right training and equipment any unit could perform elite missions.

Three very different infantry regiments were chosen to be the first wave assault troops in

This 29th Division soldier training in England has an M-7 rifle grenade launcher on his M1 Garand. Rifle grenades were generally carried in the ammunition bag as seen here, although this bag was designed as a generic bag for any type of munitions. It was made to hold a standard .30 caliber ammunition can.

Normandy. The 8th Infantry (4th Division) was a Regular Army unit that had never been tested in combat, but had taken amphibious training back in Florida. The 116th Infantry (29th Division) was a National Guard unit that had neither been in combat. The 29th Division, however, had been training in England longer than any other U.S. division. It had been there since October 1942, long enough to pick up the nickname "England's Own." The only veteran unit to be chosen for the first wave was the 16th Infantry of the 1st Division. It had already made two amphibious assaults in the Mediterranean (North Africa and Sicily).

Why these regiments were chosen from their divisions to lead the assault is an interesting question. Veterans today tend to recall that these were considered the best of their divisions at the time. There is, however, a curious tale surrounding the 116th Infantry. In the months before D-Day men from the 116th had become involved in a race riot with black troops at Ivy Bridge. Shots were fired, some men were wounded, and at formation the next day many men were sporting black eyes and bandages. General

Charles Gerhardt, the Commander of the 29th, balled them out for their behavior and remarked "*You men want to fight? I'll see you get your belly full of fighting.*" Some claim it was Gerhardt's displeasure at the 116th that caused him to select them as the assault regiment. Others claim that the 116th was considered the best of the three regiments and point to the 116th being selected for the first ATC class in 1943 as evidence the decision had been made long beforehand.

In any event, the men destined for the first waves had already gone through assault training at the ATC. In the spring of 1944 men in these divisions were put through tests for the Expert Infantryman Badge. This award, a younger brother to the Combat Infantryman Badge, not only showed that the wearer was a trained infantryman, but also earned an extra $5 a month pay. It was a small price to pay for building the morale of the infantry. The EIB was awarded after passing numerous physical tests (such as

running so far in so many minutes), qualifying on various infantry weapons, and answering questions about infantry skills. This was designed to weed out the older or weaker members of the unit so they could be replaced with younger and stronger men. Although not spoken at the time, some veterans have said they knew that if they failed the EIB tests they would be transferred to a noncombat unit and kept out of the fighting. To their credit, few chose to do so.

The Boat Teams

A standard infantry company in 1944 was composed of 6 officers and 193 enlisted men. In the company there were three rifle platoons each with 41 men armed with rifles and BARs. A fourth platoon was the weapons platoon composed of 60mm mortars and light .30 caliber machine guns. The primary requirement for an assault team was that it had to fit into a 30 man

Left.
Close inspection of this German squad will reveal an Allied Quonset hut with an American soldier standing in the doorway. These German troops are in fact members of the 1/116 communications section participating in a training program for the invasion. During the first part of the war the British Army actually manufactured reproduction German uniforms to train their men in enemy uniform and rank recognition. After the Allies had invaded Italy, captured German uniforms were brought to England. These American soldiers put on the German uniforms and marched around the 29th Division area giving their comrades a chance to see what Germans looked like before they had to face them in combat.
(Courtesy John Sullivan)

The invasion armband with American flag has long been associated with the D-Day landings. Although there is numerous photographic evidence that these armbands were used in many of the Mediterranean invasions (including Southern France), there is no evidence that any of them were worn in the Normandy Invasion. A few popular books have used photographs of men with these armbands and implied they were taken at Normandy, but the original captions always indicate one of the Mediterranean landings.

Previous page, top.
In a marshalling area in England men from the 4th Division grab what might be their last meal before boarding the transport. They have already been issued life belts and the assault gas masks. They wear HBT fatigues with rank stripes and division patches applied. A parachutist's first aid pouch can be seen tied onto the web gear of a soldier in the rear. The corporal kneeling down facing the camera has a toggle rope tied to his belt. The use of toggle ropes by the U.S. Army appears to have been limited to the 4th Division.

Right.
This 29th Div. Staff Sergeant, sharpening his knife for the upcoming invasion of France, is probably a squad leader due to the whistle chain seen on his field jacket. There is an ammunition bag of rifle grenades in their black cardboard tubes at his feet. At right is a M-1943 folding entrenching tool. This photo was supposedly taken in the marshalling area just before D–Day, so the lightweight gas mask bag hanging behind him would indicate he is part of the 175th Infantry Regiment- the 3rd regiment to land, which was not issued with the special assault gas mask.

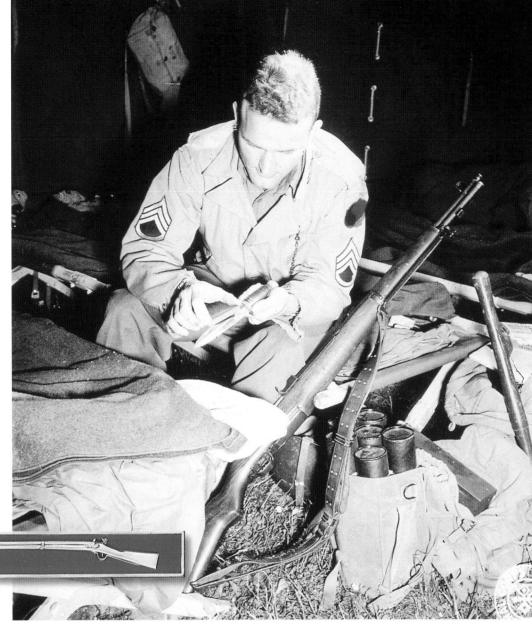

Above.
The Expert Infantryman Badge, adopted in November 1943 and described in Army Regulations of March 1944.

Right.
In the 1st and 29th Division the men painted the divisional insignia on their helmets. This was not done in the 4th Division, but at least in one unit they painted the ivy leaves on the helmet liner. Of special interest is the liner at the left marked "Eyemo Ed" with what looks like a First Army Signals marking. This may refer to a member of the 165th Signal Photo Company that operated the standard Army movie camera: the 35mm Eyemo. If so, then this photo may have been taken shortly before the invasion when the photographers had been attached to the assault units.

The most common way of communicating in an infantry company was the sound powered telephone. This marvellous invention was a lightweight handset that did not need any batteries to operate. All that was needed was a reel of wire and a sound powered phone on either end to talk up to a mile away. The heavier EE-8 battery powered telephones were too heavy for an infantry platoon to lug round. Although the U.S. Army had the best radios in the world, most communication was either by telephones or messages hand carried by runners.

LVCP. It also had to be composed of a mixture of men and weaponry so that if one or more boats were lost each boat team could continue to fight on its own.

Once safely ashore in France, the 30 man assault boat teams were to revert to their standard infantry regimental organization for the inland fighting. The assault boat team was composed of a 5 man rifle section, a 4 man BAR section, a 4 man bazooka section, a 4 man 60mm mortar section, a 4 man wire cutting section, a 2 man flamethrower section and a 4 man demolition section. They were commanded by an officer (the boat team leader) and an NCO (assistant boat team leader).

The boat teams were created by mixing the weapons platoon in with the rifle platoons, and adding extra men brought in as replacements. Each boat team was designed to be able to land on the beach and attack German fortifications without any support.

The first man off the boat was always the team leader. He was followed by the rifle team which could also provide supporting fire with rifle gre-

nades. Then the wire cutting team would advance to any barbed wire and open a gap in it with Bangalore torpedoes and wire cutters. Two bazooka teams would fan out at the sides and fire rockets at pillbox openings. Two BARs would provide covering fire, as the 60 mm mortar would provide indirect fire at targets under cover. The demolition team and the flamethrower team would advance under the covering fire, through the gaps in the barbed wire, and assault the pillbox with flame and explosive charges. The last man off the boat would be the assistant boat team leader, acting in the role of the assistant platoon leader. He made sure everyone and everything got off the landing craft and acted as second in command.

There were 6 of these assault boat teams per company, plus a command boat team formed from the company headquarters. Every man in a boat team had an assigned position in the landing craft so they could exit in a specific order.

The assault boat teams were made up from the three rifle companies, but the fourth company in the battalion (the heavy weapons company) needed its own organization. To use the skills and weapons of the heavy weapons company, it was organized into five 30-man support boat teams and one command support boat team. After the troops had gotten through the beach defenses, they were to reorganize into two rifle squads and a weapons squad. This was the first step to returning to a standard rifle company organization.

The support boat teams were to land in the second wave, once an area had been secured for them, and set up their heavy weapons. However, the organiza-

Opposite page, top.
The assault troops were given advanced combat training which included such expedients as firing a 60mm mortar without bipod or baseplate. Here a mortarman demonstrates the technique of holding the mortar tube with asbestos mittens to General Bradley during a training exercise in England.

Opposite page, bottom.
The M-7 grenade launcher was developed to fire antitank rifle grenades from the M1 Garand. It could also be used to fire a wide variety of projectiles as seen here. On the table are a practice antitank grenade, impact and time fused antipersonnel grenades, a smoke grenade, and a selection of signalling parachute flares and star clusters.

tion of these support teams indicates that the planners wanted them to have the self-contained ability to attack German positions as well. Each support team had its own 4-man wire cutting team and 5-man demolition team. Additionally it had a 5-man rifle team, a 6-man heavy machine gun team, an 8-man 81mm mortar team, and a support team leader and assistant leader.

The command boat teams of the company headquarters averaged 16 men and included the company executive officer. The company commander landed as an extra man with one of the assault boat teams. The rest of the command boat was taken up with men from other units and attachments such as the tank battalion liaison team or Shore Fire Control Parties. Two boats per company brought in a medic. Most LCVPs ended up bringing more than their 30 man teams onto the beach. It seemed that every following unit had advance parties, liaison men, or reconnaissance sections that needed one or two men to be squeezed into an LCVP. There was much juggling of space at the last minute and so it can never be determined exactly who was in each boat.

Differences in Boat Teams

Although the 1st and 29th Divisions troops seemed to follow the ATC-developed boat teams fairly closely, there were many minor differences from the established plan. In the 4th Division it appears that there was not a command assault boat team, but that the command elements were brought in on the following eight support boat teams.

In the 3rd Battalion of the 116th Infantry only two of the boat teams in each company were equipped

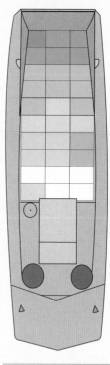

ASSAULT BOAT TEAM

Boat Team Leader (Officer)
M-1 Carbine
6 colored smoke grenades
1 smoke grenade
1 frag grenade
1 SCR-536

Rifle Team (5 men)
1 & 2. Garand
  1 smoke grenade
  2 frag grenades
  Wirecutters
3. Garand
  1 smoke grenade
  1 frag grenade
  1 grenade launcher M7
  10 smoke rifle grenades
4 & 5. Garand
  1 smoke grenade
  2 frag grenades
  1 Bangalore torpedo

Wire cutting Team (4 men)
1 - 4. Garand
  1 smoke grenade
  2 Bangalore torpedoes
  2 wirecutters
  2 large searchnose wirecutters

BAR Team (4 men)
1 & 3. BAR gunner
  BAR belt (13 mags)
  BAR spare part kit
3 et 4. Asst gunner
  Garand
  BAR belt (13 mags)
  Ammunition bag (32 M1 clips)

Basic ammo loads
M1 Rifle- 176 rounds (80 in belt, 96 in two Bandoleers)

Assistant Boat Team Leader (NCO)
  Garand
  2 smoke grenades
  8 frag grenades

60mm Mortar Team (4 men)
1. Observer: sight, cleaning staff, binocs, compass, flashlight, 12 mortar rounds, carbine
2. Gunner: mortar, pistol, 5 rounds
3. Asst. gunner: 12 rounds, carbine
4. Ammo carrier: carbine, 12 rounds

Bazooka Team (4 men)
1 & 3. Rocketeer
  Bazooka M1A1
  M1 Carbine
  8 rockets in bag
2 & 4. Loader
  Garand
  12 rockets in bag

Flamethrower Team (2 men)
1. Operator
  Flamethrower
  .45 Pistol
2. Assistant, 5 gallon fuel refill, nitrogen tank and wrenches Garand, 4 smoke and 6 fragmentation grenades

Demolition Team (5 men)
Garand, 50' Primacord, at least 4 detonators, 6 blocks TNT, 7 pack charges, 3 pole charges, 2 fuze lighters, demo kit w/crimpers, knife, tape and cord, 2 frag grenades, 1 smoke grenade.

Basic ammo loads
M1 Carbine - 75 rounds (five magazines)
.45 Pistol : 3 magazines

This series of color shots are still frames taken from a 16mm color movie shot by Coast Guard Chief Photographer's Mate Ruley during the invasion. Although it is convenient to claim this is Omaha Beach on 6 June, the scenes taken before and afterward indicate that it is more likely a day or two later. Fires in the beach area continued to burn for many days, and these often give the impression of explosions.

Right.
This 29th Division soldier stands at the water's edge on Omaha Beach. Behind him can be seen the debris of the invasion. Of specific interest is that he wears the division insignia on both his helmet and on his left shoulder. Although some have questioned if members from the assault regiments actually wore their division patch during the invasion, the evidence is clear that many did.

Bottom left and below.
It has been a matter of debate if any Amtracs (amphibious tractors) took part in the Normandy invasion. These are the only two known photographs of one that were definitely taken in Normandy. It appears that at least one Amphibious Truck Bn. may have been issued with some of these tracked vehicles. Unfortunately, the unit these amtracs were assigned to has yet to be identified. The number on the amtrac looks to be a 5-digit unit serial number normally used on bar code markings. In the background a bulldozer prepares a road up from the beach.

with bazookas and flamethrowers. It is believed that there was a shortage of these special issue weapons. In the 8th and 16th Regiments it appears there was enough equipment for the entire regiment.

The executive officer of A/116, Lt. Ray Nance, recalls that at least two of the A/116th boat teams had a light .30 caliber machine gun team that replaced one BAR and one bazooka team. There is some evidence that other companies brought their light machine guns on the assault because they provided much greater firepower than a BAR. After-action reports from the 16th Regiment indicate that light machine guns were carried by at least some, if not all, of those assault companies.

Nance also remembers that in the A/116 command boat there were only 18 men: the executive officer, 10 men from the company headquarters, 3 medics, and 4 advance men from the 29th Division recon troop. This small load let their boat ride high in the water so, unlike the heavily laden craft, they did not have to bail out water on their way to the shore. Communications from company to battalion was by SCR-300 radio carried in the command boat, while the smaller SCR-536 handie-talkie was used to transmit between the different boat teams in the company.

One F/116 boat team carried not only the standard 30 man team, but the company commander Captain Bill Callahan, his runner (with SCR-536), and a liaison officer and radio operator from the supporting 743rd Tank Battalion. The 34 man load made their boat ride deep in the water and they were worried it might swamp from the rough seas.

The careful planning sometimes went astray as was the case with a support boat team from the 16th

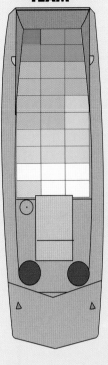

SUPPORT BOAT TEAM

Boat Team Leader (Officer)
  M-1 Carbine
  6 colored smoke grenades
  1 smoke grenade
  1 frag grenade
  1 SCR-536

Rifle Team (5 men)
1, 2 & 3. Garand
  M7 Grenade launcher
  1 smoke grenade
  1 frag grenade
  3 smoke rifle grenades
  12 AT rifle grenades
4, 5. Garand
  2 smoke grenades
  5 frag grenades
  M1938 Wirecutters

HMG Team (6 men)
1. Tripod, pistol

2. M-1917A1 HMG, carbine

3. Water chest, ammo box, spare parts kit, carbine

4 & 5. 2 ammo boxes, carbine

6. 2 ammo boxes, carbine, binocs

Assistant Boat Team Leader (NCO)
  Garand
  2 smoke grenades
  8 frag grenades

Wire cutting Team (4 men)
1 - 4. Garand
  1 smoke grenade
  2 Bangalore torpedoes
  2 M-1938 wirecutters
  2 large searchnose wirecutters

81mm Mortar Team (8 men)
1. Observer: sight, binoculars, compass, flashlight, 5 mortar rounds, carbine, sound powered phone
2. Gunner: bipod, carbine, sound powered phone
3. Asst. Gunner: mortar tube with aiming stakes in it, carbine
4. Baseplate, carbine
5. Carbine, 7 rounds, 400 yards communication wire
6, 7 & 8: Garand, 7 rounds

Demolition Team (5 men)
Garand, 50' Primacord, at least 4 detonators, 6 blocks TNT, 7 pack charges, 3 pole charges, 2 fuze lighters, demo kit w/crimpers, knife, tape and cord, 2 frag grenades, 1 smoke grenade.

Basic ammo loads
M1 Rifle- 176 rounds (80 in belt, 96 in two bandoleers)
M1 Carbine - 75 rounds (five magazines)
.45 Pistol : 3 magazines

Below.
The light colored British LCT (A) 2273 is seen here apparently with some battle damage. The 2273 is notable as it was supposed to land two standard Shermans of the 743rd Tank Bn. and a tankdozer on Dog Green Beach at H-hour. U.S. Navy vessels were uniformly painted in the standard gray color, but the British LCT(A)s stand out in their lighter colored paint scheme.

Left.
Coast Guardsmen on board a small vessel examine the damage done by German fire on D-Day. The red primer stands out where shrapnel has knocked away the outer gray paint. Behind them is the rack for signal flags.

Below.
A sailor stands in front of the pillbox at the Vierville draw. This gun looks out over Omaha from Dog Green to the east. To the right is a concrete wall that shields the gun from the sea. The German guns did not fire directly out to sea, but down the length of the beach. The wall between them and the sea prevented the Allied ships from spotting their gun flashes and knocking them out.

Infantry. Their LCVP had been damaged while loading the men and was not in shape to make the run to the beach. Col. O'Neil of the Special Engineer Task Force saw this and provided these men with one of the spare SETF LCMs for their trip to the beach.

The Overstrength

When the assault units were transformed into boat teams they were authorized extra men, known as the overstrength. Normally, each military unit has a strict number and type of men it could have on its rolls. The overstrength allowed the assault unit to leave a small cadre of men back in England to follow later. These men, known as "residues", would join the main body of their unit in France a few days after the landing with their vehicles and heavier equipment. The overstrength also strengthened the units in the assault, enabling them to take heavier casualties and still function. In the 2,500 men of an infantry division overstrength there were 126 infantry officers and 1,725 enlisted infantrymen.

The 1st, 4th and 29th Infantry Divisions were allocated 2,500 extra men for the invasion. The 1st, 5th and 6th Engineer Special Brigades were each given 925 extra men. Most of the overstrength were men trained from the infantry, artillery, engineer and medical branches.

Bill Callahan of F/116th recalls his company had 214 men in the assault (not counting any left behind in England), while other veterans feel the assault companies were 240 men. A story was making the rounds that A/116th (which took the heaviest casualties of any assault company) had been provided with

Above.
This classic photograph of 29th Division troops on their way to the embarkation points has caused some confusion in identifying the unit, as none of the men carry the black rubber assault gas mask bag. The rubber wore off the bags while marching and so had to be transported to the landing craft in vehicles. This is probably a company headquarters unit from the 115th Infantry Regiment as the men do not have the assault jackets of the 116th Regt. or the canvas lightweight gas mask bags of the 175th. Furthermore, although bazookas would generally be carried by the heavy weapons companies of the 115th, these men are could be a company headquarters as they carry Garand rifles instead of carbines, and an SCR-300 radio (far left). Of special interest is that both the early M1 ammunition bag with the open top and the closed top bazooka ammo bag are being used to carry bazooka ammunition.

Above.
Although some of the officers at the table are from the 29th Division, the men passing through this embarkation check point belong to the 1st Infantry Division, and the 'Big Red One' patch can be barely seen on their helmets. In the foreground two men are pulling a two wheeled ammunition cart that appears to hold black cardboard tubes of mortar shells.

a larger overstrength due to its tough mission. This story cannot be true because the Executive Officer of A/116, Ray Nance, clearly recalled a strength of 214 men as well.

Overstrength men were officers as well as enlisted men. Lt George Bradbury was transferred from the 100th Infantry Division to the 29th Division in May 1944. He was the officer in charge of 24 overstrength men from A/116 on D-Day. He landed with these men on the afternoon of D-Day and found only about 32 men from A company still functioning on the beach. For the first few days after the invasion he commanded a combined group of both A and B companies until an officer could be found for B company. He then led the roughly 56 men of A Company until late in June when he was wounded and evacuated. He clearly recalls that in the time he commanded the company he did not receive any replacements and lost only 5 men in combat.

Weapons of the assault troops

Most of the weapons used by the assault troops were standard in every infantry company. The rifle-

Left.
During the crossing, soldiers had to wear their life belts in all circumstances, as well as their assault gas masks and gas detector armbands (on the left arm). Their fatigue uniforms – almost new – are impregnated with CC-2, a product for neutralising the effects of blistering gas, discovered in 1924. Having been treated in the "laundries" of the Chemical Warfare Service, they were only issued to the men shortly before D-Day. The white residue of this treatment is clearly visible here.

men carried the M-1 Garand rifle. One man in the boat team carried the M-7 rifle grenade launcher that allowed him to fire rifle grenades. Officers and men carrying heavy equipment were armed with the M1 carbine. This was a lightweight weapon designed more for personal protection than for assault work. Many soldiers felt the carbine was too lightweight and inaccurate for front line work, and picked up the first discarded Garand they could find. Soldiers whose primary job was to carry a heavy machine gun or mortar were happy to carry the lighter carbine. Only a few men with the heaviest loads from the support boat team were authorized pistols. A few officers and men had acquired their own pistols before the invasion, but many more would pick them up later on from casualties in France.

The M7 rifle grenade launcher could be placed on the M1 Garand and used to fire either antitank or smoke grenades, flares or signalling flares. The M-7 was a recent development, and until mid-1944 every infantry squad had one man issued an M-1903 Springfield specifically to use with rifle grenades. When the M-7 was developed, the squad rifle grenadier traded in his Springfield for a Garand. The changeover was slow and many units continued to use

CHEMICAL GRENADES

DETONATING FUZE

BURSTER CHARGE

BURSTER WELL

SMOKE WP

WHITE PHOSPHORUS FILLING

BURSTING TYPE

IGNITING FUZE

VOID

STARTER MIXTURE

SAFETY RING

GAS CN-D

ADHESIVE TAPE

TEAR AND VOMITING GAS

BURNING TYPE

Springfields for grenade launching long after the M–7 was first issued.

The BAR teams carried the rifle squad automatic weapon: the Browning Automatic Rifle. This was a magazine fed weapon that could be fired either semi-automatic or full automatic. It was heavier than a Garand and each BAR gunner had an assistant to help keep it supplied with ammunition. A sturdy bipod was mounted on the front of the BAR to help steady the weapon, but a number of BAR gunners removed the bipod to lighten their load by a few pounds. This weapon was almost universally referred to by the troops as a "B-A-R" (letters spelled out). A second, but much less popular term for the weapon, was to call it a "bar gun", but it was never referred to as a " bar."

BAR ammo belts, with pockets large enough to hold two of the 20 round clips, were issued to the automatic riflemen and their assistants. The M-1 bayonet was carried by all men with either a Garand or Springfield. Men carrying the carbine, pistol, or BAR were issued the M-3 trench knife.

As previously mentioned, some of the boat teams substituted a light M-1919A4 machine gun for a BAR. The Garand, BAR and M1919A4 LMG all used the same ammunition. This would come in handy when rifle ammunition was low. One 250 round box of belted machine gun ammo could be broken down to supply riflemen if needed. The carbine used a lighter round that was unique to that weapon. The M1911A1 .45 caliber pistol round could be used in any of the submachine guns

AMMUNITION CARRIED IN THE LANDINGS IN ADDITION TO THE BASIC LOAD

- 6 bandoleers per rifle squad
- 4 grenades (3 fragmentation and 1 white phosphorus) for 20 men/platoon
- 1,500 rounds per HMG or LMG
- 72 rounds per 60mm mortar
- 24 rounds per 81mm mortar
- 8 rounds per heavy mortar (carried by A&P platoon)

In addition assault troops carry:
- 10 rockets, bazooka
- 2 pole charges
- 3 pack charges
- 560 rounds/BAR
- 12 grenades/AT rifle.

Above.

There were two types of American smoke grenades. The standard burning type (right) was a cylindrical metal can. Although when set off the can heated up enough to start grass fires, they posed little danger. The bursting type (left) has a rounded bottom so that men could easily tell it apart in the dark. When detonated, these grenades exploded into a rain of small burning fragments of white phosphorous. It created a smoke screen, but also burned anything or anyone that was within 20 feet of the grenade.

INFANTRY BOAT TEAM LEADER

The Boat Team Leader was supposed to be the first man off the landing craft, and lead his men onto the beach. This 1st Division officer carries the paraphernalia needed to command his 30 man boat team. He wears the standard wool uniform (impregnated against chemical weapons) and winter combat jacket with divisional insignia. His leggings would also be impregnated against gas and his boots coated with a protective dubbing. His helmet, covered with a camouflage net, is painted with the divisional insignia on the front and the vertical white stripe indicating an officer on the rear. He has chosen to wear his web gear underneath, and flotation belt over, the assault jacket. He carries the M1943 folding entrenching tool, M1938 map case, binoculars in their brown leather case, assault gas mask, and parachutist's first aid pouch. He is armed with an M1 carbine, carried in the clear Pliofilm cover. An M1911 A1 pistol in its M1916 leather holster (left) and an M-3 trench knife (right) hang from the pistol belt. Slung on his back is the SCR-536 handie-talkie used to communicate between boat teams.
(Reconstruction)

Springfields. In May 1944 the Vth Corps complained that the overstrength men being sent to it were issued with Springfields and they requested that Garands be found for these men. No records have been found to indicate what action was taken from this request and it is possible that up to 2,300 men per division landed in France equipped with the 1903 Springfield. There is some evidence that these Springfields were traded for Garands from other units.

For the actual landing, all of the weapons were carried in a thin plastic cover made from a substance known as Pliofilm. These large plastic bags were known to the troops as "elephant condoms." The Pliofilm bags shown in D-Day photographs are all clear plastic. At some point in 1944 these bags were manufactured in a dark green color, however, it is not known if any of the green Pliofilm bags were used at D-Day.

The troops were to place their weapons in the bags

(Thompson or M3 grease gun) produced by the Americans, although these SMGs were not issued to regular infantry companies or to the assault troops.

In every standard infantry platoon one man was selected as the platoon sniper with an M-1903A4 sniper rifle. This was a very accurate bolt action rifle equipped with a telescopic sight. In theory, the platoon sniper would have been allowed to carry this rifle in the landings rather than a Garand, but there is no evidence that anyone did carry an M-1903A4 rifle in any of the assault units.

This sniper rifle was based on the M-1903 Springfield rifle which had served the U.S. Army in World War One. It was possibly one of the most accurate bolt action military rifles of its day. Before WW2 the Army had plenty of time to train soldiers to be accurate marksmen and to make every round count. With the massive influx of men into the Army starting in 1940, the Army decided that it was better to arm its soldiers with a semiautomatic rifle (one that fired each time the trigger was pulled without having to operate a bolt). This new thinking emphasized massive firepower over the old theory of fewer, more accurate shots.

Outfitting the U.S. Army with millions of Garand rifles was an enormous task and a number of older M-1903 Springfields were used in the invasion. Many of the overstrength were issued with

In this rare series of photos, men from the 1st Division waterproof weapons and attach flotation belts to them in case they are dropped in the water.

Top.
A Pliofilm cover is placed over a 60mm mortar that has been tied to a life belt. The 1st Division had a great deal of experience in amphibious landings and took every precaution so their weapons and equipment would get ashore.

Above.
An inflated life belt tied to a pole charge is handed down into an LCVP. Generally the heavy equipment was pre-loaded onto the landing craft, the LCVP lowered to the water, then the men would climb down ladders into it.

Left.
A life belt has been tied to this pole charge, but the most interesting subject of this photo is the flamethrower refill found in the lower right corner. The 5 gallon can is stencilled "F.T.F. Refill No 1" (Flame Thrower Fuel). Although not visible in the photo, these refills were carried by the flamethrower assistant on packboards.

while they were on the transport ships and only remove the weapons once they were safely ashore. In actual practice this was difficult to do, as you could not use the sling when the rifle was encased in plastic. Use of the sling was necessary when climbing down rope ladders to get into the landing craft. A more common solution to keeping water out of a weapon was to just put a regular condom over the muzzle.

There were a few different types of grenades carried by the assault troops. The most common was the Mk 2A1 fragmentation grenade. This is the typical "pineapple" most commonly thought of as an American grenade. Before the war explosives like the Mk 2A1 were painted yellow to indicate the danger of a live explosive. Dummy or training rounds were always painted light blue. Once American troops entered combat they realized the

bright yellow color was a bad idea for camouflage reasons and the War Department began to paint all combat munitions olive drab, but with yellow lettering to indicate live munitions.

There were two main types of smoke grenades carried in the invasion. Colored M16 smoke grenades, which could be used for concealment or signalling purposes, came in a cylindrical metal can. Only officers in the assault troops were to use colored smoke grenades. Yellow smoke was to mark the advance of friendly troops, while violet (purple) smoke was to indicate that an explosive was about to be detonated in the area. The M8 smoke grenade was similar, but produced only white smoke.

The more fearsome smoke grenade was the M-15 (WP) white phosphorus grenade. This grenade had a tapered bottom so men would be able to tell it from a regular smoke grenade in the dark. This grenade produced a thick while cloud of smoke, while the burning white phosphorus would set flammable material on fire. A small bursting charge would scatter the burning white phosphorus particles which would cause horrendous burns on anyone they fell on. This burning phosphorus could not be extinguished by water.

Orders had been issued specifically that no tear

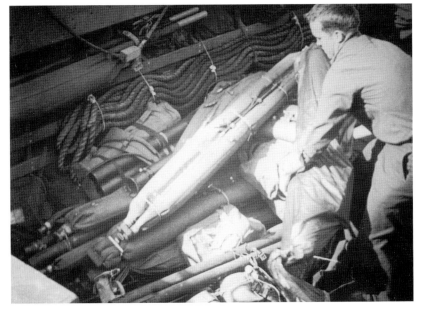

gas or other noxious gas grenades be used in the invasion. CS, or tear gas grenades, might have been helpful in clearing out German bunkers, but the Allies did not want anyone to mistake tear gas for a poison gas, which the Germans might then retaliate with. A few troops were issued with M14 (TH) Thermite grenades for demolition work. Thermite burns at a very hot temperature that would melt any metal it was in contact with. The easiest way to destroy a German artillery piece was to set off a Thermite grenade in the breech or muzzle.

Although there was a specified amount of ammunition each man was to carry, this was not always followed to the letter. In the 1st and 29th Divisions men were to carry a full ammo belt and two bandoleers. In the 4th Division only one bandoleer was specified. In practice the men carried ashore what they felt they could take and would need. This generally meant more ammo than was specified in orders. Some veterans recall carrying up to six bandoleers and many more grenades than called for.

Demolitions

Assault troops were each issued a 1/2 pound block of TNT along with an M1 pull ignitor and a short section of fuse. This was to help dig foxholes in a hurry once on the shore. All through the night of 6 June the cry of "fire in the hole", followed by a small explosion, could be heard all over the beachhead as men started digging in. After-action reports mentioning this item can be summed up by the one 29er who said: "*just one more thing to carry. More weight to our already heavy load.*"

The ATC had trained the men to make a waterproof pull ignitor from a standard M1 fuse lighter by sealing it in a condom. The waterproofed M-2 pull ignitors were in short supply, so they were issued only to the troops

The 29th Division was one of the few American divisions that regularly painted their divisional insignia on the front of their helmets. Although the size and style of the painting might vary slightly depending upon the facilities at hand, the Commander of the 29th insisted not only that his men have their helmets marked, but also that they wear the chin strap fastened at all times.

assigned to blow gaps in the beach obstacles. In K/116 everyone carried the ignitor, 6 inches of fuse, and a blasting cap stuck in their helmet net. In hindsight it was probably not a good idea to carry this so close to the head. In other units they taped the blasting caps to the outside of their entrenching tools, for the small amount of protection the metal shovel would provide if the blasting cap was set off.

Lt. Ed McNabb of H/116 recalled an interesting use for the 1/2 pound blocks of TNT. He was part of a small group of men who took cover behind the sea wall on Omaha beach. Most of their equipment had been lost getting to shore and all the rifles were jammed with sand. They expected a German counterattack to try and sweep them from the beach, so they made field expedient grenades by placing the TNT in empty K ration boxes and filled the boxes with small stones. Although they never had a chance to use their K ration grenades, it showed quick thinking and the high level of training and initiative on the part of the assault troops.

The most important job of the assault boat teams was to destroy the German fortifications on the beach to clear the way for the following troops. The primary method of destroying these bunkers and pillboxes was with demolition charges. Two demo charges were developed at the ATC specifically for the assault troops. Both the pole charge and the pack charge were not standard production items. The demolition men from the assault troops were trained to make these charges themselves from 1/2 pound blocks of TNT.

The pack charge was made by taping or wiring

All American units landing on D-Day fell under the command of the American First Army.

Before the war, the patch could be found with a branch of service color inside the "A." By 1944 they had been phased out and everyone wore this plain olive drab version. Long after the war, a red and white variety was authorized. Most Corps insignia are blue and white; white was the old color for infantry, replaced by blue. The 5th Corps used a pentagon, more commonly seen without the OD border. The VIIth Corps used a seven pointed star (a former VIIth Corps insignia) with the numerals "VII" in white on blue.

together 32 1/2-pound TNT blocks, adding a carry handle, and attaching an ignitor assembly with fuse and blasting cap. The ATC manual on demo charges suggested concealing the pack charge in a sandbag to cover the bright yellow color of the TNT labels.

The pole charge used 24 1/2-pound blocks fixed to the end of an eight foot pole. The pole could be used to push the charge into the opening of a pillbox or to hold the charge against a concrete wall. To achieve the greatest explosive effect the charge had to lie flat against the wall, so it needed to be mounted on a swivel.

Two assemblies of an ignitor, a short section of delay fuse, and blasting caps were attached to the bottom of the pole. For safety these were left unconnected until the charge was about to be set. Then the blasting caps were taped to the two lines of Primacord running up the pole and into the charge. Two fuse assemblies were used to lower the chances of a misfire after having been carried through the surf. Once the ignitor was pulled, it set off a few seconds of delay fuse. When the flame reached the blasting cap, it set off the Primacord which then detonated the main charge.

The Bangalore torpedo was the invention of a British officer serving in Bangalore, India. It was a thin metal tube filled with explosives. When detonated, the thin metal fragments would clear a

This flamethrower assistant has the responsibility to follow the flamethrower operator closely so he can open the valves just prior to firing. He carries a refill of thickened gasoline in the 5 gallon can strapped to his packboard. He would also normally carry an extra cylinder of nitrogen and the wrenches needed to change it. Due to the weight he is required to carry, this soldier from the 29th Division, recognized by the insignia painted on his helmet, has decided to discard his assault jacket and only bring the barest essentials ashore. He carries a bandoleer of ammo for his own carbine, as well as the carbine of the flamethrower operator. He has a flotation belt around his waist and has tied another belt to the refill can in case he has to jettison it before getting to shore.
(Reconstruction)

path through a belt of barbed wire. American Bangalore torpedoes were 2 1/8 inch diameter pipe of 24 gauge metal. They came in 5 foot sections. If the barbed wire was five feet deep only one section of Bangalore was needed. If the barbed wire was a wider belt, then a number of bangalores could be connected together and pushed under the barbed wire until it passed underneath all the wire.

To connect the Bangalore sections a 5 inch connecting sleeve was used to hold two sections together. A special pointed cap could be used to keep the front end of the Bangalore from getting stuck on an obstruction when being pushed under the wire. At each end of the Bangalore section was a detonating cap well. A blasting cap was placed in this well, and when set off by an ignitor and delay fuse, the explosion travelled down each section of the Bangalore opening up a 10 foot wide path through the wire.

Crew-served Weapons

The bazooka was designed as an antitank weapon, but it was used by the assault teams to fire at pillbox openings. The M1A1 bazooka was a single piece tube of metal that held a pair of flashlight batteries in the grip. The loader pulled the safety pin from a rocket, inserted it into the rear of the tube, pulled a wire out from the rocket and wound it around a special contact on the bazooka. He then tapped the bazookaman on the helmet to signify the weapon was loaded and ready to fire.

When the bazookaman pulled the trigger an electric charge was sent down the wire that led to the rocket motor. The circuit was completed through a clamp that was seated into an unpainted section of the rocket fin. The electric charge ignited the solid rocket motor and the round went on its way. The nose cone held a shaped charge that could penetrate either metal or concrete.

To provide indirect fire the 60mm mortar was used. This was a metal tube on a bipod that could fire a high explosive round 2,000 yards. The bipod could be

folded up, allowing one man to carry the entire mortar, but two men were required to aim and fire it. The mortar team was composed of four men; two men were needed just to carry ammunition.

The most unusual weapon issued to the assault troops was the M1A1 flamethrower. This weapon was normally only used by engineer troops, and the infantrymen assigned to it needed special training. Pressurized nitrogen shot a stream of gasoline 50-150 yards. A flamethrower could only fire for 10 seconds before it had to be recharged. An ignitor in the muzzle of the flamethrower gun set the gasoline on fire. A jellying, or thickening agent, in the gas caused it to stick, rather than run off as a liquid. The fire would not only burn anything it came into contact with, but when burning in a pillbox would use up the oxygen inside, forcing the occupants to either leave or suffocate.

The flamethrower was not an easy weapon to use. The pressure of the gas flow was so great that the operator had to lean forward or the pressure would push him back. This could cause the gun to be pushed up and the fire would rain back down on the operator. Accidents like this, and the realization that a single hot fragment penetrating the tanks would turn the operator into a blazing torch, made many men wonder if they really wanted to land on an invasion beach carrying five gallons of jellied gasoline. The firing wand was designed with both the flame trigger and the firing valve placed far enough apart so that two hands had to be used to fire the weapon. This prevented an untrained person from trying to use just one hand, which would not be strong enough to fight the backwards force.

Just before the invasion, a photograph showing the successful use of flamethrowers on Japanese bunkers was distributed to the assault teams in an attempt to raise morale. It is not known what the men thought of the photograph.

Each flamethrower operator needed an assistant to open the valves on the back of the weapon. He was also to carry the operator's carbine and haul a refill 5 gallon can of thickened fuel, a replacement tank of nitrogen, and all the wrenches needed to refill the weapon.

Most of the flamethrowers brought ashore in the first waves seem to have been dropped into the surf. Some men struggling ashore in deep water had no choice. One veteran confided that he took one look at all the metal flying around the beach and dumped the flamethrower right away. There has been no evidence, until recently, that any of the assault team flamethrowers were used on either Utah or Omaha. The U.S. Army official history of WW2 states that none were used on the beach.

For years there have been rumors that one flamethrower was actually used in the 1st Division sector of Omaha. This has recently been confirmed in an interview with 1st Division veteran Wally Weyant, who clearly remembers one being used to suppress a concrete emplacement. Whether or not flamethrowers were used on the beaches, they were a part of the assault troop equipment and definitely issued to the boat teams.

The only other weapons carried in the support boat teams were the 81mm mortar and the M1917A1 heavy machine gun. These were the standard arms of the heavy weapons company. The 81mm mortar was the bigger brother of the 60mm. It fired a heavier round and had a longer range. Unlike the 60mm, the 81mm had to be

broken down into three different loads (base-plate, tube and bipod). The eight-man mortar team was expected to carry only 26 rounds ashore.

The M1917A1 Browning machine gun was different from the light machine gun in that it had a water filled cooling jacket around the barrel. The water in the cooling jacket would pull heat from the barrel by boiling off. As long as there was enough water in the jacket, this heavy machine gun could keep up a constant stream of fire. A sturdier and heavier tripod, for more accurate long range fire, made this weapon a two man load.

Uniforms and Equipment

The Army was worried that Germany would use chemical weapons to repulse the invasion of France. This fear directed that all men in the assault troops would wear the wool uniform impregnated against gas. The standard wool trousers and shirt were impregnated with a substance that would keep chemicals from penetrating the cloth. The main concern was mustard gas, which is actually a liquid that causes large blisters. The impregnation made the wool smell bad and feel slightly oily to the touch. Needless to say, this caused much discomfort among

the troops who were forced to wear the same foul smelling, stiff uniform for weeks until they could get a change of clothing. Some of the non-assault troops in the invasion, such as engineers, wore impregnated herringbone twill fatigues over regular unimpregnated wool uniforms. All documentary evidence indicates that the assault troops of the 16th and 116th Regiments wore the impregnated wool uniform. The orders for the 4th Division called for the men of the 8th Regiment to wear the impregnated HBTs. It is not known why some units wore the impregnated wool and others the impregnated HBTs.

Over the wool most men wore the standard field jacket. A few of the luckier ones had acquired the warmer winter combat jacket (tanker's jacket). Some men in the 1st Division had been able to acquire this garment while serving in Italy. The 29th Division commander, General Gerhardt, called in a favor from an old friend of his who was serving as chief quartermaster of the ETO, and was able to get 50 sets of winter combat jackets and matching trousers made available for sale to his officers. Officers, unlike enlisted men, generally had to purchase their own uniforms. According to Quartermaster records the jackets sold

THE ASSAULT TROOPS' UNIFORM AND EQUIPMENT

Individual clothing

web waist belt
wool drawers
helmet with liner
handkerchiefs (2)
M1941 Field jacket or Winter combat jacket
leggings & service shoes
impregnated socks, wool, protective
flannel shirt, protective
wool trousers, protective
undershirt, wool.

Individual equipment

1928 haversack and carrier, or musette bag and 1936 suspenders for officers
canteen, cup, and cover
spoon
first aid pouch and bandage
identification tags
entrenching tool and cover

● Plus, for riflemen
cartridge belt
M-1 bayonet

● For automatic riflemen
BAR magazine belt
M-3 knife.

● For men issued the carbine or pistol:
pistol belt
carbine or pistol ammo pouch
M-3 knife
M-1916 pistol holster

**Assault troops were to leave the mess kit, knife, and fork in their blanket rolls. An extra mess kit was issued to them for use at sea. They were to leave it on board ship when they loaded into the landing craft.

Equipment to be placed in the Blanket Roll

1 Cotton drawers, short
2 handkerchiefs
1 pair shoes, service
2 pair socks, wool
1 undershirt, cotton
2 blankets, wool
1 towel, bath
1 suit HBT (either 1 or 2 piece)
shelter half, pole, rope and 5 pins
(for assault troops - include mess kit, knife, fork)

out, but few of the 29th Division officers wanted the warmer trousers. Most of the men in the assault units did wear the divisional shoulder insignia on their field jackets for the invasion as it was called for in regulations.

Under the wool uniform were worn: dog tags, long wool underwear, and wool socks that had also been impregnated against chemical weapons. Wool underwear was required by orders because it provided more protection against chemical weapons. However, it must also be kept in mind that even in June Normandy can become very cold at night and the men would need the extra warmth.

Most of the troops wore the standard combat shoes and canvas leggings. Some of the infantrymen cut the leggings down about halfway to make

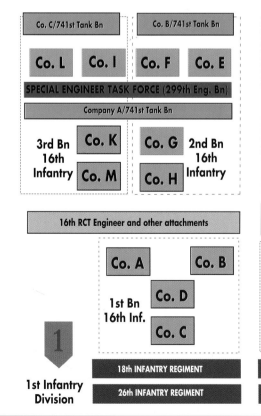

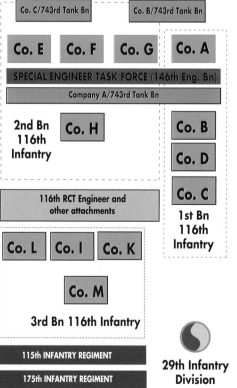

OMAHA BEACH - 16th and 116th REGIMENTAL COMBAT TEAMS ASSAULT WAVES

Co. C/741st Tank Bn — Co. B/741st Tank Bn — Co. C/743rd Tank Bn — Co. B/743rd Tank Bn

Co. L — Co. I — Co. F — Co. E — Co. E — Co. F — Co. G — Co. A

SPECIAL ENGINEER TASK FORCE (299th Eng. Bn) — SPECIAL ENGINEER TASK FORCE (146th Eng. Bn)

Company A/741st Tank Bn — Company A/743rd Tank Bn

3rd Bn 16th Infantry — Co. K / Co. M — Co. G / Co. H — 2nd Bn 16th Infantry

2nd Bn 116th Infantry — Co. H — Co. B / Co. D / Co. C — 1st Bn 116th Infantry

16th RCT Engineer and other attachments — 116th RCT Engineer and other attachments

Co. A — Co. B — Co. L — Co. I — Co. K

1st Bn 16th Inf. — Co. D — Co. C — Co. M

3rd Bn 116th Infantry

1st Infantry Division
18th INFANTRY REGIMENT
26th INFANTRY REGIMENT

115th INFANTRY REGIMENT
175th INFANTRY REGIMENT
29th Infantry Division

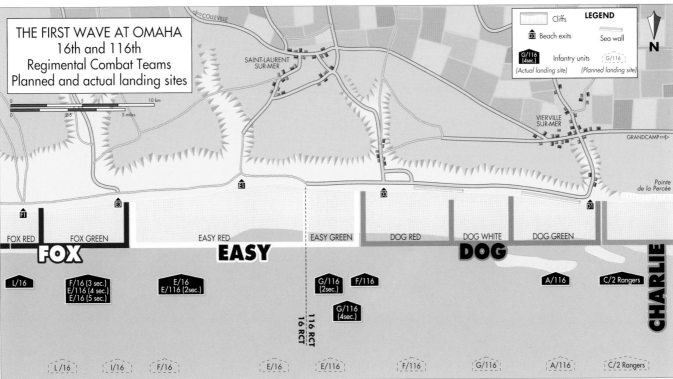

THE FIRST WAVE AT OMAHA
16th and 116th
Regimental Combat Teams
Planned and actual landing sites

LEGEND

Cliffs

Beach exits

Sea wall

G/116 (4sec.) Infantry units G/116

(Actual landing site)   (Planned landing site)

N

COLLEVILLE

SAINT-LAURENT SUR-MER

VIERVILLE SUR-MER

GRANDCAMP

Pointe de la Percée

E1

E3

D3

D1

F1

FOX RED   FOX GREEN

FOX

EASY RED

EASY

EASY GREEN

DOG RED   DOG WHITE   DOG GREEN

DOG

CHARLIE

L/16

F/16 (3 sec.)
E/116 (4 sec.)
E/16 (5 sec.)

E/16
E/116 (2sec.)

G/116
(2sec.)

F/116

G/116
(4sec.)

116 RCT
16 RCT

A/116

C/2 Rangers

L /16   I/16   F/16   E/16   E/116   F/116   G/116   A/116   C/2 Rangers

0   5   10 km
0   2.5   5 miles

Map by Morgan Gillard, © Histoire & Collections 1998   101

This extraordinary view shows an LCI landing sometime in the morning of D-Day. The tide has still not covered some of the beach obstacles. This illustrates the irregular placement of the obstacles. On shore two Duplex Drive tanks are visible. The LCI ramps are down and the passengers are moving through the surf. The gun crew at the bow seem to be tending to a wounded man.

Below.
These troops landing on Omaha beach are not from the assault regiments, as they wear the standard M–1928 haversack (albeit minus the pack carriers). Clearly visible are the clear Pliofilm bags used to protect weapons. Judging from their armament (M1 carbines and M3 trench knives, at least for the man in the right foreground), they are probably part of an LMG team. Each man is either carrying a mount, weapon or ammunition can attached to inflated life belts. Finally, note the steel helmets, with camouflage nets and with or without burlap strips.

Opposite page, bottom.
This photograph shows men from the 16th Infantry Regiment seeking cover under the cliffs at the extreme left flank of Omaha beach. A medic at the left wears a dark colored assault jacket, along with an M-1910 "T-handled" shovel. His red cross armband and medical bag are clearly visible.

them easier to get on and off. The leggings issued for Normandy were impregnated against chemical weapons. On the day before embarkation every man was to coat his footgear with an anti-gas dubbing that would prevent chemical agents from penetrating the leather. A very few men had acquired paratrooper boots. Most of those with such boots were either officers who had a chance to privately purchase them, or former members of the 29th Ranger Battalion who had been issued the boots while taking advanced training from the British Commandos.

There is a curious story about the 29th Rangers and boots. Captain Bill Callahan (F/116) was a

Above.

Members of an Engineer Special Brigade (note helmet markings and paratrooper boots) help men out of the sea onto Omaha Beach. Although there have been many claims as to the identity of the survivors, there is not enough information to confirm what unit they are from. This photo provides an excellent view of the shingle found on Omaha Beach.

former member of the 29th Rangers. He had been issued with a pair of paratrooper boots and he liked them so much that he did not want to wear them in salt water and ruin them. Instead, he chose to wear a pair of experimental British made combat boots (buckle boots) which were hobnailed. He was wounded on the beach and distinctly recalls noticing that the hobnails had started to rust by D+1 when he was being evacuated. The only men to wear such boots were rare cases such as this. No units on the beach were issued with the double buckle combat boot for the invasion.

For headgear the men all had steel helmets. Most

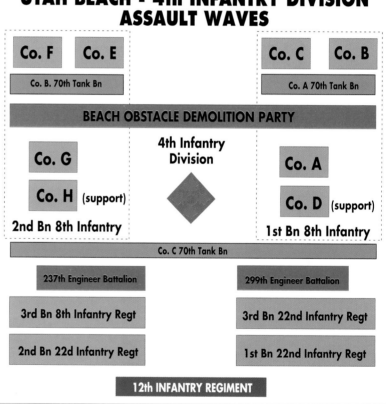

UTAH BEACH - 4th INFANTRY DIVISION ASSAULT WAVES

Co. F	Co. E			Co. C	Co. B
Co. B. 70th Tank Bn				Co. A 70th Tank Bn	

BEACH OBSTACLE DEMOLITION PARTY

Co. G	4th Infantry Division	Co. A
Co. H (support)		Co. D (support)
2nd Bn 8th Infantry		**1st Bn 8th Infantry**

Co. C 70th Tank Bn

237th Engineer Battalion	299th Engineer Battalion
3rd Bn 8th Infantry Regt	3rd Bn 22nd Infantry Regt
2nd Bn 22d Infantry Regt	1st Bn 22nd Infantry Regt

12th INFANTRY REGIMENT

The assault troops of the three infantry divisions were supposed to wear their shoulder patches on their field jackets during the invasion. The 1st Division, known as the "Big Red One" dates from WW1 when the unit was the first division to land in France and the first to fight under American command. The 4th Division used ivy leaves on its patch, a play on the Roman number four. The 29th Division was composed of troops from both Virginia and Maryland, which had fought on different sides of the American Civil War. The "Blue and Gray" insignia symbolized the merging of the former Confederate and Union units.

of the assault troops wore helmet nets. Some of the men garnished the net with strips of burlap to act as camouflage. In the 1st and 29th Divisions these helmets, and the liners, were painted with the divisional insignia. In the 4th Division it appears that only the helmet liner was painted with the divisional ivy leaf insignia. ETO regulations called for all officers to paint a 4 inch vertical while stripe on the back of their helmet. NCOs were to have a horizontal stripe on theirs. Under the helmet many of the soldiers wore the knit wool cap, commonly referred to as the "Beanie." HBT peaked caps were used only by support troops or vehicle drivers.

In a regular rifle company the men would carry the basic field equipment of a cartridge belt, M1928 haversack, canteen, cup and carrier, first-aid pouch, bayonet, and entrenching tool. In the haversack would be carried a raincoat, blanket, shelter half (half of a pup tent), mess kit, eating utensils, toiletries and whatever small items the soldier

Top.
This photo of an LCVP had to have been taken on D-Day. One man, facing away from the camera, wears an assault jacket, which was not issued until shortly before the invasion. This shot provides a good view of the armored machine gun position at the stern of the craft. The coxswain standing by the wheel, has painted his name "Jim" on his helmet.

Below.
One of the most important items issued for the invasion was a small box of seasickness pills. These were Dramamine, which is still used today for the same purpose. These pills made some soldiers very sleepy, which started a rumor that the Army had issued sleeping pills to keep the men calm on the night before the invasion.

Opposite page.
Casualties in an LCM are placed on a platform to be winched onto a ship for evacuation back to England. The debris in the landing craft includes a helmet that appears to have a 29th Division insignia on the left, and at right center a communications reel that appears to contain Primacord. This may have been one of the LCMs used to bring the Special Engineer Task Force into Omaha Beach early in the morning.

SIX
MOTION SICKNESS PREVENTIVE
U. S. ARMY Item No. 12960
Lot No. 8405-359005Z
ELI LILLY AND COMPANY, INDIANAPOLIS, U. S. A.

wanted to carry.

Officers carried the same canteen, cup and carrier, first-aid pouch, and entrenching tool as their men. However, instead of the ammo belt they wore a pistol belt with magazine carriers for the pistol or carbine. Instead of the M1928 haversack they wore the M1936 suspenders and musette bag and they also carried such items as binoculars, map cases and compasses.

For the invasion the assault troops were issued with an item that would temporarily replace their haversack and musette bags. The Assault Jacket, sometimes referred to as an assault vest, was a large canvas vest with eight large pockets. This item was designed specifically for, and only used in, the Normandy landings. As a specific Normandy piece of equipment, this item will be examined in detail later on.

Special Equipment

All soldiers carried entrenching tools. Shovels were either of the M1910 (T-handled shovel) type, or the newer M-1943 folding shovel variety. Photographs indicate that both were used. For every 10 men in an infantry company, 7 shovels, 2 pick mattocks, and 1 entrenching axe were issued. These tools were not issued by the position of the men in the squad. There is no record of a re-distribution of these tools in assault units. The men carried ashore what they had been issued before being reorganized into boat teams.

The standard first-aid packets contained a bandage with a small envelope of sulfanilamide powder and tablets of sulfa drugs. The assault troops were issued with the parachutist's first-aid packet which came in a small waterproof package. This packet contained a bandage, sulfa powder, a tourniquet, and a morphine

Men of the 4th Infantry Division move inland from Utah beach. The man in the foreground wears the anti-gas impregnated HBT suit over his regular wool uniform and field jacket, and he carries one of the 4th Division toggle ropes looped around his neck. In the rear can be seen a Duplex Drive Tank from the 70th Tank Battalion with the flotation skirt lowered. To the left are a group of medics (without painted helmets) and to the right are a few engineers moving aside some barbed wire.

List of PX ration issue for the invasion
(a week's supply)

- 7 packs of cigarettes
- 1 razor blade
- 7 sticks of gum
- 280 matches (7 x 40 boxes)
- 1/2oz pipe tobacco (on demand)

syrette. Two fabric tapes on the outside allowed the packet to be tied to web equipment or helmet netting. One veteran recalled a lecture where they were told to tie it up high on their bodies, such as the shoulder area, so if wounded they would not have to reach very far to get at it. These packets proved of great value when medics ran short of morphine during the morning of D-Day. Morphine not only dulls pain, but helps prevent the body from going into shock. Two weeks after the landing, the 1st Division issued an order for everyone to turn in any unused parachutist's first aid packets as there had been problems with untrained men giving too much morphine to wounded troops.

As previously mentioned, the Allies were afraid the Germans would use chemical weapons. To protect the men against poison gas and mustard gas, troops were normally issued with a gas mask carried in a canvas carrier. These masks became useless if they got wet during a landing. The Chemical Warfare Service had developed a small waterproofing kit to keep the masks dry, but to ensure the assault troops had protection against poisonous gas they developed a special assault gas mask.

The M5 assault gas mask was different from the standard lightweight gas mask in two ways. First, the filter was in a canister attached to the left cheek. Second, the mask was carried in a waterproof black rubber bag. This bag not only kept the mask dry, but also provided a small amount of flotation for the soldier. Examinations of photographs and interviews with veterans indicate that the first two regiments of the assault divisions were issued with the assault gas mask. The third, follow up regiment, appears to have landed with their regular M3 Lightweight masks in the canvas bags. The assault gas mask was also issued to other troops, such as engineers, scheduled

Probably taken just behind the dunes on Utah Beach, this soldier attempts to contact headquarters on his SCR-300 backpack radio. This was the standard radio used for communications from company headquarters to battalion. To the right can be seen his assault gas mask and his inflatable life belt.

CHEMICAL WARFARE STANDARD ISSUE ITEMS

● 1 tube ointment, protective
● 1 set anti dim agent
● 2 sleeve, gas detectors
● 1 8 oz can, shoe impregnite
● 1 cover individual
● 1 eye ointment, BAL
● 1 mask, assault or service, lightweight
● 2 eyeshields, (2 more kept on unit transport)

Below.
A 4th Division medic chats with some French children in the invasion area. He has not painted a red cross on his helmet, but has placed his medic's armband under the helmet netting for greater visibility. Once the aidmen learned that the Germans did not knowingly shoot medics, they started painting the larger markings on their helmets. This man carries his assault gas mask, and has made a neck scarf out of camouflaged parachute material.

to land on the first day.

When the troops were in England marching to their embarkation points it was discovered that the black rubber was wearing off the bags. The gas masks were quickly collected and transported in vehicles to the embarkation area where they were re-distributed to the men.

Other anti-gas equipment carried by each man were a tube of BAL (British Anti-Lewisite) eye oint-ment, a tube of anti-dim cloth to keep the eyepieces clear, 2 plastic eyeshields (with 2 more in unit trans-port), 1 individual protective cover, and 2 gas detec-ting brassards. These brassards were a thin paper armband coated with a chemical that turned color when exposed to chemical agents. It was normally worn on the left shoulder so as to not interfere with shooting a weapon, and thus conceals many shoulder sleeve insignia in period photographs. One of these brassards was to be worn, and the other carried in the gas mask bag as a reserve. The U.S. obtained 5 mil-lion gas brassards from the British in reverse lend-lease. To completely protect the soldier an anti-gas wool hood and protective gloves were available, but they were carried with the unit supplies.

Before boarding the transports, each man was to make up a blanket roll of equipment not needed in the initial assault. This included: 1 cotton drawers, short; 2 handkerchiefs; 1 pair shoes, service; 2 pair socks, wool; 1 undershirt, cotton; 2 blankets, wool; 1 towel, bath; 1 suit, HBT (either one- or two-piece); shelter half, poles and pins. Members of assault regiments were also to leave behind their mess kit, knife and fork. A spoon was all that would be needed for the few days until these rolls caught up with the troops. The blanket rolls were collected by the quar-termasters and eventually were reissued (although not necessarily to the original owner) at some point in France. In the 16th regiment 1,500 bedding rolls were landed in France on 10 June. More came in the next day and were distributed to the men.

When boarding the ships each man was given a pack of seasickness pills and "2, bags, vomit." Plans called for each man boarding a ship to also receive one of the small paperback Armed Service Edition books to help pass the time. Each soldier was to land with three K rations (breakfast, dinner and supper) and three D rations. They were authorized a week's worth of PX supplies. This was composed of 7 packs of cigarettes, 1 razor blade, 7 sticks of gum, 280 matches (7 boxes) and 1/2 oz of pipe tobacco. In some cases dedicated smokers brought as many car-tons of cigarettes ashore as they could carry.

Other equipment authorized for the assault were the raincoat (ponchos were not yet being issued), four 1 1/2 ounce heating units for rations, a bottle of water purification tablets, three extra pairs of wool socks, an extra a pair of gas protective socks, a 2 ounce can of dusting (insect) powder, and three pro-phylactics.

Prophylactics are not often mentioned in official

reports, but they were used extensively in the landings. They were used to waterproof everything from wallets to cigarettes and matches. Letters, currency, and other papers could be stored in them. The thin rubber could actually be stretched to hold an average sized wallet, although eventually the friction of carrying it would tear the rubber. Condoms could be placed over the muzzle of a rifle to protect it from water or sand, and then shot through with out a problem. Men with paratrooper boots used them to blouse their trousers, and everyone always kept a few extras around just in case they were needed for nonmilitary duties. As the CO of F/116 said " *We used buckets of them!* "

Medics landing with the assault troops wore the standard medical aid pouches and wide suspenders. Records indicate that they were authorized to use BAR ammo belts (with the larger pockets) but it is not known if any medics took advantage of this. Medics carried two canteens of water (one for themselves, the other for casualties). Pliofilm bags were used to waterproof the contents of their medical bags. Medics wore the red cross arm band and carried a Red Cross ID card to prove they were authorized to do so. It has been a matter of debate if medics had red crosses painted on their helmets on D-Day. Some veterans have indicated they did. Others recall they were worried about tales of Germans using the cross as a target and did not paint crosses on their helmets until after they had been in combat and found that fear to be unsubstantiated. The painting of helmets seems to have been handled on a unit basis; some did, others did not. There was

not an official regulation on how to paint medics' helmets until after the war ended, so technically they should have been left plain.

There were a few other special items carried by the assault troops. In the 8th and 12th Infantry Regiments the men had toggle ropes similar to those used by the British Commandos. It is not known if these ropes were regulation British ones or constructed by the men of the 4th Division, but they were very useful when the 8th and 12th Infantry moved off Utah Beach. The road exits off Utah were clogged with vehicles, so Col. Russell Reeder decided to move his men inland by crossing the inundated area just behind the beach. The toggle ropes were joined together to help men cross the deeper areas of water and the infantry made their way through the flooded fields.

A few of the assault companies that were to land on Omaha Beach were issued with long ladders to help them cross the antitank ditch located just behind the beach. F/116 received 12 heavy wooden fireman's ladders for this

This 4th Division soldier is possibly being evacuated from the beaches, as his arm is in a sling and his jacket has been cut open. Although shoulder sleeve insignia were not generally sewn onto HBT fatigue uniforms, this man has done so. The 4th Division assault troops wore an outer layer of HBT fatigues impregnated against chemical weapons. The men are eating British self-heating cans of soup that were issued on landing craft without kitchen facilities.

Left.
Every man taking part in the invasion was given a copy of Eisenhower's message to the troops. The other paper item issued was invasion money. Every man was given 200 Francs in these notes in an attempt to prevent inflation from destroying the economy of France.

SUPPLIES CARRIED IN THE AIDMAN'S MEDIC BAGS

12 bandages, gauze, 3"
12 dressings, Carlisle, small
3 bandages, triangular
1 bottle, metal, 2oz w/ alcohol
3 tourniquets, clasp and buckle
10 morphine Syrettes (2 boxes of 5)
6 shakers, sulfanilamide, in tieback can
6 swabs, iodine
50 tablets, sulfadiazine, in 2oz ointment box
1 roll tape, adhesive, 1"
1 pencil
1 thermometer
1 insert
NB. Bags wrapped in Pliofilm covers

mission. Two ladders were to be carried in each boat and it took four to six men to carry each ladder. The company commander, Captain Callahan, knew his men were already carrying enough equipment and would not be able to manage getting these ladders through the surf. He "accidentally" forgot the ladders in the marshalling area. While preparing to embark, his battalion commander, Col. Sidney Bingham, noticed the ladders were missing and sent Callahan back to get them. Somehow, although Callahan is not really sure how, his men got the ladders into the landing craft in the early hours of D-Day. When Company F stormed out onto the beaches they quietly left the heavy ladders sitting in the landing craft never to be seen again.

Every soldier in the invasion was issued an inflatable life belt. These belts contained compressed CO2 cartridges that would automatically inflate the belt. When the cartridge area was squeezed, it forced two levers together which pushed a sharp point into the CO2 cartridges, inflating the belt. Orders were very specific that men were to wear these belts up high under the arms so that when inflated they would not slip down low on the body and turn the soldier upside down. Even though everyone was cautioned about this, many men were drowned when their life belts did fall too low.

The 1st Division had previous experience with amphibious landings and not only issued two life belts per man, but specified that they were to be tied in place up high under the arms with twine. The assault units also tied the belts to ammo boxes, weapons, radios and other equipment so they would float to shore if dropped in the water. Orders were issued for all heavy weapons (such as mortars or items to heavy to float) to have a life belt or other float tied to the item with a 15 foot piece of rope so it could be recovered.

Assault Troops on D-Day

The tale of the assault troops on D-Day has been fairly well documented. On Utah the entire first waves drifted south to a less defended sector of the

This demolitions man from the 4th Division carries a pack charge that has been covered with a burlap sandbag to conceal the bright yellow labels on the blocks of TNT. Unlike the troops on Omaha Beach, the men of the 8th Infantry Regiment at Utah wore the regular wool uniform and field jacket underneath HBTs which had been impregnated against chemical weapons. To detect if chemical agents were being used, he wears a gas detection brassard on his right shoulder. The 4th Div. shoulder patch has been sewn to the left shoulder of the HBT jacket.
The M-7 rifle grenade launcher is attached to the rifle, and a load of rifle grenades is carried in the ammo bag hung from his left shoulder.
The toggle rope was typical of the 8th Infantry Regiment, but it is not known if they used British made ropes, or made their own on a unit basis.
(Reconstruction)

beach. Although seven landing craft in the first wave sunk, the 4th Division was able to get ashore without too many casualties and quickly linked up with the paratroops that had been dropped inland. They suffered only 197 casualties in the landings, of which 60 were men lost at sea.

On Omaha only a few boat teams reached their assigned beaches. The assault troops on Omaha took terrific casualties, but as more men piled up on the beaches, small groups were rallied and led inland by men of outstanding leadership. Most of the names of these leaders, who won the day at Omaha, will never be known. By the middle of the day the assault troops had begun to move up through the bluff overlooking the beach and break open the German emplacements.

An interesting comment on the landing is found in the 16th Regiment after-action report. It states that when the command post group landed and attempted to move inland to where they had planned to set up their C.P., they found that "*most elements were still pinned on the beach. A word might be said at this point that may in all fairness be included to explain some of the grouping on the beach. A good number of men in the small craft were deathly sea sick and needed some rest before they could continue.*"

Lt. Marvin Stine of G/16 later remarked "*when the ramps went down, some of the men couldn't move ashore, but stumbled and fell in the water. They had become so cramped because of crowding that their muscles would not respond. They lay in the water for a few minutes, rubbing their legs, then they crawled*

Above.
A heavy weapons team moves inland from Utah beach. On the left, a man carries the tripod of an M1917A1 heavy machine gun. The gun itself is on the far right with the steam condenser tube wrapped around the barrel.

OTHER ITEMS ISSUED FOR THE INVASION

2 bags, vomit
4 1/2 oz heat units
1 vial water purification tablets
1 can dusting powder
1 packet seasickness pill
3 Prophylactics
1 lifebelt (2 in the 16th RCT)
1 Pliofilm cover for weapon
Invasion currency
Ike's order of the day (see picture on page 108)

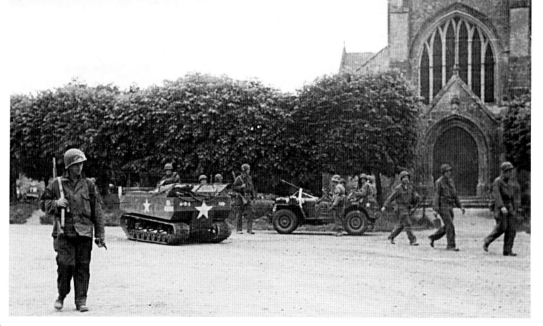

Left.
Captioned as being taken just behind Utah Beach, this may be Sainte-Marie du Mont, just off Exit 2 from Utah Beach. The M-29 weasel bears the markings of Headquarters, 8th Infantry Regiment ("4-8-I" and "HQ").

ashore." The assault troops had been crammed into the small LCVPs for hours, and it can only be assumed that some of the other boat teams that were deposited in deeper water suffered a worse fate.

There has always been a question as to how many of the assault troops became casualties. Official records indicate that in the 29th Division, which probably took the greatest casualties, 6-700 men were wounded or killed on 6 June. Historian Joe Balkoski has done an in-depth investigation of these figures and believes that a more accurate estimate is closer to 1,000 men for the 116 Regiment alone. His theory is backed by the 116th Commander, Col. Canham, who wrote in an after action report: "*The closest estimate that can be made of casualties suffered by the regiment in the initial assault was conservatively 70 officers and 900 enlisted men out of a total of about 180 officers and 3,100 enlisted men of the regiment who actually landed on D-Day. This figure arrived at after scattered and missing had reported back to the original units.*" Company A of the 116th, landing in the first wave directly in front of the emplacements at Vierville, suffered the worse with 90% casualties. To the credit of these men the survivors continued to fight in the push inland. Part of the trouble in examining casualty statistics for D- Day is that some men were not reported as killed or wounded

Above.
The first soldier in this line of 4th Division men crossing the flooded area behind Utah Beach provides an interesting clue as to how assault troops carried equipment in the invasion. He has left his rifle in the Pliofilm cover, but the Pliofilm also covers the rifle sling as well. So he has taken a short piece of rope and made a second sling so he can carry the rifle in its cover until he is firmly on dry land. On his other arm is a bazooka that has been tied to an inflated life belt.

until many days after the 6th of June. They were then listed as casualties for the days following the landing. The only other units to suffer as much were the engineers assigned to remove beach obstacles. The Naval Combat Demolition Units that landed on the heels of the first assault wave took 52% casualties on Omaha.

While interviewing veterans for this book, it became clear that the printed word can not do justice to the men who landed in the morning of 6 June. It is easy to list items carried and uniform worn, but no writing can capture the shaking voice a man has when he talks of the sea running red with the blood of his friends. One soldier from A/116 desperately wanted to talk about the landing, but each time he started he was forced away by uncontrollable tears.

Out of all the stories that have come out of the Omaha landings, there is one in particular that needs to be remembered. Cecil Breeden was a quiet young man from Iowa. He was one of the 3 medics in the A/116 command boat. As soon as they landed, one of the three medics was killed and the other severely wounded, but Breeden just went about the business he had been trained for. He walked upright between the machine gun and mortar fire helping the casualties. When a wounded soldier tried to pull him under cover, Cecil just pulled away and said, "*You're hurt now, when I get hit you can take care of me.*" He then went on looking after the wounded while enemy fire swept the beach. Cecil died in 1991, never asking or receiving any official recognition for what he did. Efforts by his fellow 29ers to award him a Medal of Honor or a Distinguished Service Cross failed.

His best reward was knowing that a number of men would live because of his actions. He is an example of the high quality men that comprised the assault troops. Cecil Breeden stands out as an example of the courage and responsibility that made the invasion a success.

There were a number of brave men who performed heroic deeds on the morning of 6 June. Sadly, many of their stories have never been recorded and their names will never be known.

The Assault Jacket

OF all the items used in the Normandy invasion none has proven to be more mysterious than the assault jacket. The history of this item can be traced back to the ATC. One of the main lessons learned at the ATC was that assault troops should not be weighed down with too much equipment when coming ashore. The ATC staff took an interest in a piece of equipment used by British troops: the assault jerkin.

The British assault jerkin was the idea of Col. Rivers-MacPherson, an ordnance officer of the British Army. He felt that a one-piece vest with large pockets to hold ammunition and equipment would be

This unusual photo shows a boat team being rail-loaded (as opposed to the men climbing down the nets) into an LCVP. The man in the left rear of the boat wears a standard M-1928 haversack, while the cross straps of an assault gas mask bag can be seen on the back of a man in the center who doesn't have an M1928 haversack or an assault jacket. The central figure clearly shows the life belt and assault gas mask bag being worn under the assault jacket, as well as a large slit cut into the jacket in an attempt to hang the canteen. He also carries the M-1943 folding shovel. Of interest are the two different styles of helmet nets, and the packboard being used to carry equipment.

a better design for the combat soldier than the standard belt, cross straps, and backpack. He developed his idea in 1942 and the assault jerkin first saw limited use with specialist troops such as the commandos. The Canadian Army followed suit and, it is believed, manufactured a limited number of assault jerkins for their own men.

A series of tests indicated that the assault jerkin was slightly superior to standard webbing equipment in terms of cost, ease of use, and comfort in battle. Col. Wayne Allen brought a sample back to the States for closer examination. The Americans thought the jerkin might be a good idea, but did not want to convert production facilities from regular belts and packs to these vest-like garments unless the British were serious about dropping the Pattern 37 web gear and converting to assault jerkins for all their troops. The cost and difficulty of converting a multi-million man army over to a new form of field gear in the middle of a war (when large stocks were already on hand) was too much and the idea was put aside.

Later on, in 1943, the staff at the ATC thought that an American version of the jerkin might be a good item for assault troops. If the soldier was dropped in deep water the vest could be released quicker than a standard ammo belt and back pack. A carefully designed vest could also be used to limit the amount of equipment a soldier would carry to the bare minimum. This would help the men come ashore with the least amount of weight possible.

Right.
These are the only known photographs of the British made prototype assault jacket at the Assault Training Center in England. Captain Charles Roten, an instructor at the ATC, is shown wearing an assault jacket made with British style fittings.

Below.
In another photo, believed to be taken shortly afterwards, a display of proposed equipment for the assault troops is laid out on the beach. This includes not only the assault jacket, but M1938 wirecutters, Garand rifle, helmet, inflatable life belt, and a British "Light Service Respirator." It seems the smaller British gas mask was tested as a possible alternative to the bulkier American mask in the period before the assault gas mask was developed.

Why an Assault jacket?

The idea for a combat vest is easy to understand today. Many modern armies are moving to the use of similar items. One developer of the current U.S. Army load carrying vest was asked if he had based any of his work on the assault jacket. He had never heard of it before and was interested to find that in a way history was repeating itself. To understand why the U.S. Army might have wanted such a garment in 1944, the question cannot be answered without looking at the history of the model 1928 haversack: the standard WW2 infantry pack.

The 1928 haversack was a slightly modified version of the 1910 infantry haversack. This pack was designed to hold a specific number and type of items. The Army did not want the troops to have free space which they could use to carry extra and unnecessary weight around. The 1910 haversack was designed for a well drilled professional army in peacetime, and the minor 1928 modifications did not change the basic size or shape. Prewar soldiers practised the difficult art of making the pack and pack roll. They knew the better it was put together, the easier it would be to carry.

In World War Two the Army suddenly found itself with new weapons, new equipment, and new tactics. With the experience of amphibious landings in the Mediterranean, the Army had started to add more and more equipment to assault troops. The equipment was too much to fit in the clumsy 1928

113

haversack, and someone needed to figure out a better way to carry it all. They just could not put all the assault gear in the same space that was designed for World War One bread cans. So a modified British battle jerkin was considered for assault troops.

Birth of the Assault Jacket

Although records on the American version of the assault jerkin are scarce, it was the ATC staff that felt that it would be a useful item for the invasion. They re-designed the jerkin based on the load they felt American soldiers would carry and had a prototype constructed in England using British materials and fittings. This prototype vest is known only by two photographs taken at the ATC in 1943. British fittings can clearly been seen on the quick release straps.

These photographs have caused many collectors to think that a British made lend-lease version of the American jacket was produced. This has been fuelled by a number of reproductions, made in British material on the American pattern, that have surfaced in recent years. After extensive research into official records there is no evidence that any American assault jackets were made in England, other than the single prototype.

It remains a remote possibility that a handful of test jackets may have been made by British companies, but the few surviving records clearly state that ONE test version was made and flown to the United States. The construction of the British made examples on the market confirm that they are of recent make. Unless someone locates a period document that proves the ordering and manufacture of an

Opposite page, far right.
Roy King on left is shown helping Joe Springman into his assault jacket in one of the marshalling areas. Through the help of the 4th Division Association, these men have been traced to Co. D, 8th Infantry Regiment. The M-3 knife in Springman's jacket indicates he carries a carbine (the carbine bayonet was not yet an issue item), as did anyone with a BAR or .45 pistol.

Opposite page, left.
This is the only photo of the assault jacket in the QMC collection and may be the official acceptance picture of the item. This dark OD jacket with light colored trim does not have any belt in the grommets or slits, and as an official photo should end any rumors of the jacket being issued with any form of belt.
(QMC Museum)

Opposite page, bottom.
This line drawing of the assault jacket is from the Marine Corps test report. No official specifications or patterns of the assault jacket have been located.

Left.
Quietly sitting in a landing craft, this member of an assault regiment may be wondering what the morning of D-Day will be like. He wears the regulation combat uniform, although his trousers are worn outside his leggings, thus negating their protective effect in case of gas attack. His assault jacket is very tight around his chest, with the adjustable front straps let out all the way. The equipment piled around him is representative of the paraphernalia required for an amphibious assault: Bangalore torpedoes, lifebelts for added buoyancy of important equipment, pack and pole charges, as well as an M1A1 bazooka.

American style assault jacket in England (which would contradict the U.S. Army records) then all of the British versions discovered in recent years are fakes.

The assault jacket shown in the ATC photograph is not a borrowed British jerkin. A close examination of the ATC prototype shows web strap quick releases. The British Army jerkins used wooden toggles as closures. The ATC jacket, pictured being worn by ATC instructor Captain Charles Roten, has sets of grommets at the waistline. This is the best proof that the pictured garment is not a borrowed British jerkin, but one designed for American troops. The British did not use equipment that can be hung from such grommets.

The design of the Assault Jacket

U.S. Army records on the assault jacket are hard to locate. Some of the best information comes from a December 1944 study of the item by the U.S. Marine Corps. Since the assault jacket was designed for invasion troops, it is logical that the Marines would at least want to consider it for their own men. The USMC test report indicates that 14,000 assault jackets had been procured by the U.S. Army quartermasters and two of them were sent to the Marines for testing.

The American assault jacket is a vest-like garment made of No. 12 cotton duck fabric. On the front are 4 large pockets, next to the bottom front pockets are 2 small grenade pockets, which came with a fabric tape sewn in to secure a grenade. These grenade pockets fit both fragmentation and WP/smoke grenades. On the shoulders are two quick release loops for attaching equipment and there are two larger pockets on the back which act as a backpack. The bottom rear pocket has two sets of fasteners so it can be firmly closed halfway or fully filled. Next to the top rear pocket is a sleeve designed to hold a bayonet. The jacket is closed in front with two adjustable web release straps.

Around the waist are four locations of two grommet holes placed just above a reinforced slit in the jacket material. Some collectors think this was for a belt of some sort, however there is no evidence of any type of belt in any period photographs, interviews with veterans, or the USMC study. Upon close examination, the spacing of the grommet holes is exactly what is needed to fit the model 1910 wire belt hanger used in most American web equipment. It is without doubt that the idea was to be able to attach equipment directly to the jacket without using a belt. For the 1910 hanger to work, it must first come through the grommets from behind. This is easy on a standard belt because the belt is not very tall, but on the jacket there must be some means of getting the hanger through to the back of the grommets so it can slip through to the front. This is the reason behind the reinforced slits: they were designed to allow a 1910 hanger to slip into the jacket and then back through the grommets. Unfortunately, somewhere along the line the distance from the grommets to the slit was not measured properly and the system does not work. Period photographs show canteens being hung clumsily by one hook or a larger slit hand cut into the jacket. This design flaw gives the impression that the assault jacket was produced in a great hurry without any time to work out the bugs.

The quick release straps on the shoulders are the subject of much debate. They are not large enough to

hold a hand grenade, and many collectors have questioned their use. The British made ETO jacket had shoulder straps added to the second pattern specifically as means of attaching the gas brassard. This may have been a partial reason for having them on the assault jacket. The loops were praised by the Marine Corps Board as being extremely useful for

Left.
Taken just before embarkation, these Rangers enjoy a last cup of coffee before boarding the LCAs that will take them to the troop transports. The two men on the right both wear assault jackets. The officer (note rank bar painted on helmet) has a parachutist's first-aid pouch tied to his right shoulder, and two map cases (M1938 dispatch case) slung in front. Uncommon for the ETO, he has a camouflage pattern painted on his helmet.

gestion that they were designed for the assault gas mask bag straps must be discounted because it would be difficult to wear the gas mask bag over the jacket and still be able to discard the jacket in a hurry.

According to the USMC study, assault jackets were made in three sizes: small, medium, and large (although no known size smalls have been located, extra large ones do exist. Possibly the record meant medium, large and extra large). All examples known have been dated 1944. Quartermaster Corps records indicate that only four American companies produced assault jackets: S.Froehlich Co., Harian Stitching Co., Tweedie Footwear, and the J.A. Shoe Co. Letters from the Chief Quartermaster of the ETO were sent to these companies thanking them for helping to expedite the production of the jackets under a very tight time frame.

These letters also indicate that the fittings for the jackets were made by the Avery Manufacturing Company. Thanks were also sent to the New York Port of Embarkation and the 5th U.S. Port for expediting shipment of the jackets to England, and to Major W.H. McLegan of the Research and

This light colored assault jacket was made by J.A. Shoe. Dark shade OD#7 versions also made by J.A. Shoe have been reported. Close examination of photographs show the vast majority of assault jackets worn at Normandy were in the darker shade.

Development Branch for his work in "*planning the garniture and making the changes needed.*" It seems the problems with the waist grommets might be due to an error on Major McLegan's part.

It appears that Harian, Froehlich, and Tweedie made them in the dark O.D. Nr.7 shade. J.A. Shoe produced them in both the dark shade and the light khaki color. On many of the dark colored jackets light colored trim or webbing was used. In period photographs the darker version appears to be more common than the lighter.

attaching the rifle sling when climbing down a net into a landing craft and it was suggested that similar straps be incorporated in the next USMC pack. The straps could be used for attaching any kind of equipment, such as binocular cases, ammo bags, or reels of communications wire. They were handy for anything that needed to be slung over the shoulder. The sug-

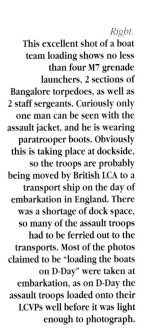

Right.
This excellent shot of a boat team loading shows no less than four M7 grenade launchers, 2 sections of Bangalore torpedoes, as well as 2 staff sergeants. Curiously only one man can be seen with the assault jacket, and he is wearing paratrooper boots. Obviously this is taking place at dockside, so the troops are probably being moved by British LCA to a transport ship on the day of embarkation in England. There was a shortage of dock space, so many of the assault troops had to be ferried out to the transports. Most of the photos claimed to be "loading the boats on D-Day" were taken at embarkation, as on D-Day the assault troops loaded onto their LCVPs well before it was light enough to photograph.

Developing the Assault Jacket

There are few records on the development of the assault jacket. An ATC memo dated February 1943 mentions "*a combat vest now in process of development.*" A later ATC memo from 18 Sept. 1943 mentions that a satchel charge could fit in the large rear pocket of the assault jacket. This was not specified in the design, but rather a discovered feature. There is no evidence that this was ever done and most men would have needed the space for rations and other equipment.

The next mention of the assault jacket is on 31 March 1944 when the 1st and 29th Division G-4s (supply staff officers) were requested to submit numbers and sizes needed for the invasion. On 1 April, Colonel Mood of Vth Corps requested 10,000 assault jackets, but said he would take as many as were available. The reply was that only 7,000 could be provided to the 1st and 29th, because some were needed for the 4th Division as well. In May a memo states the jackets would be available on 18 May 1944. This was followed by another memo saying the jackets would be delayed until 21 or 22 May. The pre-invasion Operation Neptune memo file stops at this point, so it is impossible to determine when the jackets were finally delivered.

Veterans who were issued the jacket claim they got them shortly before they left for France and did not receive any specific instructions on how to wear it or what to put in which pockets. They all claim they already had specific items to carry, but they put them in the pockets where they made the most sense. Ammunition and combat related items that would be

Above.
This still from a Signal Corps movie shows American soldiers boarding a British manned LCA somewhere in England. An assault jacket is clearly visible on the right hand American soldier. Further back, an M1A1 bazooka sticks up above the line with the metal flash protector visible at top. These men are thought to be from the 1st Division, although there is no visible evidence to confirm it. The soldier being helped aboard by British sailors has a machete at his left side.

Below.
These two G.I.s, photographed aboard an LCI, are wearing the uniform of first wave infantry troops. Their warrior-like stances, weapons at the ready, enable a good look at their assault jackets. Their M1 helmets have camouflage nets and burlap strips. The Navy M-1926 inflatable life belts are worn under the assault jackets, in order that the latter can be removed easily.

needed in a hurry went into the front, rations and non-essential items went into the back pockets. The D-Day after action report for the 2nd Bn, 16th Infantry states "*battalions and companies were assured on three separate occasions that they would have the assault jacket, and each time it changed. The assault jackets finally arrived in the marshalling area, which was three days prior to embarkation. This naturally resulted in a great deal of confusion.*" A few veterans have claimed they received the jackets up to three weeks before the invasion, but it appears that it was probably a much shorter time.

The only mention of wearing the assault jacket in the Operation Neptune orders is in a table of issue for the 16th RCT files. This states "*for troops wearing the assault jacket certain items of the above will be eliminated.*" The reference is to the list of equipment for all troops. Although not stated, the equipment eliminated would be the M1928 haversack or M1936 musette bag. These would have been put into the blanket rolls along with the other items destined to catch up with the men in France. One 29th man remembers a jeep making the rounds on 8 or 9 June issuing new web gear to those who needed it, but most claim there was enough spare gear available from casualties that they could easily get anything they wanted before that.

The Assault Jacket on D-Day

The question of who wore the assault jacket on 6 June is not easily answered. The jacket was certainly issued to troops of the first two battalions to land in each assault regiment. Yet, there are records of men not in these units having the jacket. According to the Neptune files 3,500 jackets were sent to both the 1st and 29th Divisions. A regimental combat team had a listed strength of 6,535 men including all attachments. The assault infantry regiment was 2,261 men.

These men were probably separated from their unit on D-Day, and are being led to their company area by the MP in front (note band on helmet). The rear pockets of the assault jacket can clearly be seen, as well as the bayonet holder and the model 1910 shovel. The canteen of the third man in line is hanging on its side - a result of the poor design of the grommet holes.

Thus, the initial April 1944 request for 5,000 jackets would not have covered all the men in the RCT, so the plan could not have been for everyone to get it.

There is no evidence that any of the supporting troops, specifically the engineers who followed the assault troops ashore, were issued the assault jacket. The best assumption is that the 3,500 jackets were actually delivered to the first infantry units to land, as well as some of the attached men who were in the first waves. The jackets seem to have been a trendy and desirable item, so some of them probably found their way into the hands of quartermasters or friendly officers (much like jump boots and tanker's jackets) before getting to the troops.

In August 1944 the 29th Division issued a summary of combat lessons. A comment made by a man from E/116 reads "*all men (were) not fully equipped, especially as far as assault jackets.*" As company E was one of the first wave units it is interesting that they had trouble obtaining all the assault jackets needed. It could be that the quartermasters did not take the overstrength into account when ordering the jackets, that men left them behind and claimed they never got them, or that there were not enough to go around. It is very possible that not all the assault jackets made got to England in time for D-Day. If a percentage of those issued were the small size, these would only fit the thinnest of men. It does not appear that the pattern sizing took into account the life belt and all the clothing that was worn underneath the jacket. A man would have be very small to put on his uniform and required equipment and then fit into the smallest sized assault jacket.

A few veterans have indicated that they were issued the assault jacket, but did not like it. Some left it in the marshalling areas or traded it to other troops. Harold Baumgarten, B/116, decided at the last minute he did not want to wear the assault jacket in the landing and left it on board his transport ship.

A number of photographs show men from the 2nd and 5th Ranger Battalions wearing the assault jacket. Numerous Ranger veterans reported they did not receive the assault jacket and for a long time it was not clear how some of the Rangers got them. First Sgt. Russ Woodill of the 5th Rangers finally provided the information that assault jackets were issued only to Ranger officers and senior NCOs. It was thought that the large pockets would be useful for carrying all the implements of command: compasses, maps, binoculars, etc. Close examination of the Ranger photographs confirms that the men wearing the assault jackets are almost all officers or NCOs.

A number of men, including the previously mentioned 5th Ranger NCO, found themselves in deep water on the morning of 6 June at Omaha. Some had been blown out of their landing craft, others had walked off the ramp into water over their head. An estimated 16 landing craft in the first wave were either swamped or blown up. All but one of the men in this situation that were questioned said the first thing they did was dump the assault jacket to keep from sinking.

Only one man said he kept his jacket on while in the water, and that was only because the webbing of the quick release straps had swollen when wet and he could not undo them. He was extremely fortunate, for many other men were probably drowned when their jacket, weighted down with grenades, pulled them under. One 29er recalls having someone cut his quick release straps with a bayonet so he could dump the jacket. A soldier from the 116th Inf. recalled being told to keep the top chest strap on the jacket undone until he landed, so he would only have to pull the bottom release to shed the jacket. A September 1944 report on amphibious operations states that the Army must "*devise some means of flotation of the assault jackets in case it becomes necessary for the soldier to throw off the jacket in the water.*" This would allow the discarded jackets to float to the shore and provide extra ammunition and equipment on the beach. Veterans claim they wore their assault jacket over everything else (ammo belt, life belt, bandoleers) so it could be discarded first if they went into the water. After landing it was more convenient to wear the ammo belt on the outside of the jacket.

Men did not only have problems with the

Left.
An Olive drab No 7 assault jacket made by Harian (The Harian Stitching Company), front and rear.

Below.
Close-up of the grommet holes that were supposed to allow attachment of equipment directly to the jacket, but were not properly designed. The distance from the grommets to the slit was not measured properly and the system does not work. Period photographs show canteens being hung clumsily by one hook or a larger slit hand cut into the jacket. This design flaw gives the impression that the assault jacket was produced in a great hurry without any time to work out the bugs.
(Collection of Tony Stamatelos)

The grenade pocket showing the 16 inch fabric tape used to secure the grenades. This has been cut out of many assault jackets.

Below.
Maker's stamp inside top rear pocket flap. Unlike the other manufacturers, Harian stamped the size on the inside of the jacket in large block letters.

Tweedie footwear manufactured assault jacket, in Olive Drab No 7 canvas, some elements of webbing and trimming are the lighter shade. *(Private collection)*

Below.
The "Tweedie" marking is stamped on the inside of the back of the jacket.

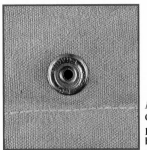

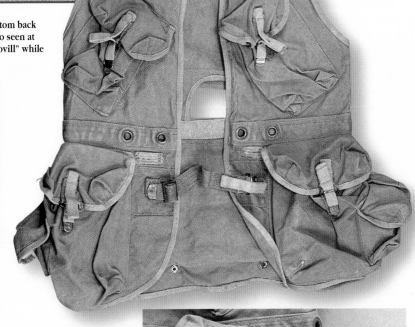

Left.
One of the snaps for the bottom back pocket extension straps (also seen at bottom right) is marked "Scovill" while the other is blank.

Above.
The top front quick release strap.

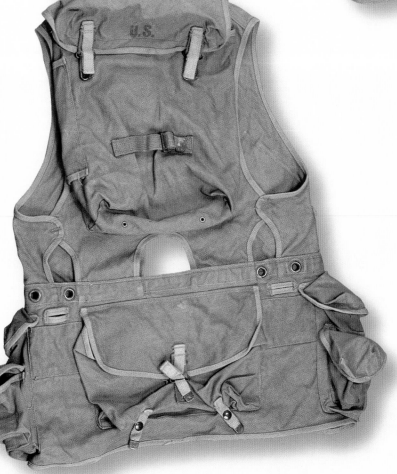

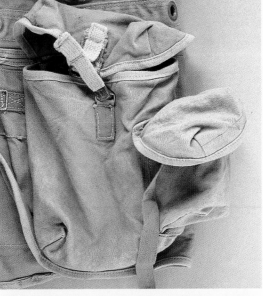

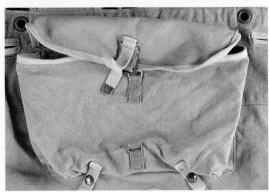

Left.
This rare photo is a still from a very brief motion picture clip. Every reel of movie film was captioned with the correct date and location, so this clip can be accurately placed as being shot on 17 June 1944 just outside Saint-Lô. Believed to be from the 29th Division, this man has drawn or painted sergeant stripes on this field jacket. In the bayonet sleeve of the assault jacket he carries a gun cleaning rod. A machete is also visible there.

Right.
This soldier looking at himself in a mirror has been identified as Pvt. Vincent Kamolz. He served as a rifleman in the 26th Infantry Regiment, 1st Infantry Division. In a recent interview he clearly recalled this photo being taken just outside Liege, Belgium. He said: "*I remember the day was very hot, and I saw this mirror. As I was looking into it I heard a noise behind me. It was a cameraman taking my picture. I later learned from my family that my picture had been in the paper.*" The original photo caption is dated 13 August 1944. But Pvt. Kamolz does not recall anything about the jacket at all. As he was in the 26th Infantry (the second 1st Division Regiment to land) he may have picked it up from a casualty. Kamolz was wounded shortly after this photo was taken, but returned to his unit just in time for the end of the war in Europe.

assault jacket when landing on the beach. The after action report for G/16 states that loading of the LCVPs "*was affected by loading all heavy equipment and ten men into the assault craft before lowering away these boats. The remainder of the boat team personnel was then loaded over the side of the U.S.S. Henrico by scramble nets. This was extremely difficult, due to the weight of the equipment carried by each man in his assault jacket, and the slippery footing created by the wooden rungs of the scramble nets.*"

After D-Day

The question of what happened to all the assault jackets, and why they were never used again cannot be answered with certainty. From veterans we understand that they found them hot, heavy, uncomfortable, and bulky. Many jackets were lost in the ocean when dropped to prevent drowning. Others were discarded in the days following the landings. Somewhere in the mass of official records there should be a report that indicates official reasons why they were never used again, but the definitive memo has not yet been found.

In September 1944, a military attaché report was filed with an interview of Staff Sgt. Leo Jereb of L/8. Jereb had been wounded on 23 June 1944 and was asked in the hospital about the assault jacket. He remarked that one problem was the poor weight distribution of the lower pockets. When loaded with

Right.
Fortunately, the wartime censor of this shot did not completely conceal the patch, and it is possible to identify these as 4th Division troops. A parachutist's first-aid packet can be seen on the left shoulder of the wearer of the assault jacket. The soldier on the right is wearing the lightweight service gas mask bag - a sign he probably came in on one of the later waves.

Below.
A column of assault troops wearing dark shade assault jackets passes some French civilians on a road thought to be behind Utah Beach. If so, this would make the troops members of the 8th Infantry Regiment. The dark shade of the assault jacket worn by the soldier at far right stands out against his lighter colored field jacket.

grenades it was difficult to move, so some of his unit cut the jacket off at the waist before the landing (and were severely reprimanded). The rest of his unit cut theirs down once ashore. He also claimed that on the shore they wore the cartridge belt outside the jacket, and this put the entire weight of the belt on the shoulders. Another problem was that men tended to load up the pockets with nonessential items, rather than use the space for grenades and ammo.

The only other post D-Day mention of the assault jacket is in QMC correspondence. On 22 July 1944 Col. Brumbaugh in the ETO sent a requisition to the Clothing and Equipment Branch for 10,000 more assault jackets. The jacket was a nonstandard item, so the request needed special approval due to

the severe shortage of cotton duck material at the time. The reply from Major General Littlejohn (Quartermaster General of the ETO) was "*I question now whether or not this jacket will be of any value other than a war souvenir.*" Although not stated, it can only be assumed that the requisition was turned down. There is no evidence that any more assault jackets were ever made or that they were used in any other campaign.

The veterans questioned about the jacket recall it was uncomfortable to wear and extremely hot. Don Van Roosen (H/115) saw a GI wearing an assault jacket in the first days after the landing. He had never seen one before and mentioned it looked like a useful piece of equipment. The GI said, "*You want it? You can have it!*" and handed

it over. Van Roosen wore the jacket for a few hours before realizing he was sweating to death in it. He dumped it by the side of the road.

One 116th rifleman questioned wore his jacket until he was wounded on 17 June. He didn't seem to mind wearing it and when questioned, he said he had never even though about exchanging it for a regular pack. It was just something he wore and never really thought about.

In all probability, most of the jackets in Normandy were lost in the ocean, left on the beach, or scattered in the hedgerows. A few of those used at Normandy have miraculously survived, but most of the jackets found in collections today were probably left in quartermaster depots until sold off after the war as surplus. Keep in mind that out of an estimated 14,000 made, 7,000 went to the Vth Corps, another 3,000 or so to the VIII Corps, and 2 to the Marines. This leaves almost 4,000 that might never have been issued.

Two pictures show an Army photographer wearing an assault jacket as a camera vest. His identity is unknown, but he was probably part of the 165th Signal Photo Company. He must have picked up a discarded jacket on the beach shortly after the landing. It was a unique item and many of the men following the assault troops ashore probably found uses for the ones they found on the beach.

The Marine Corps Tests

In December 1944 the USMC Equipment Board undertook project No. 295: Jackets, Assault. The purpose of this test was to determine the durability of the jacket under conditions likely to be met by Marine units in the field, and the practicality of the jacket as a substitute for the pack and cartridge belt in the first wave of a landing.

A Harian Stitching Co. manufactured assault jacket, marked and dated 1944 inside the top back pocket flap.
Note the wide Olive Drab shade 7 insert at waist. It appears on many other Harian vests. It is not known why Harian jackets have this, or if all Harian jackets are made in this way.
(Jim Mountain collection)

The two sample jackets were subjected to a wide variety of tests designed to simulate the battlefield conditions of a Marine first wave landing. It is interesting to note that the Marines wanted the jacket to replace both the cartridge belt and pack. No attempt was made to attach anything to the grommet holes and the report states that there was no provision for such attachments. They also made curious repeated references to the pocket sizes being designed for British ammunition and needing redesign for American troops.

The Marine tests showed that the jacket did not fit well, was uncomfortable, restricted movement, and had poor weight distribution. In addition the subjects noted it was uncomfortably hot (even when the temperature was 40-50° F) and not suited for use in the tropic climates of the Pacific. The assault jacket was turned down and never used by the Marines.

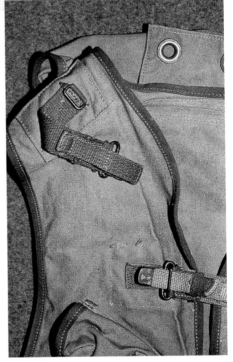

Reproduction Assault Jackets...

The question of reproduction British made assault jackets has already been addressed. There is overwhelming evidence that they are not of wartime manufacture. Soon after it was publicly announced they were fakes, an assault jacket made from American camouflage material stamped "Australian Made" was offered to the collectors' market. There is not one shred of evidence that this is an original wartime item. Everything known about the assault jacket makes the idea that, after the QMC in Europe and the Marine Corps tuned down any further production of the item, a version would be manufactured in Australia quite ridiculous. Reproductions of the British battle jerkin are now on the market as well.

and Movie Props

There have been other attempts to reproduce assault jackets in the last few years. Some obvious reproductions have originated from Europe, while at least two Americans have pro-

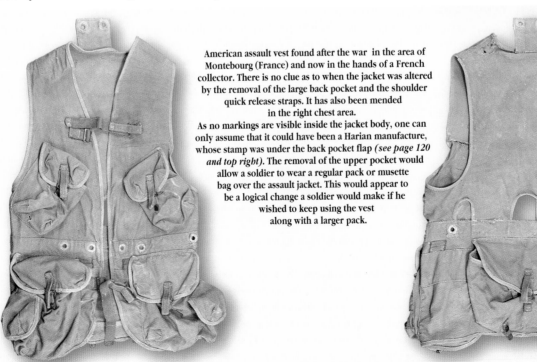

American assault vest found after the war in the area of Montebourg (France) and now in the hands of a French collector. There is no clue as to when the jacket was altered by the removal of the large back pocket and the shoulder quick release straps. It has also been mended in the right chest area.
As no markings are visible inside the jacket body, one can only assume that it could have been a Harian manufacture, whose stamp was under the back pocket flap *(see page 120 and top right)*. The removal of the upper pocket would allow a soldier to wear a regular pack or musette bag over the assault jacket. This would appear to be a logical change a soldier would make if he wished to keep using the vest along with a larger pack.

duced their own versions specifically for the reenactment community. In 1997 350 reproduction assault jackets were produced in Los Angeles for the WW2 film "*Saving Private Ryan*." These jackets are not marked in any way and come in both dark and light shades. Their construction is quite good and it is hard for an untrained eye to tell them from the real thing. Most of these jackets were ruined while filming in the ocean, but some escaped to the collectors market and have been offered as originals. As this book is being written the manufacturer is producing another run of them with authentic looking maker's stamps.

Conclusion

In the mad rush to prepare for the invasion of Normandy, 14,000 assault jackets were made and, in the last days prior to the invasion, rushed to the troops without any real testing. It is no mystery why the assault jacket idea seems to have died after D–Day. They were hot, fit poorly, useless below the waist, and probably responsible for the drowning of a number of men. The only mystery is why they have been forgotten for 50 years and why there is so little information on them.

One possibility is that the issue of assault jackets would point directly to the units that would spearhead the invasion, and throw off the plan to convince the Germans that the true landings were to be at Calais. This might mean the project would be classified, making the records harder to find. In all probability, the assault jacket was just such a minor part of the invasion that many of the records we wish had been kept slipped between the cracks. Or perhaps the paper trail is simply misplaced in the mass of government documents, which are not always as well organized as we would like.

In any event, the assault jacket is an item unique to

Right.
One of the only positive features found in the USMC test report was the usefulness of the quick release straps on the shoulder of the assault jacket. They would keep in place the weapon's sling when both soldier's hands were busy, such as here when climbing down a net into a landing craft.

Below.
An unidentified cameraman from the 165th Signal Photo Company discusses the German occupation with a French farmer. The cameraman may have picked his assault jacket up on the beach. If he was assigned to a unit in the first waves he may have been issued it in a marshalling area in England. Standing nearby is a medical captain from an Engineer Special Brigade. He wears a red cross armband, but does not have any medical markings painted on his helmet.

the invasion of Normandy. Although it must be considered a failure as a piece of military hardware, the assault jacket remains an important aspect of the D-Day story.

Chapter 4. "Fire in the Hole"

ONE of the primary concerns for the Assault Training Center was keeping track of German beach obstacles and working out ways to overcome them. The story of how these obstacles were breached starts well before the war when Draper L. Kaufman, son of a Navy officer, graduated from the U.S. Naval Academy at Annapolis in 1933.

In the midst of the Great Depression the Navy did not have enough openings for all the graduates of the Academy, so they raised the eyesight requirements to eliminate half the graduates from naval service. Kaufman's vision was not good enough to allow him a commission, so he went to work for a civilian shipping line.

In 1939 Kaufman decided he was not going to let the war pass him by, so he enlisted in the American Volunteer Ambulance Corps performing humanitarian service in France. With the collapse of the French Army in 1940, he was taken prisoner by the Germans and sent to a POW camp. Hoping to create goodwill with the Americans, the Germans released Kaufman, who then made his way to

Below.
This photograph, taken when the assault troops were boarding ships, shows Army combat engineers.
As they are not wearing the markings of the Engineer Special Brigades on their helmets, we believe that they could be engineers attached to the Special Engineer Task Force or Beach Obstacle Demolition Party.
They are wearing impregnated HBT fatigue uniforms, setting them apart from the infantry. The leggings and service shoes have also been treated against blister gas. The M5 assault gas masks are placed high on the chest.
Combat engineers, like the infantry, were armed with M-1 Garand rifles, but only the G.I. in the center has slipped his into a watertight cover. The individual equipment is also the same as for the infantry, including the cartridge belt and haversack. The M-1 bayonet is attached to the belt for easy access. The U.S. Navy M-1926 life belt is tied around the waist and would have been partially inflated on the ships, and then completely inflated just before the assault, using two CO_2 capsules.
These assault engineers carry the tools of their trade, an interesting selection of explosive charges and specialist equipment: Bangalore torpedo sections, carried in twos on the shoulders, two Satchel charges, detonators, ropes and reels of Primacord.

The Naval Combat Demolition Units, Special Engineer Task Force and Beach Obstacle Demolition Party

England. There he volunteered for bomb disposal duty and was given a commission in the Royal Naval Volunteer Reserve. While in England he played an important role in defusing unexploded bombs and developing methods to do so.

In November 1941 he was on leave in the United States when he was asked to transfer to the United States Navy (now with reduced eyesight requirements) and organize the Navy Bomb Disposal School.

After the bomb disposal school was up and running, his expertise with explosives got him the new task of starting a school to train men to deal with obstacles on landing beaches.

In June 1943 the first class entered Kaufman's Combat Demolition Unit school at Ft. Pierce, Florida. Many of the original demolitioneers, as they would be known, came from the Seabees. It had been thought that the men of the Naval Construction Battalions, the Seabees, would have previous experience with explosives in their civilian construction jobs. However, it seems that most of the Seabee volunteers had little demolitions experience at all. One veteran recalls that they actually wanted men without experience, so they would not have to break

any bad demolition habits the men might have picked up. Many books claim the obstacle demolition men were Navy Seabees. This is incorrect. Some of the men had been Seabees, but they transferred out of that unit to become NCDUs.

Naval Combat Demolition Unit School (NCDU), later to be known as UDT school (Underwater Demolition Team), started off with "hell week" where the men were pushed to their physical limits. Kaufman had been impressed with the tough standard of the Scouts and Raiders school already operating at Ft. Pierce, and adopted a condensed version of the Scouts and Raiders physical training program. "So Solly Day" took them through a day of continual explosions set off near the men in order to weed out anyone with a fear of explosives. These weeding out techniques continue to this day in current Navy Seal/UDT training.

Previously, a few Navy salvagemen had been given special demolitions training and were used to great success in the landings in North Africa. They performed a few specific demolition jobs, but for the most part had been left to themselves to figure out the best techniques. With no manual to follow, Kaufman had to develop his own demolition tech-

127

niques, equipment, and organization. He started with a small 7 man team of one officer and 6 enlisted men because they would fit into the small black rubber rafts used at the time. This team then shrank to 1 officer and 5 enlisted men so there would be room in the raft for the large amount of explosives needed.

Some members of the first NCDU class went off to assist in the invasion of Sicily in 1943, but there was little in terms of beach obstacles for them to deal with. They were primarily used as ordinary demolition engineers on land, before returning to Ft. Pierce as experienced instructors. As each NCDU team graduated, they were given a team number and took a team name based on the name of their commanding officer. Thus teams were known by names such as "Kane's Killers", "Chaney's Chain Gang", or "Heideman's Hurricanes."

Eventually the NCDU school began to place a greater emphasis on underwater demolitions, and turned into the UDT school. Many NCDU men who served in Europe later went on to the Pacific where they continued their demo work in underwater demolition teams. For his work in developing the NCDU program, Draper Kaufman would forever be known as "the father of U.S. Navy demolitions." In 1965,

Above.

**Explosives used in NCDU
training at Fort Pierce:
TNT blocks, tetrytol blocks
linked by Primacord into a
chain, the bag they were issued
in, and a roll of Primacord on
the wooden tetrytol box. In
front can be seen safety fuse,
M1 pull fuse lighters and the
cardboard tube they were
issued in, a display of electric
blasting caps, regular blasting
caps in boxes, and a roll of
safety fuse in the front.**

(then Admiral) Kaufman made a triumphant return to Annapolis as the superintendent of the school that originally kept him out of the U.S. Navy.

NCDUs in England

After the landing at Dieppe in 1942, the British had opened an underwater obstacle training center. This center was primarily designed to support the landings in the Mediterranean. In 1943 there were no obstacles yet in place on the Normandy coast. It was not until late January 1944 that reconnaissance photos showed metal hedgehogs being set up on Utah Beach. The Overlord planners became gravely concerned. If the obstacles prevented the landing craft from getting to shore, it would mean either dumping heavily weighted soldiers into deep water, or landing them at low tide, which meant they would have to cross hundreds of yards of open beach under intense machine gun fire.

Eisenhower sent Colonel O'Neil, the commander of the 112th Engineer Combat Bn., to Ft. Pierce for a demonstration of the techniques that had been worked out for beach obstacles. These included a wide array of experimental gadgets. A battery of rockets mounted onto the top of a Sherman tank was shown to be effective in eliminating many types of obstacles on land. Once the rockets were fired, the tank could jettison the rocket housing and start fighting inland.

"Apex Boats" were small radio controlled boats filled with explosives. They were designed to be sent into the middle of water covered beach obstacles. When detonated, the explosion would destroy any obstacle in the area. The "Reddy Fox" was a long tube filled with explosives. It functioned much like an underwater Bangalore torpedo. It was towed into position among the water covered obstacles, then detonated to clear a path. Although showing some promise, nothing appeared to work as well as men hand placing charges on the obstacles themselves.

Heideman's Hurricanes (NCDU Team #11) was the first to arrive in England in October 1943. The NCDUs were attached to the U.S. Naval Beach Battalions for administrative purposes. At first it seemed as though the Overlord planners did not even know or care that the NCDUs existed. Thanks to the efforts of Commander Eugene Carusi of the 6th Naval Beach Battalion, the NCDUs finally became actively involved in the invasion plans. Due to the tightness of security for Overlord, NCDUs were not

Above.
Continued from previous page.
Explosives used in NCDU training at Fort Pierce.
A close-up of a part of the display.

Left.
From left to right, back row: 1/4 pound blocks of nitrostarch in the wooden shipping case, packages of cratering explosive (ammonium nitrate), 1/4 blocks of TNT. Front row: 10 cap detonator, crimper, pocket knife, galvanometer, waterproofing compound and safety fuse.

given definitive information on the final objective and the obstacles on Omaha and Utah until mid-April 1944.

Concerns regarding the beach obstacles continued to grow. In April 1944 a bomb missed a coastal installation and fell onto some of the water covered obstacles off Omaha's Easy Red beach. The resulting secondary explosions proved that mines were being attached to the obstacles. The Allies sent a small British COPP (Combined Operations Pilotage Party) to survey the beach and check for mines. The first attempt by Captain George Lane brought back a regular German land mine that had not been water-proofed. Due to a shortage of marine mines this was precisely the type of mine the Germans were using, but the Overlord planners felt that due to the rapid deterioration these mines would suffer in seawater the Germans had to be using something different. The second attempt by COPP to bring back a mine met with disaster. The COPP member was captured by the Germans who, thankfully, did not press their interrogation as to what he might know about the invasion plans.

Because of the short period of time before the invasion, it was decided that the obstacles should be cleared using only personnel and equipment on hand in England at the time. Upon examining the beaches

and the obstacles it was decided that the best way to open up gaps in the belts of obstacles was to demolish them when the tide was out. This was the key decision needed to set the invasion date and meant D-Day would be the 5th, 6th or 7th of June. These were the only dates when low tide would occur at the right time, about an hour before dawn.

Attacking the obstacles when they were dry meant that the Apex Boats and Reddy Foxes could not be used even if available. It was decided that the troops used to destroy the obstacles would be under Army command because they would be operating on dry land. Technically the Navy was supposed to be in control of everything up to the high-water mark, but the Army won out and beach obstacle demolition was placed under overall Army control. The NCDUs were to operate in conjunction with, and under the command of, specially picked Army engineer units.

Aerial photos of the invasion beaches were finally delivered to the NCDUs on 1 May 1944. The last NCDUs for Overlord arrived in England on 6 May 1944. They had less than one month to prepare for the invasion. The NCDUs were first reinforced with men from Company C, 146th Engineer Bn. These Army engineers (5 men to each NCDU) were origi-nally given training in underwater demolition work (with diving suits and snorkels) in an indoor swim-

Above.
An NCDU class is shown working with the LCR(S) (Landing Craft Rubber-Small). The original NCDU crew size was shrunk to five men to provide room in the raft for explosives. At Normandy these rafts would be used to carry extra explosives ashore, but would prove to draw enemy fire and most were abandoned.

Below.
This is what is known in the Navy as a "hydrographic survey." It means sweeping along the surf checking for obstacles, mines or demolitions. Although technically the responsibility of the Navy Beach Battalions, the NCDUs were trained to do this as well.

ming pool. They lived with the NCDUs in Navy quarters, and when going on liberty with the sailors it was not unknown for them to swap uniforms as a joke.

Working with Army engineers and the staff of the ATC, final plans for the Normandy coast were made. One of the major concerns was exactly how beach obstacles were to be destroyed. If they were simply blown apart they would scatter debris that could injure nearby troops. Later on, the sharp metal remnants would be dangerous to landing craft attempting to come into shore. Unless the mines attached to the obstacles were disabled, they would pose a major threat to the following ships and vehicles that would have to pass through the area.

Lt(jg) Carl Hagensen developed a technique for safely reducing the most difficult obstacle - the Element C. He is credited with developing what would become known as the Hagensen Pack by putting a 2 1/4 pound block of C-2 plastic explosive in a canvas tube. This tube was about 1 1/2 inches in diameter and a foot long. When the tube of explosives was wrapped around a metal beam it could be quickly fastened by a hook and loop found at either end of the pack. When detonated, the C-2 cut right through the metal beam. By placing a minimum of 16 Hagensen Packs in carefully selected positions on an Element C, this large obstacle could be collapsed inwards upon itself with no debris sticking up more than 18" from the sand. The trick was to cut the supporting arms, then give the front face a push backwards. This technique served to eliminate shrapnel and kept the debris to a reasonable amount.

Once all the explosives were positioned, they were connected together with Primacord. Primacord looks like yellow clothesline, but it contains a central core of explosive. When set off with a blasting cap the explosion travels along the Primacord at lightning speed and simultaneously detonates anything it is connected to. In theory, all obstacles in a planned gap were to be prepared for demolition, each obstacle connected to a central string of Primacord and everything set off in one major explosion. One main explosion would prevent the

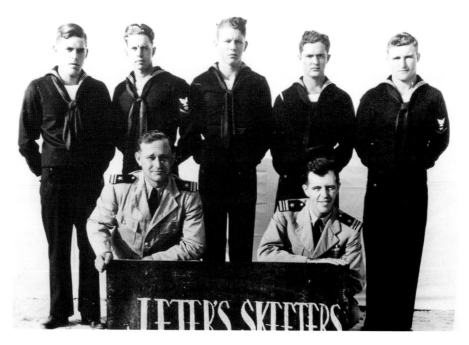

German defenders from spotting a pattern of small explosives and targeting the men working on the gap.

10,000 Hagensen Packs were ordered from British sailmakers just before the invasion, but they could not provide the necessary amount. The demo men filled socks with explosives to serve as a stopgap measure. These socks did not have the hook and eye of the Hagensen Pack, so they had to be fastened to the metal beam using either friction tape or twine. There were different ways of making the explosive-filled sock depending upon which group made them. The standard method for Force "O" was to put a small rock about 1/2 inch in diameter in the toe of the sock and tie it off with thread (forming a small knob), then add the 2 1/4 pounds of C-2 explosive. A foot long piece of Primacord was placed into the C-2 and run out of the sock. A piece of bailing wire was used to tie the sock closed. This version could be wrapped around the obstacle and the bailing wire quickly twisted around the knob at the other end. Then

the Primacord lead could be tied into the Primacord line. Some of the Force "U" NCDUs put the C-2 into a sock and tied each end with a foot long piece of Primacord. They could use this Primacord to tie the explosive to the obstacle and then connect

Above.
"Jeter's Skeeters" was the nickname of NCDU Team #26 under command of Lt Max Jeter. At front left is Max Jeter, the team commander, at front right is Commander Draper Kaufman, the father of Navy demolitions.

Opposite page.
Front and rear of Max Jeter's helmet worn ashore on Utah Beach. It bears the gray band ordered for all Navy personnel working on the beach, with a nicely stenciled "USN" in the front. An Army style Lieutenant's bar is painted above and a strip of white tape has been placed on the rear to emulate the Army officer's vertical bar. The helmet sits on a German flag taken from a Utah Beach bunker.
Max Jeter's helmet liner is bare except for his name. The U.S. Navy was insistent that all men correctly label their uniforms and equipment with their name. Thus almost all items issued to Navy personnel will have their names either stamped or stencilled on them.

Below.
Lt. Jeter's souvenirs include his medals and personal equipment.
(Courtesy Kim Jeter)

The Navy Combat Demolition Units painted a 2 inch gray band on their helmets to identify themselves as naval personnel. Some reports indicate that a few members of the NCDUs wore alpaca lined deck jackets on the morning of D–Day, but veterans recalled they wore anti-gas impregnated HBT fatigues over their standard working uniform. In the case of this officer he would wear a Navy cotton khaki shirt and trousers underneath HBT coveralls. The paratrooper boots were issued to the NCDUs because this was considered the best footgear for working in surf. He wears standard Army web gear, including M-1938 wirecutters. He carries a supply of demolitions in the haversack explosives were issued in. In his left hand is an expedient Hagensen pack made from a block of C-2 placed inside an Army sock. Slung on his back is a carbine encased in a Pliofilm bag, held by a piece of string. Navy Demolitioneers carried either a .45 caliber pistol, or a carbine, for self defense in case the Germans sent troops down onto the beach.
(Reconstruction)

the remainder to the trunk line.

C-2, a form of plastic explosive, was issued in blocks of 2 1/4 pounds. Eight of these blocks came in a thin olive drab bag. These bags would be used by some engineers to carry their Hagensen Packs, while others (mainly on Utah) used the Army M2 ammunition bag which fit over the head and provided a large pocket on the front and rear.

Along with C-2, tetrytol was used by the engineers. Both of these explosives (normally) could not be detonated by a stray bullet or piece of shrapnel. Tetrytol was issued in 2 1/2 pound blocks linked together by a single length of Primacord. Each 15 pound chain of eight tetrytol blocks was issued in a

Left.
A class portrait of the NCDU officers in the graduating class of December 1943. From their branch insignia at the bottom of the jacket sleeves, most of them belong to the CEC (Civil Engineer Corps). Seated front row center in his khaki uniform is Lt. William Flynn, one of the Ft. Pierce training officers.
(Courtesy Nate Irwin)

cloth bag. One 15 pound satchel charge of tetrytol was used to blow up each hedgehog. These satchel charges were detonated by a fuse that set off a 1/4 pound block of TNT. The explosion of the TNT triggered the tetrytol.

The most difficult problem was how to keep the fuse ignitors from getting wet. The standard M-1 ignitor was prone to failure when it got damp. An improved M-2 waterproof ignitor was available, but only in very limited quantities. Most of the waterproof ignitors did not reach the demo teams until a few days before the invasion and none of the veterans questioned recalled using them. The men were able to waterproof the M-1 ignitors by putting them in condoms, sealing the opening with asbestos grease, and tying them shut with heavy thread. The "T" shaped pull ignitor could be yanked right through the thin rubber of the condom.

The ignitor started a short length of safety fuse burning. Normally the time delay was 2 minutes, but the standard fuses made for Omaha were 8 second-, 22 second-, and 45 second-delays. Once the fuse was ignited, it took the specified time for the flame to reach the blasting cap (a small metal tube filled with a sensitive explosive). When the blasting cap went off, it detonated the Primacord it was taped to. This sent an explosive shock wave travelling along it that triggered any other Primacord it was tied to or explo-

Left.
This NCDU 139 graduation photo was taken in December 1943. During the training, the enlisted men were rotated between the officers. Upon graduation each officer could hand pick the men he wanted in his team. Ensign Nathan Itzkowitz, seated front row center, selected these men for his crew. Back row, left to right: Robert Helfrich (Gunner's Mate 3rd Class), Thomas Dille, (Gunner's Mate 3rd Class), Warren Muller (Gunner's Mate 2nd Class), and Donald McGeary (Shipfitter 2nd Class). Beside Ensign Itzkowitz are Chief Mechanic's Mate Alfred Johnson, and one of the NCDU training officers, Lt. William Flynn. These men landed on Utah Beach on 6 June and Don McGeary was one of the few NCDUs killed on that beach.
(Courtesy Nate Irwin)

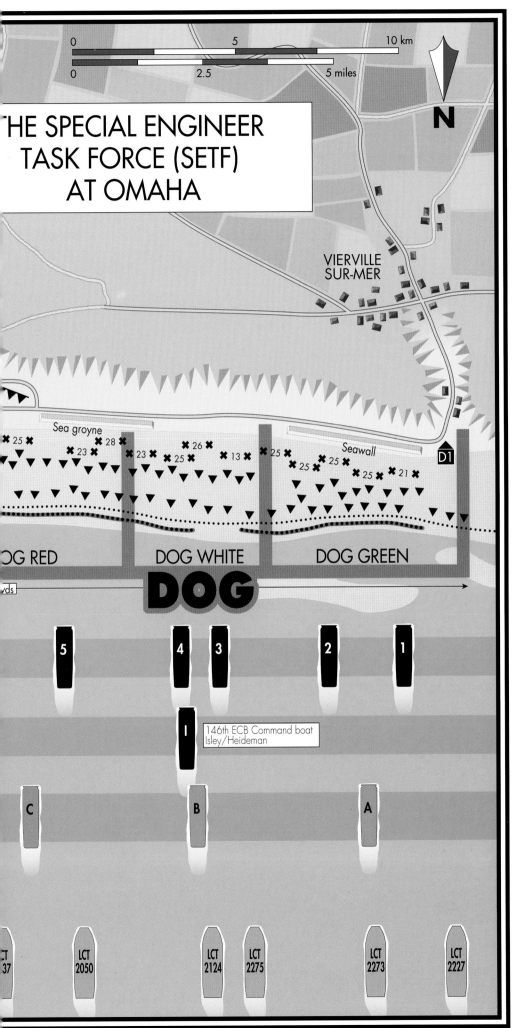

THE SPECIAL ENGINEER TASK FORCE (SETF) AT OMAHA

VIERVILLE SUR-MER

Sea groyne
Seawall

DOG RED   DOG WHITE   DOG GREEN

DOG

146th ECB Command boat Isley/Heideman

LCT 37 LCT 2050 LCT 2124 LCT 2275 LCT 2273 LCT 2227

SETF LANDING CHART CAPTION
(for map at left)

GAP TEAMS

Gap team 1
Lt. Kehaly
A/146
NCDU #11
Chief Freeman

Gap team 2
Lt. Anderson
A/146
NCDU #24
Lt(jg) Culver

Gap team 3
Lt. Schill
A/146
NCDU #27
LT(jg) Holtman

Gap team 4
Lt. Shively
A/146
NCDU#41
LT(jg) Nichols

Gap team 5
Lt. Caldwell
B/146
NCDU# 42
WO Thompson

Gap team 6
Lt. Roberts
C/146
NCDU #43
LT (jg) Jenkins

Gap team 7
Lt. Bartholomew
B/146
NCDU#140
WO Hill

Gap team 8
Lt Ross
B/146
NCDU#137
Ens. Blean

Gap team 9
Lt. Lanterman
C/146 (attached to 299th)
NCDU #44
WO Raynor

Gap team 10
Lt. Gregory
C/146 (attached to 299th)
NCDu# 45
Ens. Karnowski

Gap team 11
unknown
299th
NCDU #46
Ens. Bussell

Gap team 12
unknown
299th
NCDU#22
Lt Cooper

Gap team 13
unknown
299th
NCDU #23
LT(jg) Vetter

Gap team 14
Lt Wood
299th
NCDU #141
Ens. Gouinlock

Gap team 15
unknown
299th
NCDU#138
Ens. Allen

Gap team 16
unknown
299th
NCDU #142
Ens. Stocking

SUPPORT TEAMS

Support team A
Lt. Meier
C/146
NCDU# 133
Ens. Mitchell

Support team B
Lt. Rollins
C/146
NCDU# 130
Ens. Chaney

Support team C
Lt. Latendresse
C/146
no NCDU

Support team D
Lt. Trescher
B/146
NCDU# 128
Ens. Duquette

Support team E
unknown
299th
no NCDU

Support team F
unknown
299th
NCDU #131
Ens. Inman

Support team G
unknown
299th
No NCDU

Support team H
unknown
299th
NCDU #129
Ens. Peterson

146th command boat
Col. Isley- 146th Eng
Lt(jg) Heideman- NCDUs

299th command boat
Major Jewitt 299th Eng
Lt (jg) Cooper

SETF command boat
Col. O'Neil
Lt Cmdr Gibbons
(NCDU)

white letters USN to be painted on the front and back of Navy uniforms so there would be no question who they were while on the beach. It is not known if all NCDUs did this. Some also painted their unit number on the back of their HBTs in black paint. Again, it is not known if all teams did this. Air Force flak suits had been tested at the ATC as a means to protect the NCDUs while they operated, but these were cumbersome and not used in the actual invasion.

Special Engineer Task Force-Omaha Beach

The number of obstacles on the Normandy beaches soon grew past what the few NCDU teams would be able to handle. At first the 6 man NCDU teams were enlarged by the addition of 2 Navy seamen who were given the job of handling the rubber boat that would be filled with extra explosives, blasting caps, and fuses. Then an additional 5 Army engineers (from Company C, both 146th and 299th Engineer Combat Bns) were attached to the team to bring it to a total strength of 13 men. The Utah NCDUs used three seamen to handle the rubber boats. These boat handlers were, for the most part, brand-new sailors just out of boot camp without any special training. The exact number of men in each team varied slightly, as some might be a man or two understrength. However, the final rosters in records clearly indicate that the Force "O" NCDUs were composed of 9 Navy men. This means they were given four seamen to assist in handling the rubber boats and extra explosives.

It had also been decided to expand the mission of breaching the obstacles to an Assault Gap Team composed of the now 14 man NCDU, and a 27 man Army engineer unit (including one medic) supported by a tankdozer (a Sherman tank fitted with a bulldozer blade). A regular bulldozer could be substituted if not enough tankdozer blades were available, but it appears all Gap Teams were allocated a tankdozer. The tankdozers would land in an LCT containing two standard Sherman tanks, but not all of these LCTs arrived on time and in the right place. The crews for these tankdozers would come from the 741st and 743rd Tank Battalion, and the 610th Engineer Light Equipment Company on Omaha. The entire Gap Team would be commanded by an Army Engineer officer. These Army-Navy teams had only two weeks to practice together before the invasion.

The Omaha Assault Gap Teams were considered part of the Vth Corps Provisional Engineer Group commanded by Colonel O'Neil, former commander of the 112th Eng. Combat Bn. This group consisted of 21 NCDUs, the 146th Eng. Combat Bn. and the 299th Eng. Combat Bn. (less Company B which landed at Utah). The final composition of this group would be officially referred to as the Special Engineer Task Force (SETF) and, like other assault units on Omaha, were temporarily attached to the 1st Infantry Division.

The 146th Engineer Combat Bn. had been assigned to the ATC from November 1943

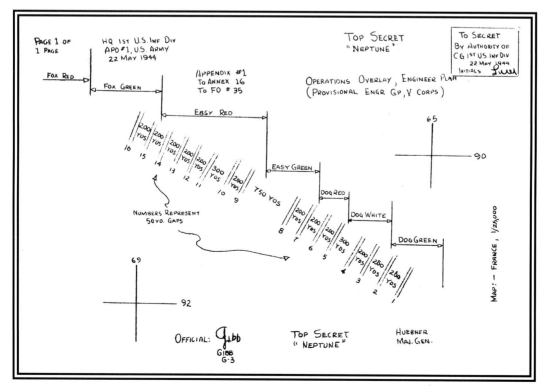

Pvt Joe Manning, mail clerk - 146th Engineer Bn., is pictured here at the Assault Training Center in England. He wears the typical uniform of the engineers based there: wool trousers and shirt, field jacket, and leggings. Although some of the engineer officers were able to obtain winter combat jackets and paratrooper boots, most of the enlisted men wore this uniform, underneath impregnated coveralls, on D-Day. As a Headquarters man, Manning would normally have stayed back in England as part of the unit residue, but he volunteered to go along on the command boat and landed on Omaha on the morning of D-Day.
(Courtesy Joe Manning)

On 20 June 1944 Manning wrote home to his father about his experience on D-Day. His letter contains a detailed description of what he carried ashore. "*When I landed I had three two-minute waterproof time fuses, also had six 20-second fuses. The 20 seconds were the best. Had all the explosives I could carry (C-2 they call it). Really cuts the steel. I did have a carbine but don't like them so got rid of it and got a good ole M1- perhaps you know it better as a Garand.*

Every man had six 20 second fuses. Was using C-2 compound. It is like clay and we had ours in sacks. I only had one pack due to the fact I was carrying a demolition kit. In it I had some cap waterproofing compound, three rolls of time fuse, friction tape, underwater fuse, lighters, several boxes of regular fuse lighters, 50 caps in a waterproof box, a ball of twine, some flea powder, some K-rations and a few other items. I believe it weighed more than my pack of explosives. Explosive and demolition kit weighed around 40 pounds. In my belt I had two rolls of Primacord, more friction tape, two pocket knives and a pair of wire cutters. On my back I had a rifle, and in my right hand I had a bangalore torpedo for blowing barbed wire."

to April 1944, where it had been involved in much of the preparations for the landings. While at the ATC the line companies of the 146th were billeted in tents on the Saunton Sands Golf Course, with Headquarters in the Golf Club clubhouse itself.

The commander of the 146th, Major Carl Isley, called his headquarters men together and asked for volunteers to go with him in the command boat on D–Day. A few stepped forward immediately as this was the job the 146th had been training for.

Company A of the 146th Engineers supplied the men for Gap Teams 1-4 and support teams "A" and "B" destined for Dog Green and Dog White beaches. Gap Teams 5-8 and Support teams "C" and "D" assigned to Dog Red and Easy Green were from Company B. Company C provided additional manpower to the NCDUs and the 299th Engineers. Headquarters and H&S company composed the command boat team and the unit residue (due to land a few days later with all the non-essential equipment).

The Special Engineer Task Force was still short of manpower so roughly 150 engineers from the 2nd "Indianhead" Infantry Division were added to the 900 men of the Gap Assault Teams to bring them up

Below.
This photo was taken in Bricqueville, France on 14 June 1944. It shows the surviving members of the 146th Engineer command boat. Lt.Col. Isley is at far left. The men are all wearing unmarked helmets and standard wool uniforms.
(Courtesy Joe Manning)

to full strength. Along with the 2nd Division engineers were a few infantrymen from the 23rd and 9th Infantry Regiments. Two to five of these 2nd Division men – whose patch they continued to wear on the field jacket – were added to each gap team that landed in the first waves of D-Day. Their contribution and presence in the initial assault has rarely been recognized.

An Army Gap Assault Team was composed of 1 officer, 25 enlisted men and one medic. Some, if not all, of the teams received a second medic from the 53rd Medical Bn. shortly before the invasion. Each team was divided into 2 demolition crews and 2 mine crews, although no records indicate the exact composition of these crews. A reserve of an extra 1,000 pounds of explosives was carried in each gap team boat. This extra explosive was stored in a rubber raft, which was pulled out of the LCM as the team landed.

The Omaha plan called for an initial wave of amphibious DD tanks to land just before H-hour and draw the attention of the German emplacements. Then a wave of assault infantry in LCVPs was to land at 0630 (H-hour). They were followed a few minutes later by LCTs, with non-amphibious tanks and the SETF tankdozers. The tanks would move up the beach, firing at pillboxes, and the infantry would keep any snipers or machine gun nests busy.

The tankdozers would begin removing wooden obstacles. Upon landing, one man from each gap team

would seek out its tankdozer and assist it on foot as it operated on the beach. Each of the four tankdozers from the 610th Engineer Light Equipment Company was to tow a 1/4 ton trailer loaded with extra explosives. Bulldozers had been assigned to the teams, but they did not land in the early morning.

The Gap Assault Teams were to land at H+3 minutes in LCMs. Each LCM held about 1,000 pounds of explosives (500 pounds in two small rubber boats), while the command boats carried a ton of extra explosives. The NCDU teams would start to demolish the obstacles closest to the sea and work in towards the beach. The Army engineers would move to the next belt of obstacles and work in to the shore.

At the time of landing the outer band of obstacles should have been in three or less feet of water. If the outer band was an element "C", then one Army demo crew was to assist the NCDU in its demolition.

If all went to plan, an entire gap would be rigged

The stencilling on this rare wartime wooden case reads "Block, demolition, C-2 in 2 haversacks." This was how the main explosive used to destroy beach obstacles was issued. Eight blocks of C-2 were packed into each haversack. These bags were designed to be blown up along with their contents, so little effort was expended on their material or construction. Once the C-2 had been removed and formed into Hagensen Packs, these haversacks were re-used to carry the packaged explosive, along with other necessary materials such as blasting caps, fuse, and Primacord. The men of the SETF and BODP used whatever types of bags were available to carry their supplies ashore on D-Day, but these haversacks were the most common. On Utah Beach a number of men preferred the over the shoulder M-2 ammo bag because it allowed them to work with their hands unencumbered. Also pictured are the crimper used to fasten the fuse into a blasting cap and a 100 foot roll of yellow colored Primacord. Over 75 miles of Primacord were used to destroy the obstacles on both Utah and Omaha.

with explosives, tied together with Primacord and set off in one major blast.

Most of the Overlord orders indicate that the Gap Teams were to use violet (purple) smoke grenades to warn off any incoming boats or troops. However the SETF plan dated 22 May 1944 clearly states that the warning smoke grenades were red ones. A handful of engineers and landing craft crew claim they recall seeing purple smoke used on the beach, but there is no explanation for the mention of red smoke in the orders. Some of the original wartime orders for the tank battalions also indicate red smoke, but have it crossed out and hand corrected to purple. Given the massive amount of paperwork developed for Overlord, it is no surprise that this error was not caught until the last minute. It remains a matter of speculation if any of the assault units did not get the correction in time and went ashore not knowing what purple smoke meant. This may explain why some men ignored the purple smoke and moved into an area ready to detonate.

There were many differences between the V Corps (Omaha) and VIIth Corps (Utah) plans for the Gap Assault Teams. On Omaha it was planned to open 2 gaps in the obstacles per beach subsector. These gaps would be 50 yards wide and run the 300 yards from the shore out to the furthest line of obstacles. Easy Red, due to its size

and location, would get six 50-yard gaps.

One man was given the task of placing a gap marker on the beach to indicate to the following boats where the obstacles had been cleared. This marker was a white triangle 2 feet wide at the bottom and mounted on a 6 foot pole. The rest of the team was to open and mark a 50 yard gap from the low to high water line. When finished with the 50 yard gap they were to continue to widen their gap until the beach was cleared of all obstacles.

There was a great fear of leaving unexploded mines scattered on the beach, as this could cause a lot of problems later on when larger ships attempted to land. The mine crews were to search the beach area between the bands of obstacles, and destroy any mines found mounted on obstacles with hand placed demolition charges. These men were also to cut paths through any barbed wire that was found strung bet-

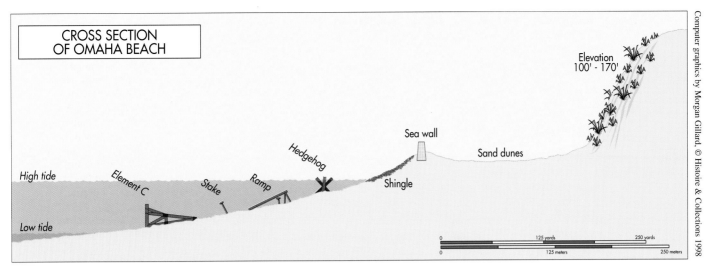

Computer graphics by Morgan Gillard. © Histoire & Collections 1998

CROSS SECTION OF OMAHA BEACH

Elevation 100' - 170'

Sea wall

Sand dunes

Hedgehog

High tide

Element C

Stake

Ramp

Shingle

Low tide

0 125 yards 250 yards

0 125 meters 250 meters

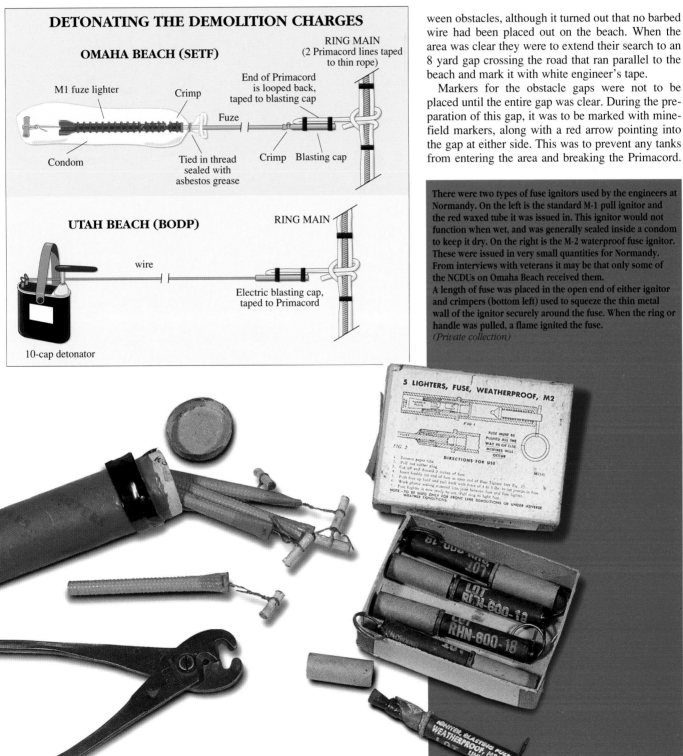

DETONATING THE DEMOLITION CHARGES

OMAHA BEACH (SETF)

RING MAIN
(2 Primacord lines taped to thin rope)

M1 fuze lighter

Crimp

End of Primacord is looped back, taped to blasting cap

Fuze

Condom

Tied in thread sealed with asbestos grease

Crimp

Blasting cap

UTAH BEACH (BODP)

RING MAIN

wire

Electric blasting cap, taped to Primacord

10-cap detonator

ween obstacles, although it turned out that no barbed wire had been placed out on the beach. When the area was clear they were to extend their search to an 8 yard gap crossing the road that ran parallel to the beach and mark it with white engineer's tape.

Markers for the obstacle gaps were not to be placed until the entire gap was clear. During the preparation of this gap, it was to be marked with minefield markers, along with a red arrow pointing into the gap at either side. This was to prevent any tanks from entering the area and breaking the Primacord.

There were two types of fuse ignitors used by the engineers at Normandy. On the left is the standard M-1 pull ignitor and the red waxed tube it was issued in. This ignitor would not function when wet, and was generally sealed inside a condom to keep it dry. On the right is the M-2 waterproof fuse ignitor. These were issued in very small quantities for Normandy. From interviews with veterans it may be that only some of the NCDUs on Omaha Beach received them.
A length of fuse was placed in the open end of either ignitor and crimpers (bottom left) used to squeeze the thin metal wall of the ignitor securely around the fuse. When the ring or handle was pulled, a flame ignited the fuse.
(Private collection)

This amazing photo has captured the LCT (A) 2273 off Omaha Beach still carrying the two standard Sherman tanks and tankdozer which were supposed to support Lt. Anderson's Gap Team #2 on Dog Green Beach. The LCT is listing and it appears it may have suffered some damage on the starboard side. It is impossible to determine the exact time this photo was taken, but there seems to be some troops already on the beach. This would indicate that these tanks did not get to the beach in time to support their Gap Team. *(See also color photo on page 89)*

The NCDUs were to place green flags on green marker buoys at the seaward edges of the cleared gap. On land the triangle range marker was to be placed at the center of the gap to guide the incoming boats. The orders called for minefield gaps to be marked with "standard mine field markers." Different veterans recall this as meaning a red triangle, a yellow marker flag, or just white engineer tape. Individual mines were marked with an 18" piece of wire with a 6x6 inch piece of red muslin attached to it. In practice minefields were cleared by enlisted men probing ahead with bayonets. Officers stood at the rear watching their progress in an attempt to figure out the pattern the Germans had used in laying the mines.

Most of the engineers carried wire cutters in case the Germans had placed barbed wire around the beach obstacles (they hadn't). Some wore the M-2 ammunition vests which would hold 20 Hagensen Packs (or explosive filled socks). Others carried their explosives in the thin olive drab bags that the C-2 or tetrytol had been issued in. Primacord was carried on the 100 foot wooden spools it was issued on or spliced into longer runs and wound onto communications wire reels. All the other demolition equipment, such as blasting caps, fuse ignitors, or crimpers, were carried as the men saw fit, either in demolition kit bags or haversacks. On Omaha alone the Gap Assault Teams required 75 miles of Primacord and 28 tons of explosives. The after-action report indicates that they ended up using all the explosives they requested.

The Gap Assault Teams were to be followed by Gap Support Teams of roughly the same composition. There was one support team for every two Assault Teams. Gap Assault Teams on Omaha were numbered from "1" to "16" and the support teams were lettered "A" through "H." Support Teams "C", "E" and "G" did not include an NCDU, but were reinforced by an additional Army mine crew and demolition crew.

Following the support teams were two command boats which each carried a ton of extra explosives. It was up to the sector commander to decide when or if his command boat team should land. He was to stay offshore evaluating how the Gap Teams were proceeding and land if he felt it was necessary. The Gap Support Teams were to land as directed, but not before H+8 minutes, and assist the Gap Teams. The support and command team boats were to retract from the beach once the men had landed, but stay in the area on call in case the reserve explosives on these boats were needed.

The SETF on D-Day

The SETF Gap Teams were to cross the Channel in LCTs. At 0300 hrs on D-Day they were to transfer to LCMs (preloaded with their explosives and equipment) for the final run into the shore. The LCMs were towed across the Channel by LCTs because the Navy did not think the LCMs had the power or flotation to make the Channel crossing while fully loaded. In case some of the LCMs floundered on the Channel crossing (and some of them did) extra "reserve" LCMs were provided. If not needed for a Gap Team, they were used to bring ashore more explosives. The Support and Command Teams of the 146th crossed the Channel in the *Princess Maud*, a small steamer converted to a British LSI(H) (the H standing for having hand hoisted davits).

Left.
Tankdozers, such as this one operating inland with the 63rd Engineer Bn, were possibly the most important vehicles on the beach. They provided greater protection for the crew than open bulldozers, could fight back if taken under fire by a German pillbox, and could open a path through most obstacles. In theory, each Gap Assault Team was to have its own assigned tankdozer, but few got to their assigned beach at the right time.

The SETF ran into a number of problems on the crossing. The LCTs were some of the slower vessels in the invasion so they started out at 0200 hours on 4 June for the originally planned 5 June invasion. They had to turn back at the last minute due to poor weather. They returned to port by 1100 hrs on the 4th much to the disappointment of the men. This meant that many of the engineers had been stuck in a small open topped landing craft for the rainy 4th of June, an aborted initial crossing, and the final voyage on the 5th of June. Some men had been seasick for almost 2 days before they got to the far shore. On the small *Princess Maud* the constant rocking made most of the men seasick while still in port. On the morning of 6 June only a few of them still had the stomach to eat breakfast. The Gap Support Teams on the *Princess Maud* were an hour late getting to shore. The four support boats of the 146th Bn. ended up landing in the 299th Bn. area.

The first men to land on Omaha may have been Gap team #14 commanded by Lt Phil C. Wood. Wood was under the impression that H-hour was 0620 (instead of 0630), and coerced his LCM to come in at 0625. The LCM was hit by an artillery shell which set off the explosives on board. Many members of team #14 were killed before they got off the boat. By the time the survivors had gotten any obstacles ready to blow, infantrymen had landed and taken cover behind the obstacles. The engineers did not want to set off the explosives where friendly troops were pinned down. This was a common problem on the beach.

It seems that roughly half the Gap Teams landed up to 15 minutes late. This meant that they did not have enough time to clear a gap before the following infantry started landing and taking cover in the obstacles. The primary reason many of the Gap Teams did not open a clear lane was they were unable to clear the infantrymen from the area so they could set off their charges.

The Gap Teams came under terrible fire from the German emplacements and had a rough time trying to perform their mission. Some of the Gap Teams were unable to clear any gaps through the obstacles, but others had reasonable success. Team 10 was able to open one 50 yard gap and one 100 yard gap on Easy Red. The rubber boats drew German fire and a number were quickly destroyed. The Gap Teams noticed this and abandoned these boats. A major problem turned out to be the green marker buoys. They were easily sunk by small arms fire. The same color was used to mark both sides of the gap, so when one marker was sunk the boat crews became unsure of which side of the remaining marker was the actual gap. As the tide rose some landing craft attempted to ram through the obstacles to get their men ashore. Some boats made it, others struck mines and were damaged.

The SETF was only able to open up a few of the planned gaps on Omaha Beach in the morning. When the tide went out in the afternoon they were finally able to clear every planned gap and continued to widen them for the next few days. On D-Day afternoon the beach was too crowded to use explosives, so most of the work was performed by bulldozers that had landed in later waves. On D+5 the engineers were relieved from operations on the beach and moved inland to regroup. For the next few weeks they performed road maintenance duties while awaiting the residues they had left behind in England. The residues finally caught up with the 146th on 24 June.

The Gap Teams suffered from 34-41% casualties on Omaha Beach. The NCDUs took 53% casualties. For their actions on the beach the SETF was awarded 15 DSCs and 7 Navy Crosses. The Force "O" NCDUs were awarded one of the only three Navy Presidential Unit Citations given for D-Day. A curious note is that technically the 146th Engineer Combat Battalion was awarded both the Army and the Navy Presidential Unit Citation. Company A and B served in the Army elements of the SETF, while Company C made up most of the Army additions to the Naval Combat Demolitions Units. The 299th Engineer Combat Battalion was one of only two units assigned to land on both Omaha (Companies A+C) and Utah (Company B) Beaches. The only other unit split between the two beaches was the 320th Barrage Balloon Bn.

The BODP on Utah Beach

The Gap Teams supporting the VIIth Corps landing on Utah Beach were called Beach Obstacle Demolition Parties (BODP) and their plan was slightly different. They were commanded by Major Herschel Linn, commander of the 237th Engineer Combat Bn. The majority of the men were from his battalion and Company B from the 299th Eng. Combat Bn. To bring the demo parties up to full strength, men were pulled from a number of different VIIth Corps units. The rest of the 299th Engineers were to land on the eastern flank of Omaha Beach with the SETF. Tankdozers were supplied from the 70th Tank Bn, with some crewmen coming from the 612th Engineer Light Equipment Company. Utah Beach had a more gradual slope, so there was more time to work on the obstacles before they were covered with water.

Lt. Commander Herbert Peterson was in charge of the 11 NCDUs on Utah. His reinforced NCDUs consisted of 1 Navy officer, 5 Navy demolition men, 3 Navy seamen, and 5 Army engineers. Records on the exact composition of these NCDUs are not clear,

Above.
Lt. Colonel Isley's serial number can be seen inside the liner. On the steel helmet, the officer's vertical white bar is visible on the back. Inside the helmet can be seen two spots where a metal major's leaf was welded or brazed to the front.

but documents indicate that they had two more sailors attached at the last minute bringing the Utah NCDUs to a total strength of 16 men.

The plan for Utah Beach called for a preliminary air and naval bombardment of the beach area. At H–20 the Air Force was to bomb the area once more in four strips perpendicular to the beach. It was hoped that these four areas would serve as a start for the engineers to open into cleared paths.

At H-hour amphibious tanks from the 70th Tank Bn, and assault infantry from the 8th Infantry Regiment, were to land on Utah. Eight NCDUs were to land in LCVPs at H+5 and open one of four 50 yard gaps in each of the two landing beaches (8 gaps total). Also at H+5 more infantry and four LCVPs of army engineers would land. These engineers were not to work on beach obstacles, but to move up with the infantry and support the assault on the German emplacements.

At H+15 LCTs with more tanks and the engineer tank-

Previous page, top.
For his courageous service on Omaha Beach, Lt. Col. Isley was awarded the Distinguished Service Cross. He is shown here receiving it from the Vth Corps commander Major General Gerow. A number of men in the 146th were awarded DSCs, Silver Stars and Bronze Stars for their actions on D-Day.

His DSC citation reads:
Lieutenant Colonel Carl J. Isley, O348085, 146th Engineer Combat Battalion, United States Army. For extraordinary heroism in action against the enemy on 6 June 1944, in France. Lieutenant Colonel Isley commanded a group of demolition teams for the removal of underwater obstacles. Landing with the initial wave, his unit was immediately met with heavy enemy rifle, machine gun, mortar and artillery fire. Completely disregarding his own safety, Lieutenant Colonel Isley promptly reorganized his teams, and though exposed to the direct enemy fire, he personally supervised the placing of demolition charges on obstacles. Undaunted by the fierce enemy fire and the large number of casualties which were inflicted, Lieutenant Colonel Isley tenaciously carried on his mission of clearing a gap in the obstacles. The personal bravery, determination and aggressive leadership displayed by Lieutenant Colonel Isley reflects great credit upon himself, and is in keeping with the highest traditions of the Armed Forces.
Signed O.N. Bradley, Lieutenant General, U.S. Army.

Above and previous page.
This is the helmet worn by Lt. Col. Carl Isley on the morning of D-Day. As commander of the 146th Engineer Combat Bn., he was in charge of obstacle demolitions for the western half of Omaha Beach. From his command boat he saw the trouble his men were having and went ashore to help rig the obstacles with explosives. Something ripped through his helmet, narrowly missing the top of his head. He survived without a scratch and sent the helmet home as a souvenir.
The helmet shows the small entrance hole, and the larger exit hole with the metal of the helmet peeled back. The original net provides an example of the style worn by the 146th at Normandy. The top of the liner is ripped open showing how close Isley came to a serious wound. Isley was promoted from Major to Lieutenant Colonel just before the invasion. On the cross-Channel trip one of his men painted over the yellow major's leaf with white paint on both the helmet and liner.

Below.
This photo was taken on 6 July 1944 of Lt. Col. Isley holding his shrapnel pierced helmet.

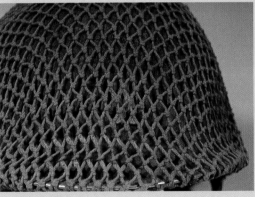

dozers would land. At H+17 the remainder of the NCDUs and the Army engineers of the BODP would land. While the NCDU teams worked on the obstacles closer to the water, 8 Army Demolition Parties, consisting of an officer and 24 enlisted men, would land in an LCM and start work on the rest of the obstacles and mines. The teams had decided that the NCDUs were to work on any obstacles in water, and the Army teams were responsible for those still dry. At H+30 two engineer platoons of 41 men would land and proceed directly to place charges on the concrete seawall. If all went according to plan, the charges on the beach obstacles and seawall would be ready by H+55. Each gap and seawall breach was to be blown simultaneously, one to two minutes after setting off violet smoke grenades to warn approaching boats that demolitions were about to be set off.

Utah on D-Day

The Demo Parties boarded their LCTs in Plymouth and had started out to sea for the planned 5 June

landing. It was not until they had gone 80 miles, at
0900 on Sunday, that they were ordered to turn back.
The men of Force "U" spent an even longer time than
the Force "O" boats seasick before finally reaching
the far shore.

Major Linn's landing craft was sunk on the way
into the beach. He was rescued, but was not able to
get to shore until the next day. Unlike Omaha Beach,
enemy fire on Utah was relatively light. Only 6 of the
Army engineers were killed, when an artillery shell
hit their boat as they came ashore.

There had been a last minute foul-up by the Navy

which resulted in no landing craft for the Gap
Support Teams. They were put into the overloaded
LCMs of the initial Gap Teams and brought in earlier
than planned. Only six of their assigned tankdozers
got ashore without being drowned out in the deep
water. Three of these were hit by artillery fire soon
after.

Some of the Navy control boats at Utah Beach
were not able to be on station as planned. The
remaining control boats attempted to keep the
landing waves sorted out, but coupled with a strong
current, the first waves came in to the left of the

Mission of Special Engineer Task Force

a. Primary Mission: to prepare sixteen (16) fifty (50) yard gaps through all obstacles with the tidal range on Beach Omaha. Two (2) gaps on Fox Green, six (6) gaps on Easy Red, two (2) gaps on Easy Green, two (2) gaps on Dog Red, two (2) gaps on Dog White, and two(2) gaps on Dog Green.

b. Secondary Mission: to remove all obstacles on Beach Omaha.

Troops in Special Engineer Task Force

The Provisional Engineer Group, V Corps, consisting of the following elements, is attached to the 1st US Infantry Division:

a. 299th Engineer Combat Bn (less Company B)

b. 146th Engineer Combat Bn

c. Six (6) Tankdozers with crews from the 743rd Tank Bn (DD)

d. Six (6) Tankdozers with crews from the 741st Tank Bn (DD)

e. Four (4) Tankdozers with crews from the 610th Engineer Light Equipment Company.

f. Twenty-one (21) Naval Combat Demolition Unit Teams.

Upon landing of 1st Eng Bn, all but 2 of the 741st tank-dozers are attached to 1st Eng.

Upon landing of 121st Eng Bn, all but 2 tankdozers from 743rd attached to 121st Eng.

Four tankdozers from 610 Eng Light Equip Co. attached 2 to 299th, and 2 to 146th.

---

planned landing beaches. This area was less heavily defended because the Germans thought it was too close to the mouth of the Taute river for a landing. This landing site had actually been the original choice by the 4th Division. The Navy had refused to land the troops there as they felt the area was too shallow for their boats. An additional advantage of the new landing area was that the aerial bombardment that morning had damaged many of the German installations where the troops finally came ashore.

Three reserve NCDUs were scheduled to land at H+17 and four reserve Army demo parties to land at H+60. In reality all Navy and Army parties landed on Utah between H+5 and H+20 with the initial forces. Commanding NCDU team #30 was Lt.(jg) Carl Hagensen, inventor of the Hagensen Pack.

The obstacles on Utah were slightly different from Omaha. There were only a handful of Element Cs. Some of these were later found on the beach being used to block the exit roads. The majority of obstacles were hedgehogs, tetrahedrons, and steel and concrete stakes. Although under direct fire on the beach for hours, and indirect artillery fire for a week,

Above.
Captain Samuel H. Ball, commander of A/146 receives the Distinguished Service Order for his actions on Omaha Beach. He is shown getting the medal from General Montgomery on 7 July 1944. Captain Ball was in charge of the four Gap Teams on Dog Green and Dog White beaches.

Below.
Officers of the 146th Engineer Combat Bn. taken in France on 7 July 1944.
1st row: Brown (S-1), Wynot (XO), Fox (Recce), Isley (CO), Pipka (S-2), Baker (S-3).
2nd row: Nichols (S-4), Stratton (surgeon), Doyle (Adjutant).
(Courtesy Carl Isley Jr.)

the engineers quickly opened up gaps in the obstacles which allowed boats to start landing. By 0800 over 700 yards of beach were cleared and by 0930 Utah Beach was essentially all clear of obstacles.

The few tankdozers that made it to the beach were useful in pushing debris aside, but in the after-action report it was claimed that almost all the obstacles had been destroyed by hand placed charges. The demo parties performed most of their work under scattered small arms and artillery fire. The Utah NCDUs suffered 4 men killed, 11 wounded ; the Army engineers 6 men killed, 39 wounded.

A final Army report on the breaching of the Utah obstacles states: *"The actual landing took place approximately 2,200 yards south of the planned location, and initially the approaching craft bunched*

to the south of the main exit road leading from the final Utah Beach. Eight engineer assault parties and twelve Naval Combat Demolition Units landed between H+5 and H+15. The four reserve engineer assault teams landed about H+15 opposite the main exit road. All of these teams executed their missions strictly in accordance with the plan except that each group of four teams first cleared a complete 200 yard band because of the fact that approaching craft were still bunched. The naval units worked on the first band of obstacles, the Army units on the second band, and both units worked on the remaining obstacles up to the high water line. Initial gaps were cleared by H+45 minutes, following which units worked to the north until the entire width of the beach area was cleared. These units also assisted the engineer platoons in the demolition of the seawall, which was blown at H+55 minutes. By H+3 hours, Utah Beach was cleared of all underwater and beach obstacles for the entire planned width, and thereafter the only obstacles to the landing were craft which had been sunk on the beach by gunfire."

Every published source about Utah Beach claims that the reason that the landing was so successful was that the men accidentally landed in the wrong place

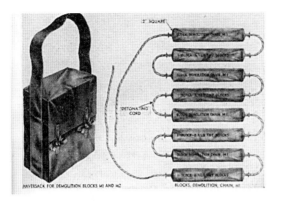

HAVERSACK FOR DEMOLITION BLOCKS M1 AND M2   BLOCKS, DEMOLITION, CHAIN, M1

Top.
Chains of tetrytol blocks were another of the explosives used by the Gap Teams. This explosive was issued in the same type of haversack as C-2. Eight blocks of tetrytol were molded around a single length of Primacord. The blocks could be used all together, or cut apart and used separately.

Above.
This jeep, with the nickname "Sophie", has a .50 caliber machine gun mounted on it. The markings on the trailer show it was one of the two jeeps authorized to Company E, 22nd Infantry Regt, 4th Infantry Division. Although captioned as boarding an LST for the invasion of Europe, the absence of extra equipment and waterproofing materials indicates the shot was probably taken during a previous exercise. Although the 22nd Infantry landed about mid-day on 6 June, the unit vehicles may not have come ashore until much later.

where there was light German resistance. One 299th veteran, James Burke, tells a slightly different story. He was one of the Army engineers attached to the NCDUs on Utah. The Naval officer in charge of the NCDUs was Lt. Commander Peterson. Burke claims that his group of support boats was guided by Peterson, who was able to navigate better than many of the less experienced LVCP coxswains and delivered them to the correct landing beaches so they could

The official report on Utah Beach demolitions
By Lt. Comdr Herbert Peterson, 26 June 1944

"1 (A) On landing at approximately 1 1/2 hours after low water, the distance from the waterline to the seawall was approximately 700 yards. The average distance from the waterline to the first obstacles was approximately 300 yards. There were a few scattered small shell holes and craters up to eight feet in diameter.

(B) Beginning from seaward the first obstacles encountered were a number of scattered wooden ramps and eight unconnected bays of element "C." Two of these were on Red Beach and six on Green Beach.

The ramps were of material eight to ten inches in diameter, comprising three legs, the two shorter legs approximately seven feet long and the seaward leg approximately 14 feet long.

The elements C were of conventional design, approximately eight feet tall, eight feet wide with rear supports approximately ten feet deep. Material was approximately 3/4 inch by six inches.

The next band of obstacles was, in some places, reinforced concrete posts, and in other places concrete tetrahedrons. The concrete posts were approximately six feet tall, with material approximately eight inches square. All had reinforcing steel rods approximately 3/4 inch thick. The tetrahedrons had bases approximately four feet to a side. Their vertical height was approximately six feet to the apex. The material was approximately six inches thick. The concrete posts were in three rows, approximately 30 feet apart, with approximately 50 feet between rows.

The tetrahedrons were, in some places, in two rows, in other places three rows. Approximately 35 feet apart with rows approximately 40 feet apart. In some places there were both posts and tetrahedrons. In other places one or the other.

The last band of obstacles consisted of wooden posts, varying from one to two feet in diameter, and varying in height from three to six feet. These were in either three or four rows, approximately 30 feet apart, with approximately 40 feet between rows. These extended the full length of the beach. They varied in distance from the seawall, being in some places as far as 200 feet from high-water mark and in others being at approximately the high-water mark.

(C) The time required to remove the obstacles is not known, but at 0800 all obstacles were ascertained to have been removed. This was one hour and 25 minutes after the first demolition team landed.

(D) In all cases, the demolition teams used hand-placed prepared charges of either composition C-2 or tetrytol, chiefly the former. For concrete posts, either one or two charges were placed at the base of the post. For tetrahedrons, two charges at the apex and one at the foot of each leg. For wooden posts, either two or three at the base. For the ramps, two were placed at the apex, and in some cases one at the base of a leg. In the case of element "C", from 18 to 22 charges were connected up to a trunk line of Primacord. Electric firing was used exclusively.

(E) In practically all cases the charges used were completely effective. In a few concrete posts, it was found that the reinforcing rods had not been cut through and as the smoke subsided, the upper part of the post was seen to be swaying back and forth, supported by the rod or rods. Each time this occurred, a single additional charge was placed alongside the rods and fired, effectively cutting them.

(F) No mines were found in connection with the obstacles on the assault beach.

(G) There were a few instances of shell fragments penetrating the prepared charges and one instance of a Primacord lead being cut by a fragment. In each case the explosive proved to be completely insensitive.

(H) Successful and speedy removal of obstacles may be attributed to:

(a) Detailed planning and preparation, and thorough training. The training received at the Assault Training Center, Woolacombe, was especially helpful.

(b) The use of prepared charges as developed by Lieut. (jg) Carl P. Hagensen, CNC-V (S), USNR, Officer in charge, NCDU 30.

(c) The use of the M-1 Ammunition Bag *, a sufficient number of which were obtained from the Army. This enabled each man to carry 32 pounds of explosive, suspended from his shoulders, and to work easily while carrying his load.

It is recommended that Primacord be put up and issued in 500 ft. reels in addition to the 100ft. reel, in use at present. The 100ft. length invariably proved too short, necessitating bonding on additional lengths, with consequent delay.

It is suggested that the original unit team composed of one officer and five men would have been too small, and it is recommended that units be increased to ten demolition men.

2. After the assault, in the evening of D-Day and on D plus 2, further demolitions were carried on, extending the original beach. Obstacles encountered were similar to those on the original beach.

On D plus 5 and D plus 6, 1000 yards were cleared on Roger White Beach. Here in addition to the types of obstacles met before, there were steel hedgehogs of material approximately 3/4 inch by eight inches with legs approximately eight feet long. Each concrete post had a Teller mine secured on top of it.

Three charges were placed at the joint of each hedgehog, with one at the base of each leg. In preparing the concrete posts, a charge was placed at the top, directly under the mine, in addition to those at the base. In every case except one, this successfully detonated the mine."

H.A. Peterson

* Although the original text mentions the M-1 ammo bag, interviews with veterans clearly indicate that they used the over the head M-2 ammo bag. Although it is possible that both styles were used, it is likely that Peterson made a simple error in his description of this piece of Army equipment.

start opening up gaps through the obstacles. There were no assault troops from the 4th Division in this area, so the engineers had to stop their work and attack a nearby pillbox (taking 25 prisoners) before they could clear a path to the beach and blow a gap in the seawall.

Although this story is not reported in after-action reports (although many of these reports are missing from the government archives) there is some corroborating evidence that a handful of Demolition Party boats did land at the correct beach, subdue the German defenders, and open gaps in the obstacles. If a handful of engineers could beat the defenders at the original landing beach, then the 4th Division assault troops should have had no problems. This little known aspect of Utah Beach may have well have been "officially forgotten" because it would make the 2,000 yard error in landing beaches seem embarrassing to the military, rather than the totally beneficial accident it has been.

After the landings

Following the assault troops and Demo Parties came more supporting engineers. These were 7 platoons from companies A and C of the 237th Eng Combat Bn, and 2 platoons from the 4th Division Engineers. These 9 platoons were not to deal with the beach obstacles, but were to blow gaps in the seawall, clear paths through the barbed wire and then help assault any enemy fortifications in the area. The seawall, a concrete wall a few feet high, was an effective barrier to any vehicle trying to get off the beach. Gaps had to be blown in it, and the rubble bulldozed clear, before any vehicles could exit the beach.

Once these engineers had opened the path off the beach, two more engineer battalions were to land on Utah. The 49th ECB and the 238th ECB landed at H+3 hours. Their job was to create exit roads across the flooded area behind the beach. They landed with a large quantity of road and bridging supplies to deal with craters in the roads from artillery fire and demolished bridges on the beach exits.

After Utah Beach was cleared, the NCDUs helped clear wreckage and pull waterlogged vehicles from the sea. One humorous story concerns an NCDU team that was poking around in the German defenses

Above.
The crew of the LCC-60, one of the control boats at Utah Beach, relax on deck during the Channel crossing of 5 June 1944. Headgear seems to be a mixture of black watch caps and Navy HBT caps. Personal photography such as this was strictly prohibited for security reasons, but examples of such rare photos constantly seem to crop up when all sources seem exhausted.
(Courtesy Howard Vander Beek)

This house on Omaha Beach shows the scars of combat from D-Day. It was targeted as being a possible location of a German strongpoint, and was therefore heavily shelled from the sea. In the days following the landing it serves as an identifiable location to station an ambulance from the 1st Infantry Division. These ambulances were not designed to travel up to the front line, so they could retain the white painted bumpers for nighttime visibility. The markings indicate it is from Company C of the 1st Medical Bn. Also on the bumper is the yellow and black tactical mark of the 1st Medical Bn and the three stripe bar code for Company C.

This photo of the crew of the LCC-60, the primary control vessel for the first waves at Utah Beach, was taken on Easter Sunday in Plymouth, England. Some of the crewmen had been to church and are wearing their dress uniforms, others have been on duty and wear working uniforms. Front row from left: Joseph Tarnowski, Sophos Lolos, Joseph Rafaniello, Robert Spenser. Back row from left: Howard Vander Beek, Thomas Williams, Wilford Yokum, Ralph Cosden, Joseph St. Germaine, Sims Gauthier, James Hopfensberger. During the landing, the two ship's officers had different duties to perform. Gauthier worked below deck in the radar and navigation room, while Vander Beek was up on the bridge. The actions of this crew, more than anything else, may well have prevented the Utah Beach landings from turning into a disaster. *(Courtesy Howard Vander Beek)*

THE DIVERTED FIRST WAVES AT UTAH BEACH

For many years the map of the first waves at Utah Beach found in the official U.S. Army history has been assumed to be accurate. Upon close inspection it portrays the two battalion landing teams heading to shore side by side. In reality, the two battalions were supposed to land with an empty stretch of beach, roughly 1,000 yards wide, between them. According to the official histories a strong offshore current, coupled with the loss of several control boats, caused the first waves to head to the wrong beach roughly 2,000 yards to the left. Popular history has it that the troops decided that since they had encountered less resistance on the alternate beaches, they would move all future landings to the new unplanned site. The Assistant Division Commander of the 4th Division is credited with stating *"we'll start the war from here."*

The story of the Utah landings has never really been thoroughly investigated. Curious details exists such as the after-action report by Col. William Gayle (8th Inf Regt) which states that *"the actual landing was 2,300 yards south of the point planned. A change was made at the last minute because the fire was so heavy on the planned landing beaches. The assault elements had no notice of this change and for a few minutes after landing were confused. This included officers and men."*

By chance both officers on board the LCC-60 are still alive, and tell a story slightly different from what is found in other records. Sims Gauthier and Howard Vander Beek were the two naval officers on board the LCC-60 which was supposed to direct the initial landing waves to Tare Green Beach *(see picture above and previous page, top)*. Vander Beek, like many

LCC officers, was a former Scout and Raider who had seen action at Sicily. Gauthier was a highly trained navigation and radar expert. The LCCs were equipped with extraordinary radar for their day. They could easily plot their location from 12 miles out using the radar signals bouncing off the high points on shore. Once they were 6 miles off shore they switched to a more accurate setting and could easily plot their position to within 50 yards. As Gauthier states, their radar set was "fantastic", and they had no problem on the morning of 6 June determining their exact location.

How then, to account for the claims they led the first waves to the wrong beach? Both Tare Green and Uncle Red had their own teams of three control boats: one PC and two LCCs. Uncle Red was assigned the PC 1261, LCC-80 and LCC-90. Tare Green was assigned the PC 1176, LCC-60 and LCC-70. The PCs were to mark the line of departure where the landing craft first started in to the beach. One LCC was to lead the waves in to shore, the other remain in the transport area.

PC 1261 was sunk early in the morning of 6 June, and the LCC-80 had been unable to make the Channel crossing due to a fouled propeller. Apparently the LCC-90 in the transport area was unaware of this problem due to all ships being at radio silence. This left Uncle Red with no control vessels at the line of departure. The LCC-60 observed the confusion and attempted to perform its own duties as well as filling in for the PC 1261 and LCC-80. The LCC-60 brought the waves in close enough to the beach so that the crews should have been able to spot their landmarks.

The problem was that there had been some delay and confusion in launching the DD tanks from the LCTs. The water was too rough to launch the tanks far offshore, so the decision was made to bring them in closer to land. The delay threw off the timing of the waves and the first wave of LCVPs were faced with passing through the line of swimming DD tanks. The sea was still rough and the freeboard of the DD tanks was so slight that any wake might swamp them. The wave commanders of the LCVPs made the decision to swing their craft out around to the left so that they would not have to pass through the DD tank line. Once out to the left there was no time left to swing back into place, so the LCVPs headed directly to shore. While the strong current may have contributed slightly to the southern drift of the first waves, the principal reason for mis-landing was the desire of the LCVP coxswains to not swamp the DD tanks. As far as is known to the LCC-60 crew, this obvious reason has never before been made public, and appears to fit the available evidence.

There is a wide variety of estimates of exactly how far off each battalion landing team was from its planned beach. Part of the problem lies with the beach sectors being renamed to fit the situation on the beach, giving the planned name to now different areas of the beach. Maps from before and after the invasion show different spots for the same beach. Vander Beek maintains that the first waves could not have landed more than 500 yards to the left, which is the estimate for the 2/8th at Uncle Red. The Army, however, recorded that the 1/8th came ashore roughly 1,500 yards from their planned target of Tare Green.

on D+1. They saw a steel shutter in a German fortification slam shut and knew there were enemy soldiers hiding inside. When they tried to report this to the Army engineers, they were told they must have been mistaken. The Navy team leader bet the soldiers $5 that there were still some Germans on the beach. He then scrounged some German explosives and blew the pillbox door open. Out came 16 Germans who promptly surrendered. The Navy man brought his German prisoners over to the Army and won his bet.

The NCDUs located approximately eight small German tracked vehicles they called "doodlebugs." Officially known as "Goliaths", these were small demolition vehicles that could be driven up to the enemy by remote control and then the 250 pounds of explosive inside detonated. The explosives were removed and the men had fun driving their mini-tanks around the beach. They would later learn that the aerial bombardment had damaged the controls of the doodlebugs, which explained why they had not been used to repulse the landings.

The NCDUs on Utah received the only Navy Unit Commendation for the Normandy landings. On 13 June the NCDUs of Force "U" left for England. There they would receive orders to clear obstacles for the invasion of Southern France. Some claim that the two commanders of the Utah and

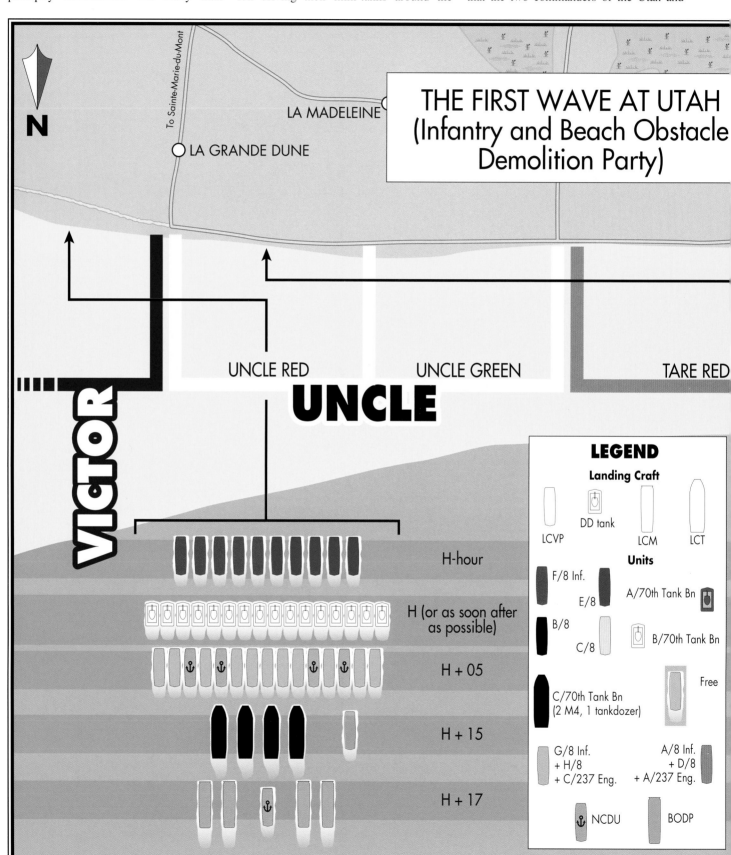

THE FIRST WAVE AT UTAH
(Infantry and Beach Obstacle Demolition Party)

To Sainte-Marie-du-Mont

N

LA MADELEINE

O LA GRANDE DUNE

UNCLE RED   UNCLE GREEN   TARE RED

UNCLE

VICTOR

H-hour

H (or as soon after as possible)

H + 05

H + 15

H + 17

LEGEND

Landing Craft

LCVP   DD tank   LCM   LCT

Units

F/8 Inf.   A/70th Tank Bn
E/8

B/8   B/70th Tank Bn
C/8

C/70th Tank Bn   Free
(2 M4, 1 tankdozer)

G/8 Inf.   A/8 Inf.
+ H/8   + D/8
+ C/237 Eng.   + A/237 Eng.

NCDU   BODP

Omaha Beach NCDUs flipped a coin to see whose men would get to participate in the next operation. However, it was clear that the Utah Beach men had suffered fewer casualties and were in better shape for another operation. In Southern France these men would get a chance to try out the radio controlled Apex Boats and the Reddy Fox demolitions. But neither would prove to be superior to charges placed by hand on the obstacles.

Conclusion

There are a great many books that give credit to Navy UDTs for clearing the obstacles on both beaches. Nothing could be further from the truth. There were no Navy UDTs at Omaha or Utah Beach. The Navy Combat Demolition Units played a major role in removing these obstacles, but only as a part of the Special Engineer Task Force and the Beach Obstacle Demolition Parties. The gaps were opened by a team effort that included not only the NCDUs, but men from the 146th, 299th and 237th Engineer Bns, as well as a handful of men from the 2nd Division, 53rd Medical Bn., 610th and 612th Engineers, 70th, 741st and 743rd Tank Bns.

British sources have been critical of the American reluctance to use their specially modified armored vehicles to open the way. Of the sixteen tankdozers to land on Omaha Beach, five were destroyed by German fire, and a few others were drowned in the surf. On Utah Beach two of the eight tankdozers never got to the beach, and three of these were soon hit by German fire. German antitank fire was both strong and accurate. It seems that the decision to use teams of men to clear the obstacles, rather than rely on special vehicles, may have been the correct one. Although not everything went according to plan on Omaha Beach, the success of the Gap Teams relied not on gadgets, but on courageous men who braved enemy fire to open the way for the invasion of France.

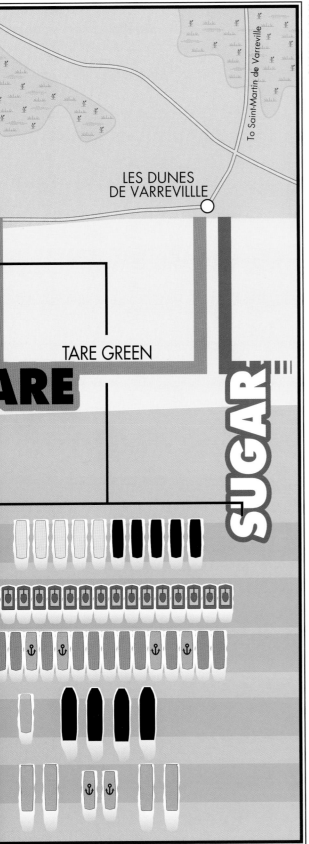

Below.
After D-Day, the NCDUs from Utah Beach were sent to the Mediterranean. This photo was taken in Salerno of James Sprouse (NCDU 135) left, and Irwin Itzkowitz (NCDU 139) right, as they prepared to take part in the invasion of Southern France. Their helmets are still painted for the Normandy assault: a 2" grey band, the letters "USN" in front, and an ensign's bar to identify them as officers.
(Courtesy Nate Irwin)

Composition of the Utah Beach Obstacle Demolition Parties (BODP)

(Otherwise known as the Provisional Battalion, 1106th Engineer Combat Group)

Unit	Officer	EM
B/299 Eng	4	139
49 Eng	1	-
238 Eng	1	3
70th Tank	1	16
612 Lt Equip Co	1	9
4 Eng	-	9
148 Eng	-	14
164 Eng	-	28
207 Eng	1	6
294 Eng	1	2
297 Eng	-	6
298 Eng	1	11
300 Eng	-	6
507 Pontoon Co	-	2
512 Pontoon Co	1	-
237 Eng	7	151
Total	**12**	**251**

E
ARLY in the war the senior commanders of the U.S. Army realized that they would have to place limits on the structure and size of the Army. The United States was thought of as having endless supplies of manpower and equipment, but the generals realized all too well their limitations. Every organization from squad up to Army Group was examined, to determine the absolute minimum of men and equipment needed to fulfil an average mission.

One of the methods used to cut back, on both men and equipment, was adding trailers. The cargo capacity of the trailers allowed for vehicles to be eliminated, which in turn eliminated their drivers, as well as the supplies and mechanics needed to keep the vehicles running. Before the war, men were assigned as drivers with no other duty when not on the road. Starting in 1943, being a driver meant that they also had another job to do when not in their truck. This not only released more men for service in other units, but also freed up the cargo space for the

Above and opposite page, top. **A tank crew loads 7.5 inch rockets into the T-40 rocket launcher somewhere in Italy. This launcher was specifically designed to use against beach obstacles, but when the 70th Tank Bn. attempted to use it at a demonstration in England the rockets did not perform as expected. This was probably caused by a failure to send installation instructions along with the launchers.**

eliminated vehicle, the driver, and all the extras needed to keep it rolling.

Not only was the job of every man examined to make sure it was necessary, but equipment was carefully checked to ensure it was only given to units that would use it more often. Engineer units would probably need to clear minefields on a regular basis, so they were allowed mine detectors. Following the same logic, not every engineer unit would need certain types of bridges, so specific bridging equipment need only be given to dedicated bridge building units. Likewise, the engineer units would not need special heavy road building equipment everyday, so the Engineer Light Equipment Companies were to provide a pool of special equipment that could be attached as needed to standard engineer units.

Weapons were looked at in much the same way. If the range of a weapon was greater than the average frontage of a unit, that weapon was generally placed in the next higher echelon so it could be used to support other units to either flank. A 60mm mortar was part of an infantry company because its range covered the average company frontage. The 81mm mortar had the range to fire throughout the battalion area, so it was assigned to the heavy weapons company supporting an entire battalion. Artillery pieces with ranges greater than the typical division frontage were placed at Corps level so they could support many different divisions as needed.

A division was usually thought of as the largest organization that had every main element of a self-contained combat team (infantry, artillery, engineer, etc.). A division was often larger than necessary for a combat task, so the U.S. Army developed the

bat Teams

Below.
This Sherman tank is carried on board an LCM during an exercise at the Assault Training Center. An officer in a trench coat uses an SCR-609 radio to communicate with the shore. Although there appears to be enough freeboard to safely carry a 32 ton Sherman in an LCM, it made the craft top-heavy and there were enough accidents in training for the Army to find it unwise to try and land tanks from LCMs.

concept of the Combat Team. They took a basic infantry element, generally a regiment or battalion, and added extra units to it depending on what was needed. If a regiment was attacking a series of pill-boxes, an engineer battalion might be assigned to support the advance and would be directly attached to the regimental headquarters. This allowed the regimental commander to issue orders directly to the

engineer battalion as though it was one of his own rifle battalions. Once the attack was finished, the engineer unit would revert to Corps or Army control and could then be assigned to any other unit or task where it was needed.

The assault divisions at Normandy were essentially Division Combat Teams. Many different types of specialty units were attached to the 1st, 4th and 29th

Right.
Waterproofing a Sherman tank called for an intake and an exhaust shroud, made of thin sheet metal, to be installed on the rear deck. These allowed the tank to operate in water with only the turret exposed. One tactic used by these tanks was to remain partially submerged when firing on the shore defenses, thus using the water to provide a hull-down position. Once ashore the shrouds were jettisoned as soon as possible so the turret could traverse freely.

Below.
Shermans of the 70th Tank Bn. are loaded onto a Royal Navy LCT at Kingswear in England. The photograph is dated 1 June 1944, which would indicate that they are preparing for Normandy. However, due to the vagueness of the photo censoring system this could have been taken months before at a practice landing and not released until June. At the front of the LCT is a T-2 tank recovery vehicle.

to assist in the mission of landing in France. Because most of the attachments were done on a regimental level, it is more common to think of the assault troops as a series of regimental combat teams formed around the nucleus of an infantry regiment. The initial assault regiments were heavier in some components such as tanks and engineers than the following regiments.

The Combat Team system is not as easy as saying that the 112th Engineer Combat Bn. was attached to the 116th Infantry Regt. This is the simplest way to understand it, but in practice the engineer unit would be broken down into smaller groups and attached piece by piece to the subelements of the regiment. Two engineer companies might be under the direct command of the lead infantry battalion, while the engineer headquarters and third company could be attached to another battalion in the infantry regiment. At times these attachments could continue down to specific engineer squads being attached to specific infantry companies or platoons.

This does not always mean that an infantry platoon leader issued orders directly to the attached engineers. Generally these attachments were mainly administrative in nature and allowed the higher command to assign tasks based on location or specific mission. In practice, the confusing nature of the Omaha landings meant that few units actually performed the missions they were assigned, on schedule and with all the correct partners. It was more of a matter of the troops knowing what had to be done and whoever was best able to perform a task did it.

In many situations the Regimental Combat Team (RCT) attachments were established because of the physical location the units were to operate in. Anti-aircraft and medical units were assigned to infantry regiments for the landing, but they had their own orders to defend a specific area from enemy aircraft, or to set up an aid station in a certain location and provide help to any casualties in the area. Their missions were not dependent upon the regimental commander issuing them any orders.

The entire question of Combat Team attachments becomes even more clouded as some units were attached to the RCT until a specific time, such as when a certain headquarters lands, or a prearranged hour. Then the attachments would suddenly report to a different headquarters. The most notable case of this kind of attachment dealt with the 116th Infantry Regiment. The 116th was given a great number of attachments, including the 2nd and 5th Ranger Battalions. During the invasion the 116th was technically assigned to the 1st Division. When the 29th Headquarters came ashore later in the day, the 116th reverted to 29th Division command. This was done so that only one divisional headquarters element

2nd Battalion Landing Team 116th Infantry

E Co +1 HMG platoon and 1 81mm section
F Co +1 81mm section G Co +1 HMG sec,
+ 1 81mm sec
G Co + 112th Eng Bn.

16th Regimental Combat Team

organic Hq+Hq Co
16th Anti-tank Co
16th Service Co
16th Medical Det
16th Cannon Co
16th 1, 2 and 3rd Rifle Bns
Divisional Det
1st Sig Co
1st Eng Bn. (less Co A, B, and one platoon of C)
7th Field Arty Bn.
Co A 1st Med
Liaison Party, 1st Inf Div attached from 1st Army Special Engineer Task Force
Civil Affairs det Liaison Party, 231st Brigade, 50th Northumbrian Div
Det L 165th Sig
741st Tnk Bn. (less Co B+C)
62nd Armored Field Artillery

197th AAA Bn. AW (SP)
det 320th Barrage balloon Bn. VLA
1 platoon 606th Graves Registration
2 prov AAA AW (SP)
4 Surgical Teams
37th Eng C Bn.
20th Eng Bn. (less Co C)
3 NSFCP
Air support party
PWI Team Lang Interp Team
CIC Det

115th RCT

Unit	men	vehicles
115th inf	3,000	236
110 FA	424	81
A/121 Eng	164	21
A/104 med	102	16
det HQ 29 ID	5	2
det 29th sig co	10	3
det 729 ord	5	2
det29 QMC	6	1
PWI team	4	1
sec,606 QM graves R	6	1
det H, 165 SPC	3	13
NSFCP	43	
det civil affairs	2	1

Once launched from an LCT the DD tanks would circle in formation, much the same as landing craft waves, until the order was given to proceed to shore. The freeboard, the distance between the water surface and the top of the flotation skirt, was normally about eight inches with a full load of ammo and fuel on board. These tanks are riding too high for them to be carrying a full load of equipment.

would have to be landed on the beach in the early hours.

The Battalion Landing Team

Experiments with amphibious assaults back at the Assault Training Center and in the States had shown that the basic unit of any landing should be the battalion. The battalion was small enough to control in the confusing atmosphere of an invasion, but large enough to have some fighting power. After the divisions had been assigned to the invasion, and the regiments given their place, the battalions were the ones to carry the weight of the fighting.

A Battalion Landing Team was formed around an infantry battalion. Attached to it was a tank company and two engineer platoons. Artillery support was

BATTALION LANDING TEAM (BLT)

Battalion (Assault)
- Battalion HQ
- Battalion Headquarters Co.
- Communications Platoon
- Anti-Tank Platoon (3 x 57 mm)
- Ammunition and Pioneer Platoon

Co. A
Co. B
Co. C
Co. D (Support)
Medical Detachment
Tank Co. (+1 platoon)
Engineer platoons (1 bulldozer)
4,2 in. CWS mortar (-1 Platoon)
E — Naval Shore Fire Control Party (US Navy)
G — NSFCP
AOP — Artillery Observation Party (Army)

2 Tank Platoons + 1 tank (11 tanks)
Command Boat Team
6 Assault Boat Teams
5 Support Boat Teams

157

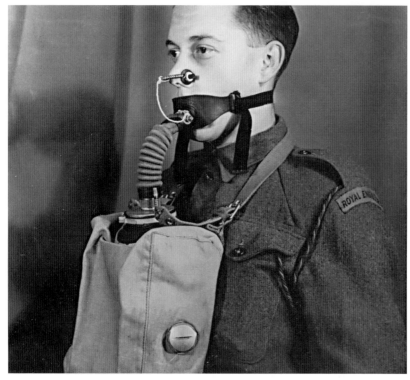

provided by a chemical company (4.2 inch mortars),
and the Naval Shore Fire Control Party (NSFCP).
Once the divisional artillery was ashore, a forward
observer would direct any needed fire from the divisional 105 and 155mm Battalions.

One of the questions that is frequently raised about
the landings on Omaha Beach deals with the 1st battalion of the 116th at Vierville. All other assault battalions landed with two companies on line and the
third rifle company following. The 1/116th landed
with only one rifle company in the first wave and the
rest following in line one after the other. Many suggestions have been made as to why the 116th did
things differently, with the most popular hypothesis
being that it was to deal with the heavy German
defenses on the extreme right flank of Omaha.

The answer appears to be much simpler and was
found in the Overlord after-action reports for the
29th Division. It seems that higher headquarters had
laid out the battalion boundaries and left it to the
division to fit the unit to the area prescribed. In the
116th area the beach was just too narrow for two
companies to land abreast, so only one was
scheduled to land with each wave. The 29th Division
was not pleased with being squeezed in this way, but
they were ordered to make it work.

The RCT and BLT concept was the basis for assigning different types of units to the same area. In the military mind every unit must have a specific superior officer to report to, even if that officer would have no reason to issue them any orders. Some of the attachments, such as the tank battalions, worked closely with the infantry. Some, such as the 4.2" chemical mortars, were directed to support the advance of specific infantry battalions. Others, such as the anti-aircraft units, were given missions where they had no reason to work with the infantry at all.

Tank Battalions

One of the most interesting attachments to each assault regiment was an independent tank battalion. The 4th Division was assigned the 70th Tank Bn., the 29th Div. the 743rd Tank Bn., and the 1st Div. the 741st Tank Bn. Early in the war, the armored troops had fought to keep tanks out of infantry divisions, arguing that tanks would be more effective when consolidated in armored divisions. Combat experience had shown that it was worthwhile to attach a single tank battalion to every infantry division. It was found that the tank battalion became more effective the longer it was assigned to the same division, as the men began to know each other and work together. It became standard procedure to give each division its own tank battalion as a near permanent attachment. After the war, the table of organization was changed to make a tank battalion a permanent part of every infantry division.

The three tank battalions used at D-Day were special. Two of their three standard tank companies had been equipped with amphibious Duplex Drive (DD) Sherman tanks. The DD tank had a canvas and rubber skirt that could be raised up around the tank. This made the tank buoyant enough to float. The duplex drive refers to the special transmission that could send power either to the treads when on land, or to twin propellers when in the water. The DD tanks were very slow in the water (4 mph), and the freeboard (the height between the water surface and the top of the skirt) was only about 8-10". The DD tanks were kept top-secret in hopes that the unusual sight of tanks crawling out of the sea would scare the German defenders.

The landing plan called for the two DD companies to cross the Channel in LCTs. If the seas were calm, they were to be launched 5,000 yards out from the shore and land on their assigned beaches just before H-hour. These tanks were to target the German pillboxes, support the initial assault companies, and draw fire away from the engineers opening gaps in the obstacles. Each LCT carried 4 DD tanks, as well as a handful of smaller vehicles from other units that were to be brought to shore later in the day.

These LCTs were specially modified to handle the DD tanks. Special "launching gear" was installed on the bow of each LCT that kept the tank from nosing under the water when it went down the ramp. No photographs of the launching gear were allowed to be taken, due to the high security around the DD tanks.

Launching gear has been described as a framework of metal that stuck out from the bow ramp about 15 feet. Two extensions were added to the front of the LCT to help lower the gear into the water with the ramp. Although crewmen on these LCTs have indicated that the launching gear would stick into the air when the ramp was raised, it seems wartime censors have eliminated any photographs that might illustrate this device.

After the obstacle clearing engineers had landed, the third company of standard Shermans was to land in LCTs. These tanks were not amphibious, but were waterproofed and equipped with air intake shrouds which allowed the tanks to function in up to seven feet of water. Once ashore, a crewman had to leave the protection of the tank to pull the pins that held the shrouds in place, or else the tank could not traverse its turret to the rear. Each of these following LCTs was to carry two standard Shermans and one tankdozer Sherman. Extra ammunition was provided so the tanks could fire at the Germans as the LCTs moved to the shore. Once these tanks were landed, the LCTs were to retract and wait until H+220 to return to the beach with the rest of their load, a handful of smaller vehicles such as jeeps and trailers.

The M5 light tanks were not scheduled to land in France until roughly H+260 minutes. Trucks from the battalion's Service Company were scheduled to land with extra fuel and ammunition around H+290.

Above.

This well-known photo of a Sherman nicknamed "Cannonball" has never been definitely identified. It is clearly a standard Sherman equipped with the air intake and exhaust shrouds, and not a DD tank or a tankdozer. It was common practice in many units to assign vehicle nicknames by matching the first letter of the nickname to the company letter, so Cannonball may be from a Company C. The only standard Sherman company to land on D-Day was C/70th, therefore is a good guess that Cannonball was one of the C/70th tanks landing on Utah Beach. The tank number painted on the side also resembles the numbers painted on other 70th Tank Bn. Shermans.

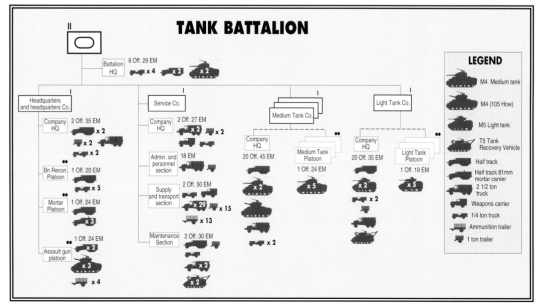

TANK BATTALION

Above.
Somewhere off Utah Beach a
soldier from the 8th Infantry
Regiment wears his assault
jacket at a crossroads. On the
left is a wagon filled with
German POWs. To the right is a
Sherman from the 70th Tank
Bn. The fixture running across
the front of the hull indicates
it is a DD tank from either
Company A or B. Of specific
interest is that the crewmen of
this tank all wear steel helmets
instead of the leather tanker's
helmet. On the gun mantle can
be seen the markings "1A" (1st
Army), concealed behind the
raised gun is what appears to be
70 ▲, and to the right is "A8"
(8th tank of Company A). At the
top right hand side of the turret
is an unreadable word that may
be the tank nickname,
and "SCR 536" which may have
been an indication to the
assault troops that this tank was
equipped with that radio and
could communicate with them.

Following later in the day were more tank battalions, and on Omaha Beach tanks from the 2nd Armored Division would start to land over the next few days.

The 70th Tank Bn. at Utah

The 70th Tank Bn. was an experienced unit. It had been the very first independent tank battalion formed (not assigned to any armored division). It had seen combat in North Africa and Sicily before being sent to England. Part of the original Company C had been sent to Iceland in February 1942 to form the 10th Light Tank Company. When the 70th was shipped to England it was altered from the earlier light tank battalion organization (of two Sherman companies and two Stuart companies), to three Sherman and one Stuart companies. The men from the 10th helped bring the 70th up to the additional strength needed for the larger crews in the Sherman tanks.

Testing and training of the DD tank crews started in March 1944 and was done under great secrecy. There are few photographs that show these weapons either in training or in action. The crews were taught to escape from a sinking DD tank with the use of the British designed Davis Breathing Apparatus. This equipment was bulky, and the crews realized that it would be very tough for them to get out of the hatches while wearing the Davis gear.

On 4 May 1944 the 70th adopted an insignia. "Joe Peckerwood" was the name given to the battalion mascot. He was a turtle wearing a tanker's helmet and goggles, standing on a globe and carrying a 75mm shell. The French words "soixante-dix" (seventy) were emblazoned across his chest - a reminder of the time spent in French North Africa. This insignia was painted on the sponson of every tank, as well as on every battalion vehicle.

Back at Ft. Pierce, Florida, the tank mounted T-40 rocket launcher had been developed for breaching beach obstacles. The T-40 mount carried twenty 7.5 inch rockets which were aimed by pointing the main tank gun. They were fired electrically, individually or by salvo, from inside the turret. Tests and demonstrations indicated the rockets would be very useful in helping to breach any obstacles or defenses the Germans had built, and a number were shipped to England to be installed on the nonamphibious Sherman tanks. These rockets were to be used to destroy any German emplacements on the beach, and blow gaps in any obstacles and sea walls. Once the path ashore was clear, the launcher could be jettisoned and the tank could function as usual. The T-40s arrived at the 70th Tank Bn. without any of the installation instructions, which detailed the electric firing system and how to zero the rocket aim.

The tank crews and their mechanics did their best, but when senior officers of the VIIth Corps and 4th Division came to observe the testing of the T-40 rockets, it was a disaster. The sighting was off and the first rockets passed over their target: a cement wall simulating a sea wall in Normandy. The second attempt hit the wall, but the rockets did not detonate and only slightly chipped the concrete.

A third attempt fired the remaining rockets simultaneously. Out of 22 rockets, five did not leave the launcher. Of those that did, half did not detonate. The wall remained intact, much to the dismay of the

observers. The commander of the 70th, Lt. Col. John Welborn, quickly ordered the tank crew to fire three rounds of armor piercing 75mm shells at the wall, and it was quickly destroyed. Based upon this poor performance of the T-40 rockets, the decision was made not to use them in the invasion. This made the tank crews very happy, as the launcher effectively blocked the turret hatches, making it almost impossible for anyone in the turret to bail out.

Training with the DD tanks continued and finally they were used in the full-scale invasion rehearsals at Slapton Sands. Everyone involved with the DD tanks was worried about their low freeboard. The crews of B/70th Bn. used their own money to purchase and

install reinforcing materials so the DD skirts could withstand rougher treatment in heavy seas.

In C/70th, as well as the 741st and 743rd, a shortage of tank crewmen was created when an additional eight tankdozers were added to the 17 standard Shermans. 24 engineers from the 612th Engineer Light Equipment Company were assigned to these tankdozers. These men had no training with tanks, but were skilled with bulldozers, so they were made the tank drivers, bow gunners, and loaders. The tank crews in the standard Sherman company had worked together long enough to operate as a team, but at the last minute they were broken up and spread around the tanks and tankdozers.

The 70th Tank Bn. was in direct support of the 8th Infantry Regiment at Utah Beach. Landing with the first waves of assault infantry were a liaison officer from the 70th (Lt. Frank Anderson) and two radiomen. A/70th were to support the landings of 1/8th, and B/70th supported 2/8th. The tankdozers of C/70th were to assist the engineers clearing beach obstacles and the standard Shermans of C/70th were to assist the 8th Regiment push inland. The light tanks of D/70th, that were scheduled to land later on, were to immediately proceed to an assembly area for attachment to the 101st Airborne Division. The sea off Utah Beach was too rough to safely launch the DD tanks, so the LCTs moved in closer to shore. One of the LCTs struck a mine and all four DD tanks on board were lost. The remaining DD tanks were launched at roughly 1,500 yards from shore and made it safely to the beach.

The standard tanks of C/70th were scheduled to land 15 minutes behind the DD tanks, but they actually landed at roughly the same time. Four tanks from C/70th were lost at sea and four of the eight tankdozers never landed on the beach. There is some confusion surrounding what happened to these tank-

Above.
This convoy of the 743rd Tank Bn. was taken just inland from the beaches. The last tank in line is a standard Sherman from Headquarters company. The bottom of the exhaust shroud is still attached to the rear of the tank. Visible on the other tanks in line is an extension around the hull just above the level of the tracks. This is the bottom seal for the DD flotation skirt, which indicates that these are tanks from either Company B or C.

dozers. No loading lists for this unit have been located but it appears that some LCTs carried either one tankdozer and two standard Shermans, while other LCTs had two tankdozers and one standard Sherman. It seems that one LCT, with two tankdozers, was sunk and another two tankdozers returned to England when their LCT developed engine trouble.

The tanks of the 70th Bn. made their way across Utah Beach, through gaps blown in the sea wall, and passed over narrow causeways crossing the inundated area. They soon made contact with the paratroopers from the 101st A/B Div. and provided a needed punch for the lightly armed paratroops. A sad incident occurred when Col. Turner, commander of the 1/506th Parachute Regt., climbed onto one of the tanks to direct it against the Germans. Exposed to enemy fire, Turner was quickly shot by a sniper, leaving the 1/506th temporarily leaderless. Turner's younger brother in the 8th Infantry Div. was later shot by another sniper, and both men are buried together at the Omaha Beach cemetery.

The 741st and 743rd Tank Battalions at Omaha

The 741st and 743rd were well trained, but had never been in combat before. Each of the battalions consisted of two companies of DD Shermans (16 tanks each), one company of standard Shermans (17), and a fourth company of 17 light M5 Stuart tanks. The M5s were fast, but lightly armored and armed with only machine guns and 37mm guns. They were used for reconnaissance and other missions where speed was important.

The plans for both the 741st and 743rd were similar. Each had two companies of DD tanks (B+C/741, B+C/743rd) that were to be launched from LCTs 6,000 yards out. These DD tanks were to land at roughly H-10, ten minutes before the assault infantry. The third company of standard tanks was to land in LCTs (two standard tanks and one tankdozer) at H-hour. The tanks were supposed to support the assault infantry, but neither tanks nor infantry had radios that could talk to one another. Only the tank battalion liaison officer could communicate the needs of the infantry to the tanks with a single bulky radio. Officers in the assault troops were told to fire smoke rifle grenades at targets they wanted the tanks to fire upon.

Throughout the training exercises with the DD tanks, everyone had been worried about the ability of the tanks to operate in anything but the calmest water. The staff at the ATC felt strongly that unless the sea was very calm, DD tanks should not be allowed to swim ashore. The orders issued for D-Day clearly indicate that if the water was calm enough the tanks were to be launched from 6,000 yards out. If the sea was too rough in the opinion of the naval commander, then the tanks would be launched from 1,000 yards.

On the morning of D-Day Lt Commander Dean Rockwell, in charge of the LCT flotilla carrying the DD tanks, saw that the sea was far too rough for the

DD tanks. He had participated in the practice landings in England and could clearly see that any tank launched would soon be swamped. He conferred with the 743rd Tank Bn. commander and the decision was made to bring the 743rd DD tanks directly to shore. Rockwell had put a naval officer he had confidence in, in charge of the section of LCTs carrying the 741st DD tanks. Unfortunately, it appears this officer could not stand up to the commanders of both 741st tank companies, who insisted that the advantage of the amphibious tanks justified the risk of launching them in the rough seas.

Out of the 32 DD tanks in the 741st, only two were able to swim to shore. On LCT 57 the first DD tank launched went out ten yards and sank. The following tank commander backed up his tank and supposedly damaged either the flotation skirt or the LCT launching gear (reports vary). The LCT 57 took the remaining three tanks directly to shore. Only 5 of the 32 DD tanks of the 741st Bn. took part in supporting the 16th Infantry Regt. The rest all sank attempting to swim in the rough water. Curiously, when salvagers explored the Normandy beaches they discovered at least two of the 741st DD tanks, sunk roughly nine miles from the coast. A possible indica-

tion that one LCT launched them far too early.

The standard Shermans and tankdozers of A/741 landed as planned, except for two Shermans and one tankdozer that had been lost when their LCT was sunk. On their way in, these tanks fired from the LCTs at German emplacements. The standard tanks in A/741 towed trailers of extra ammunition. When the tanks got ashore they were to drop these trailers at the assembly point as an emergency resupply in case the following trucks were not able to land.

The few tanks of the 741st that got ashore contributed greatly to the progress the 16th Infantry was making on the left flank of Omaha Beach. They destroyed numerous German machine gun nests and pillboxes. In the afternoon a T-2 tank retriever and support personnel of the 741st landed and began the task of salvaging the tanks that had been knocked out on the beach. Most of the crewmen on board the sunken DD tanks had been rescued by the many small vessels in the area. Unlike the majority of the soldiers, the tank crews had been issued yellow inflatable life vests instead of the gray life belts. This helped them to be spotted by the rescue vessels.

In the 743rd sector, supporting the 116th Infantry, most of the tanks got to the shore. But not every tank

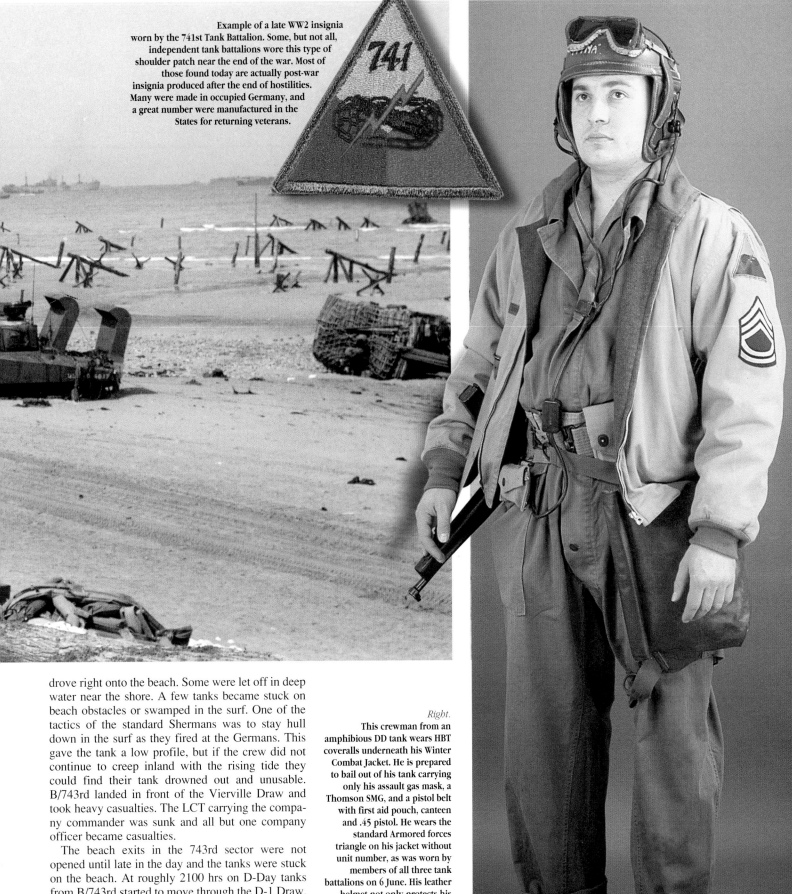

Example of a late WW2 insignia worn by the 741st Tank Battalion. Some, but not all, independent tank battalions wore this type of shoulder patch near the end of the war. Most of those found today are actually post-war insignia produced after the end of hostilities. Many were made in occupied Germany, and a great number were manufactured in the States for returning veterans.

Right.
This crewman from an amphibious DD tank wears HBT coveralls underneath his Winter Combat Jacket. He is prepared to bail out of his tank carrying only his assault gas mask, a Thomson SMG, and a pistol belt with first aid pouch, canteen and .45 pistol. He wears the standard Armored forces triangle on his jacket without unit number, as was worn by members of all three tank battalions on 6 June. His leather helmet not only protects his head inside the tank, but holds the intercom headphones in place. The amphibious tank crewmen wore a yellow inflatable vest while heading to shore, but discarded it once out of the ocean as the bright yellow color would draw German attention.
(Reconstruction)

drove right onto the beach. Some were let off in deep water near the shore. A few tanks became stuck on beach obstacles or swamped in the surf. One of the tactics of the standard Shermans was to stay hull down in the surf as they fired at the Germans. This gave the tank a low profile, but if the crew did not continue to creep inland with the rising tide they could find their tank drowned out and unusable. B/743rd landed in front of the Vierville Draw and took heavy casualties. The LCT carrying the company commander was sunk and all but one company officer became casualties.

The beach exits in the 743rd sector were not opened until late in the day and the tanks were stuck on the beach. At roughly 2100 hrs on D-Day tanks from B/743rd started to move through the D-1 Draw. During the day's fighting the commander of the 743rd, Col. John Upham, had been hit in the shoulder, but continued to direct his men. C/743rd had lost four tanks, B/743rd had lost seven, and C/743rd had lost eight tanks. In the following attempt to reach the Rangers at Pointe du Hoc, three more would be destroyed by mines. Nine men of the 743rd, including the battalion commander, would be awarded the DSC for actions on D-Day.

The after-action reports on Normandy make it clear the Army realized that DD tanks should never again be used in anything but the calmest water. The fire power of the tanks was very helpful in supporting the assault troops, but too many tanks were lost at sea to make the Duplex Drive tank anything more than an experiment that failed.

The other armored units of D-Day

The three battalions equipped with DD tanks were not the only armored units to come ashore on D-Day. As part of the 3rd and 6th Armored Groups, other Tank and Tank Destroyer Battalions came ashore later in the day. The 3rd Armored Group was supporting Vth Corps at Omaha and the 6th was supporting the VIIth Corps at Utah.

Left and opposite page.
Major General Gerow awards the Silver Star to three members of the 743rd Tank Bn. for their exploits on D-Day. These three men illustrate the average uniforms worn by the tankers of the 743rd at this time. All shoulder patches are the standard Armored Forces patch without a unit number.
Left.
T/Sgt Clifton C. Barker wears the standard M1941 field jacket not generally associated with tank crews. His black rubber assault gas mask bag is slung under his left arm.

Below.
Lt. Col. John Welborn, as the commander of the 70th Tank Bn., was awarded the Distinguished Service Cross for his actions on D-Day.
Welborn wears a standard Armor insignia on his shoulder, without the number "70" on it. Tank Battalion numbers were not added to the patch until later in the war. Barely visible, hanging from the right side of Welborn's belt, is both a standard first-aid pouch and a parachutist's first aid pouch. This confirms that at least some of the men in the assault tank battalions received this item.

On Utah Beach the 70th Tank Battalion was backed up by the 746th and 749th Tank Battalions, and the 899th Tank Destroyer Battalion. The 899th was the first Tank Destroyer unit to land in France. Two companies of M-10s came ashore on 6 June, with the remainder landing four days later. On D+11 the 899th would be attached to the 9th Infantry Division for the drive on Cherbourg. On Omaha Beach the 745th Tank Bn. was attached to the 1st Infantry Division, and the 747th Tank Battalion (officially landing on 7 June) was attached to the 29th Division. The 635th Tank Destroyer Bn. provided antitank support to both divisions.

Engineers

One of the more confusing aspects of the Normandy invasion is the plethora of engineer units. It is simpler to think of the engineer support in three main phases. First came the Special Engineer Task Force on Omaha and the Beach Obstacle Demolition Party on Utah that were given the task of clearing the beach obstacles. Then came the engineer units

Right.
S/Sgt. John S. DuQuione has the winter combat jacket, with a rather dirty armored forces patch, and also carries the assault gas mask bag under his left arm. He was awarded the Silver Star for his actions as a communications Sgt. in repairing a tank radio in the open while under enemy fire.

Below.
Pvt. Roger L. Wells wears the winter combat jacket (tanker's jacket) with knitted cuffs and collar. The three snap bag he carries is the lightweight gas mask bag. He may have lost his assault gas mask on D-Day and been issued this one as a replacement.

assigned to support the combat functions of the assaulting divisions. Each division had its own organic engineer battalion and each assault regiment had a second engineer battalion assigned for the initial landings. Lastly came the engineer units concerned with operating the beaches as a place for troops to land and for supply dumps to be established. This last function was the role of the engineer units that composed the Engineer Special Brigades.

Each division had its own permanently assigned Engineer Combat Bn. (Eng. C. Bn.). These engineers would move inland with the unit, supporting it in combat. These men wore the divisional patch and were rarely given a task that took them outside the division area.

The attached engineer units were a different story. They were separate units permanently attached to the 1st Army and assigned where needed at either corps or division level. They would land with the assault divisions, but soon after the front line passed inland, they would revert to Army control and could be assigned to any task in the entire 1st Army area.

There was a great deal of overlap in assignments given to these engineer units. This was to make sure that if one unit was not able to perform a job, then there would be another following on its heels that would be the next to try. The various assignments are confusing and can not be placed in neat lists.

On Omaha Beach each of the two divisions had an organic and an attached engineer bn. On Utah Beach the situation was slightly different. It seems that the 1106th Engineer Group was attached to the 4th Division to provide engineer support. Most of the 4th

Blowing the D-1 Wall

On the far right flank of Omaha Beach, in the D-1 exit leading to Vierville, the Germans had built a double concrete wall blocking the road. Each wall was eight and half feet high and six feet thick. The two sections overlapped in the middle of the road so that no vehicles could pass, only men on foot. In front of it was a tank trap ditch.

Sgt. Noel Dube was the squad leader of the 9th Squad, Company C, 121st Engineers. His squad was assigned to move up the D-1 Draw to a specific field, which was scheduled to be used as a vehicle transit area. His job was to make sure the field was clear of mines and ready for the vehicles when they arrived.

Due to the confusion on the beach, Dube's squad came in far to the left of the planned landing site. His men got ashore without too much trouble, but were held up at the edge of the water by German fire. Eventually, they started the long haul down to Dog Green beach and the D-1 exit. When they got there in the afternoon, they found that the concrete wall blocking the exit was still in place. Once there, an officer from the 121st (believed to be either the executive officer Major Olson, or the commander Col. Ploeger) told him: "*Sergeant, we need you to blow this wall. Go reconnoiter the other side and make sure it's safe to blow.*"

Sgt. Dube asked for volunteers to check the other side of the wall and two men stepped forward. One was Frank Wood, the other was another man from C/121st whose name remains unknown, but who was killed roughly two weeks later. The three men went halfway up the D-1 draw to make sure there were no Americans that could be hurt when they blew the wall. All they saw were some Germans moving around on the tops of the bluffs.

Returning to the wall, they found two bulldozers, each carrying ten cases of TNT. Both bulldozer drivers were from C/121st. They were Joe Drago and Al Velleco (on D+1 Drago would learn that on D-Day a bullet had struck his pack and lodged in his mess kit). The men first used Bangalore torpedoes to clear the barbed wire strung in front of the wall. Dube and one of his men, Pvt. Olenick, had no idea how much explosive would be needed to destroy the wall. They decided to use the first ten cases on the first wall and save the rest for the other wall.

Then they put a row of four cases of TNT at the bottom of the wall, then stacked three more cases on each of the end boxes *(see drawing below)*. They opened one case and put a blasting cap into one block of TNT. They pulled the ignitor, moved back to the sea wall and took cover. When the smoke cleared and the rain of concrete rubble subsided, they peered over the sea wall and saw that not only the first had been blown, but the wall behind it had also been destroyed. Sgt. Dube claims it was hard to recall the exact time this happened, but feels it was roughly 1600-1700hrs. One of the bulldozers moved in and started to fill in the remaining hole.

There is another, more famous story of how General Cota, Assistant Division Commander of the 29th Division, was instrumental in getting the D-1 wall blown. When asked about this Sgt. Dube said: "*I don't agree with the story about Cota being responsible for getting the wall blown. I'm not saying that Cota was not in the area, but that wall was not blown as a result of anything Cota said. Cota was not at that wall. I did not see him at the wall and he did not tell us to blow it. I did see Cota earlier in the day down near the center of Omaha where we landed, but not later at the wall.*"

In all the confusion of Omaha Beach, it may be that General Cota had been at the wall earlier in the day, but then moved on. However, given the details and names of the other soldiers who confirm this story, there can be little doubt that these men were responsible for blowing the D-1 wall. An after-action report from the 147th Engineer Combat Bn gives credit to one of their NCOs. Master Sgt. M. Arwood claims to have been responsible, along with an unknown Sgt. from the 121st, for blowing the D-1 wall. Arwood may have been present, and probably worked with Dube at the wall. It appears that Arwood was the only one from the 147th taking part in this action.

Yet, according to a wartime interview with Major Olson (Executive officer of the 121st Eng.) he was at the D-1 wall with General Cota at noon.

A possible answer may be that Cota and Olson were briefly at the wall and left before it was blown. Ploeger then arrived and took over supervision. Dube was sent up the draw by Olson, but when he returned the senior officer was now Ploeger. This would explain some slight confusion in his memory.

The action at the D-1 wall illustrates one of the difficult aspects of researching D-Day. Men at the same place and time sometimes recall slightly, or totally, different stories depending upon many variables. Dube was unable to clearly recall who the officer was. If it was Ploeger, who clearly recalled being at the wall and supervising its destruction, it is unusual that Dube did not know his own commanding officer. If it was Maj. Olson, who accompanied General Cota on the beach, then Cota should have been in the immediate vicinity. When under fire, and attempting to perform difficult tasks, soldiers have a very selective memory and can sometimes tune out aspects the we might find important, but to them might seem trivial at the time.

Bottom.
This photograph is often captioned as showing naval fire shelling the D-1 Draw. About noon the area was shelled by naval gunfire and this supposedly shows the result. Sgt. Dube feels that it is the smoke from his ten cases of TNT blowing the wall. While there is some evidence to support either claim, it is high tide in the photo which indicates it would have been taken closer to noon rather than late afternoon when Dube thought the wall was blown. However, the smoke patterns and proximity to the wall area are what could be expected from the demolition of the wall. It could be that Sgt. Dube is incorrect in his memory of the exact time (he was quite candid about not recalling exact times), or it could be the naval gunfire at noon. If it is the naval gunfire, then Cota and Olson's story of being at the wall at that time becomes suspect. The correct answer may never be known. What is surprising about this photo, is the total lack of any landing craft or vehicles on the beach.

Computer drawing by M. Gillard, © Histoire & Collections 1998

Engineers were not to land until later in the day. The Beach Obstacle Demolition Party was composed of a provisional unit from the 1106th engineer group (primarily composed of men from the 237th Eng. C. Bn.). Following them, the remainder of the 237th Engineers would come ashore and open gaps in the concrete sea wall. The troops assigned to breach the sea wall were seven platoons from companies A and C of the 237th Eng Combat Bn., and two platoons from the 4th Division Engineers. These nine platoons were not to deal with the beach obstacles, but were to blow gaps in the sea wall, clear paths through the barbed wire and then help assault any enemy fortifications in the area.

Once these engineers had opened the path off the

beach, two more engineer battalions were to land on Utah. The 49th ECB and the 238th ECB were to land about H+3 hours. Their job was to create exit roads across the flooded area behind the beach. They came ashore with a large quantity of road and bridging supplies to deal with craters in the roads from artillery fire and demolished bridges. The 991st Engineer Treadway Bridging Company played an important role on Utah Beach when it built a bridge on one of the beach exits where a culvert had been destroyed by shelling.

On Omaha Beach the division of labor was slightly more specific. Engineer units were given the task of clearing an eight yard wide path from the beach to the major exits, and through the exits to the transit

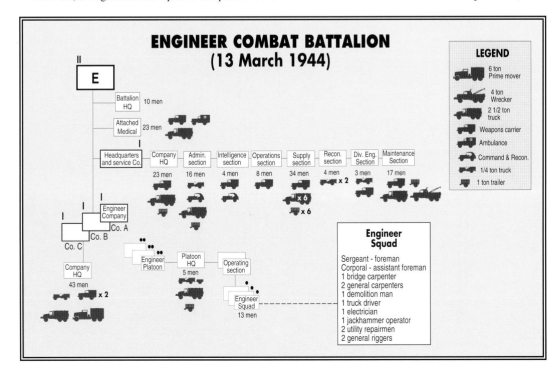

ENGINEER COMBAT BATTALION
(13 March 1944)

Above.
The SCR-625 mine detector was normally carried in the large chest. It was heavy, but the detector could locate most metallic German mines. Two of the mines it could not detect were the glass mine and wooden Schu-mine, seen at center left. The Germans often booby-trapped their mines, so the best way to destroy them was to blow them in place with a half pound block of TNT. Next to the TNT is the 10-cap detonator used to set off electric blasting caps. The yellow marker flags are a mystery. They were used to identify minefields in the early stages of the war, but by the invasion of Normandy they, and the yellow marking tape, seemed to have been dropped in favor of plain white fabric engineer tape.

Left.
The most important vehicle on the beach was the bulldozer. It could move obstacles, clear paths through minefields, push landing craft off the beach, fill antitank ditches and open up roads. It was not uncommon for bulldozer operators to be targeted by the Germans, and often the drivers had to be replaced as they were wounded. Some of the engineer units gave the drivers Air Force flak suits which protected them against shrapnel.

areas behind the bluffs. In the 1st Division sector the 1st Eng. C. Bn. was assigned the task of opening the E-1 exit and the 20th Eng. C. Bn. was to open the E–3 exit. The 20th Engineers were an experienced unit with prior service in the Mediterranean, but they had bad luck on the morning of D-Day. The craft bringing A/20th to shore was hit by German fire and only 27 men from that company got ashore. Of that number only 18 were not wounded. The commander of the 20th was lightly wounded, then later killed by an artillery blast. Due to the lack of engineers, the E–3 exit was not open to traffic until the morning of D+1. The 1st Engineers had the E-1 exit open about 1400 hours on D-Day with only 4 men killed, 6 missing and 23 wounded.

In the 29th Div. sector the 121st Engineers were assigned the D-1 exit and the 112th Engineers the D–3 exit. The tremendous confusion and powerful German emplacements on Dog Beach delayed both of these units. The 121st Engineers took severe casualties in men and equipment following on the heels of the ill-fated 116th Infantry. Of specific concern was a lack of explosives suffered by the 121st Engineers. While attempting to rally his men, Col. Ploeger, commander of the 121st, was wounded in the leg. He refused treatment for this wound until seven weeks later when it incapacitated him. The 121st Engineers, working in conjunction with elements of other engineer units in the area, finally got the D-1 exit open for vehicles in the late afternoon at roughly the same time the 20th Engineers got the D–3 exit open.

Once the beach exits were open, the engineers moved inland to specific areas where

Below.
Heavy engineering equipment such as this steam shovel, known by the Army as a "tracked crane," were needed to clear the debris from the roads. This model, with a 1/2 cubic yard bucket, was not a standard item in regular engineer companies, but was part of the equipment of the Engineer Light Equipment Company. These companies allowed such special equipment to be centralized.

Right.

The "St. Lo Special" was a Weasel from the 121st Engineers, 29th Division. This vehicle shows how the standard vehicle markings were often removed for the invasion. Only the "C" indicating Company C remains of the regulation markings. At the top left is a small square which is the 29th Division tactical symbol indicating the 121st Engineers.

Bottom.

Engineers have set up a display of the various mines and explosives they have to deal with in Normandy. This display was to help instruct new replacements just arriving in France. The material shown ranges from German grenades at left, to American antitank mines at top right. At bottom right are Russian hand grenades captured on the Eastern front.

they were to clear mines for the troops following. The 121st suffered more casualties when it found itself in the path of a German counterattack in the Vierville area on the morning of D+1.

Artillery

One problem encountered in an amphibious invasion is that field artillery units needed time to land, find a suitable spot to deploy and prepare to fire. They also needed a minimum amount of distance between the guns and the target. To provide suitable artillery support on the beach, a number of different units were assigned to the assault divisions.

The primary type of artillery support used in the initial hours of the landings was naval gunfire from the ships off the coast. These ships could fire at targets spotted along the coastline, at targets further inland spotted by the Air Spotting Pool, or could support the ground units directly through the use of Naval Shore Fire Support Parties.

The Naval Shore Fire Control Party

"I am now firmly convinced that without that gun-fire we positively could not have crossed the beaches."

1st Div. Chief of Staff Colonel S.B. Mason

Experience with previous invasions had shown the Army that it was extremely important to maintain communications between the units on shore and the ships at sea. To bridge the gap between the communications branches of the two services, the Joint Assault Signal Company (JASCO) was developed. JASCOs were composed of three elements: the Naval Shore Fire Control Party (NSFCP), the Air Liaison Section, and the largest group, the Shore and Beach Communications Section.

In theory, the JASCOs were responsible for providing an extra communications link between the units that had landed and the headquarters still afloat offshore. Eventually, enough of the Army would land to eliminate the need for the JASCOs, but in the first few days of the invasion it was important to have a unit trained in bringing signal equipment ashore during an amphibious landing, as well as in the differences between how the Army and the Navy communicated.

The main group of a JASCO was the Shore and Beach Party Communications Section. This was composed of ten Communications Teams that provided all communications in the Engineer Special Brigade. At Normandy each ESB was assigned its own JASCO: the 293rd and 294th landed on Omaha Beach and the 286th on Utah Beach. The NSFCP and ALP, although administratively part of the JASCO, trained and operated separately with the combat troops. One of the problems with examining the JASCOs, is that the 1st Army altered the official JASCO organization for Normandy by adding more men and equipment, but the records do not make it clear exactly what these additions were.

Each JASCO had an Air Liaison Section composed of 13 Air Liaison Parties. Each ALP was composed of an officer, two radio operators, and a jeep driver. According to the official organization of the JASCO, the officer was called the Air Liaison Officer and all members of the ALP were from the

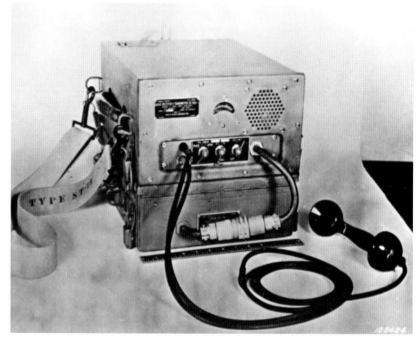

Air Force. Equipment included a jeep and trailer, carbines, .45 caliber submachine guns, and M1903 Springfield rifles. Each ALP was issued with such signalling equipment as the AP-30 identification panels, and each jeep was equipped with an AN/VRC-1 radio.

The Air Liaison Parties travelled with the headquarters of the combat units moving inland. They had a dual mission: to call for air strikes requested by the ground troops, and to also make sure that the Air Force did not accidentally attack Allied ground forces. During the initial period of the invasion the Allies expected a German counterattack led by tanks. At the time the best weapons to use against German tanks were British aircraft equipped with air to ground rockets. A handful of British Royal Air Force liaison teams were attached to the American units so

The SCR-609 (Set, Complete, Radio) and SCR-284 were the primary radios used by the NSFCPs in Normandy.

Top.
The SCR-284 was a cumbersome radio that needed a few men to carry all the components. The receiver was battery powered, but the transmitter was powered by the hand-cranked generator. The crank resistance was greatly increased whenever the transmit key was pushed. At far left is the canvas carrier for the antenna sections.

Above.
The SCR-609 was heavy, but could be carried by one man. The same basic radio could also be mounted in a vehicle without the battery as the SCR-610.

"WHO SAID THIS WAS A PORTABLE"

Left.
This cartoon was included in the Operation Neptune Orders dealing with the usage of Naval Shore Fire Control Parties. The SCR-609 radio was heavy, but it could be carried by one man. Obviously the cartoonist felt otherwise.

that if the German tanks appeared the British could direct efficient strikes against them. These RAF personnel landed in the American sector wearing blue-gray battledress impregnated against chemical weapons. The chemical treatment turned the British uniforms gray, and at least one such team was captured by members of the 29th Division who thought the gray colored uniforms were German. The RAF men were quickly issued with standard American uniforms to prevent a future misunderstanding.

The most important support provided to the troops during the first day of the invasion was from the ships sitting off the Normandy coast. The ships' guns could be fired at prearranged map coordinates; at targets visible on the coastline; as directed by the Air Spotter Pool; or most importantly as directed by the NSFCP attached to each infantry and artillery battalion of the assault regiments.

There were normally nine NSFCPs in each JASCO. This would be enough to assign one party to each infantry battalion in a division. The official organization of a NSFCP consisted of one artillery officer, three radio operators and a jeep driver from the Army, and one Gunfire Liaison Officer from the Navy. The primary radios issued to the NSFCP were the SCR-284, which was a large bulky radio that used a hand-cranked generator to power the transmitter, and the SCR-609 which was heavy, but could be carried on the back of one man.

It was decided that the standard NSFCP organization was not adequate in both men and equipment for the job they would have to do on D-Day. More men were assigned to build up the NSFCPs. The Navy supplied additional officers and installed SCR-608 radios on every fire support ship to provide additional communications links. Artillerymen from the 1st, 4th, and 29th Divisions were given intensive training in American, British, Canadian and Norwegian naval gunfire adjustment techniques. A handful of men were given special training in parachutes and jumped with a Provisional Airborne Shore Fire Control Party assigned to the 101st

Force "O" Shore Fire Control Parties

party	unit	call sign	ship	ship call sign
1	2Rgr	DJX	USS Slaterlee	TAS
2	5Rgr	FGH	HMS Glasgow	SLG
3	1/116	KRD	USS McCook	CMC
4	2/116	MKR	USS Carmick	MRC
5	3/116	SJT	USS Texas	SXT
6	11FDC	NAD	-	-
7	1/16	ZPW	USS Doyle	LYD
8	2/16	FAT	USS Endicott	CDN
9	3/16	KMA	FS Montcalm	TNM
10	7FDC	HOF		
11	1/18	CWR	USS Baldwin	DLB
12	2/18	LSG	USS Baldwin	DLB
13	3/18	DBR	USS Arkansas	NKR
14	32FDC	PBR	-	
15	1st Arty	PVA	-	
16	1/115	TBN	USS Thompson	MHT
17	2/115	BGK	USS Frankford	ARF
18	3/115	PAD	USS Thompson	MHT
19	110FDC	FRX		-
20	1/26	JBA	USS Harding	RAH
21	2/26	SDA	FS Georges Leygues	GRG
22	3/26	NSB	USS Harding	RAH
23	33 FDC	HAS	-	
24	1/175	OFJ	HMS Glasgow	SLG
25&26	no listing - spare			
27	58 arty	SVG	224 FDC	-
28	29 arty	CHW	-	
		GFS	Comdr Gunfire support	
		NCN	CTF 124 on Ancon	

Above.

This photograph is the only one catalogued by either the Army or Navy as being a Shore Fire Control Party at Normandy. The men are operating the SCR-284 radio. The central figure cranks the generator used to power the transmitter. At far right a man is using an SCR-536 handie-talkie. Behind him at the edge of the hole can be seen one of the large rubber bags used to carry radio equipment ashore.

Airborne. The 82nd Airborne jumped further inland where naval fire was not as effective, but was given nine specially trained artillery officers to call in naval gunfire when possible.

Each assault division had a naval officer serving as Naval Gunfire Liaison at every regimental headquarters and a Division Naval Gunfire Officer at division headquarters. These men were not part of the JASCO organization and were assigned separately upon demand by the Navy. Trained naval officers were not always available, so in some cases officers from the field artillery or a JASCO had to function in their place.

It appears that the final organization of the NSFCPs in Normandy was composed of three sections. The first was an observer section with one Army artillery officer, 1 Sgt., and 3 radio operators. The naval liaison section was composed of a Naval Gunfire Liaison Officer and three radio operators. A third section, scheduled to land later in the day, was composed of two radio equipped jeeps and their drivers. By splitting each NSFCP into two sections, each with an officer qualified to direct the gunfire, the chances were increased that one section would get ashore and be able to support its assigned battalion.

Once the NSFCPs were ashore, they were to remain with the headquarters of the unit they were to support and stay in touch with the ship that had been assigned to that party. Each gunfire support ship was to listen to the frequency assigned to its own NSFCP, as well as a common frequency any party could use to call for fire in an emergency.

Once a call for naval support had been made, the Navy generally fired a two gun salvo to make sure they were on target. The gunners on board ship called "splash" over the radio at the time when they predicted the rounds would hit the target. Owing to the

distance from ship to target this could be longer than expected, and allowed the observers to identify the naval shells and not confuse them with other artillery firing in the same area.

NSFCP Number Three

NSFCP Number Three, supporting the 1st Battalion of the 116th Infantry, landed in France in three sections. Captain John A. Easter, in command of the Forward Observer Section, landed at the D-1 exit with B/116 about 0700. Only one of the five men in this section survived unwounded. The Naval Liaison Section, under Lt(jg). Coit N. Coker, came ashore 1 mile to the east with C/116 about 0740. The ramp on their LCVP was jammed, so they had to go over the side. By 0830 they had their SCR-609 operating and were in contact with the destroyer McCook. Lt. Coker was lightly wounded while on the beach, but refused to be evacuated. About noon Coker directed fire on some bunkers holding up Americans at the D-1 exit. The USS McCook fired on the emplacements and about 30 Germans emerged with a white flag and were taken prisoner.

The next day, Coker and his liaison section set out to assist in the relief of the Rangers at Pointe du Hoc. German artillery fire at Saint-Pierre-du-Mont halted their advance, but local French residents gave them the locations where they had seen German artillery units. As the liaison party could not see the area where the suspected German guns were, the fire request was relayed to the USS Texas and the Air Spotter Pool. About 1300 on 7 June, the Texas shelled the suspected area around Maisy and the German fire stopped.

That night the relief group set up a perimeter in case of a German counterattack. At about 2000 hrs., more German artillery

Above.

Mortar crews of the 87th Chemical Battalion have set up their 4.2" mortars on Utah Beach. On the right is one of the unit's M-29 weasels. To the left of the photo is the two-wheeled cart that was used to carry the 330 pound mortar and its ammunition. The men wear impregnated HBT fatigues over the wool uniform and field jacket.

fire started and Coker directed both the Texas and the McCook to shell the area he suspected it came from. The German shelling once again stopped. The next morning the group reached the 2nd Rangers at Pointe du Hoc.

By this time the USS Harding relieved the McCook and took over its frequency. Coker found that the Army observer attached to the 2nd Rangers had been killed, and the Navy observer wounded and evacuated, but the enlisted men of the NSFCP had continued to call for naval support as needed. Coker had his SCR-284 set up and was soon in contact with the 111th Field Artillery Fire Direction Center. The account above comes from a report filed by Lt Coker after the invasion. It is interesting that the log of the USS McCook claims that they were never able to contact their NSFCP and only shelled targets visible to them along the coast. This is one of the frustrating aspects to investigating the Normandy operation, as very often reports contradict each other and it is sometimes impossible to figure out what the truth really is.

The other NSFCPs had mixed results. Some lost equipment on the beach or had their men separated. A particular problem was that the SCR-284 was carried in numerous pieces and if one was lost the radio was worthless. The other main radio was the backpack SCR-609, which could be carried by one strong man, but was frequent-

Right.
These men of the 87th Chemical Battalion are shown firing their mortars later on in July. The sandbags have been piled on the baseplate for added stability. The 4.2" mortar had a rifled barrel, so it did not need fins on the ammunition. Each shell weighed 25 pounds, and the 4.2 was normally used to fire either high explosive or white phosphorus.
On the belt of the soldier at right can be seen a parachutist's first-aid pouch, evidence that these troops were issued this item for the invasion.

ly split into two lighter loads. If split it too could easily become useless if the team became separated.

Once the parties had a radio operating, they were able to call for massive amounts of fire power. The *USS Nevada* fired 337 rounds from her 14-inch guns on D-Day. The *Tuscaloosa* fired 487 eight-inch, and 115 five-inch rounds. The *USS Quincy* was in contact with the observers in the 101st Airborne by 1100 hrs. and fired 585 eight-inch shells, 600 five-inch, and 53 five-inch white phosphorus shells in support. The Provisional NSFCP attached to the 506th Parachute Regiment spotted the position of German antiaircraft guns firing at Allied aircraft on the night of 6 June. They called for naval gunfire and were able to neutralize the German flak.

The role of the Naval Shore Fire Control Parties at Normandy cannot be overstated. Communications between ship and shore were not flawless, but the system had been set up to allow for flexibility. When a call for support was made there was almost always a ship able to provide it. Had the Germans

made a counterattack with tanks on the first day or two of the invasion, as the Allies thought would happen, the heavy naval guns would have been one of the primary means of defeating the Panzers. As it was, the naval gunfire support pushed the Germans back and allowed the American Army to establish a beachhead and bring in its own artillery.

Chemical Battalions

It may seem strange, but Chemical Battalions provided the means for fast and powerful artillery support. The 4.2 inch mortar had originally been designed to launch chemical weapons. Although it did not appear that chemical weapons would be used in the war, the Army was reluctant to disband these units in case they were needed.

The Chemical Battalion, motorized, was involved in the use of the different types of chemical weapons on the battlefield. The 4.2 inch mortar was just one way of delivering these weapons to the enemy. In September 1944, when it became clear that poison gas would not be playing a major role

in battle, these units were finally redesignated as Chemical Mortar Battalions.

The 4.2 inch mortars fired a heavy shell of high explosive or white phosphorus 3,000 yards. Unlike the smaller 81mm and 60mm smoothbore mortars, the 4.2 had a rifled tube which provided great accuracy. The 4.2" mortar weighed about 330 pounds, but could be broken down into three main loads for easier transport. The heaviest of the loads was the baseplate which weighed 175 pounds, not exactly a load one man could carry by himself. Generally, the mortar was transported on small wheeled carts or on jeeps.

Much less space was needed to transport the 4.2 inch mortar units than a regular artillery battalion, so a chemical battalion was assigned to land early in the day on each of the beaches. The 81st landed on Omaha and the 87th on Utah. The mortars were pulled ashore on small wheeled carts, and could be put into action almost immediately upon reaching dry land. On Omaha Beach a major problem was that these mortars needed a minimum range of 550 yards and in some places the Germans were not pushed back that far until late in the day.

White phosphorus (WP) rounds were particularly useful against the entrenched Germans. When the rounds hit, burning fragments of phosphorous were scattered around and would burn anything it then fell on. These rounds caused serious morale problems for the Germans and units were known to pull back rather than be shelled by WP rounds. The thick white smoke, although not poisonous, also forced the Germans to put on their gas masks.

In the 81st Bn, A/81st and C/81st were attached to the 16th Infantry and B/81st and D/81st to the 116th. The different companies were split up on different ships: A/81st to *USS Henrico*, B/81st to *HMS Empire*

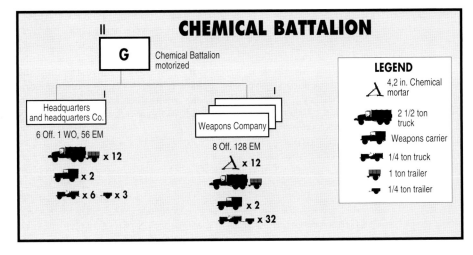

Javelin, C/81st to *HMS Empire Anvil*, D/81st to *USS Charles Carroll*, and headquarters to the LST 83. Each company was to support one of the assault battalions, but the confusion of the beaches caused two of the companies to land much later than planned. A and D/81st landed approximately H+50, B/81st at H+90 and C/81st at H+9 hours.

Problems for the 81st started early when a shell hit the advance headquarters group on an LCT and seriously wounded Col. James, the battalion commander. A/81st landed on Easy Red beach in support of 2/16th Inf. Some of their equipment was lost in the surf while getting ashore under machine gun fire, and there was no room to set up the mortars until later in the day.

B/81st was supposed to land on Dog Green in support of the 1/116th. Due to a combination of beach obstacles and enemy fire, they were redirected to Easy Green and did not land until roughly 0930. The troops moved inland through an uncleared minefield and set up their mortars. At 1700 hrs they finally fired their first round, which was at a machine gun nest near Saint-Laurent.

C/81st should have landed early in the morning, but the area they were assigned to was filled with soldiers pinned down on the beach. The company kept attempting to land and was finally successful at 1500 hrs. on Dog Red.

D/81st landed with the 3rd Bn. of the 116th Infantry on Easy Green. They took tremendous casualties while wading ashore in waist deep water, yet they were able to get one mortar tube set up on the beach and attempted to fire at Germans emplacements. However, these proved to be too close to be hit by the mortar.

Slowly the companies moved inland and began to support the infantry. At one point a mortar platoon hand-carried all equipment and ammunition across the marsh at the base of the bluffs in order to find room to set up. In the next two weeks almost 7,000 rounds of ammunition would be fired by the 81st.

The 87th Chemical Bn. was to land in support of the 4th Division at Utah Beach. A/87th was to support 1/8th Inf., B/87th the 2/8th Inf., C/87th the 3/8th Inf. and D/87th the 3/22nd Inf. During the landing

Above.
The Chemical Battalions were carried across the Channel on transport ships and brought to shore in LCVPs. They were the heaviest weapon that could be brought ashore without using a vehicle. Here a 4.2 inch mortar is hoisted aboard an LCVP attached to its hand cart. The baseplate alone weighed 175 pounds, so it was impractical to carry it by hand.

two mortars and two vehicles were lost when an LCVP was sunk, but no personnel drowned.

A and B/87th landed at H+50 and rapidly set up just behind the sand dunes. They were quickly put to work firing 100 rounds between the two units, before moving forward across the inundated area 40 minutes later. C and D/87th also landed, set up on the beach, and fired approximately 40 rounds before moving forward to keep within range of the front lines.

The 87th Chemical Bn. was one of the only land based artillery units supporting the 4th Division for the first six hours of the invasion. To quote the after-

Left.
The 4.2 inch mortar weighed over 330 pounds for the baseplate, barrel, and mount. This load was too much to be hand carried over any distance so a two-wheeled cart was used. This photo, taken in April 1944, illustrates the 4.2 mortar broken down for movement on the cart. For long distances the mortar was placed in the 1/4 ton trailer and secured using the wooden blocks shown here.

action report: "*the infantry was amazed at the rapidity and accuracy with which our mortars replied.*"

Armored Field Artillery

The majority of artillery in the U.S. Army were towed field pieces. These took a while to set up and prepare to fire. Self-propelled guns were developed to provide the armored divisions with a mobile artillery force that could keep up with the leading tanks and took much less time to support them.

Experiments at the ATC had concluded that 105mm guns could be chained to the deck of an LCT and shell a landing beach with a reasonable degree of accuracy. The problem was that it then took time to get these guns unchained, turned around and hooked up to their trucks to leave the landing craft. A similar experiment was conducted with the self-propelled M7 Priest. This was a fully tracked, open topped vehicle with a 105mm howitzer. The M7 Priest, so named because of a machine gun position that resembled a minister's pulpit, was even more accurate in shelling the beach and then could drive off the LCT as soon as it got to shore.

Three Armored Field Artillery battalions, equipped with the 105mm M7 Priest, were assigned to the assault divisions at Normandy. On Omaha the 62nd AFA supported the 1st Division and the 58th the 29th Division. On Utah the 65th AFA supported the 4th Division.

The plan called for LCTs to be loaded with four M7s that would shell the beach as the craft proceeded to shore. The Priests would start firing at 8,000 yards offshore, or roughly H-30. They would lift their fire at H-5 or when the LCTs got to 2,500 yards off shore. At this range the M7 could no longer fire over the front ramp of the LCT. Each M7 was allocated an extra 100 rounds of ammunition for this role, that the Navy referred to as "Gunfire Support Group Five."

The LCTs carrying the M7s were to follow astern of the rocket firing LCTs by 200 yards. When they were too close to shell the beach, or at H-5, the LCTs were to pull back from the coast and wait until it was their turn to land. Once the LCTs did get to shore, some of the M7s would then tow a halftrack through the surf to shore, and each halftrack in turn pulled a jeep. The heavy pulling power of the M7s was considered enough to pull all three vehicles safely onto shore.

The 62nd AFA

The 62nd AFA fired 349 rounds at the beach in the morning of D-Day. The LCTs then returned to 10,000 yards off shore to

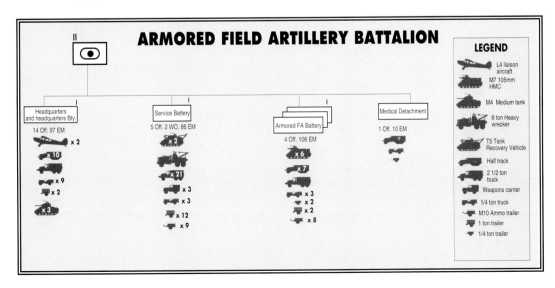

Top.
The self-propelled M7 was developed to allow the artillery to keep up with a rapidly moving tank assault. The 105mm gun was mounted to allow for a rapid set up, which made it the perfect artillery piece to use in an amphibious assault.

Above.
The crew of an M7 prepare to load onto an LCT in one of the embarkation areas. One of the crew, with his back to the camera, wears a parachutist's first-aid pouch just above his standard first-aid pouch.

Left.
A casualty is transferred from an LCT to another vessel for medical treatment. The markings on the heavily loaded jeep and M7 indicate that these are from the 62nd Armored Field Artillery, which supported the 1st Division on D-Day. Behind the lead tank is one of the trailers used by each M7 to tow additional ammunition ashore.

Below.

An M7 from the 2nd Armored Division rumbles down a road in Normandy. The 105mm gun on the M7 was designed for indirect fire, however it was sometimes used for direct fire against German tanks. Even if its 105mm High Explosive round did not penetrate the armor, the concussion would cause some damage and stun the crew.

wait for the assigned landing time of H+90. At H+30 a small advance party of observers, including the battalion commander, landed to select the initial positions for the guns. When the rest of the battalion attempted to land at H+90, the LCTs were turned away by heavy German fire. Numerous attempts were made to find a quiet point for the guns to land, but it was not until 1500 that the first M7s came on land. As soon as Battery B got three guns ashore, they were placed in firing positions right at the high water line. One M7 was immediately destroyed by enemy fire. A fourth gun was brought ashore from Battery A and soon a composite battery of four M7s was in operation at the water line.

These guns fired at the bluffs until roughly 1800 hours when they were able to move off the beach. At 1830 two more M7s from Battery B landed and were positioned opposite Saint-Laurent-sur-Mer. These six guns were not given any fire missions, but awaited the expected German counterattack while trying to locate their missing men and equipment scattered up and down the beach.

Each AFA battalion was equipped with two light observation planes. These aircraft did not have the range to fly across the Channel by themselves, so they had been broken down into a single 2 1/2 ton truck load for the cross-Channel voyage. At 2000 hrs. one plane was brought ashore but damaged by floating wreckage. The next day the second aircraft also became damaged when being brought ashore. Eventually the two aircraft were cannibalized to make one operational plane.

Not all of the LCTs that had landed vehicles had totally discharged their cargo. Some had only landed a handful of vehicles and were still waiting off shore for a chance to land the remainder. It was not until 7 June that all the equipment of the 62nd got ashore. On the same day, the battalion started firing missions in support of the 16th Infantry and in conjunction with the 33rd Field Artillery Battalion.

The 58th and 65th AFA

The 58th AFA had planned to work under Col. John Cooper of the 110th Field Artillery (29th Division). They ran into the same difficulties the 62nd did in locating clear areas to bring the guns ashore. Three LCTs hit mines and suffered casualties. The LCT 364 sank in seven feet of water, which later allowed the men to salvage four guns and much of the equipment. The LCT 197 capsized with a loss of all material aboard. The LCT 332 was forced to push one M7 and one halftrack off the front ramp to stay afloat. It was not until the exit road at D-1 was opened late in the day that the M7s could make their way off the beach and prepare to support the 29th as had been planned.

No guns of the 65th AFA fired from the LCTs offshore in the morning due to confusion among the forward observers. In any event, the morning aerial

bombardment had damaged much of the beach installations and the 65th came ashore between 0930 and 1030 without much difficulty. The battalion remained on the beach firing only a few missions until they moved forward at 1730 to take up a better location inland. During the day they had been subjected to constant harassment from German guns, but only two men were killed.

Divisional Artillery

Every infantry division had four battalions of artillery: three 105mm and one 155mm battalion. In practice, each infantry regiment had a 105mm batta-

lion in direct support, and the division's 155mm battalion had the range to support anywhere in the division area. Each infantry regiment also had its own organic cannon company of six short barrelled 105mm guns. The 155mm guns were too heavy to be brought onto the beach except on the larger LSTs and LCTs. A clever method was developed to get the 105mm guns of the artillery battalion and the cannon company to shore early in the invasion.

The 105mm guns were placed aboard Dukws, along with their ammunition and gun crews. The Dukw had just enough flotation to carry this heavy load unless the water was very rough. Fortunately, each Dukw had a bilge pump that continually pumped out any water that splashed inside.

The plan called for the Dukws to bring the guns and crews ashore, then use an A-frame to hoist the guns into a firing position. The problem with this concept was that the water off the Normandy coast was too rough for the low freeboard of the fully loaded Dukws and many of them swamped. Some of the Dukws were forced to stay at sea for a long period of time and their bilge pumps quit from overuse. Once the pump stopped it was only a matter of time before the Dukw went under.

At 0200 on D-Day, 13 Dukws with the 111th Field Artillery Battalion were launched from an LST seven miles off Omaha. Twelve of the Dukws carried the battalion's 105mm howitzers and the last Dukw carried the battalion headquarters. The Battalion commander was scheduled to land on Omaha with an advance party during the morning.

Each howitzer-carrying Dukw also carried the 13 man artillery crew, 50 rounds of ammo, and a large amount of other gear such as camouflage netting and

105mm FIELD ARTILLERY BATTALION

	LEGEND
	L4 liaison aircraft
	105 How.
	2 1/2 ton truck
	Weapons carrier
	1/4 ton truck
	Ammo trailer
	1 ton trailer
	1/4 ton trailer

Headquarters and headquarters Bty.
14 Off. 117 EM
x 2
x 3
x 2
x 11
x 10
x 5

Service Battery
4 Off. 1 WO, 72 EM
x 13
x 3
x 9
x 3
x 2

105mm Battery
4 Off. 96 EM
x 4
x 7   x 2
x 4
x 3   x 2

sandbags. The weight of all this made the Dukw ride very low in the water and two of them sank only minutes after they were launched. The Dukws had been ordered to circle about 600 yards off the LST until the order was given for them to proceed to shore. Before long all but six of the Dukws had sunk and they had not even started for shore yet.

It became apparent that the rest of the Dukws would sink unless something was done. Under direction of Captain Louis Shuford, commander of Battery B, a Navy LCVP started to guide them to shore. Two more Dukws sank and Shuford decided to unload 12 of the 13 cannoneers from one Dukw, that was ready to go under, onto the Navy LCVP. Continuing to the shore, by 0900 only two of the Dukws were still afloat roughly 1,000 yards off Omaha Beach. The two Dukws were lashed together. The crews could see that Omaha Beach was still under heavy artillery fire, but they decided they would try for shore. Machine gun fire disabled the engine of one Dukw and it quickly swamped.

The remaining Dukw carried a 105mm gun that had been nicknamed the "Chief." An Indian chief on a shield had been painted on its gun shield. This Dukw was now leaking where machine gun fire had pierced the hull. Passing Navy boats told the artillerymen that there was no safe sector to land at, so finally the Dukw pulled up alongside a Rhino Ferry. On the ferry there were other men from the 111th Field Artillery Battalion, who were dismayed to hear that all but one gun had been lost. Unfortunately, the Dukw was still taking on water quicker than it could be pumped out and the Rhino Ferry had no crane on board to lift out the artillery piece.

Shuford spotted a nearby Rhino Ferry that did have a crane and jettisoned everything he could from

Below.
Taken in Hawaii, this photograph shows how artillery pieces were loaded and unloaded from Dukws. An "A" frame, the two poles attached at the top, forms a simple crane which can be used to lift the cannon into, or out of, the Dukw.

Above.
Only one of the 105mm guns of the 111th Field Artillery Bn., 29th Infantry Div. did not sink on the morning of D-Day. The surviving gun was nicknamed "chief." It was pulled from a sinking Dukw by a crane on a Rhino Ferry. This rare photograph may show the Chief being pulled to safety by an ESB crane. Records indicate that the only other 105mm gun saved in this way was one of the short barrelled guns from the 16th Regt. Cannon Company. From this view it is difficult to tell which variety of 105mm this is, but a number of artillery experts feel that it is the model of gun issued to the 111th F.A. The Chief was turned over to men from the 7th Artillery Bn. and saw action in Normandy supporting the 1st Infantry Division.

181

the Dukw to lighten the weight. He brought the Dukw over to the Rhino Ferry, and convinced the men on board to pull the Chief from the sinking Dukw. By chance, this Rhino Ferry was carrying men from the 7th FA Bn., which was supporting the 16th Infantry assault. Six of its twelve guns had already gone down on other Dukws. The men of the 7th gladly accepted the Chief as a replacement for one of their lost guns. After it had been landed later that afternoon, the Chief went into action with the 7th Artillery before the end of the day.

The men of the 111th no longer had any artillery pieces, but they went ashore and served as guards for the division headquarters using small arms they found scattered on the beach. The loss of three quarters of all 1st and 29th Division artillery that was supposed to land on the morning of the invasion was a severe blow, but the support provided by the naval guns, self-propelled artillery and 4.2 inch mortars filled the gap. The 155mm guns of the divisions were landed on D+1, but in the case of the 29th Division the ammo for their guns was not brought ashore until D+2.

Also being brought ashore in Dukws were the shorter barrelled 105mm guns of the regimental cannon companies. These units were originally designed to provide direct fire on the front lines, but in practice tended to be used as an extra artillery unit firing from well behind the lines. Records of the cannon companies are not complete, but the activities of the 16th Infantry Regiment Cannon Co. are probably average.

Two forward observer teams landed at H+50 on Easy Red. Some of the men were wounded, but the remainder continued to advance with the 1/16th Headquarters. The cannon company commander landed with his party at H+100 to coordinate the landing of the rest of the unit. The company half-tracks attempted to land in LCTs at H+60, but were driven off with machine gun fire. One LCT landed its halftracks at H+120, the other at H+360. Four half-tracks were destroyed on the beach by enemy fire.

At H-3 hours the six howitzer sections on board Dukws drove off the LST 376 ramp into the water. While heading to shore two of the Dukw engines

stopped, and because this stopped the bilge pumps, these trucks quickly sank. A third Dukw was swamped when attempting to rescue the survivors. A fourth Dukw was able to get its cannon lifted by crane onto a Rhino Ferry. Despite lightening the load and continuous bailing, the final two Dukws finally went under.

Most of the gun crews had been rescued by small boats in the area and gathered on board one of the LSTs. At about 1300 they were able to get to shore and the one surviving cannon was finally reclaimed

Above.
This time exposure photograph, taken at night looking out to sea from Omaha Beach, shows the massive firepower used against German aircraft. For each tracer seen here there are at least 3 or 4 other nonvisible shells. It is no wonder that men in the area always wore their helmets to protect against the projectiles when they fell back to earth.

Left.
The 90mm antiaircraft gun is shown here in both travelling and firing position. There were times in Normandy when the 90mm was used in a ground role against German armor, but that was relatively rare. Although similar to the German 88mm gun, the American 90mm antiaircraft did not normally have sights and ammunition designed for antitank use.

Right.
"The Luftwaffe's Nightmare" is an M4 tractor towing a 90mm antiaircraft gun from Battery D of the 110th AAA Bn. These heavier guns followed the self-propelled antiaircraft units ashore as soon as there was space on the beachhead for them. The card hanging on front of the tractor indicates the specific LST and position on the LST for the cross-Channel voyage. The numbers found on these cards were assigned by the Army. Once the vehicles for LST 454 were at the embarkation port, the Navy could assign any LST to take on the "LST454" load. Thus every loading list for Normandy has both an arbitrary Army number and the actual Navy ship number.

Below.
Taken in the same series as above, this side view of the M4 tractor is in the same unit as the Luftwaffe's Nightmare. It pulls the 90mm antiaircraft gun in the towed position. The semicircular metal plating at the front of the gun folds out into a round metal platform so the gun crew has a stable surface to work on.

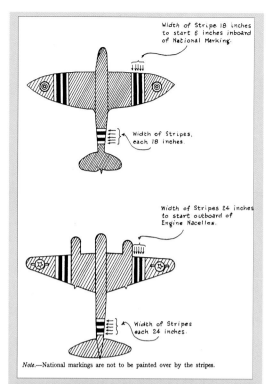

Width of Stripe 18 inches to start 6 inches inboard of National Marking.

Width of Stripes, each 18 inches.

Width of Stripes 24 inches to start outboard of Engine Nacelles.

Width of Stripes each 24 inches.

Note.—National markings are not to be painted over by the stripes.

To prevent Allied antiaircraft units from shooting down their own planes, special "Invasion Stripes" were painted on every Allied aircraft. This diagram is from the original order sent out to all aviation and antiaircraft units illustrating the black and white stripes. As an added measure, the fighter cover over the convoys was composed of P38s, which had a distinctive twin boom unlike any German aircraft.

when the Rhino Ferry brought it ashore. However, it was not in any shape to fire. The surviving gun crews picked up weapons and helmets from the beach, and were formed into a provisional rifle company attached to the 1/16th Infantry. They served with it until replacement cannons were available.

Each rifle battalion had an organic antitank platoon of three 57mm antitank guns. Although these guns were not powerful enough to destroy the heavier German tanks, they could still hurt lighter vehicles. The antitank guns in the assault regiments were also carried to shore by Dukws. The 57mm was much lighter than a 105mm, so the Dukws rode higher in the water.

In the 16th Infantry one of these Dukws had its engine quit while travelling to shore. Without the pumps working this Dukw quickly went under. The other 57mm guns in the 16th Infantry did get to shore, but needed to find vehicles to tow them, and then had to wait until the beach exits were opened. The regimental antitank companies of nine 57mm guns were brought ashore on LCTs. In the 16th Infantry two of them were lost to enemy fire while attempting to land on Easy Red Beach. These guns were later salvaged and returned to use.

All of the 57mm antitank guns in both the battalion level antitank platoons and the regimental level antitank company were given the primary mission of finding good positions to defend the beachhead against the expected German counterattack. Most of the antitank guns were ashore and in position by nightfall, but the expected German armored attack did not materialize.

Antiaircraft Artillery

By June 1944 the German air force had been all but eliminated from the skies over England and Normandy. The Allies had achieved near total air superiority. But the cross-Channel convoys were a very tempting target with a mass of ships filled with men and material in one place. It could not be taken for granted that the Luftwaffe would not throw every available aircraft against these ships; either in the embarkation ports, the convoys, or the beachhead area.

The beachhead presented an even better target than the ships. There were so many troops and supply dumps in here that bombs could be dropped anywhere in the area with a good chance of hitting something. So a large concentration of antiaircraft

Bottom.
This M16 quad fifty half-track was photographed at the AAA Replacement Training Center. During WW2, anti-aircraft units were considered part of the Coastal Artillery Corps. It was not until 1968 that the anti-aircraft units would finally be considered their own separate branch.

Organization of the 49th AAA Brigade

320th Barrage
Balloon Bn. VLA

11th AAA Group (Utah Beach)
116th AAA Gun Bn.
535th AAA AW Bn.
474th AAA AW Bn. (SP)

16th AAA Group (Omaha)
413th AAA Gun Bn.
457th AAA AW Bn.
197th AAA AW Bn. (SP)

18th AAA Group (Omaha)
110th AAA Gun Bn.
447th AAA AW Bn.
467th AAA AW Bn. (SP)

207th AAA Group
109th AAA Gun Bn.
118th AAA Gun Bn.
411th AAA Gun Bn.
440th AAA Gun Bn.
552nd AAA Gun Bn.
634th AAA Gun Bn.

ANTIAIRCRAFT ARTILLERY
Auto Weapons Battalion (Mobile)

defenses were scheduled to go ashore early in the landings to provide a defense against any aerial attacks that might take place.

The British port defenses had been developed since 1939 and were able to prevent the Germans from sending reconnaissance missions to photograph the build-up of troops. The ships in the Navy convoys were all provided with antiaircraft weapons. This was augmented by placing every available anti-aircraft weapon (mainly .50 caliber machine guns) on deck in a location where they could also fire at enemy aircraft.

Antiaircraft Artillery (AAA) battalions were divided by types of weaponry and how they were transported. The two basic types of AAA battalions were the AAA Automatic Weapons Bn. and the AAA Gun Bn. The AW Bn. was armed with rapid-firing machine guns and 37mm or 40mm guns. The Gun Battalions were armed with slower firing guns, generally the 90mm. Each battalion could be classed as semimobile or mobile, depending upon how well equipped it was to move from one location to another. Auto-weapons battalions could also be classed as self-propelled, if the guns were all mounted on halftracks so they needed no setup time before firing. Depending on the circumstances, two or

more AAA battalions were assigned to an AAA Group. Normally, two AAA Groups composed an AAA Brigade. The exact organization was flexible to allow the battalions to be shifted around as needed.

In France, the first AAA units ashore were armed with a handful of air-cooled .50 caliber machine guns. These were tied to flotation belts so they would not sink if dropped in the ocean. Following right behind them were the self-propelled battalions. with both M15 and M16 mounts in halftracks. The M15 carried a 37mm gun and twin .50 caliber MGs. The M16 had quad mounted .50 caliber MGs. At this point in the war most of the gun mounts in the self-propelled unit were M45s. The crews disliked this mount and replaced as many as possible with the newer M51 mount used on the M17 trailer.

Each AAA Bn. had a specific sector to cover once ashore. As more units landed, these sectors would shrink until there was a solid ring of antiaircraft fire around the beachhead. Following the self-propelled units, the semimobile battalions with 40mm and 90mm guns would land and their longer range would be added to the defense of the area. Many of the AA halftracks are seen in photographs with signs on them saying either "Beach defense" or "AA." This was to show that they were assigned to antiaircraft duties in the beach area and were not to be commandeered for ground support missions or ordered off the beach.

One of the more unusual forms of AA protection came from the guns on board the "Gooseberries." These obsolete freighters had been scuttled off the beaches to form a protective breakwater. These ships still had their upper decks above water, and served as antiaircraft positions protecting the ships offshore.

On board a burnt-out LCT are the remains of an antiaircraft unit. On the left is an M16 quad .50 caliber mount, with an M15 mount of 37mm gun and twin .50 caliber MG behind it. Another M16 quad .50 is on the right front of the LCT. These vehicles are probably from the 1st Platoon of Battery B, 197th AAA Bn. Most of their equipment was lost when LCT200 was struck by an artillery shell and caught fire.

The crews slept in the cabins above water and the galleys continued to operate. The U.S. Navy Armed Guard manned these guns until the ships were sunk, then men from the 397th AAA Bn. replaced them. The Phoenix Units were large concrete blocks that were also sunk off shore to serve as part of the artificial harbor. They were each equipped with a 40mm antiaircraft gun and living space below for the crew. Some of these guns were destroyed when the Phoenix Units were badly damaged by the storm of 20 June.

The 197th AAA Automatic Weapons Bn. (Self-Propelled) went ashore around H+120 supporting the 16th Infantry Regt. During the landing they lost six M-15 halftracks, seven M-16 halftracks, one M-2 halftrack and three jeeps. Only 16 men, however, became casualties. The largest amount of equipment was destroyed when LCT 200 was hit by artillery and the vehicles of 1st Platoon, Battery B were burned in the fire.

Once ashore, the halftracks found themselves trapped on the beach until the exits were cleared. With nowhere to go they supported the ground advance as best they could, while keeping a careful eye on the skies. Once off the beach, the guns were set up to defend their assigned sector, where the battalion stayed until 25 June when they were given the specific task of protecting airstrip ARL 9, just south of Omaha Beach. From 6 June through 15 July, German air activity was light and the unit was credited with only one definite, and two probable, kills.

The 457th AAA Automatic Weapons Bn. (Mobile) was equipped with both quad .50 MGs and 40mm guns. It was scheduled to land at H+14 hours on

D–Day and take up position between the 197th AAA Bn. on the left, and the 467th AAA Bn. on the right. Due to the congestion on the beach the 457th did not come ashore until 1500 hrs on 7 June. Battery D took up positions behind the D-3 exit, Battery A behind the E-3 exit, and Batteries B and C near the E-1 exit. Part of the assigned area for the 457th was still in enemy hands by the night of 7 June, so the 457th found the best possible sites for their guns and waited until the ground troops had pushed the Germans back.

The 320th Barrage Balloon Bn. (VLA) (Colored)

The 320th Barrage Balloon Bn. was unique at Normandy for two reasons. First, it was the first barrage balloon unit in France and second, it was the first black unit in the segregated American Army to come ashore on D-Day.

Below.
Lt. Ray Karcy says mass for men from the 327th Glider Infantry Regt. Due to a shortage of gliders and glider pilots, the 327th came ashore in landing craft. Two black soldiers are watching from the ramp of the LCI on the left. One wears the shoulder patch of the 1st Army. There were very few black contingents in the early days of the invasion, and these men are probably a balloon crew from the 320th Barrage Balloon Bn.

The VLA in the 320th designation stood for "very low altitude." These units used smaller barrage balloons that could easily be moved by a few men and transported across the Channel on landing craft. A standard balloon crew was normally four men, but trained personnel were in short supply and the 320th reduced the crews to three men to get as many balloons in the air as possible.

The barrage balloon concept was simple. Lighter-than-air balloons were tethered over an area that the Army wished to protect against air attack. The balloons were flown at irregular intervals and altitudes. If an enemy plane attempted to fly into the area, it ran the risk of striking one of the wire cables holding the balloons. This could be enough to slice off a wing or the cable could become tangled in the propeller. It was a passive form of defense which forced the enemy aircraft to fly above the balloons where it would be harder to hit the target. Many of the ships taking part in the Channel crossing flew barrage balloons to prevent low level attacks.

A few types of balloons had small explosives attached to them. If a plane caught on the cable the explosive package would be cut loose and fall down the cable to the aircraft, where it would detonate. There is no evidence that any of these were used at Normandy.

In 1944 the U.S. Army segregated their units by race. Almost all of the combat units were made up of white soldiers, while the blacks were assigned to the less glamorous support units. In the thinking of the times barrage balloon units were considered one of the jobs that black troops could handle (under white officers). The 320th had the official Army designation 320th Barrage Balloon Bn. (VLA) (Colored) to indicate racial composition.

The men of the 320th were not second-rate soldiers. They were highly trained and took pride in their job. When they were told they were going to land in France to protect the invasion beaches, they quickly realized that the standard VLA balloon winch was too heavy and cumbersome to lug ashore from a landing craft. The M-1 US Army winch had a

A VLA barrage balloon flies over Omaha Beach. Barrage balloons were used to prevent enemy aircraft from flying over an area at low altitude. By forcing the planes to fly high, it reduced the accuracy of any aerial attacks. The 320th Barrage Balloon Bn. claimed only one definite kill when a JU-88 ran into the wire of one of their balloons shortly after D-Day.

The standard VLA winch assembly seen here was considered too heavy for an amphibious invasion. The men of the 320th Barrage Balloon Bn. developed a lighter weight winch by modifying Signal Corps field telephone wire reels.

Right.
The VLA (Very Low Altitude) barrage balloon did not have great lifting power. Sandbags were used as ballast and the VLA balloon could be easily moved by a few men. The standard balloon crew was four men, but at Normandy this was reduced to only three men.

CORPS AND DIVISIONAL AAA UNITS

Vth Corps
103rd AAA
AW Bn. (1st Div)
459th AAA
AW Bn. (29th Div)
462nd AAA
AW Bn. (28th Div)

115th AAA Group
430th AAA Bn.
460th AAA Bn.
461st AAA Bn.

VII Corps
376th AAA
AW Bn. (4th Div)
377th AAA
AW Bn. (9th Div)
537th AAA Bn.
(90th Div)

109th AAA Group
438th AAA Bn.
453rd AAA Bn.

Weapons
● *AAA Gun Bn.- 16 90mm guns, 16 water-cooled .50 MG*
● *AAA AW Bn. - 32 M51 quad .50 MG, 32 40mm, 32 water-cooled MG*
● *AAA AW Bn. (SP) 32 M15 37mm/.50 cal H/T, 32 M16 Quad .50 H/T*

gasoline motor and weighed 1,000 pounds. The British Mark VII winch weighed almost 400 pounds. They developed an expedient by adding two handles to a Signal Corps RL-31 Winder and putting the balloon wire on the DR-4 drum. This new winch weighed only 50 pounds and could be easily carried ashore by one man.

The plans called for a balloon unit of the RAF to fill the balloons with gas in England, then put them on the ships leaving for France. The 320th would meet the vessels on the shore and transfer the balloons to locations on the beachhead. This provided protection for the ships crossing the Channel and allowed the 320th to not have to carry the bulky gas equipment ashore until the beaches were secure.

The 320th Headquarters and Battery A were assigned to the 1st Div. at Omaha, and Battery C to the 4th Div. on Utah Beach. This makes the 320th

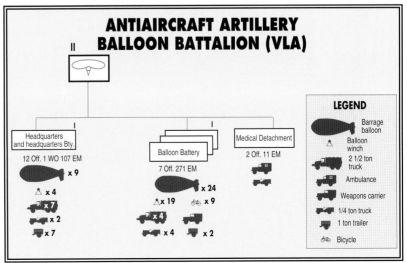

ANTIAIRCRAFT ARTILLERY BALLOON BATTALION (VLA)

Headquarters and headquarters Bty.
12 Off. 1 WO 107 EM
x 9
x 7
x 2
x 7

Balloon Battery
7 Off. 271 EM
x 24
x 19   x 9
x 4
x 4   x 2

Medical Detachment
2 Off. 11 EM

LEGEND
Barrage balloon
Balloon winch
2 1/2 ton truck
Ambulance
Weapons carrier
1/4 ton truck
1 ton trailer
Bicycle

Right.
Of all the units to land on D-Day, the medical troops possibly performed the best. The reports of medics and doctors braving German fire to carry wounded men to safety are too numerous to mention. There were many different echelons of medical units, but they all worked together without problems to provide the best possible care for the casualties. Some of the medics in the background have the full arc of the 1st Engineer Special Brigade painted on their helmets, indicating this was taken on Utah Beach.

Below.
A First Army doctor treats a local French inhabitant. Both the captain and lieutenant wear red cross arm bands, but neither has any red cross markings on his helmet. Within a few days medics realized that snipers did not shoot at neutrality markings and many began to wear red cross arm bands on each arm for increased visibility.

Right.

These men from the 165th Signal Photographic Company are the ones responsible for the majority of the photos in this book. Normally working in teams of one still photographer and one motion picture cameraman, they covered every aspect of the invasion. The two most commonly used cameras are shown here. Still photos were almost exclusively shot in 4x5 inch format on a Speed Graphic. Official motion picture film was always shot in 35mm in an Eyemo camera. The motion picture film was destined for the newsreels shown in theaters, and 16mm footage had too much grain when enlarged.

Below.

Many photos were taken on the invasion beaches, but few were taken of the area just inland. This shows one of the exits from Omaha Beach with a Dukw from the 460th Amphibious Truck Bn. bringing a load of cargo to one of the supply dumps. In the field to the right some of the supporting elements are setting up around the hedge line. Typically the troops stayed to the edges of the fields where they could have some cover and be able to camouflage themselves against aerial observation. It was quite typical for a large field to seem empty, but have the edges packed with men and equipment.

one of the very few units to be assigned tasks on both Omaha and Utah. Battery B was part of the follow-up force that landed over a period of time from D+1 to D+4. The area they had to cover was so great they reduced each balloon crew from four to three men, and some records indicate that they even used two man balloon crews at times.

The 600 men of the 320th were scattered throughout 150 landing craft on D-Day. The first element ashore on Omaha was the medical detachment which set up a first-aid station. It was followed by 12 crews with balloons and another 43 crews without balloons. The crews without balloons were to take the barrage balloons from the incoming ships and bring them ashore. Sandbags were tied below the

balloons as ballast, allowing the three man crew to easily move the inflated balloons ashore. According to the official report of the 320th, the first balloon to fly on Omaha Beach went up near the E-3 exit at approximately 2315 hrs. on 6 June. This means that any photograph showing a barrage balloon ashore in daylight could not have been taken on D-Day.

By the evening of 7 June there were 12 balloons over Omaha Beach. These were listed as all being destroyed by enemy fire, however it can now be revealed that one was destroyed by a member of one of the engineer units on the night of 6 June. The engineer was sitting in a foxhole looking up at a balloon and wondered what would happen if he fired a tracer into it. He tried it, the balloon was destroyed,

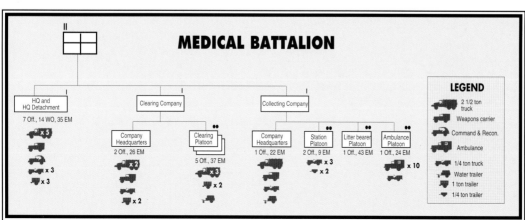

MEDICAL BATTALION

LEGEND

- 2 1/2 ton truck
- Weapons carrier
- Command & Recon.
- Ambulance
- 1/4 ton truck
- Water trailer
- 1 ton trailer
- 1/4 ton trailer

HQ and HQ Detachment
7 Off., 14 WO, 35 EM
x 5
x 3
x 3

Clearing Company

Company Headquarters
2 Off., 26 EM
x 2
x 2

Clearing Platoon
5 Off., 37 EM
x 3
x 2

Collecting Company

Company Headquarters
1 Off., 22 EM
x 3
x 2

Station Platoon
2 Off., 9 EM
x 3
x 2

Litter bearer Platoon
1 Off., 43 EM

Ambulance Platoon
1 Off., 24 EM
x 10

The engineers were often called upon to make sure Allied and German casualties had not been booby-trapped. The Germans were known to booby-trap not only bodies, but anything they felt the Americans might have an interest in. This could be a tempting souvenir such as a pistol or dagger, or just a common helmet placed in a tempting location. The Allies continually tried to teach their men not to go souvenir hunting until the area had been carefully checked for booby-traps.

and an angry officer from the 320th went in search of the responsible party. This officer found the engineer in a foxhole and asked if he had any idea what had happened to the balloon. In fine Army tradition the engineer replied he had no idea, and the balloon was officially listed as destroyed by enemy fire. In all probability most of the lost balloons were hit by the tremendous amounts of antiaircraft fire that was flung into the air whenever one of the few German aircraft came nearby.

On Utah Beach the men of Battery C brought 25 barrage balloons ashore and got them set up over the beach area. It soon became apparent that these balloons were being used as aiming points by the German artillery and they were all cut loose. According to one story, the German gunners must have thought these balloons were attached to ships, as they continued to shell the area below one balloon as it drifted out to sea.

The 320th had their maximum number of balloons flying over the beaches on D+15 when 141 were flying. The only plane confirmed destroyed by the balloons of the 320th was a JU-88 that became tangled in a balloon wire and crashed on 16 June 1944. The 320th remained on the beachhead with their balloons until 11 November 1944 when they left Normandy and were returned to the USA.

Medical units

The medical plan for Normandy called for the best possible care being provided to casualties. An evacuation system was developed to get wounded men off the beach and back to hospital, as fast as possible. There were also provisions to get as many medical supplies ashore as early as possible in case the invasion ran into problems.

There were basically three main types of medical units providing care on the beach. Every combat unit had its own medical detachment permanently assigned to it. These medical personnel moved forward with their unit and provided immediate care to casualties. Then came the medical battalions permanently assigned to the divisions. These men worked just behind the lines getting the casualty evacuated back to the hospitals. At Normandy there was also an additional layer of medical units. These were attached to the Engineer Special Brigades and were concerned with taking care of the casualties in the beach area and getting them evacuated by sea.

The first medical personnel to deal with a casualty were normally the medics attached directly to a combat unit. The best example of this were the three medical aid men attached to each infantry company. Extra medical personnel were provided to each combat unit as part of their overstrength and extra medical equipment was given to the assault units. Each man in the assault regiments, as well as other soldiers landing in the first waves, carried not only the standard first-aid pouch with bandage and sulfa powder, but was also issued the parachutist's first-aid pouch. This small waterproof pouch contained another bandage, a tourniquet, and a Syrette of morphine. There are many stories of medics running out of morphine in the early hours of D-Day, and having to scrounge extra Syrettes from these pouches.

Morphine was considered one of the most important medical supplies to provide to the first waves. It not only served as a pain killer, but also helped prevent the body from going into shock. Shock was what killed many casualties that otherwise would have survived with proper medical treatment. The morphine Syrettes were small lead tubes, much like toothpaste tubes, with a needle at one end. To use them you had to push a small pin down the needle to puncture a seal, remove the pin, then stick the needle into the casualty and squeeze the morphine out. Too much morphine could kill a man, so when a casualty was given morphine the medic was to pin the Syrette

Dirt roads such as this one
might have been suitable for
local farmers, but when
subjected to military traffic they
soon deteriorated into a sea of
mud. One of the least
glamorous, but most important,
tasks of the engineers was to
improve and maintain the
roads. Without constant
maintenance the supply of men
and equipment to the front
lines would slow to a halt.

Below.

When the fighting had passed
an area, discarded weapons
were picked up and brought to
ordnance repair units that
stripped everything down,
repaired and rebuilt the
equipment. Every time a rifle
could be repaired and reissued
saved valuable shipping space
on the transatlantic convoys
which could be used to bring
more supplies to the ETO.
Ordnance units played a vital
role by supplying a steady
stream of repaired weapons
and vehicles
to the combat troops.

to the wounded man's jacket, or write the letter "M" on his forehead, so another medic would not come along and give an overdose.

In normal practice, once the casualty was given initial treatment by an aidman, he would be transported away from the front lines by stretcher-bearers from his battalion and brought to the battalion aid station. There he would be given brief treatment by a doctor and handed over to the Regimental Collecting Company. This unit would, in turn, bring him to the Division Clearing Company. The casualty would then be sent to either a field hospital or specialty hospital, depending on his wounds.

Since the greatest number of casualties would probably be suffered on the first day of the landing, medical personnel had to be sent ashore as early as possible. But during the first few days of the invasion, the beachhead was too small for full-scale hospitals to be brought ashore.

To ensure that there would be an adequate amount of medical equipment on shore, all medical units scheduled to land in the first three days carried special "Waterproofed medical units." These were eight waterproof containers that would float ashore if dropped in the water, and provided a stock of supplies above and beyond what was normally carried by the unit. They were issued one to each battalion medical detachment, two per collecting company, four per clearing company, and six per Engineer Special Brigade medical battalion. Each special medical unit contained:

50	dressings, first-aid, large
50	dressings, first-aid, small
50	packages, gauze, plain sterile
50	bandage, gauze, 3 inch.
10	packages, sulfanilamide crystalline
25	boxes, morphine tartrate Syrette
7	packages, dried human plasma

1000   sulfa tablets
1   bottle halazone water purification tablets
1   sterile gauze packet impregnated with vaseline.

To make sure that there were enough stretchers to evacuate the expected casualties, every medical unit carried extras ashore. Extra stretchers were issued 12 per battalion, 24 per Ranger battalion, and 180 per medical battalion. Additional Medical chests No. 1 were issued on the basis of two per collecting co., four per clearing co., and six per ESB medical battalion. Extra splint sets were issued one per battalion, five per collecting co., and ten per ESB medical battalion. Extra blanket sets, small, were issued three per battalion, four per collecting and clearing cos., and ten per ESB medical battalion. It was hoped that all this extra medical equipment would make the medical units self-sufficient for a few days in case the worst happened and more supplies were not able to be landed on the invasion beaches.

Medical units in the assault formations were also given extra surgical teams to help deal with casualties until the hospitals could get ashore. Once the beachhead had room for field hospitals, the standard casualty evacuation system would take over. As soon as airstrips could be constructed, casualties would be evacuated by aircraft to well-equipped hospitals in England. Until then, wounded men were brought aboard the specially designated LST hospital ships

Above.
A joint Anglo-American Civil Affairs team operating in a Norman town. These men were responsible for handling any problems the local population might have, so that the combat commanders would not have to deal with farmers complaining about their barns being destroyed. They also dealt with such problems as tracking down collaborators and spies, as well as making sure the civilians got enough to eat. This is probably a Type "D" detachment consisting of two American and two British officers: two administrative officers (Food and Civil Administration) and two Public Safety Officers (Police Civil Defense and Fire).

and transported to England once the ships were full.

The medical plans for the Normandy invasion were carefully worked out to cover any eventuality, including a disaster on the beaches. The high proportion of medical personnel and equipment in the first day greatly contributed to the saving of many lives. There were many things that did not go right during the invasion, but there are few, if any, complaints that can be made against the medical service.

Detachments

There were a number of small detachments assigned to the Combat Teams. These ranged from photographers sent to record the invasion on film, to civilian journalists reporting for newspapers. Intelligence units provided prisoner of war interrogation teams to question captured German soldiers, and Counter Intelligence Corps men to prevent the Germans from sending spies into Allied lines. Language Interpreting Teams and Civil Affairs Teams were used to deal with the local French population. Supplies provided from British Civil Affairs sections were labelled with "CA" in red paint, supplies from U.S. Civil Affairs were to be labelled "CA" in black paint.

The 1st Div. had a British Liaison team to prepare for the link up between the American and British sectors. These detachments were usually no more than two to four men with a jeep or two, but nonetheless played a vital role.

Chapter 6. Rangers and

FOR the Normandy landing, both the 2nd and 5th Ranger Battalions were attached together under command of Lt. Col. James E. Rudder. The Provisional Ranger Group was officially formed on 9 May 1944 and consisted of the 2nd and 5th Rangers, along with two Naval Shore Fire Control Parties, one Air Liaison Party (both from the 293rd JASCO), and a Ranger Cannon Company consisting of four half-tracks mounting 75mm guns.

This photo of British LCA 1377 shows a lot of the detail of the front armor. A Ranger patch can be seen on the arm of one man - indicating this is part of the same series taken of Rangers boarding at Weymouth (see following pages). It is interesting that a few of the helmets have red crosses painted on them. It is often debated if American medics at D-Day wore painted helmets, and here is proof that at least some of the medics assigned to the Rangers did so.

The Provisional Ranger Group

The Ranger half-tracks were not scheduled to land in France until D+2. Technically, the Provisional Ranger Group was under the command of the 116th Regimental Combat Team, which in turn was officially attached to the 1st Infantry Division for the initial phase of the assault.

The mission given to the Ranger Group was to make sure that the battery of six 155mm guns on Pointe du Hoc were destroyed. Pointe du Hoc was perfectly positioned to allow these guns to shell either Omaha or Utah Beach, or to fire on the transport ships waiting offshore. If these guns were used against the beaches they would be firing parallel to the shore, causing more destruction than guns placed inland firing perpendicular to the coastline. The Overlord planners felt that the Pointe du Hoc guns were "the most dangerous battery in France."

arines on D-Day

The problem was that these guns were emplaced on top of an 85 to 100 foot cliff. The Germans did not think anyone could scale it, but had placed mines and sentries around the area just in case. The Air Force had subjected the area to heavy bombing and the invasion plan called for the 14" guns of the *U.S.S. Texas*, along with the guns of the destroyers *Satterlee* and *HMS Tallybont*, to bombard the gun

positions with 250 14" shells on the morning of D–Day. The danger from even one operational gun on Pointe du Hoc was so great a unit had to be assigned to capture the gun battery and make absolutely sure none were able to fire on the beaches. If the guns were destroyed in the shelling, it was

(Continued on page 203)

Above.
Careful inspection of this photograph shows it to be men from the 2nd Ranger Battalion marching down the waterfront at Weymouth, England, ready to leave for Normandy. The Rangers boarded their ships on 1 June 1944 and spent the next five days stuck on British transports, unable to disembark for security reasons. Some Rangers can be seen carrying the 5 foot long Bangalore torpedoes. All appear to wear the standard canvas leggings. Close scrutiny shows a few men wearing the dark colored assault jackets. Since these jackets were not issued until 10 days before the landings, the photo could not have been taken at an earlier practice invasion and must have been taken just prior to the real invasion.

Left.
The last stop on shore for the Rangers was this tent with the sign "*check rosters here.*" Transportation officers would double check the men against the official unit roster before letting them board the ship. Signal Corps movies taken at the same time show that coffee and doughnuts were handed out by the Red Cross on the other side of the tent. In the background can be seen the Weymouth Pavilion.

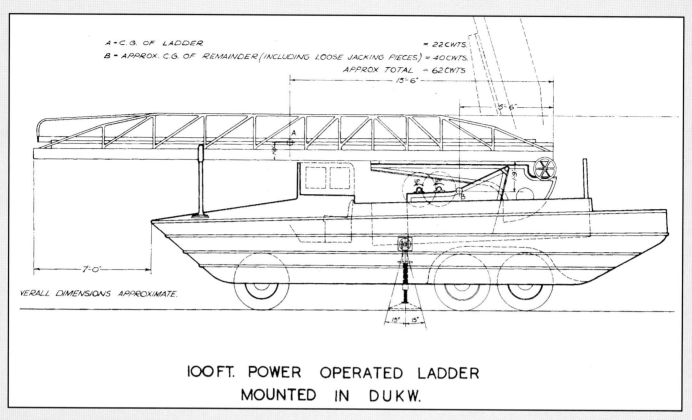

A = C.G. OF LADDER = 22 CWTS.
B = APPROX. C.G. OF REMAINDER (INCLUDING LOOSE JACKING PIECES) = 40 CWTS.
APPROX TOTAL = 62 CWTS

15'-6"
5'-6"
7'-0"
VERALL DIMENSIONS APPROXIMATE.
15° 15°

100 FT. POWER OPERATED LADDER
MOUNTED IN D.U.K.W.

Left.
General view of the ladder equipped DUKW.

Below.
On either side of the DUKW, approximately amidships, steadying jacks were fitted. The baseplates are made out of aluminium to keep the weight to a minimum.

Bottom left.
The ladder elevating gear.

Opposite page, top.
DUKW disembarking from an LCT (5) into deep water.

Opposite page, center.
DUKW landing: gunner manning the two MGs. Armor protection for the gunner is not shown in this model.

Opposite page, bottom left.
DUKW stationed at foot of cliff. The ladder being elevated with gunner in position.

Opposite page, bottom right.
Men climbing extended ladder.

or scaling cliffs"

The following photographs are from a Top-Secret Combined Operations Headquarters report called "*Mechanical aids for scaling cliffs.*" The report evaluated a number of the devices used at Pointe du Hoc.

The ladder-carrying Dukw

" *The first experiments with powered ladders were made using a 100 ft ladder turntable (water tower) used by Fire Brigades. It was mounted on a 13-ton six-wheeled vehicle. The ladder worked well, but the vehicle used was hard to handle on difficult beaches. This led to the concept of placing the ladder on a DUKW, which proved far superior to the water-tower design. A suggestion was made that the 13-ton water towers might still be useful as portable artillery observation posts.*

This equipment consists of a standard fireman's ladder mounted in the hold of a DUKW. The power for extension and elevation is supplied from the DUKW engine, the ladder being operated in place of the normal DUKW winch. To give greater stability and safety when the ladder is extended, particularly on uneven or soft surfaces, jacks which can be rapidly placed in position are fitted to each side of the DUKW.

Two automatic weapons can be mounted and fired from the top of the ladder. The gunner, who is protected by armor plating and linked to the bottom of the ladder by telephone, can be elevated with the ladder. Special waterproof covers were made to fit over the guns. These could be removed after the run in, and just before the craft touched down.

Provision has been made for six spare pans of ammunition at the ladder top. It is most important not to exceed the maximum weights given or there will be a danger of the ladder being strained when fully extended. These weights are: armor 80 lbs; machine gun with full pan 31 lbs; spare ammo pans 11 lbs each; plus weight of man. The total weight should not exceed 450 lbs. The arrangement of guns and spare ammunition must be adjusted accordingly.

To save time, it is possible to elevate the ladder 10°-20°(degrees) while the DUKW is in the water, or crossing the beach to the foot of the cliff. The ladder must not be elevated more than 20° whilst the DUKW is afloat. Although greater angles than this have been used successfully, the craft does not have great stability and if there is any swell it might capsize if higher angles are used. Elevation to the full amount can commence immediately as the wheels touch bottom.

When the ladder is fully extended five men are able to ascend at the same time providing they are spaced out along the length of the ladder. With the ladder stowed, performance at sea is very similar to that of a DUKW fully laden. It can disembark in calm water safely from an LCT(5). The position of the DUKW relative to the bottom of the cliff is important. If the DUKW is brought so that the bow is against the cliff it will not be possible to get sufficient elevation for the ladder to clear the top. The best position is one where the elevation of the ladder is about 70°. "

Left.
Standard 2" rocket and
modified projector type "J"
showing position of rope
boxes. The pigtail of the rocket
has been plugged into the 20
foot firing lead. One side of the
projector is left open to give a
free run for the wiring strap.

Rocket Fired Grapnels

"*The original development of the principle of projecting a rope by means of a rocket consisted of a 2" rocket fitted with a grapnel head fired from a modified type "J" projector. The tail of the rocket was connected by an 8 foot wire strap to 90 fathoms of 2 1/2" rope packed in two boxes. The rocket was fired electrically by a four volt battery through a firing lead 20 feet long.*

The various parts of this equipment could be stowed in a small boat, such as a dory, carried ashore and set up on the beach. Alternately the projector could be attached to the gunwale of the dory and fired from the boat.

Subsequently, rope ladders and 2 1/2" ropes fitted with wooden toggle bars were tried. The rope ladders were for use when the cliff was vertical or had an overhang, and the toggle ropes on sloping cliffs in place of plain rope. It was found that often on a sloping cliff there would be a short vertical face to climb and the toggle ropes were easier to climb than the plain. The rope ladders were packed in rectangular boxes, and the toggle ropes in the same size box as the plain ropes.

The original ladders were made with the object of reaching a height of 200-250 feet and it was necessary to keep the weight to a minimum. When firing from the beach an

Right.
Close up of the type "J" projector. The grapnel, which will hold the weight of three men, is screwed into the top of the rocket in place of the usual head. To use this equipment the operator holds the projector by the handle and points it in the direction he wishes the grapnel to go. The rope box is laid down on the ground in front of the projector.

Below left.
LCA fitted with six 2" rockets type "J" projectors firing.

Below right.
As above, a second or two later. Note toggle ropes and rope ladders.

extra 50 feet of ladder should be used, unless it is possible to fire from the foot of the cliff.

The ladders consist of two one inch manila ropes with wooden rungs one inch diameter by nine inches long, spaced 18 inches apart. One half-inch rope and 1 1/2 inch diameter rungs were used in equipment supplied to the U.S. Rangers. The additional weight is acceptable with low cliff height. A one inch tail rope was attached to the bottom of the ladder in case the ladder overshot. The toggle rope consists of five inch wooden toggles spaced every three feet.

In addition, and as an alternative method, six rocket projectors were fitted in an LCA. The standard Type "J" projector was used. They were fitted on each side of the deck and they could be rapidly detached and taken ashore if necessary. Each LCA was to fire two each of rope ladders, toggle ropes, and plain ropes. Used operationally this method is suitable only when the beach is narrow and the angle of fire and range can be carefully judged."

Above left.
Firing the portable lightweight grapnel equipment: the Schermuly mortar. This was developed specifically for the U.S. Rangers. The requirement was for a complete equipment which could be carried by one man. The grapnel was to carry a 1" line to a height of 100 feet.
Above right.
Grapnel with toggle rope attached, fixed in position at top of cliff.

Performance of the different ropes and rockets		
Rocket Type	Rope size and type	approx. vertical height reached
Standard 2"	1" plain	600 feet
Rocket Grapnel	2 1/2" plain	300 feet
	2 1/2" toggle	275 feet
	Rope ladder (light)	250 feet
	Rope ladder heavy	200 feet
Light Schermuly Equipment	1" rope	200 feet
	1 1/2" rope	150 feet

Below.
This shows the proper positioning of the rope in the boxes. The rope has to be flaked (coiled) in a special way if it is to run clear. The rope should be flaked from one corner of the box to the other and then snaked back as shown in the diagram. Snaking and flaking should be continued alternately, care being taken that the layers of flaking (which should be quite slack) cross each other. The pin base, which is only used for stowing the rope, must be removed before firing. Care must be taken to see that no pins have been broken off and left in the rope box as this would result in the breaking or fouling of the rope when the grapnel was fired.

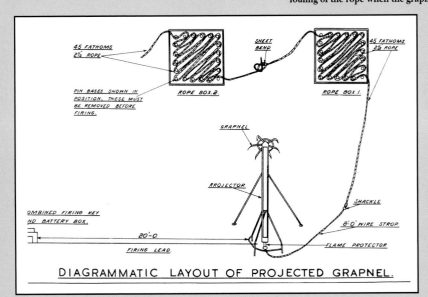

DIAGRAMMATIC LAYOUT OF PROJECTED GRAPNEL.

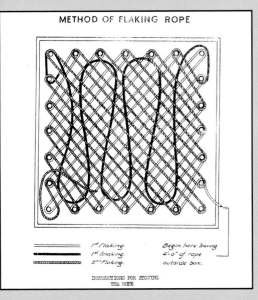

METHOD OF FLAKING ROPE

"Mechanical aids for scaling cliffs"

Light Tubular Steel Ladders

"These ladders are manufactured in 4' sections. Each section is carried by one man and assembled at the bottom of the cliff. As the ladder is built up it is hauled to the top of the cliff by men already at the top, the necessary lengths being added until the required height is obtained. On the top section of the ladder there are warp hooks which give security when the ladder is placed against the cliff. A line with a grip fast is also used, while steel supports hold the ladder away from the cliff face. When in position, the steel ladder hung vertically like a rope ladder and assistance in scaling it can be obtained by the use of an additional rope.

As it has to be hauled from the cliff top, it is suitable for follow up troops only, but its attractions are that it is light and handy, easy to scale, quickly erected, works well up to 80 feet, and is very suitable for overhangs. Its main disadvantage is a tendency to come apart in the middle which in most cases is probably due to faulty assembly. However, "S" hooks used at the joints serve to overcome this difficulty, and if the climber has a rope round him which is held by men at the top of the cliff he can come to little harm."

Other items were mentioned in this test report, but not photographed. This included a "special roller" placed at the top of the cliff. The soldier tied one end of a rope under his armpits. The rope ran up to the roller at the top and back down again. The rest of the soldiers pulled on the other end of the rope to take the weight off the first soldier so he could "run" to the top of the cliff.

Standard climbing irons and pitons were tested, but were considered impossible to use on vertical cliffs or where there were overhangs. Another trial used naval kite balloons. A man in a parachute harness was attached to the balloon cable at a height slightly more than the cliff face. The balloon was flown at a suitable operation height (500 ft). Up to three balloons might be needed to obtain the necessary lift depending on the force of the wind. The soldier was supposed to drop out of the harness once over the cliff. The balloons could then be winched back down and another man sent to the top.

The report states that the disadvantages of the balloon method outweighed any advantages. It was very difficult to handle, the winds had to be on-shore and the balloon was vulnerable to small arms fire. The advantages were that it was a silent operation, the first man was on the cliff quickly, and that it could be used on any height cliff.

almost as important to deny the Germans the use of Pointe du Hoc as an observation post overlooking the Allied fleets.

Given the task of landing on the rocky coast below the cliffs and scaling them under German fire, the Rangers experimented with a number of devices they thought might be of help. In the end it was decided to use only a few of the suggestions. Lightweight four foot sections of metal ladders were designed that could be connected together to climb to whatever height was needed. Each LCA used by the Rangers would carry 100 feet of these ladder sections, pre-assembled in 16 foot lengths. These ladders were designed to be used only after the cliffs had been captured, but the Rangers trained to climb a partially assembled ladder, push themselves out from the cliff wall, and add another 16 feet of ladder to the top. They would keep repeating this until they were at the top.

Dukws were to be used to carry some of the heavier weapons, such as 81mm mortars, as well as more ammunition and supplies ashore. Four Dukws were equipped with special fire fighting ladders that could be raised to 100 feet. At the top of these ladders twin Vickers K machine guns were mounted. It was hoped that these guns could rake the top of the cliff and keep the Germans from dropping grenades down on the men climbing. These Dukws were transported across the channel in an LCT and launched when the LCAs were ready to head to shore. Men from the 234th Engineer Combat Bn. were assigned as drivers and crew for these Dukws.

Rocket-propelled grappling hooks were developed that trailed ropes and rope ladders up the cliff. Each of the ten LCAs that would land the Rangers was

Below.
Colonel James Rudder is at front right leading the 2nd Ranger Bn. to the embarkation point at Weymouth on 1 June 1944. At the far left is Captain Harvey Cook (Intelligence officer) next to Lt. James Eikner (Communications officer). In the front row is a First Sgt. wearing a helmet net, who has painted his stripes on his field jacket. The officer outside the column following Rudder is Lieutenant Robert Edlin of Company A.
Colonel Rudder is wearing a dark shade assault jacket over his inflatable lifebelt. The assault gas mask bag is on his chest and the map case hanging on his right side is quite full. Although it was thought that the 2nd Rangers were issued paratrooper boots, every man in this photo wears canvas leggings.

equipped with six of these two-inch rockets: two in the bow, two astern, and two amidships. Behind each rocket was a box holding a carefully coiled rope or rope ladder. The first two rockets carried plain 3/4 inch ropes, the second had ropes with wooden toggles at one foot intervals, and the last two were fitted with light rope ladders.

When the rockets were fired the grappling hooks were shot up over the cliff. In testing, the rockets propelled the grapnels 200 feet in the air. With luck the hooks would catch on an obstruction and provide the Rangers a way to climb to the top. If the LCA rockets failed, each landing craft also carried two lighter Schermuly rocket grapnels attached to lighter ropes that could be hand carried to the base of the cliff for another attempt.

The Rangers given the task of climbing Pointe du Hoc were stripped of all unnecessary equipment. They carried only their rifles and a few grenades. Officially each man was to carry only 16 clips for his Garand, and four grenades. The only food they were to carry was one D-bar: a chocolate bar fortified with vitamins. The Rangers' packs would follow in one of the supply boats, along with more ammunition and extra rations.

The most common weapons carried up the cliff were the Garand rifle, the BAR, and the Thompson submachine gun. The heavier weapons were to follow later when the top of the cliff had been secured. First to follow would be light machine guns, 60mm mortars, and a few bazookas. Later would come heavier 81mm mortars which were carried in the supply boats.

The landing plan called for the Ranger Group to split into three forces. Force A, of roughly 225 men, would land Companies E and F of the 2nd Rangers on the eastern side of Pointe du Hoc, while Company D landed on the western side. Ten LCAs, two supply LCAs, and four ladder carrying Dukws were to land the men. Also attached to Force A was Lt. Col. Thomas Trevor of the British Commandos. This experienced officer went along as both an observer and advisor.

Force B consisted of Company C, 2nd Rangers under Captain Ralph Goranson. They were to land on Omaha's Charlie Beach on the right flank of the 29th Division at H+1 minute. These Rangers were to scale the smaller cliffs between Omaha and the Pointe de la Percée. They were then to eliminate the German strong points and gun positions from the right flank of Omaha Beach out to the Pointe de la Percée. Once this area was secured, they were to link up with Force A at Pointe du Hoc.

Force C consisted of the 5th Ranger Bn. and Companies A and B of the 2nd Rangers. Under the command of Lt.Col. Max Schneider, the 5th Ranger Bn. commander, these men were to wait offshore until it was known if Force A had successfully captured Pointe du Hoc. If the assault was successful, then Force C was to reinforce Force A at Pointe du Hoc at approximately H+30. If Force A was not successful, Force C was to land at H+60 behind Force B

Above.
Technician 5th Class (Technical Corporal) Jack Bramkamp - the barber, and his client T/5 Elmer Olander, were members of Company B, 2nd Ranger Battalion. They were killed on D-Day before they even got off the beach.

Opposite page.
Another view of Company B of the 2nd Ranger Battalion. On the ground is the assault jacket issued to specific units taking part in the Normandy invasion. This canvas vest with many pockets was worn by the assault regiments, as well as the NCOs and officers of the Ranger Battalions. Tied to the assault jacket is the parachutist's first-aid pouch which held a bandage, a tourniquet, and a Syrette of morphine. Next to it, under the helmet, can be seen the black rubber M5 assault gas mask bag. The man squatting down at center is holding a gray can of boot impregnite, which was applied just prior to embarkation as protection against possible chemical attack.

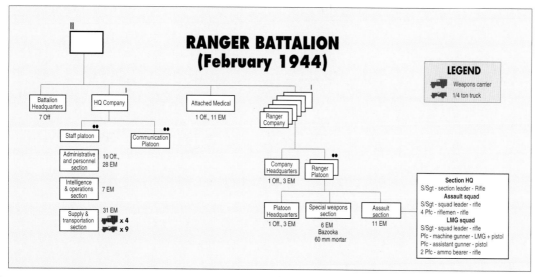

RANGER BATTALION
(February 1944)

LEGEND
Weapons carrier
1/4 ton truck

Battalion Headquarters
7 Off

HQ Company

Attached Medical
1 Off., 11 EM

Ranger Company

Staff platoon

Communication Platoon

Administrative and personnel section
10 Off., 28 EM

Intelligence & operations section
7 EM

Supply & transportation section
31 EM
x 4
x 9

Company Headquarters
1 Off., 3 EM

Ranger Platoon

Platoon Headquarters
1 Off., 3 EM

Special weapons section
6 EM
Bazooka
60 mm mortar

Assault section
11 EM

Section HQ
S/Sgt - section leader - Rifle
Assault squad
S/Sgt - squad leader - rifle
4 Pfc - riflemen - rifle
LMG squad
S/Sgt - squad leader - rifle
Pfc - machine gunner - LMG + pistol
Pfc - assistant gunner - pistol
2 Pfc - ammo bearer - rifle

at Omaha Beach and press on to capture Pointe du Hoc by land. Schneider was no stranger to Ranger operations. He had previously taken part in three landings with the 1st Ranger Bn, then served as Executive Officer to the 2nd Ranger Bn. before assuming command of the 5th Rangers.

The Rangers boarded British transport ships on 1 June and remained on board during the postponement of D-Day to 6 June.

There was a last minute change in the command structure once the men were on board the transports ships. When Col. Rudder had been given command of the Ranger Group, his executive officer, Captain

Above.
Lt. Robert T. Edlin was a platoon leader in Company A, 2nd Ranger Bn. He was credited with being the first Allied soldier to board a landing craft for the Normandy invasion. He is shown here on board the British LCA that will take the Rangers out to their transport ships. Curiously, Edlin wears a BAR ammo belt. He may have found its larger pockets more useful than the standard cartridge belt. Later, while fighting in Brittany, Edlin would earn the D.S.C.

Left.
Taken within moments of the picture above, this photo of Lt. Edlin was filmed by a motion picture cameraman from the opposite angle on board the LCA. The small ladder was needed for the men to get into the LCA due to its overhead cover. Edlin wears the typical Ranger uniform of impregnated HBTs under the M41 field jacket.

Cleveland Lytle, had been put in charge of Force A. It appears that Rudder wanted to lead his men ashore at Pointe du Hoc, but was forbidden to do so by a higher authority. The records of exactly what happened were ignored until long after the war and today there are different versions of the story.

It appears that once on board the transports, Captain Lytle was given an updated map of the German installations which clearly indicated that the guns at Pointe du

(Continued on page 210)

Above.

The British LCA was roughly the same size as the American LCVP, but the armored sides and top made it more cramped for the passengers. These Rangers are about to be brought out to the transport ships waiting in Weymouth Harbor. A high percentage of the men in this boat wear assault jackets. Ranger diamonds can be seen on the back of two helmets. Close examination reveals they have the number "2" painted on them.
The white stripe running down the middle of the helmet has not yet been identified.

Left.

The bombardment and shelling of Pointe du Hoc caused some of the cliffs to collapse, leaving piles of debris that shortened the climb to the top. This climb is only about half of what it was before the cliff collapsed.
This is to the left of the point, just below where Rudder's command post is thought to be. The pile at the bottom of the cliff is actually composed of slippery wet clay.

These two close-ups show Rangers in an LCA at Weymouth. A 60mm mortar can be seen on the overhead cover next to a conical mesh bazooka flash shield. A white pack of Lucky Strikes cigarettes is being handed around. The Lucky Strikes pack was originally green, but green dye was desperately needed for the military, so the company changed to white and got a lot of advertising mileage out of their slogan "Lucky Strikes has gone to war." The diamond shaped Ranger patch is worn on some of the M41 field jackets, and in one case can be seen (in the upper right hand corner) worn on the right shoulder. The men all wear their M5 assault gas mask bags on their chests, and the M1928 haversack is visible on a few of them.

Opposite page.
In this photo the bazookaman carries a gray cardboard box, the box the lifebelts were issued in, which is covered with pencilled games of tic-tac-toe. At the top left can be seen a Bangalore torpedo with a center hole on top designed to hold the detonator.
The diamond shaped Ranger patch was worn by the 2nd and 5th Rangers in Normandy. The black scroll patch for each Ranger Battalion had not yet been adopted. The shape and colors of the diamond patch were similar to the sign used by the American Sunoco gasoline company, thus it was quickly termed "the Sunoco patch."

Left.
This is a close-up view of the area shown on page 207. Visible in this photo are two thin ropes, one toggle rope, and one tubular ladder. The climb here is cut in half due to the pile of debris at the bottom of the cliff. Thus it was a logical spot to concentrate the Rangers' climbing effort. It is thought this is the location where Tech. 5 George Putzek became the first man to reach the top of the cliffs.

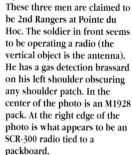

Left.
These three men are claimed to be 2nd Rangers at Pointe du Hoc. The soldier in front seems to be operating a radio (the vertical object is the antenna). He has a gas detection brassard on his left shoulder obscuring any shoulder patch. In the center of the photo is an M1928 pack. At the right edge of the photo is what appears to be an SCR-300 radio tied to a packboard.

Below.
This shows Col. Rudder's command post next to the cliff at Pointe du Hoc. Lt. Eikner, the communications officer, is in the center drinking from a canteen. Seated just to the right of Eikner is Sgt. Leonard Goodgal of the 101st A/B Div. His 101st patch and helmet marking are clearly visible. Goodgal was one of three paratroopers dropped on the Pointe du Hoc area who fought with the Rangers. In the bottom right corner is British Commando Col. Trevor who went ashore as an observer. At the far left edge of the photo a Ranger is seen wearing an assault jacket. The officer's stripe on his helmet is barely visible. This may be Col. Rudder.

Hoc had been dismantled and removed. The mission to eliminate these guns was considered by many a suicide mission, and Lytle was quite upset about throwing the unit away for nothing. According to recent books, he started drinking very heavily and began to make his feelings about the ill-fated mission known to his men.

Rudder was on the command ship *U.S.S. Ancon* when he heard this was happening. He told his superior that the mission would be jeopardized if it was led by a man with no faith in what they were doing. Permission was finally granted for Rudder to relieve the officer of his

command and to lead Force A ashore himself. Captain Lytle was sent back to England and disappeared into obscurity. Some books claim he was relieved for drunkenness, but it seems more likely it was because of his lack of faith in their mission. Exactly what happened, and why, remains unclear. However, this last minute change of plans left no one on the command ship with a direct interest in the well-being of the Ranger Group.

In the early hours of 6th June, the Rangers boarded the LCAs and started in to

shore. The sea was much rougher than expected. One LCA headed to Pointe du Hoc, carrying Captain Slater and men from D/2nd, swamped and left the men adrift. It was soon followed to the bottom by one of the two supply boats. The men in the other LCAs had to bail with their helmets to keep their boats afloat.

Ranger Force A was supposed to be directed to Pointe du Hoc by LCS-91, LCS-102, and ML-304 (Motor Launch). While heading to shore, LCS-91 was hit be enemy fire and sunk, and LCS-102 had problems with its rudder and was unable to continue. This left the navigation of the LCAs to the boat crews, who were not prepared for the mission.

Once the sun started to rise, Colonel Rudder realized that the British LCA crew had mistaken Pointe de la Percée for Pointe du Hoc and were miles off course. He ordered them to turn right and head for the correct landing point. As Force A travelled along the coastline they came under fire from German emplacements and five men in one of the Dukws were hit. The error in navigation meant that Force A could not follow the timetable. Instead of landing on the heels of the naval bombardment, when the Germans were crouched in their shelters, the Rangers would face an enemy who would have had 30 minutes to reorganize. Fortunately, the destroyer *Satterlee* realized what had happened and continued to provide fire support as the Rangers travelled along the shoreline back to Pointe du Hoc.

D Company had lost its commander and a third of its men when their LCA swamped. Rudder thought it would be unwise to send this under strength unit to the other side of Pointe du Hoc all by itself. He ordered all remaining boats to land on the eastern side of Pointe du Hoc. It was not until 0708 that Force A actually got to Pointe du Hoc. Schneider never

received the prearranged signal, so he made the decision to divert Force C to the alternate landing site on Omaha Beach near Vierville.

At Pointe du Hoc the Rangers in Force A discovered that the ropes attached to the rocket grapnels had become wet with spray. This additional weight caused the grapnels to fall short of the cliff. Most of the rockets mounted on the LCAs fell short, with only a few of the hooks clearing the top of the cliff and holding firm. The lighter Schermuly rockets were carried ashore and fired with better success. Some of the unfired rockets on the LCAs were removed and carried ashore to be fired closer to the cliff, which allowed them to clear the top. The Rangers took 15 casualties just getting across the 30 yard shingle beach. As he was leaving the landing craft, Col. Trevor was struck by a German bullet that penetrated his helmet and left him with a light wound on the forehead.

The shore in front of the cliff was pockmarked with shell craters from the air and sea bombardment. The Dukws were unable to get ashore and attempted to raised their ladders while still in the surf. Only two of the Dukw mounted ladders were deployed. One Dukw was stuck at a bad angle and the ladder could not be raised enough. The other went up roughly 80 feet and drew a lot of enemy fire. S/Sgt William Stivison found himself swaying back and forth as the waves hit the Dukw, but was able to use the twin Vickers K MGs mounted on the ladder to distract the Germans away from the men climbing the cliffs. The previous bombardment of Pointe du Hoc also caused some of the cliff to collapse, leaving large piles of debris which gave the Rangers a shorter climb.

At 0745 the top of the cliff was secure enough for Rudder to move his command post to a shell hole on top. His men fanned out and captured the fortified complex. They were dismayed to find the guns had been removed and

Although most officers were issued submachine guns, this Ranger Captain has chosen to carry an M1 Garand ashore due to its better accuracy and power. He wears the standard uniform shown in photographs on D-Day. HBT fatigues with anti-gas impregnation are worn over wool shirt and trousers. Over this he wears a Winter Combat jacket, and a dark shade assault jacket. The assault jacket was issued only to officers and NCOs in the Rangers. Photos indicate that assault jackets issued to the Rangers were all of the dark shade. He has a pistol belt with .45 and carries extra Garand ammo in a bandoleer. He has strapped an assault gas mask bag to his chest, and tied the parachutist's first-aid pouch to his left shoulder. He wears leather gloves to protect his hands while climbing up the rocky cliffs. His helmet is marked with painted rank insignia, as is seen on photographs of the Rangers boarding their LCAs. Although most photographs of Rangers show them wearing standard boots and leggings before D-day, photos taken after the landings show them with paratrooper boots. Many soldiers issued paratrooper boots preferred to save them for dress occasions, and continued to use their boots with leggings during combat.
(Reconstruction)

Previous page, top.

Previous page, top.
These ten Rangers were awarded the DSC for their actions on D-Day. From left to right are: Col. James E. Rudder, Major Richard P. Sullivan, Capt. Otto Masny, Captain Edgar L. Arnold, Captain Ralph E. Goranson, Capt. Joseph R. Lacy, Lt. George F. Kerchner, T/Sgt. John W. White, Sgt. Julius W. Belcher, and Pfc. William E. Dreher. Of interest is that they all wear paratrooper boots and most have used sections of camouflage parachute material as helmet covers. Rudder's dark colored shirt was optional for officers, but was not supposed to be worn in the field.

Previous page, bottom.
Joseph Lacy was the Chaplain for the 5th Ranger Bn. He landed on Omaha Beach with the rest of his unit and provided assistance to those who were wounded. For his actions on the beach he is being awarded the Distinguished Service Cross. The officer making the presentation is believed to be Lt. Col. Max Schneider, commander of the 5th Ranger Bn.

dummy wooden gun barrels had been left in their place. Patrols headed out to scout the surrounding area and at 0830 Sgt. Lomell and Sgt. Kuhn found a battery of five guns unmanned but ready to fire on Utah Beach. They quickly destroyed the gun barrels with thermite grenades. Some sources claim that these were the 155mm guns previously stationed at Pointe du Hoc. Others claim these were smaller guns, possibly 75mm, which would not have posed much of a danger to the beaches. No definitive source has been found that confirms what size these guns were,

Above.

This is one of the LVCPs that brought German POWs out to the USS Texas. Wounded Rangers can be seen on the right, and the German POWs are at the left by the bow of the craft. The soldier sitting on the edge of the LCVP at top right is a sergeant from the 29th Division.

Left.

A doctor from the U.S.S. Texas has gone down to the LVCP to evaluate the wounded. He is visible in his U.S. Navy khaki uniform about the center of the craft. At the lower right, the soldier with the helmet net wears the Ranger diamond on his field jacket.

although Ranger veterans strongly claim they were the 155mm guns that had been pulled back from the Pointe du Hoc emplacements.

Initially the Rangers cleared the fortified area around Pointe du Hoc and pressed inland to secure the vital Grandcamp road. Col. Rudder suffered his first of three wounds when at 1000 he was shot in the thigh. Communications between the Rangers and the ships offshore were confused due to a last minute change in procedure that had not been sent to the Rangers. The Ranger communications officer, Lt. Eikner, along with the NSFCP and forward observer from the 58th Armored Field Artillery, was able to get some supporting fire which helped the Rangers hold their ground. Three paratroopers from the 101st Div., who had been accidentally dropped nearby during the night, joined the Rangers defending Pointe du Hoc. Two of these paratroops had actually landed on the beach underneath the cliff.

The *U.S.S. Barton* could observe the Rangers moving around the cliff and could see many were bandaged. A wooden whaleboat was sent to shore in an attempt to evacuate some of the casualties. But a German machine gun post a few hundred yards to the east spotted them and fired upon the small boat. One crewman was wounded and the whaleboat returned to the *Barton* without landing.

Even though the German guns were not emplaced on Pointe du Hoc, it was still very important for the Allies to control the area. It provided one of the best views of both of the American beaches, as well as prevented the Germans from using the coastal road to move reinforcements and messengers from one beach to another. About 2100 hrs on the night of 6 June a small group of 23 men, under command of Lt. Charles Parker from the 5th Rangers, made their way to Pointe du Hoc from Omaha. They had cut cross-country and been fortunate in not running into any German resistance. Throughout the night the Germans attempted to infiltrate the Ranger lines and

Right.
A German POW climbs on board the *USS Texas*. In the foreground is a Marine holding a Reising SMG. On the back of this Marine's HBT jacket can be read the words "Marine Detachment." On his helmet is stencilled "M3," the meaning of which remains unknown.

Below.
A U.S. Navy officer on board the *Texas* gives directions to one of the German NCOs captured at Pointe du Hoc.

drive them back. The Rangers continued to hold their positions, running low in ammo and without any food to speak of. The Rangers started using captured German weapons. Finally, about 0400 on 7 June the Germans penetrated the Ranger defenses and drove them back to the fortified area on the Pointe itself.

While Ranger Force A was capturing Pointe du Hoc on D-Day, Force B of Company C managed to climb up the smaller cliffs of Charlie Beach to the right of Omaha. They were joined by men from the 116th Infantry Regt. who had landed off course. Force B moved to the Pointe de la Percée where they found the German emplacements had been destroyed by naval gunfire. At one point they were mistaken for German soldiers by the ships and were shelled by their own Navy until they could signal the ships they were Americans.

Force C, consisting of the 5th Rangers and two companies of the 2nd, had waited offshore as long as possible without getting the signal to land at Pointe du Hoc. As planned, they were diverted to Omaha Beach. When Max Schneider saw Omaha he realized that Dog Green was still under a great deal of enemy fire, so he directed the boats to land further left at Dog White where it appeared quieter. They came ashore at roughly 0740. These Rangers got ashore without too much trouble and, working with the men of the 116th who had already landed, pushed up through the German defenses. It was at this point where General Cota coined a famous Ranger phrase. Although versions differ as to exactly what Cota said, "Rangers lead the way" is used to this day as the official motto of the U.S. Rangers.

With no word on what had happened to Col. Rudder and the men at Pointe du Hoc, Schneider formed a task force on the morning of 7 June to relieve or rescue them. This force was composed of all available men from the 2nd and 5th Rangers, troops from the 116th Infantry, and a handful of tanks from

(Continued on page 218)

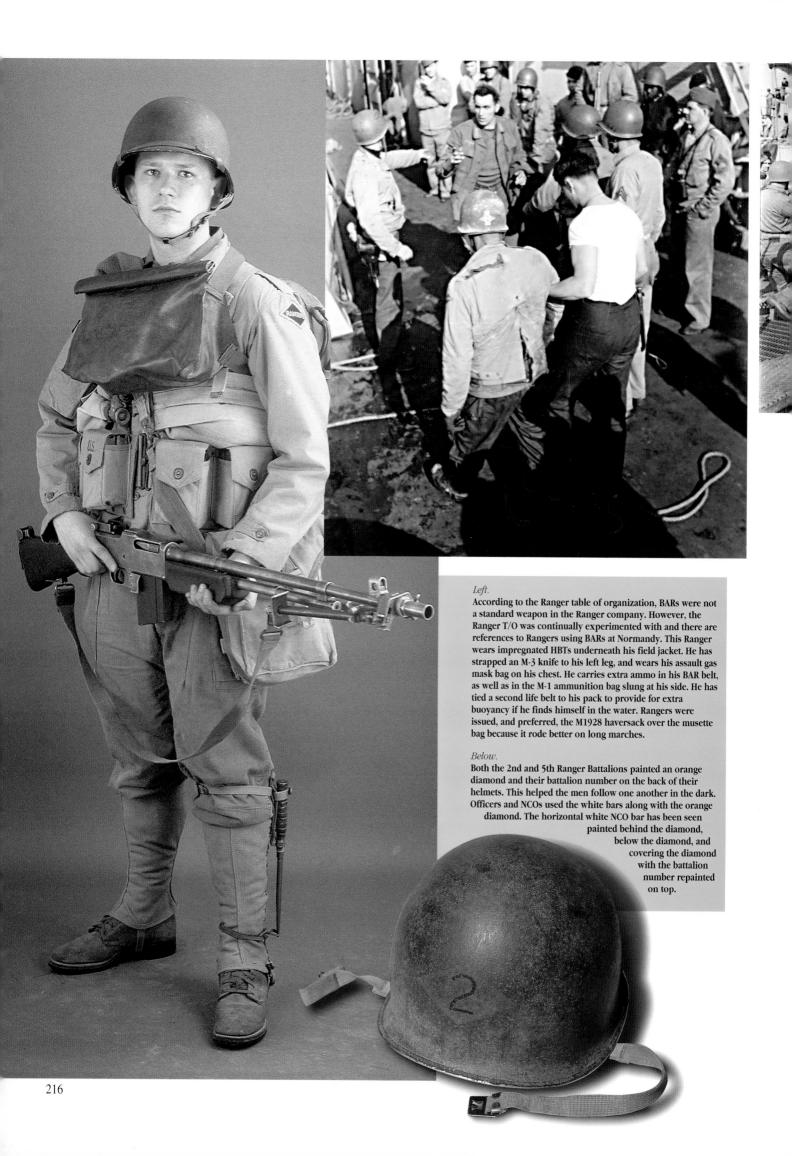

Left.

According to the Ranger table of organization, BARs were not a standard weapon in the Ranger company. However, the Ranger T/O was continually experimented with and there are references to Rangers using BARs at Normandy. This Ranger wears impregnated HBTs underneath his field jacket. He has strapped an M-3 knife to his left leg, and wears his assault gas mask bag on his chest. He carries extra ammo in his BAR belt, as well as in the M-1 ammunition bag slung at his side. He has tied a second life belt to his pack to provide for extra buoyancy if he finds himself in the water. Rangers were issued, and preferred, the M1928 haversack over the musette bag because it rode better on long marches.

Below.

Both the 2nd and 5th Ranger Battalions painted an orange diamond and their battalion number on the back of their helmets. This helped the men follow one another in the dark. Officers and NCOs used the white bars along with the orange diamond. The horizontal white NCO bar has been seen painted behind the diamond, below the diamond, and covering the diamond with the battalion number repainted on top.

Previous page.

A 2nd Ranger Bn. officer is being led to sick bay on board the *Texas*. This photo provides some of the best evidence of the uniform the Rangers wore at Pointe du Hoc: HBT fatigues underneath a field jacket. The Ranger's diamond shaped patch and helmet marking are clearly visible. It was regulation in the ETO for all officers to have a vertical stripe on the back of the helmet.

Above.

Sgt. Joe Sivy is handing earplugs to the POWs. The *U.S.S. Texas* was still providing fire support to the troops on shore, so anyone on deck had to protect their hearing from the 14" naval guns. Sgt. Sivy wears the standard Marine Corps shirt with the distinctive pointed pocket flap. On his pistol belt is a knife scabbard carried just behind the holster.

Right.

This Seahorse insignia was worn on the forest green wool dress uniform of Marines assigned to shipboard duty. It was not worn on the working or combat uniform. Although technically these men were part of the ship's crew, they were first and foremost members of the Marine Corps.

The typical uniform of the Marine Detachment on board the *U.S.S. Texas* on the morning of 6 June was HBT trousers, khaki shirts, and rough out boots. The Marines referred to the HBT trousers as "dungarees," and the boots as "boondockers." The Marines were not scheduled to go ashore, so their HBTs were not impregnated against chemical weapons. A helmet was required above deck due to the danger of not only being shelled by the German coastal guns, but also of falling pieces of anti-aircraft shells. Marine NCOs were issued with .45 caliber pistols, while the enlisted Marines received M1 Garands. Special weapons such as grenades and Reising submachine guns were taken from the armory only on special occasions.

the 743rd Tank Bn. The Allies were still not positive the guns at Pointe du Hoc had been eliminated.

Throughout the day on 7 June (D+1) the Germans continued to press the Rangers trapped at Pointe du Hoc. Thankfully, communications were now working better and the Rangers were able to call for supporting fire from the Navy. Since Col. Rudder had left the *U.S.S. Ancon* to lead the action ashore, there was no one back at headquarters to look out for the Ranger force. One of the staff officers for Admiral Hall, however, was Major Jack Street. Major Street had previously served as commander of Company G, 1st Ranger Battalion. As a Ranger himself, once he learned of the men at Pointe du Hoc trapped without food and running short of ammunition, he had to take action. He was able to get two LCVPs to bring 30 reinforcements, food, and ammunition ashore. The LCVPs then evacuated the worst of the Ranger casualties and the German POWs. No records have been found that identify where the reinforcements came from. One source claims they were men of the 5th Ranger Bn., but one photograph of the POWs

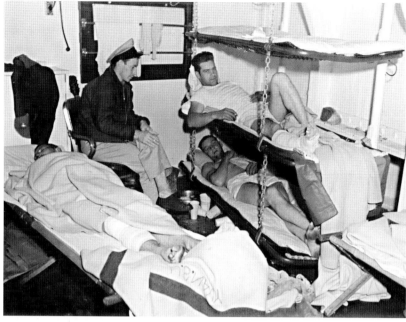

Above.
Wounded Rangers were treated in the *USS Texas* sick bay before being transferred to a hospital ship. Their uniforms have been cut off them in order to get at their wounds. They would later be issued with Navy clothing from the ship's stores.

Left.
It seems like the entire crew of the *Texas* has turned out for their first look at the German Army. Standing on a ventilator, one of the Marines guards the POWs with a Reising SMG. The Reising is thought of as a weapon used only in the Pacific, but it has been issued to the Marine detachments on board ships in the ETO. The Marine wears both the USMC HBT jacket and trousers, but no leggings.

ammo, the Rangers were able to hold on to their small perimeter by the cliffs. At nightfall patrols from the task force relieving them overland were heard nearby. Just after dark some of the advance men for the task force shot on a position where they had heard German weapons being fired. They had no way of knowing the Rangers were using captured German weapons due to their ammo shortage, and wounded one of the defending Rangers. The mistaken identity was rapidly cleared up, but the official relief of Force A at Pointe du Hoc was not conducted until daylight on 8 June, roughly 48 hours after the men had landed.

The Provisional Ranger Group was given one of

being evacuated on the LCVPs clearly shows a soldier wearing a 29th Division patch.

During the day the Rangers at Pointe du Hoc blew up a small ammo dump located in the fortified area to deny it to the Germans if the area was recaptured. Col. Rudder's command post was still in the shell crater next to the cliff, and that cluster of men drew the attention of some Allied aircraft. When it looked as if the Rangers were about to be strafed by their own planes, an American flag was laid out to indicate the area was under Allied control. The aircraft saw the flag, realized their mistake, and moved on.

With the reinforcements and a new supply of

Right.
Marine Captain Herbert Merillat was an observer on board a British LCG at Normandy. He is shown here between Royal Navy Lt. Hugh Ashworth (left) and Royal Marine Lt. George Hardwick. The 4.7 inch guns on the LCG were manned by Royal Marines, which made this vessel a natural place to station an American Marine observer.

the toughest assignments during the Normandy landing. Although they did not find the German guns on Pointe du Hoc, they denied the Germans that important observation point, kept the Grandcamp road closed for much of the first day, and destroyed a German battery that could have caused great damage to Utah Beach. During the first two days they suffered 77 men killed, 152 wounded, and 70 missing.

The United States Marine Corps at Normandy

Amphibious landings were the primary mission of the U.S. Marines, so the question is often asked why the Marines did not take part in Normandy? The answer dates back to the First World War, when the American Army was short of trained soldiers and desperately trying to build up its forces in Europe. Two Marine regiments, the 5th and 6th, were sent to France as half of the four infantry regiments in the U.S. Army's 2nd

Above.
Officers of the 29th Ranger Bn. pose for a group photo in August 1943.
Back row, left to right:
Lt. Davidson, Lt. "Doc" Heffner, Lt. Callahan, Lt. Grass, Lt. Kordymar, Lt. Farrell, Lt. Clemner.
Front row, Left to right:
Lt. McNabb, Capt. Hille, Major Millholland, Capt. Marr, Capt. Ernst, Lt. Dance.
Lt. Eugene Dance was the only Ranger officer to participate in the raids on Norway.

Left.
29th Rangers make their way inland during a beach landing exercise at Bude, England. Much of the special training the Rangers received was in amphibious operations.

Division. A popular tale indicates that the strong inter-service rivalry between the Army and Marine Corps supposedly dates from this time period.

Strict censorship rules in WW1 forbade journalists from mentioning specific units, but allowed the mention of branch of service. When the 2nd Division entered combat, newspapers gave headlines to the Marines, ignoring the Army troops that had fought alongside them. This public relations victory for the Marines left a bitter taste in the mouths of the junior officers of the American Army. When they rose in rank to high command in WW2, it is claimed they kept the Marines out of Europe to make sure the glory went to the Army. The Marines kept to the Pacific, which is thought of as the Marine's war, even though more Army Divisions than Marine Divisions fought there.

There were a handful of U.S. Marines that were sent to Europe. They served three primary functions: guards at U.S. embassies, Marine detachments on the larger U.S. Navy ships, and observers and liaisons to other Allied nations' Marine forces. With a speciality in amphibious operations, the Marines naturally had an interest in the Normandy landings and sent observers to learn what lessons they could from the Anglo-American attempt to land in France. As far as is known, none of these observers took part in combat.

USMC detachments were placed only aboard battleships (2 or 3 officers and roughly 100 enlisted men), heavy and light cruisers (1 officer and roughly 45 enlisted men), and carriers and light carriers (1 or 2 officers and roughly 80 enlisted men). Smaller ships only had a Marine Detachment when the vessel was used as a flagship.

Each of the battleships providing gunfire support at Normandy had a Marine detachment of roughly 84 men. Although they could be used as a small landing party, they generally served as antiaircraft gunners when called to combat stations. On the *Texas* they manned four quad 40mm mounts (two on the fantail and two amidships). By chance, the Marine detach-

Pvt. Jack Womer of the 175th Infantry Regiment is shown here shortly after graduating from the British Commando School. This is one of the few photographs that shows the correct wearing of the 29th Ranger tabs on both shoulders in the British style. Womer was one of the men so upset with the disbanding of the 29th Rangers that he volunteered to join the paratroops so that he could stay in an elite unit. He jumped into Normandy as a member of the 506th demolitions platoon. He firmly believed that his Ranger training was superior to that received by the paratroopers, and could specifically point to incidents where things he learned in the Rangers saved his life.

ment from the battleship *U.S.S. Texas* came very close to playing an historic role in the fighting at Pointe du Hoc.

The 2nd Rangers took heavy casualties at Pointe du Hoc. They held the German gun emplacement, but had no contact with the American forces ashore at Omaha Beach. The planned reinforcements for Pointe du Hoc were diverted to Omaha and the 2nd Rangers grew very short of men. At some point in the afternoon of 7 June they called for the evacuation of casualties, a resupply of ammunition, and reinforcements. The *U.S.S. Texas* was ordered to provide the ammunition for the Rangers and made preparations to get it ashore on a handful of LCVPs sent by the Force "O" Commander. The Marines got the word to prepare to go ashore and reinforce the Rangers defending Pointe du Hoc.

The Marine detachment on board the *Texas* consisted of 83 enlisted men and three officers. It was commanded by Marine Captain Bernard. It appears that one of his lieutenants, Lt. Hammerbeck, pushed hard to be allowed to lead his men ashore to help out the Rangers. The Marines who served on the *Texas* recalled breaking out weapons and grenades and getting ready to go ashore. Most of these Marines had no combat experience and had only been in the Corps for a few months. One of them commented: *"This is going be the biggest goddam slaughter since Custer got his at the Little Big Horn."*

At the last minute an order was given that the Marines would not be allowed to go ashore. They were not even to be allowed to ride shotgun on the LVCPs. There is some debate as to who gave this order. It was passed to the Marines by the Gunnery Officer of the *Texas*, but some veterans recall a rumor that it originated from the senior Army commanders on board the *U.S.S. Ancon*. The rumor indicated that the Army commanders were horrified at the idea of headlines reading *"Marines save Rangers at Normandy."*

The LCVPs pulled aside the *Texas*, loaded up on

Left.
A group of 29th Rangers are shown eating 5-in-1 rations during the testing of field rations. The men wear the typical Ranger outfit of HBT coveralls, paratrooper boots, and the knit wool cap. Clearly visible at top left and lower right is the first pattern British made ETO jacket (with attached belt and slash pockets).

food and ammunition, and took it ashore. What then happened is one of the few cases where the U.S. Marines would face German soldiers. Once the supplies were unloaded at Pointe du Hoc, the Rangers sent the German POWs they had captured back to the *Texas*. The Rangers were so short of manpower, they could not spare guards for their prisoners. This load included 20 Germans, four Italians, and three Frenchmen. 35 wounded Rangers and one dead Coast Guardsman were also evacuated at the same time.

The waters were rough off the coast and the German POWs became seasick. When they pulled up alongside the *Texas*, the coxswain of one of the boats called up to the *Texas* to toss down some buckets and mops. He was not going to allow the Germans to get off his LCVP until they cleaned up the mess they had made. The mops went down, the boat was cleaned, and the Germans climbed up onto the *Texas* to be guarded by the Marine detachment. They were kept on board the *Texas* for only a short while before being transferred to LST 266, which was more appropriate for holding POWs.

As far as is known, the only Marine to set foot in France on D-Day was Col. James E. Kerr. He was a member of Admiral Moon's staff, and was sent in to Utah beach at 1015 hours to evaluate the landing. The *Texas* incident is perhaps the only time where armed U.S. Marines faced German soldiers.

29th Rangers

The exploits of the 2nd and 5th Rangers at Normandy are well known. What is generally not remembered, however, is that there was a large part of a third Ranger Battalion that also landed on Omaha Beach. The men of the 29th Ranger Bn. were scattered through the ranks of the 29th Division, pro-

A handful of veterans recall some, but not all, men continued to wear the 29th Ranger tab on their uniforms at Normandy. This example of the British produced 29th Ranger tab was worn by Lt. Eugene Dance, the only Ranger officer to participate in the raids into Norway. Below it is a British manufactured 506th Parachute Infantry Regiment insignia given to him when he joined the 101st A/B Division just prior to the Normandy invasion.

Right.
The typical uniform worn by the 29th Rangers in England was composed of the one piece HBT coveralls, underneath a British Made wool field jacket. The paratrooper boots were issued to the Rangers after they had completed their Commando training. The American service gas mask was quite bulky, so this Ranger officer carries a British lightweight gas mask in its small green canvas bag.
(Reconstruction)

Below.
Every man in the 29th Rangers was weighed once in the morning and again at night during the ration test. This information could be used to track the dietary effects of eating a constant diet of specific field rations.

viding a highly trained and motivated cadre of NCOs and junior officers. There is no way to determine what impact the 29th Rangers had on the landing, but it appears they may have played a valuable role.

When the 1st Ranger Bn. was sent to the Mediterranean in October 1942, there were no replacements for them in the United States. The War Department was not able to send another Ranger Bn. to England, so the theater command decided to form one out of troops already in England. The order authorizing the formation of this unit stated that the men should *"receive training and experience in actual combat, after which they will return to their organizations."*

Major Randolph Millholland, of the 29th Div., was selected to command this provisional ranger unit. It was generally referred to as the 29th Rangers due to its strong tie with that division. The 29th Rangers was formed on 20 Dec 1942, primarily of volunteers from the 29th Division. A handful of men from other units in England, including at least one from the Air Force, were also accepted. The unit was built around a cadre of three officers and 15 enlisted men from the 1st Ranger Bn. who had been left behind in England for medical reasons.

The first two companies, A and B, consisted of ten officers and 170 men. Before heading to the British Commando School they underwent strenuous physical training to get the men into top shape. At one point the 29th Rangers broke the ETO speed marching record by travelling 27 miles in 7.5 hours.

On 1 Feb 1943 the 29th Rangers arrived at the British Commando School at Achnacarry, Scotland. There they underwent a five week commando course given by Lord Lovat's No. 4 Commando. Ranger veterans have many different memories of this training, but they all agree it was very hard and very good. At Achnacarry the Rangers were trained in all types of Commando work, which included small boat handling on nearby Spean Lake. During the exercises the Commando instructors would fire live rounds near the Rangers to accustom them to the sound of gunfire. One Ranger recalled being hurt during a boat exercise and asked to go see a medic.

Left.
Major General Gerow (then commander of the 29th Division) speaks with Sgt. John O'Brien during an inspection visit to the Commando School in February 1943. In the foreground is the school commandant, Lt. Col. Vaughan.

The instructor's response was: *"You don't stop in the middle of a real landing for sick call, do you?"* and sent him back to finish.

All evidence of the 29th Rangers indicates they were as good as, if not better than, the 1st Ranger Bn. that had passed through the same school. The few remaining records have nothing but praise for these men and their dedication to their training. Upon completion of the school the men were issued paratrooper boots and the 29th Ranger tab. This red insignia was worn on both shoulders, British style, of the dress uniforms.

Two more Ranger companies, C and D, passed through the Commando school in March 1943. From then on the 29th Rangers were never given a rest. They were used to test experimental uniforms including the short wool ETO jacket and combat boots (buckle boots) with both hobnailed and composition soles. The ETO jacket is often mistaken in photographs for the British battledress blouse. This has given rise to the erroneous belief that the Rangers wore British uniforms while serving with the Commandos.

As soon as the first group had finished Commando School, a small detachment of four men, under command of Lt. Eugene Dance, was attached to Northforce as participants in raids on Norway. One

Above.
Pfc. Bill Steadman and Sgt. Heywood, both from Company A, 29th Rangers, demonstrate the typical uniforms worn by the unit. Both men carry the lightweight gas mask bag and wear paratrooper boots, which were issued to the men after they had graduated from the Commando School.
Pfc. Steadman carries the BAR and Sgt. Heywood has a Thompson submachine gun. He has wrapped a rag around the magazine well opening to prevent dirt from getting inside.

of the enlisted men became ill at the last moment, so only Dance and three enlisted men took part. Northforce, under the command of Commando Captain Gilcrist, was a composite group of British Commandos and Norwegian volunteers in Motor Torpedo Boats (MTB) given the task of harassing German shipping off the Norwegian coast.

Most published sources claim the small group of Rangers took part in only four raids into Norway. In a recent interview with Lt. Dance, he claims that he personally took part in at least five raids. Three of the raids were relatively simple. The MTB would make the 90 mile run to Norway and then be tied up and camouflaged in a fjord. The commandos would climb to high ground and observe local shipping movements. A fourth operation was unsuccessful due to faulty intelligence. The German installation had been abandoned long before the operation took place and the raiders went home empty handed.

For these operations the British lent the Rangers white snow parkas for camouflage and leather jerkins for warmth. Lt. Dance was quite firm in his statement that at no time did they wear British battledress while in Norway. The Rangers always wore their own American equipment and uniforms and carried M1 Garands. So taken were the commandos with the Garand, that they traded a Thompson submachine gun for a Garand.

Operation Roundabout was the 5th raid into Norway. On 23 March 1943 Captain Gilcrist of No. 12 Commando, the four Rangers, five Norwegians from No. 10 Commando (IA), and two men from No. 12 Commando went ashore at Landet near Roydenfjord. The published accounts differ, but Dance recalls that intelligence claimed the Germans were supposed to withdraw from the area at night to a more secure base inland. As the raiders crept up to the supposedly empty buildings, a German soldier came out a door. One of the Norwegians went to fire his Thompson, but the clip had not been seated right and fell out, alerting the German. The second man in line shot the German, but the garrison was alerted and a brisk fire fight ensued. Realizing that the element of surprise had been lost, the British commander of the raid ordered the men back to the boats.

In an after-action report, the British unjustly criticized the Americans for their lack of aggressiveness and singled out Lt. Dance for leaving his pack behind. Dance later recalled that he had dropped his musette bag while diving for cover and every time he went to reach for it, "it jumped" a little from German bullets. He decided it was better to just leave it there, as it contained nothing of importance.

While Dance and his men were in the North, other Rangers were attached to various Commando units as well. A few Rangers were assigned to instruct French Commandos on the use of American weapons. One Ranger veteran, Walter Hedlund, recalls crossing the Channel with the French Commandos to raid the French coast, but at the last minute the operation was cancelled and the boats returned to England. There are unsubstantiated rumors that a handful of other Rangers took part in Commando operations during this time period, but none have been confirmed.

In July 1943 the Quartermaster Corps selected the Rangers to test combat rations for a 22 day period. The Rangers were put through constant field exercises while their weight and health was monitored. Each company was allowed to eat only a specific type of ration: Company A- C rations; Company B- K rations; Company C- a mixture of C, K, and D

rations; and Company D- 5-in-1 rations. As a control group the headquarters troops ate 12-in-1 rations. The Rangers hiked an average of 15 miles a day in combat conditions. Eleven men were hospitalized from injuries. At times the moors were so dense with fog that scouts would become lost for hours at a time.

In September the 29th Rangers took advanced assault training at Dorlin House with Commando and Royal Marine units. One aspect of this training was a competition with other units where they tried to take the other teams' weapons away. The Rangers beat all the other teams they played, which included not only Commandos and Royal Marines, but French Marines as well. It was noted by their instructors that the 29th Rangers were the best group of soldiers to have ever passed through the school.

While at Dorlin House, a group of Rangers took part in a raid on a German radar station on the Ile d'Ouessant, off the Brittany coast. The radar station was destroyed, 20-30 Germans killed, but no prisoners were taken. This time the Rangers purposely left behind a helmet and cartridge belt marked with the name *"Millholland"* and *"U.S. Rangers."* This was to make the Germans think that American Rangers were now becoming active in raids and divert more manpower to protecting their coastal installations in Brittany.

A larger 100 man raid was being planned when the unit was suddenly disbanded on 18 October 1943. This came as a shock to the Rangers, who had gone through some of the most rugged training in the ETO and felt their unit was second to none. They had earned nothing but praise and thought they would be playing an important role in the coming invasion of France. No reason was given for the disbanding of the 29th Rangers, but it was clear from the original orders that it was always intended to give this group of men special training and experience, then return them to their units to increase each unit's effectiveness.

When returned to the 29th Division, most of the Rangers were given a promotion in rank and were expected to pass on what they had learned. A few Rangers were so disappointed in going back to a regular infantry

unit that they transferred to airborne divisions. Lt. Dance was ordered to set up a sniper school for the 175th Inf. Regt. When no students were sent to the school, he felt he was wasting his time and was readily accepted into the 101st Airborne Division. He earned his jump wings by making five

jumps in one day in England, then reported to an assembly area in preparation for the Normandy jump. He took over as a platoon leader in the 506th Parachute Infantry Regt. only one week before D-Day.

When the 29th Division landed on Omaha Beach there were former Rangers scattered through all its combat units. Many of the NCOs and junior officers had gone through the toughest training the British Commandos could provide and had developed a great deal of personal initiative. There is no way of knowing what impact this had on the 29th Division, but from numerous interviews with veterans it seems clear that the former Rangers were thought of as some of the best men in the Division.

There are many stories that tell of a former Ranger taking charge and pushing the attack when others hesitated. It may be that the Army deliberately chose the 29th Division for their temporary Ranger unit, to provide a strong backbone to this untested National Guard unit. They may have known the 29th Division would play a major role in the most important operation of the war. A few hundred ex-Rangers, placed in leadership positions through the 29th Division, toughened to the sound of gunfire and explosions, may have made all the difference on the morning of the 6th of June.

Major Randolph Millholland

In 1944 Major Randolph Millholland was a 36-year-old accountant from Cumberland, Maryland. He had enlisted as a private in the Maryland National Guard in 1924, was commissioned as a Lieutenant in 1932, and made captain of Co. G/1st Maryland Infantry in 1935. When his unit was federalized, it became company G, 115th Infantry Regt. Once in England he was selected to attend the British Battle School. Millholland was in top physical condition and had been heavily involved with the divisional fitness training program. His company had set many of the 29th Division's fitness and military training records. When the orders were issued to form a Ranger Bn., Millholland was the logical choice.

After the disbanding of the 29th Rangers, Millholland was made Executive Officer of 2/115th. When someone noticed he had a civilian pilot's license, he was sent to the 9th Air Force to help develop new procedures for ground support tactics. Frustrated with missing D-Day, Millholland finally got back to the 29th Division in July 1944. He was then assigned to command 3/115th. In November 1944 he was wounded in the leg by artillery fire and was sent to a hospital in England.

Millholland recovered and after the war continued to play an important role in the Maryland National Guard. He was finally promoted to the rank of Brigadier General and the National Guard Armory in Hagertown, Maryland is named after him. Almost unknown outside the circles of the 29th Division, "Randy" Millholland will always be as important to the 29th Ranger Bn. as Col. Darby is to the 1st Ranger Bn., and Col. Rudder to the 2nd Ranger Bn.

OF all the special units that took part in the Normandy operation, none have been so forgotten as the Navy Beach Battalions. These sailors, serving under Army command, played a vital role on the beaches not only on D-Day, but for the weeks that followed. The Navy, for the most part, has all but forgotten them.

When the U.S. Navy commissioned the *U.S.S. Normandy* in 1989, they invited dozens of Army

U.S. Navy Beach Battalions

Above.
This highly staged photo of a beachmaster operating on a hostile shore was taken at an American training base. It was part of the Navy's effort to publicize the importance of the Beach Battalions. Although period newspapers and magazines do occasionally feature articles on these units, for the most part the Navy Beach Battalions of the ETO have been largely ignored for the past 50 years.

veterans of the invasion, but none from the Beach Battalions.

Amphibious operations in World War Two were handled differently in the Pacific and European theaters. The rationale for this is often confusing, but stems from the Army-Navy rivalry that dates back for many years. The U.S. Army had never been faced with an amphibious landing in modern warfare. In World War One the troops were able to land at Allied held ports. In theory, any beach landings would be handled by the U.S. Marines, who would capture a beachhead upon which the Army would later land and press inland.

Faced with the possibility of an amphibious war in

the Pacific greater than anything previously considered, it was apparent that the tiny Marine force could not be called upon for every amphibious operation. The Army and Navy held manoeuvres in 1941 to test their ability to land on enemy held territory. Due to lack of experience and trained manpower, the first attempts were not good. The Army blamed the Navy, and vice versa.

The Navy realized that a war in the Pacific would be much more of a naval war than the fight in Europe, and wanted to dominate in the fight against Japan. The Army did not want a repeat of World War One, where the Marines received a greater share of credit for their fighting in France than the Army felt they should have.

In most of the amphibious landings in the Pacific, the coordination of landing craft was handled by "beach parties" formed from the regular crews of the transport ships. These beach parties, of about 30 men, served as regular ship's crew until "condition 1A" was called (invasion stations). Then they made their way to the beach and took care of all ship-to-shore functions. When the landing of the troops from their ship was finished, the beach party returned to their vessel and left. The beach operations would be handed over to an Army unit that would stay until a port system had been set up. In the southwest Pacific, amphibious operations were handled by General MacArthur's three Engineer Special Brigades.

Generally, landings in the Pacific were small in size, no more than a few divisions. In Europe, Operation Torch in North Africa called for a number of divisions to be landed, followed up by corps and then armies. There was a great deal of confusion in these landings and it became clear that in large operations such as this there must be a stronger link between the Navy and the Army. The result was the Navy Beach Battalion: a unit specifically designed to bridge the gap between the sea and the land. These units would be independent of any ship and able to handle all necessary functions on an invasion beach.

The first Naval Beach Battalion (NBB) landed in North Africa in late 1942. The battalion was given instruction by one of the Army Engineer Special Brigades (ESB). From that point on, NBBs were to be attached as part of an Engineer Special Brigade. The specific duties assigned to the NBBs were to handle all shore to ship communications, clear and

Above.
Training at Ft. Pierce, Florida, these officers wear their visored caps because they are not in a combat situation. It is interesting to note that the unit was using Army issue coveralls even before they were shipped overseas. Enlisted men in this situation would have worn the typical white sailor's hat.
(Courtesy Ken Davey)

Below.
Taken in 1943 at Camp Bradford, Virginia, officers from Company C, 6th NBB wear the one-piece HBT coverall with "USN" stencilled on the front. With close examination the number "6" can be seen painted on their helmets. The "six" was worn while training in the States, and was replaced by the red arc and gray band for Normandy.
(Courtesy Ken Davey)

mark sea lanes for landing craft, perform minor repairs on small boats, and treat and arrange for evacuation of casualties from the beach.

The commander of the NBB was the Beachmaster. He was in charge of everything up to the high tide line on the beach he was assigned to. Some beaches were too large for one man to control, so NBB company and platoon leaders were given the task of being beachmasters of their own specific sector of the beach. Beachmasters have been called "the traffic cops of the invasion" because they directed the landing of every craft, no matter how large or how small.

Organization of the Naval Beach Battalions

An NBB was composed of three companies (A, B, and C). Each company had three platoons, referred to by their company letter, and a number from one to nine. Thus the first platoons of each company were A-1, B-4 and C-7. During landing operations each NBB would be attached to an Army ESB. Each NBB company was then attached to an ESB battalion, and in turn each NBB platoon was then attached to a specific ESB company. Each sector of an invasion beach assigned to an Army Regimental Combat Team was run by a "battalion beach group." This beach group was composed of an ESB engineer bn. along with its assigned NBB company. The NBB platoons took care of matters below the high tide mark, while the Army engineers were responsible for problems above it. This is the theory of how the NBBs were supposed to function, but it could be modified depending upon the local circumstances.

In order to fulfil its assigned duties, each NBB platoon had four sections: communications, hydrographic, medical and small boat repair. The communications section handled all Navy related ship-to-shore messages by use of blinker lights, flags, and radios. The hydrographic section was responsible for marking sea lanes, removing obstacles, and handling the ropes of landing craft. Each medical section had a doctor to take care of casualties before they could be evacuated, and the Navy corpsmen were in charge of getting casualties from the beach out to the evacuation landing craft. The small boat repair section initially repaired only minor breakdowns in their

sector. After the first landings all repair sections would group together to form one large unit to perform major repairs.

An NBB platoon was commanded by a Navy Lieutenant, who had at his disposal a small headquarters and mess section, as well as 5 jeeps, 1 radio jeep, 1 truck, and 2 bulldozers. Specific types and quantities of vehicles appear to fluctuate from unit to unit during the war. At Normandy the 6th NBB was listed as having 32 vehicles and 373 men, while the 7th had only 15 vehicles and 541 men. The difference in organization has not been explained, but these units were frequently tailored to fit a specific landing.

For the Normandy invasion the 6th NBB (under the 5th ESB) was assigned the eastern sector of Omaha Beach. The western sector of Omaha was given to the 7th NBB (under the 6th ESB). Utah was handled by the veteran 2nd NBB (under the 1st ESB). There are some records that appear to indicate the 5th NBB was in England during the invasion and was supposed to reinforce the others at Normandy, or take part in a later operation planned for Brittany. No information on the actual plans for the 5th NBB have

been located. Some veterans theorize that the references were a typographic error stemming from the "5th ESB," and had never heard of the 5th NBB ever being in England.

Uniforms and insignia of the Naval Beach Battalions

While in the USA NBBs trained wearing Army HBT one-piece coveralls, rough-out boots (which they called "beach shoes"), and leggings. They were not given any special insignia or patches, and only wore their standard Navy ratings. The 8th NBB, which saw action in the invasion of southern France, did design a shoulder patch while training at Camp Little Creek, Va. Soon after this patch was made and distributed to the men, the base commander ordered it removed because it looked "too Army." As far as is known, no other NBB ever made a unit insignia. The 9th NBB did come up with a design, but it was only used once, on the plaque given to its commander when the unit was disbanded.

On 20 January 1944, the 6th NBB under Commander Eugene Carusi arrived in Salcombe, England to prepare for the invasion of France. Shortly after arriving at the Assault Training Center, the unit was issued paratrooper boots and M41 field jackets. Tests by the Army amphibious forces had determined that the high paratrooper boots were the best footgear to use in surf because they kept out sand better than lower boots. The sailors were given M3 trench knives to add to their Army webbing equipment and some were able to exchange their long Navy bayonets for the shorter Army ones. At first the NBBs carried the Navy MK IV double hose gas mask, but by June they had turned these in for the

Above.
A signal unit from the 7th NBB training in England. This picture illustrates the three major types of communications the men were trained in. In the center a team sends a message in Morse code on the blinker light. At right a lieutenant (the equivalent to an Army captain) uses an SCR-536 Handie-Talkie to communicate with the beachmasters to either side. On his Navy issue gas mask bag can be made out the letters "CARPEN.." This identifies him as Lt. Carpenter of the 7th NBB. The white arm band with letter "B" is an early attempt to indicate the beachmaster of an area. These were not used in Normandy. On the left waits a sailor ready to use his red and yellow semaphore flags. Their helmets have been painted with "USN 7" in red. Shortly before D-Day they would add a red arc and gray band.

Right.
On the East Coast most of the Navy amphibious forces were trained at Little Creek, Virginia.

Army assault mask that came in a black rubber bag. Medics were issued the Army medical pouches with wide suspenders. These men were authorized to wear the red cross armband, but it seems that few (at least in the 6th NBB) actually did. The men were also issued Navy foul weather clothing (lined dark blue jackets, trousers, and hat) but it was not worn in the invasion as it was too bulky.

The NBBs were in the curious position of being Navy sailors under Army control and their source of supply was confusing. Photos exist showing NBB men with early Army style gas masks, alongside men with the Navy issue gas masks. This is explained by the fact that any items needing replacement were made up out of Army quartermaster stocks. The Army was not always willing to part with the needed materials, so the 6th earned the nickname "Commander Carusi and his four hundred thieves."

In the 7th NBB it seems many of the men were not issued paratrooper boots, but they were given winter combat jackets. Some of the men stencilled USN in 3" high red letters on the back. A number of them added extra touches such as their name and hometown.

The men of the NBBs were sailors first and foremost. They tried their best not to lose their Navy identity while surrounded by the Army. While on liberty (on pass) they wore their dress blue uniform and bloused their baggy trousers into the high
paratrooper

Left.
This rare photo shows one of the platoons from Company A, 6th NBB while training in England. Most of the men wear the Army style rubber foul weather gear with the metal buckle closures. The NBBs were issued a mixture of Army and Navy uniforms and equipment.

Right.
A NBB communications section in action at a Slapton Sands practice landing. The signalman is wearing the Navy foul weather oilskin coat and both men have the dark blue foul weather cloth helmet. Taken before issue of paratrooper booots, this sailor has pulled up his socks in an attempt to keep sand out of his boots. Note the blinker light being held by the sitting man.

Left.
This 2nd NBB signalman directs a ship heading for shore. He stands in front of the Utah Beach sea wall. A few of the steel hedgehog beach obstacles are visible in the background. They were probably bulldozed up out of the way and it was easier to just let them sit there. Eventually the steel beams would be welded onto the front of tanks to help break through the hedgerows. The sailor wears the rubberized foul weather jacket and trousers for protection against the wind and sea spray.

boots. They took delight in telling curious British civilians that they were "Navy paratroopers."

At one point someone decided that the 6th NBB should supply men for guard duty at the Army base where they were stationed. The sailors turned out in their dress blue uniforms with white hats and black scarves to man the gates. The base commander decided he did not want anyone to see sailors manning his gates and never again assigned them guard duty.

Each NBB section was armed differently. The hydrographic section carried M1903 Springfield rifles. The small boat repair crews carried M1 carbines. The medical section had been issued with .45 pistols for guard duty in England, but did not bring them to France. The petty officers (NCOs) leading each section were given Thompson SMGs, and the platoon commander carried both a carbine and a .45 pistol.

Above.
A signalman of the 7th Beach Bn. uses a blinker during a practice landing somewhere in England. The NBB Communications Section was responsible for naval messages sent from the shore out to ships waiting off the coast. Their primary function was to direct vessels to land at the correct time and place. The helmet has been painted with the red "7 NBB," but has not yet gotten the gray band or red arc.

Above.
This beachmaster command post on Utah Beach reveals a number of unusual details. A pile of explosives, in the thin fabric satchel they were issued in, is stacked in front of the sea wall. The post is equipped with both a blinker light and a loudspeaker system to direct the incoming landing craft. An electric generator powering the systems can be seen to the left of the post. Both sailors lying on the beach hold their black rubber gas mask bags.

Right.
Platoon A-2, 2d NBB, medical section at Utah. This mixture of signalmen and medics shows various methods of painting the helmet. This battalion was a veteran unit with service in the Mediterranean, so that may account for their being able to obtain tanker's jackets and the different helmet markings. The paratrooper boots are quite visible in this shot.

NBB distinguishing marks

While training in the States, the sailors of the 6th NBB tried to ensure that they were not mistaken for Army troops. The entire unit stencilled the letters "USN" on their field jackets and coveralls. Shortly before the invasion, an order was given to all Navy troops who might operate on the beaches to paint a gray band (2 inches high) around their helmets and paint "USN" in large letters on the front and back of their uniforms. It is believed that at the same time the men of Company A, 6th NBB painted the waist belt of their coveralls in the same gray color. This order served two purposes: it identified the sailors who might be wearing unfamiliar uniforms to any nervous and trigger-happy soldiers, and prevented the sailors from being pressed into the inland fighting while they still had a job to do on the beach.

At some point another order directed both the 6th and 7th NBBs to paint red arcs on their helmets. This was to signify they were members of the beach organization and had essential duties in the beach area. The 7th NBB, under Commander Leaver, had previously painted a red "7" and "USN" on their helmets. They added the red arc and covered up part

(Continued on page 234)

This member of the 2nd NBB on Utah Beach wears a Navy rubberized parka (note the metal buckles) to protect against the offshore winds and salt spray. He continues to carry his assault gas mask in case of German chemical attack. The SCR-536 is used to communicate with the beach units to either side of him. He has picked up a section of camo uflage parachute to use as a scarf, which was commonly done on Utah Beach.

Below.

These men of the 2nd NBB on Utah Beach have a hand-lettered "USN" on their helmets. Clearly visible on each man are the amphibious assault gas masks. The sailor at the left is wearing the tanker's jacket under his foul weather parka, and the central figure has obtained some camouflage parachute material to wear as a neck scarf. This may have been obtained from the Mediterranean, the drop zones directly behind the beach, or from a casualty being evacuated. In the foreground lies an indispensable "Handie-talkie".

A tale of two helmets

Ensign Joe Vaghi, commander of platoon C-8, 6th NBB, wore the helmet pictured below as he went ashore on 6 June. While bending over to move a 1st Div. casualty out of the path of some vehicles, an artillery blast swept this helmet off his head and knocked him unconscious. When he came to his clothing was on fire and he had to beat out the flames. He picked up the closest helmet to him, which came from the casualty he had been moving. Then Vaghi noticed a nearby jeep, filled with gasoline and ammo, that was on fire. The jeep was surrounded by wounded men unable to move. Ensign Vaghi charged into the flames and removed the ammo and gasoline before it could explode. For this action Vaghi was awarded the Bronze Star for valor. Vaghi continued to wear the 1st Division helmet *(right)* for the next few weeks until one of this men found the original helmet and returned it to him. Vaghi retained the 1st Division helmet as a souvenir, with an idea of trying to return it to its original owner someday.

The blue "6" on Vaghi's original helmet *(below)* had remained a mystery until recently. It seems that the 6th Beach Bn. used this marking while training in the USA. For some reason Ensign Vaghi never repainted his helmet with the correct D-Day markings.

The story of the 1st Division helmet continued. The 1st Div. Association, using the partial serial number written on the chinstrap, claims to have traced the original owner of the helmet to a veterans' hospital. This veteran had no interest in getting his helmet back because he did not want to remember being wounded on the beach. The helmet was then presented to the 1st Division Cantigny Museum in Wheaton, Illinois.

Below.
This photograph of Ensign Vaghi was taken in Colleville-sur-mer about 10 June 1944. Vaghi had spent the first 36 hours of the invasion working without sleep, and in the three weeks he spent directing boat traffic he was only able to get off the beach once for a quick visit to the nearest town. A *Stars and Stripes* photographer caught him on film trading invasion money to local residents. On his left shoulder a gas brassard can be seen indicating that the threat of gas was still taken seriously. The strap of his assault gas mask bag is around his left leg. The helmet in this photo is the exact same 1st Div. helmet pictured above. Ensign Vaghi wears an M41 field jacket over HBT fatigues and wool shirt.

of the "USN" with the gray band. The men used the width of a playing card to mark an even band around the helmet, and painted it by hand.

The 2nd NBB (on Utah Beach) also painted the gray band on their helmets and painted the letters "USN", but did not use an arc of any kind. Photographic evidence clearly shows the gray band broken in front with either black stencilled or hand lettered "USN" on the front. NBBs taking part in the Southern France landings would use similar gray bands on their helmets, but only the 6th and 7th NBB would ever use the red arc.

These helmet markings may vary from company to company. The commander of platoon C-8 (6th NBB), Ensign Joseph Vaghi, had only his name and a blue number "6" on his helmet, However his men had helmets with the standard gray band, red arc, and USN. In the next platoon the men had

stencilled the number of their platoon on the back ("C-9"). The blue "six" had been painted on their helmets during training in the States, and it is unknown why Vaghi did not repaint his helmet in the typical Normandy style. It may be that he was busy with other duties on the day everyone painted the helmets.

Just prior to the invasion these sailors were issued with a two piece gas impregnated HBT suit. Some of the men were given gas brassards to wear along with the assault gas mask. On D-Day it appears that most of the men wore the two-piece HBTs, their M41 field jacket, lifebelts and their own personal field gear. The HBT coveralls were carried in their packs as a change of clothing. Some of the men in the 2nd NBB had obtained winter combat jackets during their service in the Mediterranean. These had the

letters "USN" added on the front and back.

Everyone had a special load to bring ashore. The signalmen had their radios and blinker lights and the medics their litters, blankets and extra medical supplies. To aid in communications between the different sectors of the beach, the platoon commanders carried an SCR-536 handie-talkie so they could talk with the beachmasters on either side of them.

At some point after the initial landings the NBB men obtained the Navy rubberized foul weather jacket and pants. It is assumed this was part of their unit supplies brought ashore by their headquarters. The foul weather uniform helped to keep them dry while working in the surf. It seems that the more experienced men of the 2nd NBB may have worn their foul weather clothing ashore, whereas the 6th and 7th seem to have picked them up sometime after 6 June.

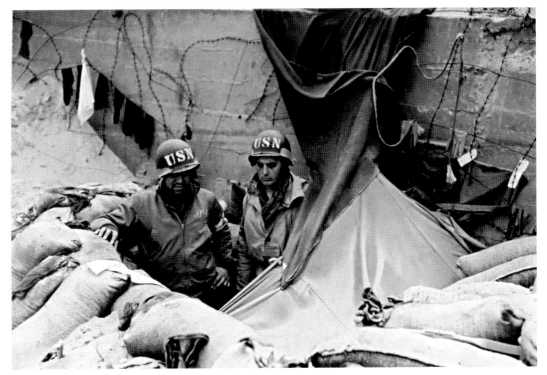

Left.
Two men from the 2nd NBB stand in their dugout on Utah Beach. Note the laundry drying on the barbed wire behind them. These men would frequently have to work in the surf helping disabled landing craft. One sailor has a camouflaged neck scarf from parachute material. This was much more commonly seen in units operating in the Utah Beach area due to the airborne landings that took place inland from them.

Below.
This 2nd NBB sailor writes home on a box marked to the "Wrigley Gum Company, January 1944." The unit had previously served in the Mediterranean and that is where many men obtained the winter combat jacket. Of interest is the black "USN" stencil on this jacket. White letters were added just before D-Day for greater visibility.

Demolitions

Technically, the hydrographic sections were in charge of clearing and marking all obstacles below the high-water mark. The hydrographic men received training in demolitions, but there were too few of them to clear the large number of obstacles on Utah and Omaha Beaches. The Navy sent specially trained Naval Combat Demolitions Units (NCDUs) to England to assist in the obstacle clearance, and placed these NCDUs under administrative control of the NBBs.

The NCDUs were, at first, ignored by the Army engineers in England. The NCDUs issued a report that a handful of NCDUs and hydrographic men would not be able to open up the proposed landing beaches due to the ever growing number of obstacles. The report was ignored by higher command until Commander Carusi put his career in jeopardy by bringing this information to the senior commanders. Carusi's efforts were successful and the NCDUs were transferred to Army control for

Left.
This Navy recovery and repair station may be the combined small boat repair group from the 2nd NBB on Utah Beach. During the initial hours of the invasion each platoon's small boat repair section operated alone on its stretch of the beach. Once the beach was secure their heavier equipment would arrive and they would all join together to form a larger repair group to handle tougher boat repair jobs.

Above.

This is the field jacket worn by Joe Geary, 6th Naval Beach Battalion, on D-Day. The right sleeve is ripped where he was hit by shrapnel. He had stencilled "USN" on the back in black paint before the invasion, possibly even before arriving in England. Geary was able to keep his Normandy uniforms because he had reported everything lost on Omaha Beach, and was provided a new issue by the Navy. He left his Normandy souvenirs at home during his first leave.

D–Day in the Special Engineer Task Force. After the landings, the NCDUs would again revert to the NBBs for administrative control.

NBBs on D-Day

Beach battalion units were to be among the first waves to land on the shore. The strong eastward currents, as well as enemy fire, caused many of them to land in the wrong location. The Army engineers had such a hard time opening the exits from Omaha Beach that by 0830 a 7th NBB beachmaster (in the 29th Division sector) sent out an order to temporarily cease all landings of vehicles on the beach. There was no more room on the beach and no way to get vehicles off it. Landings were restricted to infantry and engineers on foot until the exits were open.

Since the NBBs were considered very important to the landings, they did not come in as complete units. They were split up among a number of ships and

Above right.

Lt. J. Russell Davey was the Navy doctor in the medical section of Ensign Joe Vaghi's platoon C-8, 6th NBB. This selection of Lt. Davey's wartime souvenirs includes his HBT coveralls, assault gas mask, M1928 haversack, some of his medals and ribbons, as well as his helmet.
(Courtesy Ken Davey)

Right.

The commander of the Beach Battalion was the primary beachmaster for the whole beach, but each junior officer had his own subsector of beach he was responsible for. Each beach area would have its own command post to direct operations in that area. The sign is in a special box that allows for dim back illumination at night.

Lt. J. Russell Davey's helmet is painted with the typical gray band and red arc. Unlike other officers who painted a lieutenant's bar on the front to signify rank, Davey painted a thick and thin stripe (taken from the sleeve braid worn on his Navy dress uniform) with a small white oak leaf above signifying Navy Medical Corps. *(Courtesy Ken Davey)*

BEACH BATTALION HELMET MARKINGS IN NORMANDY

FRONT		
6th NBB A Company	6th NBB B Company	6th NBB C Company

BACK		
USN		TAYLOR
6th NBB A Company	6th NBB B Company	6th NBB C Company

FRONT		
USN 7	USN	✚ USN
7th NBB	2nd NBB	2nd NBB Medical Section

6th Naval Beach Battalion helmets

Left and right.
Herbert Goodrick was one of the sailors in Platoon C-9. His helmet also has the two-inch gray band and red arc typical of the 6th and 7th NBB on Omaha Beach. On the rear of his helmet he has added "USN" in black and in red "C-9." From the way the grey band is painted it appears the USN was done first. The helmets of the Beach Battalions were all painted slightly different. The painting was done on a section or platoon basis and there was enough leeway for men to add their own small touches.
(Courtesy Herbert Goodrick)

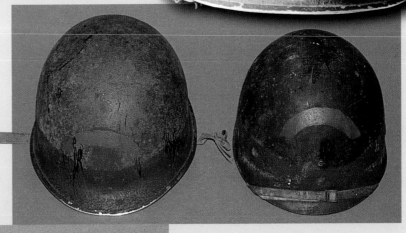

Right.
Front of helmet shell and liner worn by Joe Geary of platoon A-2, 6th NBB on Omaha Beach. The chinstrap was cut by shrapnel on the beach, which also ripped off the helmet net. Each helmet and liner in the unit was hand-painted by the owner. The red arc was worn only by members of the 6th and 7th NBBs on Omaha Beach.

Left.
Rear view of Joe Geary's helmet. The "USN" appears to have been worn only by members of A Company in the 6th NBB.

assigned to different landing waves. This ensured that a lucky hit would not knock out an entire beach control section. Many of the Omaha units were therefore scattered, but gradually the men made their way to their proper destinations and started to put the original plans into action.

By 1200 on 6 June the first ship-to-shore communications net was established. Three more were in place later that day. Slowly the fighting moved inland, the shelling on the beach slowed down, and the NBBs were able to work unhampered by sniper fire. By 2200 all platoons of the 6th NBB had reorganized and were operating their assigned beach sector.

At first the medical sections provided some of the only aid to casualties on the beach. They started moving the wounded to casualty points and gave what care they could. Once more medical units had come ashore, the NBB medics turned over the casualty collection areas to the Army and started their main job of evacuating the wounded. The medical units of the ESBs began to collect and treat the wounded. The NBB medics took care of bringing the casualties to the landing craft which would take them out to a hospital ship. In some cases this meant

Above.
The gray band on the helmet and lack of red arc identifies this man as a member of the 2nd NBB on Utah Beach. The sign next to him can be lit from behind after dark. No open lights were allowed at night, but dim lighting in signs like this allowed beach operations to continue long into the night.

Below.
This area has been marked as one of the casualty collection points on the beach. One of the primary functions of the Beach Battalions was to coordinate the evacuation of casualties on landing craft. They attempted to make sure that every landing craft that unloaded on the beach took on as many wounded as possible and delivered them to specified hospital ships. This service allowed the Army medics to concentrate on treating the wounded further ashore.

carrying a stretcher out into deep water to get a man on board a craft for evacuation.

The communications men were not the only ones concerned with signals on that day. Army communications were handled by the ESB JASCO units (Joint Assault Signal Companies). Each JASCO handled all communications for their Engineer Special Brigade. Normally, the Navy would have attached a naval communications unit to the JASCOs, but it had been decided that the NBB communications sections were sufficient for all Navy signals. The JASCOs handled signals from the Army troops ashore to their headquarters on ships, the NBB men handled communications dealing only with Navy matters such as where a ship was to anchor or at what beach a landing craft should come in. This separation of communications networks did allow for a redundancy of communications links between shore and sea, but did add some confusion regarding who was supposed to speak with who.

Men of the invasion

Sailor Joe Geary's story is typical. He landed early in the morning of 6 June as a member of the hydrographic section, platoon A-2, 6th NBB. Leaving his landing craft, he was forced to swim part of the way to shore and found cover behind a broached LCVP. The Germans shelled the craft that he, and a few other men, were hiding behind. One blast caused him multiple shrapnel wounds, ripped off his helmet net and cut his chin strap. As he ran for the cover of the dunes, Geary heard a wounded man crying for help. He went back through the German fire to pick up this badly wounded casualty and carried him to safety. He then made his way, with the casualty, to an aid station. There they were both treated. Geary spent the night in a shallow foxhole and was evacuated the next morning. Although his wounds prevented him from performing his hydrographic section tasks, he nevertheless saved the life of another man.

Clyde Whirty of the 6th NBB came in later driving a bulldozer on which he had hung a small American flag. Whirty was pushing some of the beach obstacles into a pile when the Germans knocked out his dozer. He took down his flag and found another bulldozer not in use, rehung his flag and went back to work. Again the bulldozer was hit by the Germans.

He recovered his flag a second time and was about to put it on a third dozer when his Lieutenant said "*I'm not telling you to take down that flag, but that's what they're shooting at.*" So Whirty carefully folded up the flag and went back to work. The Germans did not shoot at this bulldozer and Whirty continued to help clear the beach.

One of the seamen from platoon C-9, 6th NBB, was Bob Guigere. He struggled to shore and found himself separated from his unit. A number of infantrymen from the 16th Infantry Regiment were trying to break through the German defenses and kept yelling "*Get off the beach!*" Guigere decided that since he had lost contact with his own unit, the best thing to do was try and help some people who seemed to know what they were doing. Instead of sitting by himself on the beach waiting for someone to tell him what to do, he pitched in and soon found himself crawling under barbed wire to get at some pillboxes. The infantrymen tossed him grenades across an antitank ditch and he relayed them to an infantryman by a pillbox. This man was able to toss the grenades right into the pillbox opening. Guigere moved up with the infantry into Colleville-sur-Mer and helped evacuate a number of Frenchmen hiding in the church shortly before the steeple was shelled by the US Navy. He brought the French civilians back to the relative safety of the beach where he was wounded by mortar fire. He was evacuated the next day. While in the hospital he discovered that one of the infantry officers had jotted down his name while he helped them break off the beach and he had been awarded the Silver Star for those actions. After he had recovered, the Navy noticed he had received special "invasion training" and assigned him to a Marine Raider unit. He went behind the Japanese lines in the Philippines to help scout for the planned amphibious assault. He

Above.

These men take a break on Utah Beach. The man in the center, with helmet net, has the Navy gray band on his helmet. Two men are visible looking up out of their dugout. In the foreground a space has been marked with white engineer tape. This normally signified an area not cleared of mines, but in this case the sandbags are probably the top of another shelter. The white tape would keep any vehicles from accidentally driving over, and collapsing, this dugout.

The 9th NBB insignia

This insignia was designed by the men of the 9th NBB while training at Ft Pierce. The tail of the black cat is curled into a number "9." The cat symbolized the men's desire to have nine lives. About it are the Navy insignia representing the four major functions of the Beach battalions: seamanship, communications, medical, and repair work. On top is the amphibious force alligator and tanks. This plaque hung on the wall of the Ft. Pierce officer's club. No shoulder patches were ever made from the design because the 9th NBB was broken up into separate platoons. Some were sent to Normandy as replacements in other NBBs. When the 9th was finally disbanded the plaque was presented to Commander E.L. Adams in recognition of his service.
(Photo by Carl Hutto. Courtesy Larry Adams)

spent several weeks there working with the Philippine guerrillas and Marine Raiders.

Frank Thompson was a radio operator in B-6, 7th NBB. Just prior to the invasion he and two friends had decided to duck into the local town without a pass. Their absence was noted and their platoon leader decided to reassign the landing rosters "due to their unreliability." Thompson found himself moved from the first wave to the second. As

it turned out his group was held off shore until the morning of D+1. When Thompson finally got to the beach he ran into Robert Callahan, who had been moved from the second wave to the first to replace Thompson. There were no hurt feelings, but Callahan did ask for some water. A bullet had pierced his canteen on D-Day and he had not had anything to drink for 24 hours. That night Thompson was wounded in the hand during an air raid. It was probably a piece of flak falling back to earth. He was sent to a hospital in England and eventually took part in the invasion of Okinawa. There he was surprised to see many faces he remembered from the 7th NBB in other beach parties.

In the 2nd NBB, on Utah Beach, there was little need for such heroics for Commander Curtin's men. They had a relatively clear beach and an enormous number of men to bring across it. Their job was made slightly more difficult as the primary landing beaches were 2,000 yards south of where all the charts said they should be. The lack of enemy resistance on Utah Beach meant that the 2nd NBB was able to get its beach markers up relatively quickly, but there were still some craft coming in that were puzzled by the apparent difference between what their charts said and where they were told to land.

After the landings

For the first few days the NBB men went about their duties directing landing craft to

239

the correct beach and bringing in as much manpower and equipment as possible. Many of them worked around the clock for the first few days without any sleep. It seemed there was always one more landing craft to direct or one more transport that needed to know where to anchor.

The transfer of supplies from the larger ships to the smaller ones, and then to the beach by way of LCVPs or Dukws was not fast enough to keep the Army supplied. Work on the artificial "Mulberry Harbor" progressed, but the appetite of the Army for more men and ammunition was insatiable. In a desperate move the beachmasters tried bringing the LSTs up onto the beach at high tide and letting them "dry out" as the tide went down. LSTs and other landing craft had flat bottoms, but the Navy was still concerned that this manoeuvre would break the back of these ships. The strong construction of the LSTs held up to this abuse, but this meant that the LST could only unload every 14 hours. Other ships transferred their cargo to Dukws who brought the cargo ashore and drove it right to the supply dump, thus eliminating a transfer from Dukw to truck. Vehicles could also be transferred at sea to the Navy Rhino Ferries and then unloaded in shallow water. All of these methods had to be watched over by the careful eyes of the Navy beachmaster and his assistants to make sure no one caused a traffic jam at sea or on the shore.

A few days after the landing a new naval officer was supposed to take over control of all naval operations on the beaches. The NOIC (Naval Officer in Charge) was supposed to direct movements of every ship and craft off his beach. On Utah this change seemed to cause few problems, but it was different on Omaha. The NOIC for Omaha claimed he was unable to perform his job because much of his equipment and notes had been lost at sea. Things worsened when it was discovered that the transport manifests, listing what cargo was on which ship, had been sent to the British sector and lost. The most embarrassing problem was when the 30th Infantry Division was "lost" off shore. The NOIC knew that the division was waiting to disembark, but had no idea which ships they were on. Precious time was lost going ship to ship to locate the missing units.

Right.
Originally, the only insignia allowed by the Navy was a small embroidered "Strike" worn on the sleeve. This was a stylized view of an alligator disembarking tanks from his mouth. A full color shoulder patch of the same design came into use at some point in the war, but was never given wide distribution. The popular feeling among naval officers was that shoulder patches were an Army concept. A few weeks after D-Day the Navy finally authorized the yellow and red shoulder patch (below) that used the same design as the Army Engineer Special Brigades. The only known shoulder patch worn by any of the Beach Battalions was this design (bottom), privately manufactured by the 8th Naval Beach Battalion while training at Little Creek. Within days after it was first worn by the men, the base commander ordered its removal and it was never worn overseas.

Although the story is muddled, it seems that the Beach Battalions had a more difficult time working under this new authority than if they had been left on their own. Eventually the NOIC Omaha was relieved, and the new officer (the former Gunfire Support Officer) proved easier to work with. The backlog of ships was dealt with by the simple process of unloading every transport regardless of the priority of its cargo. The main goal was to get the material on shore and send the ships on their way. The quartermasters would have to sort things out at the supply dumps. It was not the best solution, but the men of the Special Brigades and Beach Battalions worked long hours to clear up the mess. By D+9 the backlog had been cleared up. An ESB after-action report suggested that in future operations the Beach Battalion commander should be given a larger staff and allowed to serve as both beachmaster and NOIC of his beach.

By 12 June the beachmasters had the total tonnage of Omaha and Utah up to 9,452 tons per day: far above what had been expected. On 15 June the Seabees completed the Mulberry Harbor and the first vehicles rolled off an LST onto the floating piers and onto dry land. This meant that unloading LSTs was no longer dependent on the tide. An LST could now unload, return to England for another cargo, and be halfway back to France in the same time as it took to dry out. The Beachmasters were ready to turn the whole operation over the men of the 11th Port when disaster struck.

On 19 June, a storm hit the Normandy coast. Incoming supplies were negligible for the next three days and a serious ammunition shortage developed. Artillery ammunition was in such short supply that 600 tons a day were airlifted in from England at tremendous expense. Many small craft and vessels were beached by the storm and damaged beyond repair. The cry for supplies became so desperate that some of the smaller transport ships were beached and their hulls cut open to unload them. The storm had left the beaches in worse shape than after the initial landings. The Beach Battalions, along with other units stationed on the shore, cleared the debris in record time and got many small craft repaired and back into operation.

The Army's Lifeline

The Mulberry Harbor, upon which so much depended, was ruined. A decision was made to cannibalize the American Mulberry at Omaha to create spare parts for the British Mulberry at Arromanches. Knowing that the Army depended upon their ability to bring in supplies and reinforcements, the amount of tonnage landed by the Navy went up beyond what had been expected. An average of 20,000 tons a day, much higher than with the

artificial harbor, was brought onto the American beaches by the end of June.

This amount rose until winter storms forced a closure of the beaches on 19 November 1944. Had it not been for the skilled and dedicated men keeping the supplies flowing over the beachhead, the combat troops would have faced a severe shortage of food, ammunition and replacements. By November the Beach Battalions had been sent back to the United States, but they had left behind them a functioning beach operation that kept the supplies moving.

Of the 42 officers and 368 sailors that had gone ashore with the 6th NBB, four officers and 18 sailors were killed. 12 officers and 55 sailors were wounded. Included in this figure is Commander Carusi, the battalion com-

manding officer. He was accidentally wounded by friendly 20mm antiaircraft fire while standing on the bluffs overlooking Omaha Beach.

The surviving men of the Beach Battalions stayed on the beaches until the end of June, when most of them were transferred back to the States as instructors at the new Navy amphibious training base at Oceanside, California. Most of these men went on to serve as members of shore parties from transports in Pacific landings. On 19 August all of the remaining 104 men of the 6th NBB turned their duties over to the Army ESBs, and returned to the States.

The 6th NBB was awarded the French Croix de Guerre with palm for its service on Omaha Beach. As the unit was attached to the 5th ESB at the time, all paperwork went through Army channels and to this day many of the sailors have never received notification of this award. A proposed Navy Unit Citation for the NBBs was turned down on the basis that the men had been put in for an Army Citation for being assigned to the ESBs. Due to the confusion of being a Navy unit attached to an Army unit, only Companies B and C of the 7th NBB were officially awarded the Army Unit Citation.

These shore based sailors have never received the recognition they deserve. The NBBs played a critical role not only in the initial landings in Normandy, but in continuing to keep a steady flow of men and supplies moving swiftly across the beaches. Had it not been for their expertise, the wrecking of the Mulberry harbor might have spelled doom for the Allied armies.

Below.

After the Normandy invasion most of the men from the 2nd, 6th and 7th Beach Battalions were sent to the Pacific by way of the Amphibious Training Base at Oceanside, California. Vince Perrin and some of his men from C-9, 6th NBB are seen here at Oceanside awaiting their next assignment.

❝ IN Operation Neptune, the Provisional Engineer Special Brigade Group under Army command, will support the assault landing of the Vth U.S. Corps and subsequent debarkation of the XIXth U.S. corps and other First United States Army and Communications Zone troops in the Omaha area beginning D-Day, and organize and operate all shore installations necessary for debarkation, supply, evacuation, and local security in order to insure the continuous movement of personnel, vehicles, and supplies across the beaches, and through Mulberry "A" and the minor ports of Grandcamp and Isigny."

The Engineer Special Brigades are the best known of all the special units taking part in the invasion. This is possibly due to their unique helmet markings which stand out in many photographs, but primarily because these Brigades composed the main supporting elements of the invasion. The ESBs were the backbone of the invasion.

Although referred to as Engineer units, the ESBs were, in fact, a logistical structure composed of all the different types of noncombat units needed for a successful invasion. It must be kept in mind that although the ESB's primary mission was to get the combat troops and supplies across the beach, many units of the ESBs did take part in the fight to get ashore. The elements of the 5th and 6th ESBs, that landed on the morning of 6 June, played important roles helping to push the Germans off the beach and securing the area.

The ESBs originated in May 1942 as the Engineer Amphibian Command. During the rapid expansion of the U.S. military at the start of 1942, the Navy had been unable to keep up with demands for small boat crews to help train the Army in amphibious landings. The Army and Navy had a previous agreement that they would not put any restrictions on the weapons or

equipment the other service used. The Army decided that if the Navy was unable to supply the boat crews, then the Army would form its own amphibious units. Thus the 1st Engineer Amphibian Brigade was organized in June 1942.

Engineer Amphibian Brigades were originally formed out of one Boat Regiment (trained in handling landing craft), one Shore Regiment (to provide the beach organization), a Quartermaster Bn., Medical Bn., Boat Maintenance Co., a Signal Co. and Ordnance Platoon. In August 1942 the 1st Engineer Amphibian Brigade took part in the invasion of North Africa. In the Center Task Force, where the 1st EAB was assigned, the transport ships

Below.

Members of the 1st ESB check their newly issued assault gas masks. These were not issued to the troops until just prior to the invasion. Thus any photographs showing men carrying this mask, or its black rubber bag, are probably from the actual invasion and not one of the practice landings. The full white arc on the helmets was used only in the 1st ESB.

and landing craft were from the British Navy. With no landing craft for them to use, the Boat Regt. served as extra shore personnel and as additional cargo crews on the transport ships. The Shore Regt. formed the beach organization that assisted the 1st Inf. Div. and 1st Arm. Div. landings. The landing operation was not handled well and a number of landing craft were damaged by poor seamanship. If not for the early capture of the nearby port of Arzew there might have been a serious problem in keeping the Army supplied. However, valuable lessons were learned and future landings went smoother.

In April 1943 the War Department had decided upon a division of labor for future amphibious ope-

;ineer Special Brigades

rations. The U.S. Navy would procure all equipment and conduct all amphibious training in the States. It would then be up to the individual theater commander to decide who would provide amphibious training and support in their area. This ruling was influenced by General MacArthur in the Southwest Pacific. He did not want to give up his three Engineer Amphibious Brigades. This decision let him keep his Army units, but allowed the Navy to be used in the rest of the Pacific and in Europe. Possibly due to the heavy influence of the British Navy, the decision was made that landing craft in the ETO would be under the jurisdiction of the Navy.

The EABs in Europe were stripped of their Boat Regiments. They were technically no longer amphibious, but the Army wanted to indicate their specialty training in beach operations. The Engineer Amphibian Brigades underwent a name change to Engineer Special Brigades. The 1st EAB's 591st Boat Regiment was transferred to the Transportation Corps (that still operated some cargo and small boat services). Most of these men served in port units,

Left.
These men from an Engineer Special Brigade have hung their dartboard on a camouflaged truck. Different shades of burlap strips have been woven into the camouflage net to help break up and conceal the outline of the vehicle. The white arc is clearly visible on their helmet liners and they wear the paratrooper boots that were issued to the ESBs. One man has an M1903 Springfield rifle which, due to a shortage of Garands, was issued to soldiers who were not expected to take part in combat.

American Army Supply Classes:

● Class I Food
● Class II equipment prescribed by the T/O&E (clothing, weapons, and vehicles)
● Class III oil and gasoline
● Class IV special materials not prescribed by the T/O&E (barbed wire, lumber, special clothing)
● Class V ammunition and

General Missions of ESB units

It can be difficult to keep track of the many different functions of the units in an Engineer Special Brigade. The following is a listing of primary responsibilities from a wartime report issued by the Provisional Engineer Special Brigade Group.

● **Brigade, reinforced**- Insures the continuous movement of personnel, vehicles, and supplies across the beach in support of a landing operation.

● **Brigade**- Insures the movement of personnel, vehicles and supplies across the beach in support of a landing operation involving one division.

● **Brigade Headquarters and Headquarters Company**- Establishes and operates forward and rear Brigade command posts.

● **Battalion Beach Group** - Organizes and operates all shore installations necessary for debarkation, supply, evacuation and local security in support of a regimental combat team or combat command.

● **Engineer Combat or Shore Battalion**- Commands Combat or Shore Battalion and attached service troops and performs all engineer work in beach maintenance area assigned to the battalion necessary to facilitate debarkation, supply, evacuation, and local security.

● **Engineer Headquarters and Service or Shore Battalion Headquarters Company**- Organizes, operates and secures all Headquarters and service or shore battalion headquarters company installations necessary for supply, control, coordination, and maintenance of the battalion beach group.

● **Engineer combat or shore company**- organizes operates, and secures all combat or shore company beach installations necessary to debark all personnel, vehicles and supplies in support of a battalion combat team.

● **Quartermaster headquarters and headquarters company, Engineer Special brigade**- Coordinates operations of class I II, and II dumps; furnishes intra-brigade supply personnel.

● **Ordnance Battalion Headquarters and**

Headquarters detachment- Coordinates activities of Ordnance Companies.

● **Ordnance Platoon Engineer Special Brigade**- maintenance of all weapons of the brigade.

● **Quartermaster Gas Supply Company**- Organizes, operates Class III dumps, including storage, issue, and inventory of Class III supplies.

● **Quartermaster Railhead Company**- Organizes and operates Class I and II dumps including the receipt, storage, issue, and inventory of Class I and II supplies.

● **Quartermaster Service Battalion**- Furnishes personnel to assist in vehicle, dump, and unloading operations.

● **Headquarters and Headquarters Detachment Quartermaster Battalion Mobile**- Coordinates activities of Amphibian Truck Companies and Quartermaster Truck Companies, transporting equipment and supplies from ship, craft, or shore to dumps; coordinates activities of dump operating companies.

● **Amphibian Truck Company**- Transfers equipment, and supplies from ships or craft to dumps.

● **Ordnance Ammunition Company**- Organizes and operates Class V dumps including the receipt, storage, issue and inventory of Class V supplies.

● **Medical Battalion Headquarters**- Coordinates activities of medical companies in collecting, clearing and evacuation of casualties from beach to ship or higher medical echelons in accordance with medical plan; supervises medical supplies.

● **Medical Company**- Collects and/or clears beach casualties in conjunction with medical detachments and naval beach sections.

● **Signal Company**- Establishes and maintains radio and telephone communications and message centers for Brigade Headquarters, intra-brigade communications to shore-to-ship, air-ground, and naval gunfire observers.

● **Military Police Company**- Guides and enforces traffic and military police regulations; guards and evacuates prisoners of war.

● **Medium Automotive Maintenance Company**- Maintains all Brigade transportation.

● **Decontamination Company**- Executes chemical decontamination of equipment, vehicles, supplies, areas, roads, bridges, and other military objects but not personnel or clothing and/or operates chemical dump.

● **Attached Engineer Contact Platoon**- maintains Engineer equipment in Brigade.

● **Attached Engineer Depot and Map Detachments**- Receives, stores, and controls issues of Engineer Class II and IV supplies and maps.

● **Attached Air Corps Supply Detachment**- Receives, stores and controls issue of Air Corps supplies of all classes including special parts, gasoline, lubricants and bombs.

● **Attached Naval Beach Battalion**- Surveys beaches, marks and removes underwater obstacles, assists landing craft, makes emergency boat repairs, operates naval shore to ship communications, controls landing craft traffic, evacuates casualties and prisoners of war to ships and assist in shore operations when necessary.

● **Attached Storage and Issue Section**- Organize and operate Signal dump including receipt, storage, issue, and inventory of Signal Supplies.

● **Attached Ordnance Depot Platoon**- Establishes depot and controls issues of all Ordnance material except ammunition.

● **Attached Medical Supply Section**- Establishes depot and controls issue of all medical supplies.

● **Attached Graves Registration Platoon**- Complete graves registration forms, handles effects of casualties and supervises burial in designated cemeteries.

● **Attached Quartermaster Truck Company**- Transports personnel, equipment, and supplies from shore to dump.

One of the few color still photographs of the invasion, this shot was taken by the Signal Corps team of Ardean Miller and Steve Stevens. The bulk of their photos disappeared after Stevens was killed in a post-war airplane crash. They were the only official color photography team sent into Northern Europe by the Army.

This photograph is thought to have been taken on Utah Beach. One of the men wears the blue patch of the Army Engineer Special Brigades, which would make him a member of the 1st ESB. The two men in front wear the paratrooper boots issued to these units. The man in the rear has a blue arc painted on his helmet which has not been identified. The full arc is typical of the 1st ESB, so it is probable that this is Utah Beach and it denotes a unit of the 1st ESB. Most arcs in the ESBs were white, while the 6th and 7th Navy Beach Battalions had red arcs. It was previously thought that the blue arc might have been used by the Navy demolition units, but NCDU vets claim they only had the gray band. The white bags underneath one soldier, once thought to be Hagensen packs, are far too large to be this type of demolition. Unless someone is able to come forward with evidence as to who wore the blue arc, it will remain one of the mysteries of the Normandy Invasion.

although a number later played an important role as assault boat crews in the Rhine River crossing. The Boat Maintenance Company continued to function, under the jurisdiction of the Navy, and repaired not only landing craft, but assisted in repairs of major warships when needed.

The remainder of 1st Engineer Special Brigade participated in the invasion of Sicily. Bolstered by the 36th and 540th Engineer Regiments (both with amphibious experience), the 1st ESB was concerned only with activities on the shore. At Sicily each invading division was supported by a Battalion Beach Group (BBG). These BBGs were organized around the nucleus of an engineer or shore regt. Additional elements, such as quartermaster, medical or signal, were attached as needed. Each BBG was assigned a Naval Beach Battalion to assist in dealings with the Navy. The BBG concept was considered a success and used in the later landings in Italy. In November 1943 the 1st ESB was transferred to England in preparation for the invasion of Normandy.

Plans for Normandy

The invasion of Normandy was an amphibious landing unlike any before. The logistics of moving entire armies and their supplies across a few beaches was enormous. Although it was hoped that the port of Cherbourg would be quickly captured, plans had to include the possibility that they might not capture a usable French port. As the Normandy plan grew, the organization of the ESBs swelled with attached units to handle a multitude of tasks, both during the initial landing operation and in the following supporting phase.

The overall plan called for the veteran 1st ESB to provide the beach structure for Utah. Omaha Beach would be supported by the 5th and 6th ESBs. To provide overall control of these two units the Provisional Engineer Special Brigade Group was formed. Originally, this was to be only a small head-

Battalion Beach Groups

149th Battalion Beach group, supporting 116th Infantry Regt.	37th Battalion Beach Group, supporting 16th Infantry Regt.
149th Engineer Combat Battalion	37th Engineer Combat Bn.
Company C, 147th Engineer Combat Bn.	298 personel attached
461st Amphib Truck Co.	from 348th Engineer Combat Bn.
Company A, 7th Naval Beach Bn.	459th Amphib Truck Co
293rd JASCO (less 3 teams)	4141st QM Service Co
500th Medical Collecting Co.	97th QM Railhead Co
1 platoon, Company B, 7th Naval Beach Bn.	391st Collecting-clearing Co, 61st Med Bn.
1 platoon, 31st Chemical Decon Co.	Company C, 6th Naval Beach Bn.
1 platoon, 88th QM Railhead Co.	1 Platoon, Company A, 203rd QM Gas Supply Bn.
1 platoon, 214th MP Co.	1 Section, Magazine Platoon, 616th Ord Ammo Co.
1 platoon, 618th Ordnance Ammo Co.	1 Section, Depot Office, 616th Ord Ammo Co.
1 platoon, 634th Medical Clearing Co.	1 Section, Shop Plat, 3466th Ord MAM Co.
1 platoon, 3205th QM Service Co.	1 Platoon, 210th MP Co.
1 platoon, 3820th QM Gas Co.	1 platoon, 30th Chem Decon. Co.
Recovery Sect, 3565th Medium Auto Maint Co.	1 platoon, 294th JASCO
Det, HQ, 6th Eng Special Brigade	26th Ord Bomb Disposal Squad
Det, HQ & Service Co., 147th Eng C Bn.	2 Surgical Teams, 3rd Aux. Surgical Group.
1st Team, 293rd JASCO (less 2 sections)	
3rd Team, 293rd JASCO	
27th Ordnance Bomb Disposal Squad	

quarters and command unit of 30 men. As plans progressed, elements continued to be attached to the Provisional Group Headquarter, until it numbered almost 1,400 men.

Operations for the ESBs were divided into four phases:

" *Assault Phase: Support of the initial assault elements and exploitation of the primary landing beaches.*

Initial Dump Phase: Establishment and operation of initial beach supply installations, and development of maximum unloading capacities. The supply dumps in this phase were within 1,000 yards of the shore.

Beach Maintenance Area Dump Phase: Establishment and operation of permanent Beach Maintenance Area installations, maximum unloading operations across the beaches, and construction of the artificial port. Supply dumps in the phase could extend up to 5 miles inland.

Port Phase: The final phase covering capacity operation of the Artificial Port 'Mulberry A" and minor ports of Isigny and Grandcamp when completed, in addition to maximum operations over the beaches."

Thus it can be seen that after the initial landings the ESBs would have no combat duties. They would

---

Engineer Combat Battalions assignments for D-Day

37th Engineer Combat Bn supports 16th RCT on Easy Red and Fox Green Beach

348th Engineer Combat Bn supports 18th RCT on Easy Red and Fox Green Beach

149th Engineer Combat Bn supports 116th RCT on Dog and Easy Green.

147th Engineer Combat Bn supports 115th RCT

1st Engineer Special Brigade

The various elements of the ESBs changed over the period between June through November. The following is as complete a roster as possible for when the brigade was at its largest size.

1st Engineer Special Brigade, Hq & Hq Co.	577th QM Bn.	262nd QM Bn.	3683rd QM truck Co.	52nd Finance Disbursing Section
531st Eng Shore Regt, 3 Shore Bns	363rd QM Serv Co.	4061st QM Serv Co.	3684th QM Truck Co.	Det, 8th AF Intransit Depot Group
24th Amphib Trk Bn.	3207th QM Serv Co.	4083rd QM Serv Co.	4002nd QM Truck Co.	Det A, 11th Port
462nd Amphib Trk Co.	4144th QM Serv Co.	4088th QM Serv Co.	4041st QM Truck Co.	490th Port Bn.
478th Amphib Trk Co.	261th Med Bn.	4090th QM Serv Co.	815th Amphib Truck Co.	226th Port Co.
479th Amphib Trk Co.	449th MP Co.	4092nd QM Serv Co.	816th Amphib Truck Co.	227th Port Co.
306th QM Bn.	286th JASCO	4190th QM Serv Co.	817th Amphib Truck Co.	228th Port Co.
556th QM Railhead Co.	33rd Chem Decon Co.	244th QM Bn.	818th Amphib Truck Co.	229th Port Co.
562nd QM Railhead Co.	3206th QM Service Co. (1 section)	552nd QM Railhead Co.	3615th Ord MAM Co. (att'd 191st Ord Bn.)	518th Port Bn.
3939th QM Gas Supply Co.		3877th QM Gas Supply Co.	175th Sig Repair Co.	278th Port Co.
191st Ord Bn.	**Attached troops**	3878th QM Gas Supply Co.	Det 215th Sig Depot Co.	281th Port Co.
3497th Ord MAM Co.	2nd Naval Beach Battalion	308th QM Railhead Co. (att'd to 306th QM Bn.)	Det 999th Sig Serv Co.	298th Port Co.
625th Ord Amm Co.	23rd Ord Bomb Disposal Sec	3877th QM Gas Supply Co. (att'd 306th QM Bn.)	Det 980th Sig Serv Co.	299th Port Co.
161st Ord Plat.	38th Eng Gen Serv Regt, 2 Eng GS Bns	4132nd QM Serv Co. (att'd 577th QM Bn.)	Det 3111th Sig Serv Co.	300th Port Co.
	467th Eng Maint Co., 1st plat 440th Eng Depot Co.	607th QM Graves Reg Co., 4th Plat (att'd 577th QM Bn.)	Det 165th Sig Photo Co.	301st port Co.
	1 plat 1605th Eng Map Sect	537th QM Bn.	Det E 1st Med Co., 2 Sec	519th Port Bn.
	1217th Eng Fire Fighting Plat	3692nd QM Truck Co.	6th Surgical Group (12 teams)	280th Port Co.
	1218th Eng Fire Fighting Plat		3rd Aux Surgical Group	279th Port Co.
			301st MP Escort Guard Co.	302nd Port Co.
			595th MP Escort Guard Co.	303rd Port Co.
			Company D, 383rd MP Bn.	304th Port Co.
				305th Port Co.

first be concerned with engineering and construction tasks, then become more involved with quartermaster and transportation functions.

The basic plan for the assault phase was to provide a Battalion Beach Group, based around an engineer combat battalion, for every assault regiment. As more troops came ashore additional BBGs would land and develop their own sector of the beach. By attaching small elements of specialized units to each BBG, each beach sector of roughly 1,000 yards could be self-sufficient. This policy of dispersing men and equipment was also important so that one sunk transport ship would not be carrying, for instance, all of the chemical decontamination troops for Omaha Beach.

The initial elements of the ESBs to land were reconnaissance parties. These were not concerned with locating enemy forces, but with making an ini-

tial examination of the beach area and deciding where to locate command posts and important installations. If all went as planned, the ESBs would not be involved in combat at all.

According to the normal table of organization, each engineer combat battalion had one bulldozer per company. For the Normandy assault this was raised to one bulldozer per platoon and one per company headquarters (four per company). Additional heavy equipment, such as cranes, were also added to bolster the strength of the units. All members of the ESBs were issued paratrooper boots to better allow them to work in the surf. Many men did not want to ruin these fine boots and preferred to keep them for dress purposes. These men wore the standard Army boot and canvas leggings ashore.

Inset.
The Engineer Special Brigades' shoulder sleeve insignia. The design was patterned after that of British Combined Operations. The eagle, gun, and anchor symbolized the air, land, and sea aspects of combined operations.

Below.
The main command post of the Provisional Engineer Special Brigade Group was in the German pillbox overlooking the E-1 Exit. The sign has been censored in this print, but in the original negative it reads "MARS-CP." Mars was the code name for the Provisional ESB Group. The 5th ESB was "Marble," The 6th ESB "Mentor" and the 11th Port was "Macaroon."

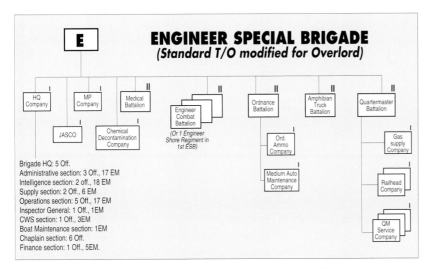

ENGINEER SPECIAL BRIGADE
(Standard T/O modified for Overlord)

| E |

- HQ Company
- MP Company
- Medical Battalion
  - JASCO
  - Chemical Decontamination Company
- Engineer Combat Battalion *(Or 1 Engineer Shore Regiment in 1st ESB)*
- Ordnance Battalion
  - Ord. Ammo Company
  - Medium Auto Maintenance Company
- Amphibian Truck Battalion
- Quartermaster Battalion
  - Gas supply Company
  - Railhead Company
  - QM Service Company

Brigade HQ: 5 Off.
Administrative section: 3 Off., 17 EM
Intelligence section: 2 off., 18 EM
Supply section: 2 Off., 6 EM
Operations section: 5 Off., 17 EM
Inspector General: 1 Off., 1EM
CWS section: 1 Off., 3EM
Boat Maintenance section: 1EM
Chaplain section: 6 Off.
Finance section: 1 Off., 5EM.

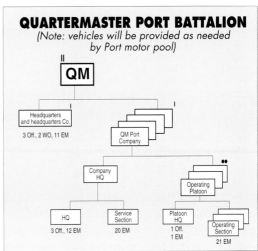

QUARTERMASTER PORT BATTALION
(Note: vehicles will be provided as needed by Port motor pool)

| QM |

- Headquarters and headquarters Co. — 3 Off., 2 WO, 11 EM
- QM Port Company
  - Company HQ
    - HQ — 3 Off., 12 EM
    - Service Section — 20 EM
  - Operating Platoon
    - Platoon HQ — 1 Off. 1 EM
    - Operating Section — 21 EM

ESB TABLE OF MEN AND VEHICLES
(Total per unit)

	Men	Vehicles	trailers
Hq Provisional ESB Group	1393	172	11
5th Eng. Spec. Brigade	8722	916	304
6th Eng. Spec. Brigade	8708	919	304
11th Port	8631	597	15

The 1st Engineer Special Brigade

The 1st ESB was composed of veteran troops from the Mediterranean landings. The basic structure for an ESB in Europe called for three engineer combat battalions, but the 1st ESB was allowed to retain the 531st Engineer Shore Regiment, which consisted of three engineer battalions (by this time most engineer regiments had been converted to engineer bns.). The only real difference between this organization and the way the 5th and 6th were set up was the 1st ESB had an addition Regimental Headquarters section.

The most notable incident for the 1st ESB in England took place during Operation Tiger on 28 April 1944. This was the final dress rehearsal for the Utah landings. German torpedo boats sunk two LSTs, and damaged a third, as they were moving to

Above.
In June, 1945 a ceremony was held on Utah Beach to dedicate a monument to the 1st Engineer Special Brigade. The color guard wear the small oval seahorse patch on their shirt pockets. The two local girls wear dresses representing both the American and French flags.

Left.
Dukws from the 460th Amphibian Truck Company, 6th ESB on Omaha Beach. Above the beach exit flies a barrage balloon from the 320th Barrage Balloon Bn.

a practice landing at Slapton Sands. 429 of the roughly 700 casualties were from various elements of the 1st ESB. The ESBs had been allowed 22% overstrength to allow for events such as this and most of the units were able to fill the losses with replacements. The 557th QM Railhead Co. and 3206th QM Service Co. suffered such heavy losses during the Tiger sinking, however, that both units were pulled from the invasion and replaced by the 562nd QM Railhead Co. and the 363rd QM Service Co. The German attack was to have an unplanned for effect in the command of the 1st ESB. Col. Eugene Caffey was in command of this unit during its time in England. Throughout that period the 1st ESB had performed well in spite of a shortage of equipment when it first arrived. The 1st ESB did not, however, perform as well as expected during Operation Tiger.

This appears to have been caused by the loss of the two previously mentioned units, as well as the loss of men from other elements of the 1st ESB that had been on the three LSTs.

Beach operations were also hampered by the realization that a few of the casualties had been "Bigot'ed" (given the top secret Bigot clearance which allowed them knowledge of the date and location of the actual invasion). The Allies were afraid that one of these men might have been rescued from the water by a German boat. If so, the plans for the invasion could have been compromised.

A systematic search for of all Bigots in the affected units was undertaken. Corpses were meticulously identified. Divers were sent down to the sunken LSTs to search for the dog tags of men trapped below decks. Eventually, all Bigots were accounted for and the search was called off. However, the loss of men and confusion of the Bigot search had a negative impact on the 1st ESB's performance.

General Omar Bradley, commander of the First Army, had been observing the beach operations that day. He was greatly concerned about the problems he saw and

directed the VII Corps commander, General J. Laughton Collins, to replace the 1st ESB commander. On 9 May 1944 Caffey was relieved of command without explanation and General James E. Wharton was assigned command of the 1st ESB. Col. Caffey was kept on as deputy commander of the brigade. Later in France, on 2 July 1944, Wharton would be transferred to the 9th Infantry Division, and Caffey would once again command the 1st ESB. General Wharton was made assistant division commander of the 9th Infantry Division but was killed soon after he arrived.

Provisional Engineer Special Brigade Group

Headquarters and HQ Co.	619th QM Bn.		31st Chem Decon Co.	467 Eng Maint Co.
Signal Platoon	97th QM Rhd Co.	**Attached upon**	293rd Joint Asault Sig Co.	607th Graves Reg Co.,
Det A, 255th Sig Const Co.	559th QM Rhd Co.	**landing**	74th Ord Bn.	3rd Plat
Co C, 783rd MP Bn.	Co. A, 203rd Gas Supply	487th Port Bn.	618th Ord Ammo Co.	1220th Eng Fire
302nd MP Escort Guard Co.	Bn.	184th Port Co.	3565th Ord MAM Co.	Fighting Plat
2nd Bn., 358th Gen	131st QM Mobile Bn.	185th Port Co.	538th QM Bn.	1st Med Depot, one Squad
Service Regt	453rd Amphib Trk Co.	186th Port Co.	3204th QM Serv Co.	Det Q 165th Sig Photo Co.
Det A, CIC team	458th Amphib Trk Co.	187th Port Co.	3205th QM Serv Co.	Det C CIC Team
440th Eng Dep Co. (- 3	459th Amphib Trk Co.	282nd Port Co.	967th QM Serv Co.	Civil Affairs Det
plats)		283rd Port Co	95th QM Bn.	Det B AF Intratransit
	Attached units	502nd Port Bn.	88th QM Rhd Co.	Depot Gp
5th Engineer	4042nd QM Truck Co.	270th Port Co.	555th QM Rhd Co.	1602nd Engr
Special Brigade	6th Naval Beach Bn.	271st Port Co.	3820th QM Gas Sup Co.	Map Depot Grp
	26th Bomb Disposal Squad	272nd Port Co.	280th QM Bn.	
5th Engineer Special Brigade	3rd Aux Surgical Group	272rd Port Co.	460th Amphib Truck Co.	**Attached upon**
Hq & Hq Co.	(6 teams)		461st Amphib Truck Co.	**landing**
37th Engineer C Bn.	S&I Sect,		463rd Amphib Truck Co.	494th Port Bn.
336th Engineer C Bn.	Det 1215th Sig Dep Co.	**6th Engineer**		238th Port Co.
348th Engineer C Bn.	Det, 175th Sig Repair Co.	**Special Brigade**	**Attached units**	239th Port Co.
61st Med Bn.	467th Eng Maint Co.,			240th Port Co.
210th MP Co.	one plat	6th Engineer Special Brigade	3704th QM Truck Co.	241st Port Co.
30th Chemical Decon Co.	440th Eng Dep Co., one Plat	Hq&Hq Co.	7th Naval Beach Bn.	517th Port Bn.
294th Joint Assault Sig Co.	607th Graves Reg Co.,	147th Eng C Bn.	27th Ord Bomb	284th Port Co.
251st Ord Bn.	2nd Plat	149th Eng C Bn.	Disposal Squad	285th Port Co.
616th Ord Ammo Co..	1219th Fire Fighting Plat	203rd Eng C Bn.	3rd Aux Surg Group	797th Port Co.
3466th Ord MAM Co.	1st Med Supply Depot Sec	60th Med Bn.	(4 teams)	799th Port Co.
533rd QM Service Bn.	Det P 165th Sig Photo Co.	453rd Col Co.	Det S&I	800th Port Co.
4141st QM Serv Co.	British VHF Signal Det	499th Col Co.	Sec 3 215th Sig Dep Co.	
4142nd QM Serv Co.	Civil Affairs Det	500th Col Co.	Det I&O 175th Sig Rep Co.	
4143rd QM Serv Co.		634th Clearing Co.	440th Eng Dep Co., 3rd Plat	
		214th MP Co.		

Right.
This 1st ESB jeep, from the 261st Medical Bn, has been outfitted with brackets to hold four stretchers. The Army entered the war expecting stretcher bearers to carry wounded men back to a point where regular ambulances could pick them up. It was soon realized that the jeep could get much closer to the front lines than an ambulance, and this would and speed up the evacuation of casualties. The faster a wounded man got to medical attention, the better his chances of survival. Blankets were needed for casualties because loss of blood caused shock, and it was vital that men suffering from shock be kept warm.

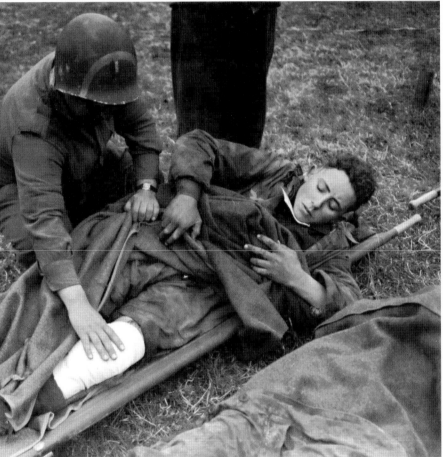

Although the casualties resulting from these torpedo attacks were commonly known among the brigade, Caffey had never been told the reason for his relief. It was not until many years later that Caffey would learn that Bradley had suggested the action before he had learned of the attacks on the LSTs. Bradley later implied that had he known about those losses he would not have relieved him. To his credit, Col. Caffey made no complaint about what must have been a tremendously embarrassing situation. He continued to serve in his former unit as best he could. Finally, he was restored to command and continued to run the 1st ESB in an efficient manner.

The 1st ESB plan for Utah Beach was for two of the BBGs to support the initial two landing beaches. Later on, the third BBG would open up Sugar Red Beach when possible. The executive officer of the 1st ESB landed in the first waves alongside the assault companies. Along with his small recon party, he started to evaluate the area they were to work in. The previous plans called for the landing beaches to be 2,000 yards further west, but this was easily altered to fit the situation.

What they found on the beach was a reinforced concrete sea wall 50 feet from the high-water mark. Behind that was a 15 foot sand dune followed by minefields. After the minefields were a handful of one lane roads crossing flooded fields. It was not the best situation for moving men and equipment inland, but unlike Omaha they did not have to contend with an enemy firing down upon them. First to land were the 1st and 2nd battalions of the 531st Shore

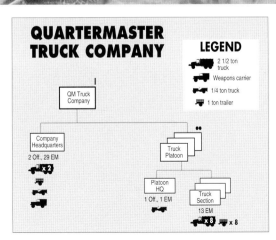

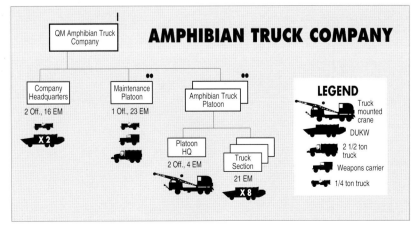

251

Regiment. Along with engineers attached to the 4th Division, they opened paths through the sea wall, cleared gaps in the minefields, and improved the beach exits. By noon the 1st ESB Headquarters was ashore and had set up their command post in a pill-box at La Grande Dune near Exit U-5.

Only half the ESB road building equipment expected came ashore on D-Day. The area was still in range of German artillery and three of the LCTs carrying engineering equipment were hit offshore. But compared with Omaha Beach, the Utah landings went smoothly. D-Day casualties for the 1st ESB were only 21 killed and 96 wounded. All caused by German artillery, or strafing from a few German planes in the evening.

The 1st ESB performed very well and they had few problems. Unlike the difficulties with the NOIC at Omaha, the men at Utah adapted to having a new naval officer to work with. The work continued smoothly even though the beaches were under sporadic German artillery fire for the next few weeks. As time passed the 1st ESB grew to become the Utah Beach Command composed of 25,000 men. Eventually it became the Utah District covering the entire Cotentin Peninsula with over 70,000 men operating in the area. In December the 1st ESB left for the States. Later on in the Pacific it would participate in the invasion of Okinawa.

The 5th and 6th Engineer Special Brigades

Both the 5th and 6th ESBs were organized in England from existing Engineer Combat Groups. The 5th ESB was formed in November 1943 out of the 1119th Eng Combat group (37, 336, and 348th Eng. C. battalions). The 5th ESB was commanded by General William Hoge. The 6th ESB was formed in January 1944 from the 1116th Eng. Combat Group, (147, 149, 203rd Eng. C. battalions). In March 1944 Col. Paul Thompson, former commander of the Assault Training Center, was given command of the 6th ESB.

To provide for overall control of the two brigades on Omaha Beach, the Provisional

Right.
Clearing mines was one of the main jobs of the engineer units. The Germans had laid an enormous number of mines, using both German and captured French stocks. A pile of concrete German Stock-mines are piled by the SCR-625 metal detector carried by Lieutenant Merle Kirsten. In the foreground are French anti-tank mines captured and reused by the Germans. The white tape marks the edge of the area that has been checked.

Below right.
An ambulance from the 1st Medical Bn, 1st Inf. Div., comes ashore from a Rhino Ferry. The Engineers are staking down Sommerfeld track so it will not shift when the vehicles cross it. In England the ambulance would have been marked with the ship number it was to board. Once across the Channel a card placed on the front grill would indicate the transit area it should be directed to.

Amphibious units patches

The blue and yellow insignia of the Engineer Special Brigades was based upon the British insignia designed for Combined Operations units. It was composed of an eagle, a submachine gun, and an anchor. These three elements were supposed to represent combined operations on air, land and sea.

In late 1942 the blue and gold insignia was authorized for units of the Engineer Amphibian Command. On 8 April, 1944 the same insignia was authorized for:
– Amphibian Tank Battalions
– Amphibian Tractor Battalions
– Engineer Amphibian Units
– Joint Assault Signal Companies
– Headquarters Ships Detachments (Type A and B)
– Headquarters Section (Army) Amphibian Training Command.

A small white pocket patch with a blue seahorse was also worn by members of the ESBs on the left pocket of their dress uniforms. This is one of the few pocket patches authorized by the U.S. Army during the war. White tabs with the different brigade numbers were a postwar addition, and not used during WW2.

Above.
The officer in front of this memorial service has an excellent example of a medical helmet worn in an ESB unit. The helmet has red crosses outlined in white, but no white background. Captain's bars are painted under the ESB insignia.

This ESB medic is prepared to wade ashore from a landing craft on D-Day. Like most men in ESB units he wears jump boots, and impregnated HBTs under his field jacket. As an aidman, he wears the medical aid pouches and special suspenders. A life belt has been tied to his stretcher so that it will float to shore if he has to drop it in the water. Like most medics pictured on D-Day, he wears the red cross on his armband, but not his helmet (which does have the ESB markings). Goggles are worn as protection against the sea spray, and a parachutist's first-aid pouch is tied to his leg for easy access.

Left.
Engineers lay down a road of Sommerfeld trackway on Omaha Beach. This was a roll of wire mesh, reinforced with steel inserts, that allowed vehicles to move on beach sand without getting stuck. In the background is a damaged LCVP and two different models of bulldozers.

Bottom left.
A small rock quarry was opened near the D-1 exit at Vierville. In the background is a portable rock crusher. Crushed rock was considered essential to provide a solid base for roadwork. After the beaches were opened, most of the engineering work performed by the ESBs was continual road maintenance.

Engineer Special Brigade Group was formed in March 1944. The original intention had been to provide a small headquarters group to coordinate the activities of the 5th and 6th ESBs. It soon became apparent that the plans for Omaha were so immense that additional staff was needed to work out all the details. This led to a headquarters company to support the staff, then other units were deemed necessary and attached to the Provisional Group.

First to be attached to the Group HQ was a communications unit, then a military police company. A finance section was included to handle the payrolls of both the soldiers and the expected civilian workers.

Eventually, the Provisional Group Headquarters grew to include almost 1,400 men. General Hoge was promoted from the 5th ESB to command the Provisional Group. Col. William D. Bridges was given command of the 5th ESB.

The 5th and 6th ESBs were designed to support the landings and subsequent supply operations over Omaha Beach. They were not designed to support the operations of the artificial Mulberry harbor or the minor ports in the Normandy area. To handle those activities the Provisional Group was assigned the 11th Port in April. The 11th Port, essentially a Transportation Corps unit, did not have a specific military designation such as battalion or brigade. It was a collection of units needed to run a full-fledged naval port. The 11th Port contained over 8,500 men, but they were trained to handle supplies landing on docks in a real harbor. They were to land in France after the area was secure and take over supply operations on the beaches, minor ports, and hopefully the captured port of Cherbourg.

The 5th and 6th ESBs participated in Operation Fabius, the dress rehearsal for the Omaha landings. There were a few problems that needed correction, but for the most part their performance was good. Unlike the 1st ESB, the German torpedo boats did not interfere with their operations.

The first element of the Brigade ashore on Omaha was a recon party from the 37th Engineers at 0700 hrs. Although the entire area had been carefully mapped, and locations for beach installations and supply had been planned out in detail, the area had to be checked in case of surprises that did not show up in aerial photos. In the morning hours the 6th ESB was temporarily attached to the 5th ESB. Both units would later report to the Provisional Group Headquarters when it landed at roughly 1500 hrs near the E-1 exit.

The unexpected enemy firepower, coupled with the confusion resulting from misplaced landings, resulted in a delay for most of the plans for Omaha. ESB engineers

Right.
A bulldozer tows a Dukw ashore onto a roadway of Sommerfeld tracking. To the left is a second track of Chespalling. This was length of canvas reinforced with wooden slats. A rack on the side of the bulldozer holds spare cans of gasoline.

Below.
A white officer (with vertical helmet stripe) leads a group of black soldiers on a sniper hunt in the Vierville area. Along with the 320th Barrage Balloon Bn., there were a number of Port and transportation units composed of black troops in the Engineer Special Brigades. These may be members of the 3565th Ord. Medium Auto Maintenance Co. that was used to help clear the area.

found themselves helping out the assault troops in the fight for the beach. A number of ESB units took heavy casualties and the commander of the 37th Eng. C. Bn. was killed by mortar fire early in the day.

Col. Paul Thompson attempted to rally men in an assault against a German emplacement at the D-3 exit. His experience at the Assault Training Center had prepared him to handle the job of any of the assault troops. He was helping some engineers blow the barbed wire with Bangalore torpedoes when he was badly wounded. His executive officer, Col. Chase, had previously been badly burned on his face and arms when the craft he was on (LCI-92) was hit. Chase helped evacuate this ship, which contained men from the 147th and 149th Engineers and two platoons of the 214th MP Co., then took over command of the 6th ESB. Chase was an infantry officer, so he was later replaced by an engineer, Col. Timothy Mullins, the deputy commander of the Provisional ESB Group.

Upon landing, the men of the ESBs found the situation ashore did not allow them to start the planned construction of roads and supply dumps. Instead of waiting for the infantry to clear the beach, the engineers and their attached troops pitched in to help drive the Germans from the bluffs overlooking Omaha. A great many men from the 5th and 6th ESBs were cited for heroism in this fight. One such example was a group of men from the 95th QM Bn. They had landed on Easy Red Beach with trucks loaded down with gasoline and ammunition. A few of the trucks were hit and caught fire. The drivers did not leave their burning vehicles, but drove them down the beach so they would not pose a danger to the rest of the unit.

A lieutenant in charge of the dump trucks of the 37th Engineer Combat Bn. decided that he was not able to perform his assigned mission, so he organized a group of men sheltering in his area and led them up the bluffs to sweep through the German positions above Easy Red. Although the 16th Infantry had

Left.
Somewhere in the Beach Maintenance area behind Omaha Beach, these men tap into a barrel of cider. One soldier, at left, had liberated a double-barrelled shotgun as a souvenir. In their search for cider, many American soldiers discovered the extremely powerful kick of the locally brewed Calvados.

Above.
An MP on Utah Beach speaks with a German POW being evacuated off the beach. Each ESB had an MP company to guard POWs in the beach area. Escort Guard companies were attached to guard the prisoners during the voyage back to England. Note the 1st ESB arc painted on his helmet.

already been through this area, the impromptu unit killed or captured 25 German soldiers that had been overlooked. Men from the 3205th QM Service Co. found themselves assisting the Rangers in the fight for Vierville.

Working together with the engineers attached to the 1st and 29th Divisions, units of the ESBs gradually opened up the beach exits, cleared the area of mines, and began setting up the transit areas behind the bluffs. The roads leading inland started to fill with vehicles and the engineers began their task of converting this quiet farming community into a massive supply depot designed to support the entire American First Army.

ESB helmets were painted by whomever in the unit had the most artistic talent, or was simply picked by the Sergeant for this task. This means that there is no one correct style for the markings. Some appear to be hand painted, others airbrushed or stenciled. Many ESB helmet liners were also painted with the markings. Some of the engineer units wore helmet liners that were marked with the soldier's name on the front, and white engineer castles on each side. With so many different units in the three ESBs, a wide variety of markings and styles can be found.

Left.
This portrait of an unknown Ordnance Lieutenant, probably from the 191st Ordnance Bn., provides a classic example of the full white arc painted on helmets of the 1st ESB. Although no documentation has been located indicating exactly what units used this marking, careful examination of photographs from the invasion show with great certainty that it was the organic units of the 1st ESB. It is not known if the attached units used this marking.
(Courtesy Jean-Yves Nasse)

Top.
The 5th and 6th ESBs used the smaller arc with blue and yellow amphibious engineer insignia.
This helmet has also been camouflaged with wide brush strokes.

Bottom.
Another Provisional Engineer Special Brigade helmet and liner, found in Normandy.

Engineer Special Brigade Helmets

The most commonly asked question about the Engineer Special Brigades is why did they have special markings on their helmets. No official document has been found explaining these markings, but there is a suggested reason that most experts agree on.

One of the major concerns in an amphibious landing is to keep the beach clear of men and equipment that are not needed there. Beaches are confusing enough without excess men getting in the way. It is also well-known that landing beaches provide a good target for enemy artillery fire and aerial bombardments. In a Jan. 1944 document, the British specifically called for a special marking to signify authorized beach personnel. British troops serving in the same function as the ESBs were identified by a band painted around their helmet.

Veterans of the ESBs do not recall ever being told why they had helmet markings. Some recalled it was a matter of pride to have their blue and gold patch painted on their helmet, but most never gave it any thought. From examination of period photographs it seems that only the men of the Provisional ESB Group (5th and 6th ESBs) had the amphibious engineer insignia painted on their helmets, underneath a small white arc. The men of the 1st ESB on Utah Beach did not have the insignia, but used a larger edge to edge white arc.

Pfc William Ashley, in the 147th Eng. C. Bn., had been made the sign painter for his battalion due to his artistic expertise. He recalls that he painted all the helmets in his battalion, but never wondered or asked about the markings. No instructions were given as to the method he should use, so he developed his own. Using a template, he chalked the outline the various elements. Then he painted them in by hand. He had no knowledge of how the other battalions painted their helmets, so it is possible that other units used different methods. After the invasion Ashley was asked to put his talents to a different use when he painted the sign marking the first American cemetery at Omaha Beach.

The short white arc is sometimes referred to as the "high-water mark" by ESB veterans. It is not clear if this was a wartime term or one developed in the post war years. The short white arc was used by men in the 5th and 6th ESBs, as well as the Provisional

Group Headquarters. The attached sailors of the 6th and 7th Naval Beach Battalion had a short red arc on their helmets.

Curiously, one of the few color photographs to have been taken on either beach shows a man wearing a helmet with a full blue arc. No one has been able to identify what unit used the blue arc. From the style of the arc it probably was a unit in the 1st ESB on Utah Beach. It had previously been erroneously identified as belonging to one of the Naval Combat Demolition Units. It has now been proven that the NCDUs wore only the gray Navy band with the letters USN.

Above.
This ESB colonel has had a larger than normal rank insignia painted on his helmet. The brush strokes are clearly visible in these markings.

Below.
This helmet liner and shell were found separately in France. The blue arc of an unknown 1st ESB unit is painted on both.

After the invasion

At first, supplies of all types were placed in emergency dumps on the beach itself. In case the expected German counter-attack pushed the Allies back, they wanted to make sure that they would have a reserve handy. The Dukws of the ESB were preloaded with supplies in England. On their first trip to the beach they brought ashore the basis for these emergency dumps.

By D+1 the initial dump phase had started, with small supply dumps being placed just behind the beach. Opening these dumps was not a simple task. The entire area had to first be carefully checked for mines. Then information on the exact location of the

Above.
An Engineer Light Equipment Company operates rock crushing equipment in a quarry near Carentan. Crushed rock was used to upgrade and repair roadbeds. A steam shovel drops rocks into the portable crusher. The rocks are crushed into gravel, then travel up the conveyor belt into the truck at right.

dump sent to the proper headquarters and signs posted. Individual German soldiers were scattered throughout the area and the men were constantly interrupted by sniper fire. Eventually, on D+3, the 3/23rd Infantry Regiment was given the task of clearing all German snipers and stragglers from the Omaha area. The 3565th Ord. MAM (Medium Auto Maintenance) Co. assisted them in sweeping a 3,000 yard path. No Germans were found, but a number of casualties were caused by land mines.

About D+6 the troops had pushed inland enough to allow for expansion of the supply dumps to further inland. As soon as possible the assigned units of the ESBs continued to develop the area up to five miles

Right.
The engineers decided that the bulldozer was the most useful item they had. It is hard to believe that only a few years prior the U.S. Army did not want to purchase bulldozers, as it thought men equipped with pick and shovel could do the same job. Dozers, without the blade, could be used for pushing or towing, but the addition of a blade made it a very versatile machine. This bulldozer clears rubble off the road in a local town.

Left.
This photograph is officially captioned as being half-tracks and 57mm antitank guns from the 1st ESB. Close examination of the markings (1-18-I, 3-13) reveal this is the antitank squad of the 3rd Bn, 18th Infantry Regt, 1st Inf. Div. The table of organization states this unit should have 1 1/2 ton trucks to tow their guns, but there is evidence in printed memoirs that the 18th was issued with halftracks. Note the round tactical sign for the 18th Infantry on the bumper and side of the halftrack .

Special Equipment issued to 1st ESB Engineer Shore Bns.

Item	per Bn
Ardante loud hailer equipment	3
Bucket, clamshell, 3/4 yard	1
Bucket, drag line, 3/8 yard	1
Button, traffic, radioactive	1,000
Conveyor, roller, 8 foot length	25
Crane, truck mounted, 7 1/2 ton 25 t boom	3
Crane, crawler mounted, 7 1/2 ton	6
Net, cargo 12 x 12 foot	300
Sign box, interior illuminated	24
Shovel attachment for crane	1
Tape marker, luminous, 1,000 yard roll	27
Tank, canvas, 1,000 gallon	3
Trackway, Chespalling, 25 foot rolls	5,000 yards
Trackway, Sommerfeld, 25 foot rolls	3,000 yards
Tractor, crawler, w/bulldozer blade	9
Tractor, Ord, M1 w/winch	4
Trailer, full flat bed, 20 ton	6
Trailer, 6-ton Athey flat bed	9
Truck, 6-ton, 6x6 prime mover	6
Compressor, air, portable, 350 cubic ft	3
Burlap, 30-36" wide	25,000 yards
Beach marking panel and light set	2
Electric arc welding set	1
Electric lighting set	1

inland. A massive project was the construction, improvement, and continual repair of the road system. The constant heavy traffic, including many tracked vehicles, continually wore down the small Norman roads. This was a problem that never ended until the area was finally abandoned in November 1944.

The Germans did not use chemical weapons in Normandy, so there was nothing for the Chemical Decontamination Companies to do. They were put to work performing all types of jobs that came up at the last moment. Some of them were used to assist the de-waterproofing of vehicles. The chemical decontamination trucks were used to spray oil on the roads to keep down the dust. The chemical companies were frequently given these extra assignments because they were the only troops that could not claim to be overworked. They were used to clear the beaches of non-essential personnel in the nights following 6 June, and often helped the Graves Registration Companies collect bodies.

One of the most important jobs assigned to the ESBs was road maintenance. In August they had to

Above.

Brigadier General James Wharton, commander of the 1st ESB, escorts Admiral Harold Stark, commander of naval forces in Europe, on an inspection of Utah Beach. Seated is Rear Admiral Alan Kirk. This was probably taken about 14 June when Stark visited the beaches. Waterproofing compound is still covering the headlights of the command car.

Below.

Members of the 1st ESB leave a small, war damaged church after services. Most of the men have the full arc of the 1st ESB on their helmets and carry the assault gas mask. Those in front are trying to avoid tripping on the communications wire that has been strung along the road.

contend with clouds of dust stirred up by the constant traffic. Later in September the roads turned to mud. There was not enough crushed rock available to use as a base for the road, but the engineers knew it was vitally important to keep the flow of supplies moving inland. Somewhere, buried under a road in Normandy, lies roughly a quarter mile of lead-cased batteries that were used in place of crushed rock. On other occasions the shingle from the beach was scooped up and used for roadbeds. Starting on 11 June, the 11th Port began taking over the task of getting supplies to shore.

But the job of the Engineer Special Brigades did not end for many months. The storm of 20 June destroyed the Mulberry harbor. The landing of men,

equipment and supplies over the beaches had to be improvised. What had been considered a stopgap approach until "Mulberry A" and the port of Cherbourg were available now became the life line of the American Army. The task was harder than before due to the many landing craft that had been damaged in the storm.

Men of the Provisional ESB Group continued to assist in the operation of the beaches until late in the fall. One by one the attached units were transferred away. In October the 348th Eng. C Bn., 487th Port Bn. and 4141st QM Service Co. were sent to take over the Arromanches Mulberry harbor from the British. Ammunition was one of their highest priorities and they were able to send six fully loaded trains of ammo a day to the front lines. In November 1944 the 5th ESB was reassigned to the Paris region to take charge of all engineer operations in that area. Eventually they would be given the job of constructing the redeployment "cigarette camps."

At the start of December 1944 a curious role reversal occurred in the 6th ESB. Prior to D-Day they had

Left.
The 616th Ordnance Ammo Co. salvage German munitions on Omaha Beach. The area needed to be cleared of dangerous materials and the ordnance troops were the best prepared to deal with enemy ammunition. The weapons carrier behind has bumper markings for "Det-1, 162nd Signal." It was not uncommon for photographers to park their vehicles in a photo to make sure they got credit for the shot, or to later burn in their unit information on another unit's vehicle.

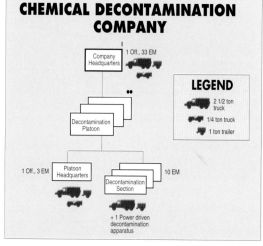

Below.
This Chemical Decontamination Company practised cleaning chemical agents off vehicles in England, but never had a chance to use this skill in France. The best use found for their equipment was using the chemical decontamination trucks to spray a film of oil on the dirt roads to keep the dust down. The oil had been provided for the smoke generators, in case it was necessary to create a smoke screen over the beach area.

been prepared to invade the French coast against German defenders. Now the 6th was assigned the task of defending the French coast against a possible German invasion organized by the estimated 20,000 German troops stationed on the Channel Islands. The 6th ESB patrolled the entire west coast of the Cotentin Peninsula until just before Christmas. Then the 156th Infantry Regt., stationed in Paris, was sent to relieve them and the three engineer bns. were rapidly shipped to assist in the defense against the Germans in the Ardennes.

Eventually, the 6th ESB was sent to the Verdun-Metz area to construct hospitals and other facilities. In March they became the Advance Section Engineer Rhine Coal Control, in charge of getting the German coal mines back into operation. By the time they turned the mines over to the British in June 1945, the 6th ESB, with the assistance of some mining specialists, had put 200 mines back into operation. They had raised coal production from nothing to 2 million tons a month. The 6th ESB was sent back to the States for redeployment to the Pacific, but when Japan surrendered the unit was disbanded.

JASCO- Joint Assault Signal Company

The communications plans for the invasion revolved around the Engineer Special Brigade communications companies. These were generally referred to as JASCOs. The Joint Assault Signal Company was composed of three different sections. The main part of the unit, the Beach Communications Section, provided all communications for the Engineer Special Brigade. The other two sections, Air Liaison and Naval Shore Fire Control Parties, were administratively part of the JASCO, but in practice trained and operated separately. These two groups were attached to the infantry unit they were to support long before the invasion and rarely had anything to do with the main section of the JASCO.

The first JASCOs were organized as under the name of "Signal Company, Special" at Camp Bradford in March 1943. In December 1943 they were reorganized with the addition of the Air Liaison and Naval Shore Fire Control Parties. The term "joint assault" replaced the "special" category due to the inclusion of Air Force personnel in the air sections, and naval personnel in the gunfire parties.

In Normandy, the 293rd JASCO was attached to the 6th ESB, and the 294th JASCO to the 5th ESB. On Utah Beach the 286th JASCO worked under the 1st ESB. In March 1944 each company was provided an extra 125 men for both the shore fire and beach communications sections. In April 1944 the air and Naval Shore Fire Control Parties were placed on detached service with their assigned assault divisions, and had little contact with their parent JASCO. The U.S. Navy was supposed to provide a contingent of signalmen to the JASCOs, but the naval authorities in England decided that the communications sec-

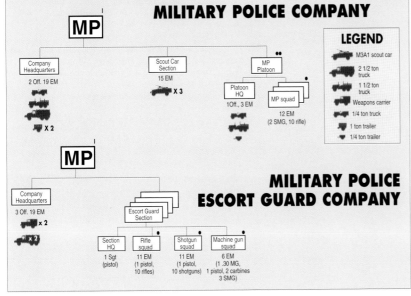

JASCO detachment assigned to each engineer company

Army personnel
1 Communications chief
3 linemen
2 switchboard operators
2 radio operators
1 message center clerk
1 messenger

Equipment
2 SCR-609
1 M-209 converter
1 eight drop switchboard
4 miles, W-130 phone wire
6 EE-8 field telephones
500 feet W-110 phone wire
Spare batteries for the
first 24 hours of operation

Left.
A JASCO unit sets up an SCR-609 during a practice landing. Behind them an antiaircraft unit manhandles two water-cooled .50 caliber machine guns off an LCM. These were the first antiaircraft protection to be set up on the beachhead.

tions of the Navy Beach Battalions could provide the same service and refused to release the manpower. This left the JASCOs understrength for their assigned tasks and placed a great reliance on their ability to work in conjunction with the Beach Battalions.

Each JASCO beach communications section was grouped into four operating units. A Brigade Signal Platoon was to provide all the communications services to the Engineer Special Brigade Headquarters. Each of the three engineer battalions in the ESB were assigned a JASCO battalion signal platoon. These platoons provided a 24-man team to the engineer battalion headquarters, and a ten-man signal team to each of the engineer companies.

The signal teams were to accompany their assigned units ashore and immediately start to set up radio and telephone links with their comrades to either side. The standard operating procedure was for each signal unit to be responsible for providing the link down to the next lower echelon and to the unit on their right. Once the initial radio nets and phone lines were in place, these units were to provide communications systems for the entire beach maintenan-

JOINT ASSAULT SIGNAL COMPANY (JASCO)
(First Army modification, 31 March 1944)

```
                    Company
49 (Off. & EM)      Headquarters

Air Liaison      Naval Shore Fire                    Brigade Signal
Party            Control Party (NSFCP)               Platoon         4 Off., 96 EM
13 Off., 34 EM   9 Off., 39 EM

                 (One attached
                 per Engineer      Beach
                 Combat Battalion) Communications
                                   Section

(Attached                                (Attached
to Engineer      Battalion Signal        to each Engineer
Combat Battalion HQ) Platoon             Company HQ)
                 2 Off., 22 EM   Company Signal
                                 Detachment
                                 10 EM
```

ce area. Each JASCO unit had been told what fields were scheduled to be used as transit areas, or supply dumps, and what types of communications lines needed to be run to these areas. Over the following weeks an impressive amount of telephone wire was strung all across the beach maintenance area.

Each of the ten-man company level detachment was equipped with a special eight line switchboard, six telephones, two SCR-609 radios, an M-209 converter (a decoding unit), and a large supply of telephone wire. The 24 man team assigned to the engineer battalion was equipped with larger switchboards, more telephones, SCR-609 and SCR-284 radios. The brigade support platoon was provided with a central office switchboard, multiple radios, and at least four miles of phone wire. The ESB section had even more equipment, including an SCR-399 radio to provide cross Channel communications with England.

The first beach communications team ashore was attached to Company C, 149th Eng C Bn. It landed at H+45 minutes on Easy Red Beach. Their SCR-609 was lost when their landing craft was hit, but by 0730 contact had been made with the 116th Infantry Regt. on an SCR-300. German fire was too heavy to permit the men to start running telephone wire, so the signalmen dug in and provided what help they could to the infantry.

By 1000 hrs the beginnings of a basic telephone wire system was being put into place on Omaha. Infantry units were desperate for working radios, so many of the JASCO radios were handed over to the combat units. The communications plan for Omaha had not gone as expected and a great deal of equip-

Five different sizes of waterproof black rubber bags were made to keep signal equipment dry during amphibious assaults. The largest had two shoulder straps and could be worn as a backpack. The SCR-609 radio, one of the more commonly used radios at Normandy, was too large to fit into this back. It had to be broken down and carried in two different bags.

Above.
A group of signalmen waiting to board an LST in Portland harbor. Two of them use the large rubber backpacks, designed to carry signal equipment and keep it dry while coming ashore. These rubber bags had the official designation "bag, waterproof, special purpose." They were made in five different sizes, the largest being the full backpack worn here.

Left.
Members of the 286th Joint Assault Signal Company (JASCO) set up their signal equipment in an abandoned German trench on Utah Beach. The 286th provided all communications for the 1st Engineer Special Brigade. They have the 1st ESB arc on their helmets, but are not wearing the amphibious engineer shoulder insignia.

The activities of the Marine Corps Navaho Code Talkers in the Pacific have been well documented. A unit of Native American signalmen also took part in the Normandy invasion, but their story remains almost unknown.

Although many historians have theorized how the Comanche Code Talkers may have been used at Normandy, it was thought that their use was so secret that records of the unit would never be found. The truth is actually much simpler, and it may come as a surprise that the Comanche Code Talkers were never the classified unit some have made them out to be.

The origins of the Comanche Code Talkers is unclear. It seems that during the First World War there had been attempts to use Native Americans to send messages over field telephone lines. The Germans had developed sophisticated listening equipment and could eavesdrop on Allied telephone lines. American Indian languages were difficult to both speak and understand unless one was raised in the correct tribe. Many of the dialects were unlike any other language spoken and few, if any, outsiders could comprehend them. After WW1, it seems that a few German language students took a particular interest in

learning Native American Tongues, but the Indians refused to instruct them. It was fairly clear this interest had more to do with military intelligence than linguistics.

Although the use of Indian languages in WW1 has not been fully documented, it seems that someone in the 4th Infantry Division in 1941 had known about it, and thought it might be good to try again.

Lt. Hugh F. Foster, a brand-new second Lieutenant out of West Point, was given the job of developing the use of the Comanche language in the 4th Infantry Division Signal Company. Foster was able to locate 17 Comanche speakers in the Division and they were transferred to the 4th Signal Company. At the time no one had heard of the Navaho Code Talkers the U.S. Marines were training.

Many of the military terms that would be needed had no matching word in the Comanche language. For months the men discussed substitute words they could use. The word turtle would stand for tank. Bird meant an airplane, and a pregnant bird stood for a bomber. For words that needed to be spelled out, such as the name of towns, a strange phonetic alphabet was used. The Comanches would first say a word meaning "*I am spelling*," then use Comanche words of which the first letter of their English meaning would spell out what was needed. Finally another word was used to indicate "*I am not longer spelling*." Eventually a military vocabulary of about 250 words was developed.

What is unusual about the Comanche Code Talkers is that these men had normal Signal Corps duties to perform in addition to working on the code. They had to put in their shifts as switchboard operators or telephone wiremen. Many of them were in Lt Foster's wire platoon. One of the stranger tasks they had was to string field telephone wire between the various radio stations in the unit. The

The Comanche Code Talkers

A group photo of some of the Comanche Code Talkers stationed with the 4th Signal Company, 4th Infantry Division, at Ft. Benning in 1941. Front L-R Forrest Kassanavoid, Charles Chibbitty, Larry Saupitty, Roderick Red Elk. Rear L-R, Edward Nahquaddy, Haddon Codynah, Ralph Wahnee, Willis Yackeshi, Perry Noyobad.

Left.
A Comanche signalman stringing telephone wire at Camp Gordon, Georgia in December 1941. The Comanche Code Talkers each had a regular job in the Signal Company along with any Code duties. They were not treated any different from the rest of the men.

Below.
Comanche Private Wellington Mihecoby, a telephone switchboard operator, stands beside his BD-72 twelve line switchboard during the Carolina Maneuvers of 1941. It appears he is wearing the blue denim fatigue trousers in use by the prewar Army.

radio operators needed to use telephones to get help get their early pattern radios tuned to the same frequencies.

Out of the 17 Comanches trained only 14 or 15 went overseas in the Signal Company. All 15 served in the 4th Infantry Division. The plan called for teams of two Comanches to be available at divisional and regimental signal units in case a message had to be sent in code. Although not kept a strict secret, the use of the Comanche language was not publicized before the 4th went overseas, Lt. Foster was sent to a special radar school and eventually commanded all radar installations along the North African Coast. He stayed in the Army and eventually commanded the 1st Signal Brigade in Vietnam.

On D-Day

A team of Code talkers landed with the first waves of the 8th Inf. Regt at Utah Beach. The first message sent back to 4th Division HQ stated "*Red beach, wrong place.*" The Comanches continued to serve throughout the ETO with the 4th Division in dual roles as regular signalmen, and as specialist code talkers when needed.

In 1989 the Comanche Code Talkers were officially recognized for their contributions by the French Government. Lt. Foster (now a retired General)was made an honorary member of the Comanche tribe with the name "*Poo-hee-wee-tek-wha Eksa-bahn*" meaning "Telephone Soldier." It was the closest the Comanche language could come to "Signal Officer."

This shoulder patch is thought to be an insignia of the Joint Assault Signal Companies. The design contains signal flags for the beach communications section, crossed naval cannon for the Shore fire control party, and an eagle for the air liaison party. An anchor signifies the amphibious nature of the unit. Although clearly associated with the JASCOs, veterans of the three D-Day JASCOs have no knowledge about it. It is thought that this patch was used by the JASCOs operating in the Pacific, but no evidence has been located to substantiate this theory. This rare patch has only been found with a blue twill background.

ment had been lost or destroyed. Most of the heavy equipment had been held back until the beach was secure, and things progressed rapidly after the first day. On D+1 more men and equipment were landed and the radio and telephone links were in place. There was continuous trouble with vehicles breaking the phone wire and wire teams were continually sent out to fix the phone lines.

There were a few other signal units landing later that were not part of the JASCOs. Signal Photographic Company teams took still and motion pictures of the invasion. British VHF radio detachments provided a special radio link to England. Detachments of the 175th Signal Repair Co. took over maintenance of the telephone wires. The 215th Signal Depot Section ran the Signal Corps supply dumps. At the Provisional ESB Group headquarters communications were operated by the 246th Signal Co. When the area had been secured, the 255th Sig Construction Co performed all the heavy telephone line construction in the Beach Maintenance area, and the 990th Signal Port Service Co supplied communications for the 11th Port. In the Utah Beach area over 200 telephones were installed in June. These, similar to the system at Omaha Beach, linked the various beach sectors and headquarters with transit areas and supply dumps inland.

This signalman from one of the JASCOs has a black rubber radio bag on his back. In the ammo bag strapped next to his entrenching tool he might be carrying a mixture of grenades and supplies he will need to get the signals network operational on the far shore. Signalmen were trained to dig large foxholes while their comrades were setting the equipment set up. As soon as the radio or switchboard was operational they would have a protected place to operate it from.
(Reconstruction)

Below.
The Army developed five different sized black rubber bags to protect radio equipment from getting wet during a landing. The BG–160 is the largest of the bags. It could be worn as a backpack and carry a complete SCR-300 radio.

Chapter 9.
"Making It Stick"

THE original plans for the invasion were based on the Army capturing the nearby port of Cherbourg soon after the initial landing. An artificial harbor was planned for the Omaha area, but it was not expected to be as useful as an actual port with docks, cranes, rail yards, and warehouses. The Engineer Special Brigades (ESBs) were trained to bring supplies across a beach, but had no training specific to operating a real port.

Above.
LCT 550 has a side mounted superstructure which identifies it as an LCT(6). This model of LCT could marry up to the ramp of an LST at sea and take on a load of vehicles much the same as a Rhino Ferry. These ambulances are from the 19th Corps' 546th Medical Bn. They probably crossed the Channel in an LST and were transferred to this LCT for the trip ashore.

Below.
Ammunition and food were vital to the combat troops, but their morale had to be thought of as well. The first Red Cross clubmobile to land in France is shown here. Clubmobiles provided hot coffee and doughnuts to soldiers near the front line. More importantly, they were staffed by the first American women some of the troops had seen in years.

The 11th Port

The 11th Port was attached to the Provisional Engineer Special Brigade Group to handle the actual port operations. It was hoped that once the major ports in France were operating, the ESBs could be released for other duties.

The 11th Port was essentially a mixture of Quartermaster Corps and Transportation Corps units. Port companies unloaded the transport ships. Amphibious truck companies of Dukws were used to bring supplies ashore. Truck companies were used to move supplies on shore. Quartermaster units were then used to sort, inventory, and issue the materials.

Logistical support troops in the area behind the front lines were normally considered to be part of the Communications Zone, or COMZ as it was called. The logistical plans for the invasion called for the advance group of COMZ to be ready to take over control of installations as soon as the First Army moved inland away from the beaches. The Advance Section of COMZ was known as ADSEC. ADSEC troops started to land roughly a week after D-Day, but discovered that the front lines had not advanced as far into France as planned. The Quartermasters of the First Army could not move forward, so they did

not wish to hand over their installations to ADSEC control. Eventually, the First Army moved on and ADSEC took over all logistical facilities near the beaches. About three months after the invasion, COMZ headquarters finally moved from England to France and took over from ADSEC.

The first ADSEC unit at Utah Beach was the 38th Engineer General Service Regt. It arrived on 10 June, marking the transition to the beach maintenance phase with supply dumps extending inland up to five miles. About this time a fourth beach on Utah, Roger White, was opened up but it was a few more days before operations there started because the Germans were still able to shell the area. The inability of the Americans to work in the northern Utah beaches also hampered repair of the northern sluice gates which

Elements of the 11th Port

The elements of the 11th Port changed over time. The following list contains all major units when the 11th Port was at its maximum strength.

11th Port Hq&Hq Co
Col Whitcomb commanding

1594 Eng Utility Plat.	535rd Port Co.	4093rd QM Service Co.
334th Harbor Craft Co.	536th Port Co.	3263rd QM Service Co.
990th Port Signal Serv Co.	537th Port Co.	554th QM Service Bn
1st Bn, 358th Eng GS Regt	509th Port Bn	4058th QM Service Co.
302nd MP Escort Guard Co.	306th Port Co.	4145th QM Service Co.
3531 Ord MAM Co.	307th Port Co.	4191st QM Service Co.
40th Sig Const Co.	308th Port Co.	4146th QM Service Co.
516th Port Bn .	309th Port Co.	512th QM Bn.
534th Port Co.	514th Port Bn .	4009th QM Trk Co.
	526th Port Co.	3582 QM Trk Co.
	527th Port Co.	3583 QM Trk Co.
	528th Port Co.	512th QM Group
	529th Port Co.	467th Amph Trk Co.
	688th QM Bn.	468th Amph Trk Co.
	91st QM Serv Co.	469th Amph Trk Co.
	145th QM Serv Co.	174th QM Bn .
	4058th QM Serv Co.	470th Amph Trk Co.
	556th QM Service Bn .	821st Amph Trk Co.
	4183rd QM Service Co.	819th Amph Trk Co.
	4182nd QM Service Co.	

controlled the flooding of the inundated area. The infantry pushed the Germans back to Cherbourg and allowed the gates to be repaired, the fields drained, and Roger White Beach to be used to bring in supplies. On 13 June supply dumps on the road to Isigny were opened.

The troops of the 11th Port did not expect to operate on the beaches. They planned to take over operations at Cherbourg and the artificial harbor at Omaha. By 8 June only 17,000 troops had landed, far short of the planned amount of 22,800 men. Supply tonnage was running at only 9,896 instead of the planned 12,700. Only 2,645 of the 4,000 expected vehicles had been brought ashore. Most of these shortages were caused by the unexpected delay in getting the Omaha Beach exits cleared of fire and the roads open to traffic. A severe shortage of ammunition, specifically artillery shells, developed. At times ammunition was unloaded and brought directly to the front lines instead of passing through a supply dump.

"Mulberry A," the artificial harbor at Omaha, started to operate on 16 June. It took only two hours

Above.

to unload the first LST that pulled up to the pier. With practice the average unloading time for an LST was only 40 minutes. This was a vast improvement over the 12 to 14 hours it took to dry out an LST on the beach. The 11th Port took over operations of Mulberry A as planned and the supplies started to flow ashore. But the Mulberry operations were short lived, as on the night of 19 June the wind started

Above.

Looking ashore from one of the floating piers, the Omaha D-1 exit can be seen on shore to the right. The first LST to discharge cargo took two hours. The average for the first day was roughly 60 minutes per ship, but later on the crews were able to get it down to only 40 minutes per LST. This saved an enormous amount of time considering it took 12 to 14 hours to disembark an LST directly onto the shore by drying out.

Members of Advance Section units wore the standard ETO patch with the ADSEC tab above. The patch is a typical embroidered on felt version as was commonly produced in England.

to pick up. The storm that was approaching was about to bring the American Army to the brink of disaster.

Navy Seabees

The Navy Construction Battalions, sometimes referred to as C.B.s (or Sea Bees) were an unusual group of men. Many of them were older than the average soldier, and had experience in the construction trades. The Seabees recruited men up to 50 years old, as opposed to the lower age of 31 for most of the armed forces. The Seabees were formed when the Navy worried what would happen if civilian construction workers were asked to function in a combat zone. According to international law such civilian workers could not carry weapons and defend themselves. It seemed logical to enlist construction workers into the service and provide them with basic military skills. The Seabees were expected to be able to continue to work under enemy fire and defend themselves if necessary.

The Seabees were thought to perform miracles when it came to construction of naval facilities. At Normandy they were involved with a number of construction projects including the artificial harbors, the sunken causeways, and the Rhino Ferries.

A popular misconception regarding the Seabees is that they took part in the clearing of beach obstacles on D-Day but this is not true. Many of the sailors forming the Naval Combat Demolition Units had been Seabees prior to going to NCDU school, but they no longer wore the "CB" insignia on their uniform, and were not considered part of any Seabee outfit.

The story of the artificial Mulberry harbors is, however, closely tied to the Seabees. One of the major problems with amphibious operations is that

Left.

This photo shows one of the sunken causeways on Omaha Beach. The landing blisters on each side of the causeway are clearly visible. An LCT is unloading at the second set of blisters. As the tide came in or went out, LCTs would use the blister that was at the right water level for them. The Gooseberry blockships are visible in the background.

ships can not get close enough to the shore to unload their cargo. In the invasion of Sicily, LSTs could get as close as 300 feet from shore. The Navy used pontoons to build 300-foot floating causeways to bridge the gap and allow men and vehicles to drive from the LSTs to dry land. The pontoon sections were assembled by the Seabees and either towed, or carried on the sides of the LSTs until arrival at the Sicilian coast.

In Normandy, the closest an LST could get to the shore at high tide was 1,100 feet. It would have been impossible to maintain an 1,100-foot pontoon causeway due to the rough Channel waters. Coastal freighters would need a pier extending 3,000 feet out to sea and Liberty

ships would need one 4,500 feet long. An additional complication was the extreme tides which rose and fell roughly twenty feet twice a day.

The British developed an idea that would be known as the Loebnitz pier. This pier was a floating barge secured to four legs planted firmly in the sea-bed. As the tide rose and fell the pierhead would always stay the same level above the water. The Loebnitz Pier was designed to be planted 3,100 feet offshore. A floating roadway known as a "Whale" would connect it to the shore. Concrete pontoons, nicknamed "Beetles" supported the floating road-way. This design worked, but only if the water was reasonably calm.

To save on steel, the Beetles had been made of concrete in both 25 ton and 40 ton versions. The idea

Top.
Rhino Ferry 2 is assisted with the extra horsepower of Rhino Tug 3, nicknamed "Hell's Angels." The original concept was that the Rhino Ferries would need the extra power of the tugs to make headway in the rough water. It turned out that the addition of a Rhino Tug made little difference to the speed or performance of the ferry and their use was discontinued.

Above.
The commander of RHF-15 (Rhino Ferry), William O. Davies, was photographed while repairs were being made to his vessel. Davies was a warrant officer, his trade being that of carpenter. He wears Army HBT coveralls over the khaki Navy working uniform. He has pinned the Navy insignia for the Civil Engineer Corps to his Army knit wool cap.

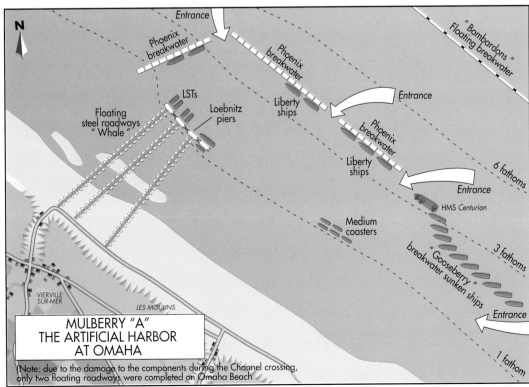

MULBERRY "A"
THE ARTIFICIAL HARBOR
AT OMAHA

(Note: due to the damage to the components during the Channel crossing, only two floating roadways were completed on Omaha Beach)

was to construct one roadway to support heavier vehicles, such as the 32 ton Sherman tank, and two others for the lighter trucks and jeeps. The problem was that many of the Beetles had been damaged in the Channel crossing. By carefully alternating 25 ton with 40 ton floats, the crews were able to allow the Shermans to disembark over the Loebnitz pier. However, it meant that only two of the planned three piers could be built at Omaha.

To protect the pier from rough water, a reinforced concrete breakwater was constructed, in sections, in England. The large concrete blocks were called "Phoenix" caissons. Each mounted a 40mm gun for antiaircraft defense with space inside the Phoenix for the gun crew. There were different sized Phoenixes, with an average of 200 feet long, 58 feet wide, and 60 feet high. They weighed over 7,000 tons, but could be pumped dry and floated across the Channel. Once at Omaha they were to be put into place and flooded. They would serve as an

effective breakwater for the Loebnitz piers. To quiet the waters out to the sixty foot depths, where Liberty ships would anchor, a floating string of steel structures, called "Bombardons," was developed that reduced wave action by one third.

The components of the artificial harbor were towed across the Channel and the first elements arrived on D+1. Each section had a small contingent of Seabees aboard for the trip. Three 3,300 foot floating piers were planned for Omaha Beach. The Phoenix caissons were sunk in place, and the Bombardons moored further out. This artificial harbor was not expected to be permanent, but only to serve as a temporary solution (roughly 90 days) until a larger port could be captured and put into service. A second artificial harbor, "Mulberry B," was constructed in the British sector at Arromanches.

As an additional aid to provide a sheltered harbor for the unloading of ships, a breakwater of blockships was constructed by

sinking older vessels to one side of the planned harbor. At Omaha 14 ships were sunk in a line to the east of the Phoenix breakwater to form a "Gooseberry." These sacrificial ships, code named "Corncobs," were nearing the end of their useful life. The cornerstone of the Omaha blockships was the former British battleship *HMS Centurion*, which had been used as a target ship, then as a dummy battleship to fool the Italian Navy in the Mediterranean. There were two 200 foot openings in the line of blockships to allow smaller vessels to pass through.

On Utah Beach, where there were no plans to construct a floating pier, only ten block-ships were sunk offshore to provide shelter for the beaches. The blockships were unusual in that they were sunk so that the top decks remained above water at high tide. The antiaircraft guns mounted on the ships continued to be manned and the crews lived on board. Most of the construction of the American harbor and breakwaters in

Right.
The tide is out and a Rhino Ferry is stranded on the beach alongside a few LCTs. In the foreground is a group of sailors with the distinctive gray band on their helmets. The light bulldozer in the background has padding on its blade so it can be used to push landing craft back to sea.

Bottom.
This shot shows the use of a bulldozer in Rhino Ferry landing operations. Each ferry brought its own bulldozer to shore on its first trip. The dozer would then be used to pull the ferry as far ashore as possible to unload. If the tide was going out this could leave the ferry stranded on the beach, so the bulldozer was used to push it back out to sea for another load.

Normandy was performed by the Navy Seabees. Back in England they had constructed a number of different structures out of steel pontoons. The standard pontoon, the T6, was five by five by seven feet. They were watertight, and when bolted together could be formed into floating structures of almost any size. Earlier in the war an experimental floating airstrip had been constructed out of these pontoons. A slightly smaller pontoon section, the T7, could be used at the end of a structure for a tapered bow.

One of the first things the Seabees constructed out of pontoons were pontoon causeways. These were towed to Normandy in sections, set into place, then the pontoons flooded to create what would be known as the sunken causeways. At high tide the top surface was only a few feet under water. Vehicles could still travel from an LCT to shore even if they were slightly under water. Each causeway had clusters of four by twelve pontoon sections spaced at intervals on each side forming landing platforms. Known as "Blisters," these platforms allowed vessels to moor and discharge their cargo.

The 1006th CB Bn. assigned detachments to construct two sunken causeways at both Utah and Omaha Beaches. At Omaha the first causeway, 1,400 feet long, was put into operation on 11 June. From 11 to 17 June almost 8,700 personnel and 3,500 tons of cargo were unloaded over this causeway. The second, only 1,100 feet long, was finished on 16 June. Until traffic was halted by the storm the next day, 4,700 troops disembarked there. At Utah Beach a 2,200 foot long causeway was operational by 8 June. The second was finished on 14 June. Before the waves grew too high on the 19th, over 750 vessels of all types had used them to unload.

The Seabees used the same pontoon sections to construct self-propelled barges, called Rhino Ferries. These barges were six pontoons wide by 30 pontoons long (41 by 176 feet) and powered by two outboard engines.

They were named after the rhino due to their large size and slow lumbering speed. The 111th CB Bn. constructed a special Rhino Ferry equipped with a crane and storage on board for spare parts and workshops. This repair barge proved very useful in keeping the Rhino Ferries, as well as many other vessels, operational. The Americans had 32 Rhino Ferries at Normandy (and provided the British with another 32). At Omaha Beach the 111th CB Bn. provided the crews for the Rhino Ferries and the 81st CB Bn. manned the Utah Beach Rhinos.

Smaller versions were constructed to serve as glorified tugboats, and these were called Rhino Tugs. These were three by seven pontoons in size. In normal use each Rhino Ferry was assisted by a Rhino

Seabee Pontoon Equipment		
Name	crew	number of pontoons
Rhino Ferry	18	6x30
Rhino Tug	7	3x7
Causeway Tug	7	3x7
Warping Tug	8	3x7
Causeway	80	2x30
Causeway Blister	-	4x12
Repair Barge	40	6x40
Dry Dock	unknown	7x30

Left.
RHF12 heads to shore on what may be the morning of D-Day. Each Rhino Ferry carried one bulldozer on the first cross-Channel trip, which would then be used to pull the ferry closer to shore and push it back out to sea. It appears this Rhino is preparing to attach itself to the bow of an LST to take on a load of vehicles.

Right.
Each Rhino Ferry had two powerful outboard engines. Here the engines are being overhauled by the Seabee repair barge off Omaha Beach. Outboard engines were designed to be easily replaced, an advantage over the inboard engines used on the Rhino Tugs, which had to be repaired in place.

Tug adding the power of its two engines. The Rhino Tugs were given inboard engines, which did not prove as useful as the outboard engines on the Rhino Ferries. Eventually, the Seabees decided that the Rhino Tugs were a waste of material, and it would have been better to have built more standard Rhino Ferries instead of the tugs. In the construction of the pontoon equipment, including Rhinos, causeways, tugs, barges and pontoon floats, 22,806 pontoons were used.

The Seabees also constructed Rhino Warping Tugs and Rhino Causeway Tugs out of the pontoons. The Warping Tugs were three pontoons wide by seven long. They were designed to help pull landing craft off the beach after they had been unloaded. The Causeway Tugs were also three pontoons wide by seven long. These were used to pull landing craft away from the causeway blisters after unloading.

The concept behind the Rhino Ferries was that they had a very shallow draft. This meant they could move in close to the shore to unload. The Rhino Ferry was

Below and bottom.
The Warping Tugs were the smaller brother to the Rhino Tugs. They were designed specifically to assist landing craft retract from the beach.
(Courtesy Seabee Log)

designed so it could be attached, or married, to the ramp of an LST. The standard method for unloading LSTs was to marry a Rhino Ferry to the LST ramp, drive the vehicles onto the ferry, then bring them to shore. The stern of the LCT(6) could also be married to the LST ramp and many vehicles were also moved from LST to LCT, then to shore. Each Rhino Ferry could hold up to 18 trucks and jeeps, or ten Sherman tanks. It usually only took two Rhino Ferries to unload each LST. The Rhino Ferry would then pull up to shore and normally a bulldozer would be used to tow it as close to the beach as possible. Vehicles would unload over a ramp designed by, and named after, Lt. C.E. Olson. The Olson ramp was 14 feet wide by 20 feet long. It could support up to 60 tons. Shortly after his ramp was adopted, Lt. Olson was killed during the landing at Salerno.

For the first three days in Normandy most of the vehicles unloaded came ashore on Rhino Ferries. Then, with the Germans no longer able to shell the invasion beaches, the drying out of LSTs was tried. This technique proved successful and afterwards most of the LSTs unloaded their cargo by drying off, allowing the vehicles to drive right onto the beach. The Rhino Ferries took over unloading the cargo of Liberty ships. They became, in effect, floating docks which moved out to the ships and took on cargo, then moved to shore and unloaded on the beach. From 8 to 16 June the Rhino Ferries delivered 14,749 vehicles and 33,091 tons of cargo to the shore.

The crews of the Rhino Ferries had a tough job. They frequently worked up to 18-hour days exposed to the wind and spray without any shelter or warm food. Some of the crews became angry when they were refused even a cup of hot coffee by some Liberty ship crews. The ship *Bernard Carter* was assigned as a mother ship for the Rhino crews for a short while, but it was eventually needed for other

purposes and the Rhino crews had to fend for themselves.

An interesting aspect to the Seabees was that prior to the Normandy invasion there were no signalmen in the standard CB Bn. organization. The ability to read semaphore flags and Morse code on blinker lights was considered important to the crews of the various ferries and tugs. A special school was set up in England that provided a crash course in such matters to 60 Seabees from the 81st and 111th CB Bns.

All of the Seabee battalions operating in Normandy were part of the 25th CB Regiment. The 81st and 111th manned the Rhino Ferries. The 108th CB Bn. was in charge of construction and maintenance of the Loebnitz pierheads and floating roadways. The 146th CB Bn. was assigned the task of constructing and manning a POL (Petrol, Oil, Lubricants) barge. Three lines would be run to shore: a six inch diesel fuel line, a four inch gasoline line, and a four inch water line. The barge would be anchored at the two fathom line and provide refuelling capacities for ships in the area.

The Seabees wore the same uniforms as the rest of the U.S. Navy. The only distinguishing mark on their dress uniforms was a small embroidered insignia (called a "strike") worn on the left sleeve. On the blue dress uniform the strike was the letters "CB" embroidered in white. The letters were dark blue for wear on the dress white uniform. It was not until October 1944 that a shoulder patch was authorized with the famous fighting bee insignia.

Navy Seabees were issued standard Navy work uniforms, but as they spent time in Normandy, could be seen wearing more and more items obtained from the Army. This Rhino Ferry crewman wears a Navy deck jacket over impregnated HBT Army coveralls. Rubber overshoes keep his feet dry while helping vehicles disembark from his craft. Leather work gloves and a wool watch cap were necessary in the cold offshore breezes. In 1944 the U.S. Navy was in the midst of changing many of its foul weather uniforms from the early dark blue color to olive drab.

273

Seabee enlisted men would normally wear the standard Navy work uniform of dungarees (denim trousers) and the light blue chambray shirt. Officers had a khaki working uniform. The Seabees were issued Army HBT coveralls impregnated against gas for the invasion. However, due to the cold, wet work performed by the men, most Seabees were commonly seen wearing a wide selection of Navy foul weather and rubberized garments. Steel helmets were mandatory on the beaches to protect against falling flak, and the Seabees painted the gray band around their helmets. Many also painted "USN" on the front and back of their outer jacket, as required by a last minute order.

Some Seabees added artwork to their uniforms, in particular the fighting bee logo. It should be pointed out that this was not the norm and many uniforms

Above.
Shermans from the 66th Armored Regiment, 2nd Armored Division, disembark from a Rhino Ferry. Each ferry could carry ten of these tanks. The 2nd Armored was the first full Armored Division to land in Normandy. The main elements came ashore starting on D+3.

U.S. Navy Construction Battalions in Normandy

13th CB Regt. in charge of all CB operations in England

25th CB Regt.
28th CB Bn- Utah RHF crews
5 Off 270 EM
69th CB Bn- split in detachments to support other Bns.
81st CB Bn Utah RHF Crews, beach camp and shore admin
108th CB Bn Omaha- Phoenix

and Whales 19 off, 315 EM
111th CB Bn Omaha RHF, beach camp and shore admin.
6 off, 245 EM
114th CB Bn arrived August 1944
146th CB Bn. POL Barge, 5 off 97 EM
1006th CB Bn. Utah and Omaha sunken causeways
30th Special Bn.

Seabee Rhino Ferry units

(LST assigned for cross-Channel tow)

Omaha Beach
Group 1
Division 1
RHF 1 (LST314), 2 (LST357), 3 (LST376) , 4 (LST374) , 5 (LST375)
Division 2
RHF 6 (LST 6), 7 (LST316), 8 (LST310), 9 (LST 315), 10 (LST317)

Group 2
Division 3
RHF 11(LST502), 12 (LST51), 13 (LST133), 14 (LST34),

15(LST285)
Division 4
RHF 16(LST286), 17 (LST157), 18 (LST347), 19 (LST350), 20 (LST75)

Utah Beach
Group 3
Division 5
RHF 21 (LST282), 22 (LST230), 23 (LST48), 24 (LST47), 25 (LST281)
Division 6
RHF 25 (LST281), 26 (LST311), 27 (LST346), 28 (LST371)
Division 7
RHF 29 (LST283), 30 (LST49) , 31 (LST501)

Rhino Ferry crew
1 Officer in Charge
1 Boatswain (CPO)
2 Coxswains
1 Shipfitter
1 Motor Mechanic
1 Signalman
1 Corpsman
8 Deckhands
1 Bulldozer Operator
1 Bulldozer Attendant

Rhino Tug crew
1 Boatswain (CPO)
2 Coxswains
1 Signalman
3 Deckhands

Opposite page, top.
The 111th CB Bn. constructed a special repair barge from pontoon sections. The name "*USS Can-do*" has been painted on a storage unit. The deck of the barge is so filled with equipment that a jeep has been put on top of the unit for the cross-Channel trip.

Opposite page, right.
Rhino Ferry number 14 brings a load of trucks and personnel ashore. The slope of the T-7 pontoon section is clearly visible. Bulldozers are available to pull stuck vehicles ashore and will be used to push the Rhino Ferry off the beach when unloading is finished.

Left.
Two five-ton cranes were placed aboard the CB repair barge, which proved invaluable in working off the invasion beaches. As it turned out, the beaches were so clogged with incoming men and supplies there would have been little room to spare for this repair equipment. The Repair Barge was specifically designed for working on Seabee pontoon equipment and replacing motors in the Rhino Ferries.

Cargo handled by Rhino Ferries over Omaha and Utah Beaches		
	Vehicles	**Bulk Cargo**
6 June to 21 October	94,495	422,195 tons
Peak day during invasion period	2,382	8,084 tons
Peak day during follow-up period	1,144	2,857 tons
Average per day for period operation of beaches (136 days)	695	3,100 tons

found today with these insignia were made after the war. As time passed in Normandy, it is assumed that the Seabees adopted more and more articles of Army clothing because it was much easier to obtain in the beachhead.

The storm of 20 June

On the afternoon of 19 June 1944 the wind started to pick up off the coast of France. By nightfall it was clear a storm was on the way. For the next three days the invasion area was subject to near gale force winds. The winds averaged 30 knots and waves were eight to ten feet high on the beach.

The flow of supplies dropped to almost nothing. The smaller vessels were lucky just to keep from get-

Above, left.
In this sequence of photographs we can observe a Rhino Ferry attaching, or marrying, to the LST 357. The equipment to attach a ferry to an LST was designed to be used in seas with no greater than three foot waves, but off Normandy the crews had to deal with up to six foot waves.

Left.
A Rhino Ferry has "married" to the LST 357, and has started to take on a load of vehicles for the trip to shore. The pattern of the pontoon sections is visible on the deck of the ferry.

Below, left.
The Rhino Ferry has started to fill up with trucks. The load has to be spread out evenly to each side to keep the weight properly distributed.

Below.
A five-ton crane travels from the LST onto the Rhino Ferry. Note the rack containing extra gasoline cans. There is some evidence to indicate that this is the crane that lifted the surviving 111th F.A. Bn. 105mm howitzer from a sinking Dukw.

Opposite page, bottom.
The view from the top of the trucks looking toward Omaha Beach. Smoke is rising from the shore and LCTs can be seen searching for a place to land.

ting swamped or dashed ashore. When the skies cleared a large number of small boats had been destroyed and many more larger vessels were sunk or damaged. The main problem was that supplies of ammunition, food and fuel for the combat troops fighting inland were now days behind schedule. The American troops were running short of items such as mortar shells and artillery ammunition. Had the storm lasted any longer the stocks might have dwindled low enough to have posed a serious threat to the success of the invasion.

To get material to the front lines quickly, artillery shells were flown into France on whatever aircraft were available. Transport ships that had been grounded in the storm were cut open and unloaded through their hulls. One such ship had been flooded, so the fire fighting unit of an ESB put its pumps to work emptying the compartment so it could be unloaded. The crew soon discovered corpses aboard and the ESB graves registration unit was called in to take care of the bodies before the unloading could commence.

For most of the men stationed on shore it meant clearing the beaches of new debris, and rebuilding what they had just completed. A special 475-ton floating dry dock that had just been brought over from England had been thrown ashore and ruined. The sunken causeways were damaged and needed extensive repairs. The CBs refloated them, and then re-sank them in better locations. The worst loss was the artificial harbor at

Above.
The LCT195 lands a group of soldiers onto a sunken causeway. The standard procedure was for the LCT to approach a Blister at a 45° angle, then lower the ramp and discharge the passengers. A Causeway Tug, made from pontoon sections, would be available to pull the LCT off the Blister if the tide was going out.
(Courtesy Seabee Log)

Omaha. The British "Mulberry B" at Arromanches had been spared the worst of the storm, but "Mulberry A" was almost totally destroyed. Many thin-walled Phoenix caissons had collapsed under the force of the storm. A number of Gooseberry blockships had shifted out of position or sunk further into the sea bed. The repair barge and a few LCTs had been forced into the Loebnitz piers, twisting them out of shape.

Vessels driven on the beaches in the 20 June Storm			
Utah Beach		**Omaha Beach**	
LCI	1	LST	2
LCT	45	LCT	78
LCVP	45	LCI	12
Rhino Ferry	10	LCF	1
Rhino Tug	11	LCM	83
LCF	3	Rhino Ferry	19
LCM	64	Rhino Tug	22
LBV	25	Rhino Repair Barge	1
POL Barge	1	LCVP	39
Liberty Ships	5	Liberty Ship	3
		LBV	17
		LSC	2
		POL Barge	1
		Repair Barge	1
		Food Barge	1

It was decided to not repair "Mulberry A," but to use the surviving material to rebuild "Mulberry B." Additional blockships and Phoenix caissons would be sunk in position to create a more sheltered area at Omaha for unloading. Most of the Rhino Ferries were damaged in the storm and it would be a few days before they were back in operation. What saved the Allies' supply line was that the amphibious Dukw companies had been able to park their vehicles ashore, out of the storm's fury. For the next few days the Dukws provided the majority of cargo brought ashore.

The question as to how severe the storm of 20 June really was has come under some discussion. Popular books claim that it was the worst storm on the Normandy coast in 40 to 80 years. Some of the local population feel that it was just an average storm, and that the claims of severity were made to justify the amount of damage to the small boats and Mulberry Harbor. This question will remain unanswered until someone is able to perform the meteorological research needed to finally confirm, or deny, the force of the storm.

The Amphibian Truck Companies

The after-action report of the 1st ESB states "*The Dukw is worth its weight in gold in an assault landing such as Neptune. No self-respecting invasion*

Above.
The floating piers were heavily damaged in the storm of 20 June. A number of landing craft, including five LCTs, were driven by the force of the storm into the pier on the right. With not enough spare parts in England to repair them, the American floating piers were taken apart and whatever sections still usable transferred to the British artificial harbor at Arromanches.

Left.
The Seabees worked with the Beach Battalion repair sections to keep ships and landing craft operating. This dozer has a special attachment so it can transport LCVPs to repair shops on the shore.

Previous page, top.
This view of the floating road shows how the metal sections twisted under the force of the craft being rammed into it. A key factor in the decision to scrap these piers was that the Beetles, the floats for the pier, were made of reinforced concrete which had a tendency to crack. In the background can be seen the vertical columns the Loebnitz pierhead floated up and down on in the tides.

Right.
This Dukw is from one of the Amphibian Truck Companies operated by black soldiers, possibly the 463rd Amphibious Truck Company. Normal crew for a Dukw was the driver and a "swamper" attached from a QM Service Company. The swamper's duties were to moor, cast off, and to guide the Dukw, allowing the driver to concentrate on operating the vehicle.

should be without them."

With the Mulberry harbor destroyed, the sunken causeways damaged, the beaches jammed with debris, and Cherbourg still in German hands, a unique vehicle took on great importance. The Dukw (pronounced "duck") was basically a two and a half ton truck that could float. A special drive train and single propeller gave the Dukw a speed of 6 mph in water. The term Dukw came from the production code assigned to this GMC product. "D" indicated the year of design (1942), "U" meant Utility, "K" four wheel drive, and "W" indicated two rear-driving axles.

Dukws were used on D-Day to carry ashore the guns of the assault regiment's cannon company and the 105mm howitzers of the support artillery battalion. In normal practice the Dukw could carry a cargo of two to three tons. Fully loaded, however, there was little freeboard and it was susceptible to swamping in rough seas. Most of the Dukws carrying artillery pieces on D-Day sank either from being

Above.
Spare parts for the Dukws were hard to come by. The constant use of the vehicles caused many components to wear out more rapidly than expected. Here a member of the 463rd Amphibious Truck Company makes a replacement bearing for a Dukw propeller shaft out of wood. The insignia on his helmet liner is cruder than seen in other units. This painting was done on a company or battalion basis, thus it could have been done in many different ways.

Left.
The standard method of loading a Dukw was to put the cargo into a net, then lower it down into the hull of the Dukw. The censor has tried to block out the name of this coastal freighter, but it is the *Kyle Queen.*

overloaded or from engine failure. If the Dukws engine should stop working for any reason, the bilge pumps also stopped and the Dukw would start to take on water.

A major design problem was that it was difficult to refuel the Dukw at sea without allowing some sea water to get into the gas tank. This would cause the engine to stop and possibly, the Dukw to sink. This caused many problems on D-Day when there was no room on shore for any more vehicles. Many Dukws circled in the water offshore until they either swamped or ran out of gas.

For the initial cross-Channel trip, the Dukws were

Left.
Another field expedient used by the 463rd Amphibious Truck Company was this homemade rudder assembly. Many rudders and propellers were damaged by the wreckage found on both beaches. Unable to get replacements, the 463rd was forced to make their own.

Below.
The Dukw was essentially a six wheeled, two and half ton truck inside a flotation hull. Here, "Darling Lou" heads out to a Liberty ship to pick up a load of cargo. Four Navy sailors, note the painted gray band on their helmets, accompany the driver.

Below.
The Dukw (pronounced "duck") was a 2 1/2 ton truck mounted in a flotation hull. The cargo compartment holds either 25 men or a 5,000 pound payload. It is able to travel at 45 m.p.h. on land, or 6 m.p.h. in the water.
(Computer graphics by C. Camilotte, © Histoire & Collections 1998)

Bottom.
"Jesse James" was the name given to this Dukw from the 462nd Amphibian Truck Company, part of the 1st Engineer Special Brigade. A load of boxes inside cargo nets can be seen heaped inside. In standard weather a Dukw would haul three cargo nets worth per trip, or roughly two tons. Both crewmen have the full 1st ESB arc painted on their helmets.

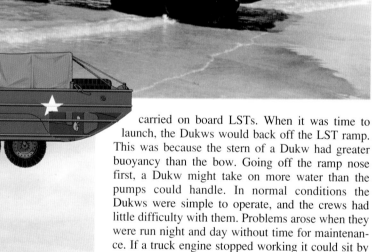

carried on board LSTs. When it was time to launch, the Dukws would back off the LST ramp. This was because the stern of a Dukw had greater buoyancy than the bow. Going off the ramp nose first, a Dukw might take on more water than the pumps could handle. In normal conditions the Dukws were simple to operate, and the crews had little difficulty with them. Problems arose when they were run night and day without time for maintenance. If a truck engine stopped working it could sit by the side of the road. If a Dukw engine stopped, the Dukw would soon fill with water and sink unless

Dukw turnaround times at Utah Beach		
	Coaster	Liberty Ship
Distance offshore in miles	1/2	3
Distance, shore to transfer point	1/2	1/2
Average speed in water	3 mph	3 mph
Average speed on land	6 mph	6 mph
Loading time in minutes	10	15
Unloading time in minutes	10	10
Travel time in minutes	30	130
Theoretical turnaround time	50	155

immediately towed to shore. Many of the ships the Dukws were unloading were miles out to sea, so it was not always possible to save a sinking Dukw.

Dukws were organized into Amphibian Truck Companies (see table on page 251). Each had 48 Dukws, divided into two platoons. One problem with the organization of a Dukw company was that no provisions had been made for relief drivers. In practice the units tried to rotate shifts every twelve hours, but at times men were asked to work nonstop to get vital cargo ashore, or else the Dukws had to sit idle while the drivers slept.

Dukws were normally used to unload cargo from coastal freighters or Liberty ships. These were unable to come onto the shore and dry out, or pull up to the causeway or floating pier. A Dukw would pull up alongside a freighter and two or three nets full of cargo would be lowered by crane into it. The Dukw would head to shore, drive up onto land, and bring the cargo directly to a supply dump. This technique skipped the step of moving the cargo from Dukw to truck and saved time.

As the supply dumps moved further inland, a new technique was used to save wear on the Dukws and allow them more trips offshore. A loaded Dukw

Above, right and below.
Launching a Dukw from the ramp of an LST was not an easy task. The Dukw had more flotation in the stern, so the driver had to back the Dukw down the ramp into the water. As soon as he felt the propeller bite into the water, he would use that force to pull the Dukw back off the ramp. These are Dukws from the 462nd Amphibious Truck Company practicing in England.

would pull up to a transit station. A crane would lift the cargo nets out of the Dukw and hold them suspended. Then the Dukw would leave and an empty truck would pull up in its place. The nets and cargo would be lowered into the truck, which would then head off to the inland supply dump.

The rule of thumb was that Dukws should not travel to supply dumps more than a mile inland. Every Dukw had landed with six cargo nets aboard and Dukw crews were careful to always exchange full loads for empty nets. These nets were in constant use and shortages developed. Until replacement nets were obtained it became another bottleneck in getting cargo ashore.

The Dukw was essential to the Normandy invasion. Without these vehicles the flow of cargo would have dried up after the storm, causing tremendous shortages for the combat troops. From June through

November 1944 most of the Dukws attached to the ESBs had travelled 75,000 miles bringing supplies ashore. However, the Dukws did not perform this function all by themselves. It took a group of skilled drivers, and even more skilled mechanics, to keep these vehicles in operating condition.

The minor ports

Allied planners had examined every mile of coastline for places they could use to bring materials ashore. A few coastal towns could be used to unload small transports. These minor ports were to be the responsibility of the 11th Port.

The 1055th Port Construction and Repair Group, along with the 342nd Engineer General Service Regiment, were given the assignment of preparing the minor ports. Isigny was captured on 10 June. To the Americans' delight, the Germans had done very little damage to it. The first coastal freighter arrived on 24 June with 486 tons of supplies. For the rest of

Above.

"Lady Leighton," a Dukw from the 479th Amphibian Truck Company, unloads a cargo of gasoline cans at a cargo transfer point. Once the supply dumps were moved more than one mile inland, it was more practical to transfer the cargo to a normal truck for the journey inland.

Below.

This diver prepares to check one of the Minor Ports for possible booby traps. Men from an ESB operate the hand powered air pump to provide a steady supply of oxygen to the diver. In the foreground is a Mauser rifle- possibly a souvenir picked up by one of the men.

the summer and fall the average daily rate for Isigny would be 740 tons.

The Transportation Corps had expected to have the minor port of Grandcamp opened by 20 June. When the town was liberated on 9 June it was discovered that the waterfront was in bad shape. Five small vessels had been sunk in the basin by Allied air attacks and the Germans had sunk two ships across the Channel. The worst news was the discovery that the channel had not been dredged in six years. Instead of the expected eight foot depth it was only four and a half feet deep. The crews worked hard and had the port ready by 17 June. No ships arrived until 23 June when the Dutch coaster *June*, that was heading to Isigny, accidentally ended up in Grandcamp. There was only a skeleton crew of men from the 11th Port available, but these clerks and officers enlisted the aid of the local population and unloaded 158 tons of cargo.

Fifty ton landing barges were later used to bring cargo into Grandcamp. Although it was planned to move 500 tons per day through this area, the average was closer to 675 tons a day. The minor port of Saint-Vaast was also cleared and manned by troops from the 11th Port. Later on, the 4th Port would take over the minor ports of Saint-Malo, Barfleur, and Granville. The delay in capturing and opening Cherbourg put added strain on the minor ports and beaches. The small detachments operating these minor ports may have only dealt with a fraction of the cargo brought in over Omaha and Utah, but the tonnage added up and helped to keep the flow of supplies moving.

Aviation Engineers

An important aspect of the invasion was to provide airfields in France as soon as possible. These airfields would be used to bring in vital supplies and evacuate seriously wounded men that might not survive a voyage back across the Channel. Due to the special demands in building airfields, the Army had developed specialized Aviation Engineer Battalions for this function.

Aviation Engineers were trained not only to construct airfields, but also to repair damaged enemy airfields and restore them to operation. These units had the heavy equipment necessary to repair bombed runways, or grade and pack down fields to construct

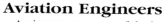

new ones. Initially the runways were surfaced with either Square Mesh Track (rolls of wide wire mesh) or Pierced Steel Planking sometimes referred to as Marston Matting (strips of interlocking metal with holes for drainage and traction).

There were also specialized units of Aviation Engineers who had been trained to land in cargo planes or by glider. These airborne units had smaller and lighter equipment and could be sent behind enemy lines, following paratroops, to construct emergency airfields. Although a few Airborne Aviation Engineer units did later serve in Normandy, they did not perform any such special missions and were not landed by aircraft.

One company from each of the two Aviation Engineer Bns. were scheduled to land on either Utah and Omaha Beach on D-Day. These companies were to construct an emergency landing strip just behind each beach. These strips would give damaged Allied aircraft a place to safely land. This would not only

Above, center.
The caption for this photograph claims this is the first P-38 to land at the Saint-Laurent airstrip. The light observation aircraft at right bears the codes of the 2nd Infantry Division.

save the lives of a few pilots, but preserve their aircraft as well.

On D+1 more elements of the Aviation Engineers were to come ashore and start construction of full-fledged airfields. Once completed they would provide a place for aircraft to land and refuel. As the Allied Armies moved inland, the aviation engineers would continue to move forward constructing, or repairing, airfields close behind the front lines. This

Above.
Pierced Steel Planking, otherwise known as Marston matting, was used to construct runways quickly. The lengths of metal planking were joined by clips and the engineer crews could assemble them rapidly. The holes allowed for drainage and traction. Grass growing underneath would keep dust down in dry areas.

Left.
Aviation Engineers lay down square mesh track for the runway at A-6, just outside Sainte-Mère Eglise. The men wear standard HBT fatigues for this hot, dirty work. Before the track could be laid down the area had to be carefully graded, with any low spots filled in. Note the aircraft with invasion stripes against the hedgerow at far left.

Aviation Engineer Battalions in Normandy		
	Omaha	**Utah**
D-Day	1 Co of 834th aviation	1 co 819th
+1	834th remainder	-
+1	820th	-
+2	816th	-
+3	-	819th remainder
+5	-	826th
+12	-	850th

units had started to drain the inundated area, but the planned landing strip location was still too wet to begin construction. The men of the 819th scouted around and found another location where they constructed a sod landing strip (LS-1) at Pouppeville. Three days later they finished another landing strip at Beuzeville just outside Sainte-Mère Eglise.

On Omaha Beach one company of the 834th Aviation Eng. Bn. came ashore and started construction of an airfield at Saint-Laurent-sur-Mer

way aircraft supporting the ground troops would have less distance to travel before getting to their targets.

The Emergency Landing Strips first constructed would be developed into "Refuelling and Rearming Strips." Then dispersal facilities were added to make it an "Advanced Landing Ground." If the facilities continued to be improved and the runways lengthened, it was considered an "Airfield." Eventually the runways would be given a hard surface so it could be considered an "All-weather Airfield" that could be used in wet weather.

The advance company of the 819th Aviation Eng. Bn. landed on Utah Beach about 2100 hrs on D-Day. They moved inland to start construction of an emergency landing strip just behind Utah Beach. However, the planned location for the strip had been flooded by the Germans. On D+2 other engineer

Above.
Unfortunately the censor has been hard at work blocking out the unit information on this truck's bumper. Aviation Engineer units had a large amount of heavy equipment to help them construct airstrips. This truck has a boom mounted in front to help move rolls of SMT to the runway area.

Inset.
The 9th Air Force Engineers were not authorized this patch until after the invasion of Normandy.

between the D-3 and E-3 exits. They were interrupted in their work by having to divert bulldozers to dig defensive positions to help defend against the expected German counterattack.

This emergency landing strip was 3,400 feet long and 120 feet wide. It was opened to light observation aircraft on the afternoon of D+2. It was ready to handle larger aircraft on the evening of D+3. Another airstrip was constructed afterwards at Saint-Pierre-du-Mont. A confusing aspect of these two airfields near Omaha Beach is that originally the strip at Saint-Laurent was named "A-1." Later on it was renamed "A–21" and

ENGINEER AVIATION BATTALION

```
        II
      [ E ]
        |
    ┌───┴───────────┐
    I               I
[Headquarters   ┌───┴───┐
and HQ Co.]     I       I
            [Engineer Aviation
14 officers      Company]
226 EM
            5 officers
            183 EM
```

- 1-air compressor truck-mounted
- 3- four-wheel tandem dolly
- 1-12-foot grader, motorized
- 1-asphalt kettle trailer
- 1- lubricator trailer
- 1- steam roller
- 2- roadscraper
- 3- low bed semi trailer
- 3- Bulldozer
- 1- M16 half-track
- 4- Jeep
- 4- 1/4-ton trailer
- 2 -water trailer
- 4 -1-ton trailer
- 3- 3/4 ton truck
- 2- 2 1/2 ton truck
- 9 -2 1/2 ton dump truck
- 3- 4-ton dump truck

One of the more unusual patches worn on D-Day was this red bomb. Patterned after the British insignia, it was worn on the left sleeve by members of unexploded ordnance disposal units. These men were supposed to disarm booby traps left behind by the Germans. However, it seems that most of their duties in Normandy were dealing with unexploded Allied munitions from the pre-invasion bombardment.

The operator of this grader is protected by a fellow engineer who keeps an eye out for German snipers. The invasion had left many German stragglers in the area behind the beaches. They knew that a few shots fired at equipment operators could slow down, or stop, the progress of a vital project such as this airfield.

Previous page, right.
Clips were used to hold rolls of Square Mesh Track (SMT) together. One of the benefits to using this open mesh material was that grass could easily grow underneath. This helped keep dust down, and provided added camouflage to the runway.

the Saint-Pierre-du-Mont strip became "A-1." It seems the Saint-Laurent airstrip should have originally been called an "ELS" (Emergency Landing Strip) the same as the Utah Beach landing strip (ELS-1). Possibly for publicity reasons it was erroneously referred to as A–1, which would have stood for the first American airfield on the Continent. Numerous photographs were taken of the Saint-Laurent landing strip, which was erroneously acclaimed as the first American airfield in France.

Below.
An American NCO checks the POW tag of a German soldier before sending him onto a landing craft to be taken back to England. 65,000 POWs were evacuated over Utah Beach in the five months it operated.

Left and right.
German POWs are brought down the E-1 exit on Omaha Beach for evacuation. Behind them can be seen MPs from one of the ESBs. The Provisional ESB Group Command Post is visible in the pillbox behind the MPs. Note how a large number of foxholes have been dug into the side of the bluff.

Below.
On board an LST, this Military Police Lieutenant has his picture taken with a member of the German Air Force. Many of the first prisoners captured on Utah Beach were part of a Luftwaffe antiaircraft unit. This officer has pinned his MP armband to his sleeve with a Lieutenant's bar.

The first American Air Force unit to permanently move to Normandy was the 397th Fighter Squadron, which landed at the Cardonville Airfield (A-3) on 16 June. They were followed by the 366th Fighter Squadron which took over Saint-Pierre-du-Mont (A–1) on 17 June. By the end of June there were six completed airfields in the American sector and four more that were almost finished. The work of the Aviation Engineers proved itself after the storm of 20 June. The airfields were used to bring in vitally needed supplies and ammunition while the beaches were clogged with debris and damaged craft.

Conclusion

The invasion of Normandy could not have succeeded without many of the supporting units that followed the assault troops ashore. The war for the beaches was not won when the infantry pushed the Germans back inland. It was won only when the first major port in France was operational, and a steady stream of supplies was assured. Without a strong logistical network supporting the invasion, the sacrifice of the combat troops might well have been in vain.

Many of these supporting troops took part in combat on D-Day. On the following days they were hounded by German snipers and stragglers. They continued to perform to the best of their ability, and in true American style continued to streamline and improvise their methods until they were able to land more cargo across the beaches than had originally been planned for the artificial harbor.

Above.
A crowd has turned out to see this group of German POWs escorted off the LST 47 onto English soil. The guards are armed with Garands and Thompson submachine guns. Specific LSTs were designated as hospital ships, and others as POW ships, for the return trip to England.

Left.
On the left a soldier guards these POWs with a shotgun. Shotguns were issued to the MPs only for guard duty and were not to be used as an everyday weapon. In the rear a group of medics are on hand in case any of the prisoners are in need of medical attention.

Acknowledgments

There are an enormous number of people I'd like to thank for their assistance in doing this book. I'm sure I've forgotten someone. I apologize, but you know who you are and I thank you.

A special thank you to the principal veterans that assisted me:

William Ashly 6th ESB
John Barnes 29th Div
Harold Baumgarten 29th Div
Sid Berger 1st ESB
Sidney Bingham 29th Div
George Bradbury 29th Div
Francis Bradley 4th Div
Felix Branham 29th Div
August Bruno 29th Div
James Burke 299th Eng. C. Bn.
Bill Callahan 29th Rangers
Gerald Carver USS Charles Carroll
Fred Corey 4th Div
Gene Dance 29th Rangers
Joe Drago 29th Div
Noel Dube 29th Div
Ed Dyer LST-266
Hugh Foster 4th Div
Bob Garcia 29th Div
Sims Gauthier LCC-60
Joe Geary 6th NBB
Herbert Goodrick 6th NBB
Bob Guigere 6th NBB
Walter Hedlund 29th Rangers
Arthur Hill 146th Eng. C. Bn.
Roy Holmes 146th Eng. C. Bn.
Charles Hurlburt 299th Eng. C. Bn.
Nathan Irwin NCDU
George Itzel 147th 6th ESB
Vincent Kamolz 1st Div
Lamar Keith 146th Eng. C. Bn.
James Knight 299th Eng. C. Bn.
Vincent Kordak 6th NBB

Ed Long 348th ECB
Ernest Lusebrink 29th Div
Paul Malachowski 29th Div
Joe Manning 146th Eng C. Bn.
Ed Marriot 6th NBB
Albert Mazza 4th Div
Ed McNabb 29th Rangers
Jack Metternich USS Charles Carroll
Don Miller 299th Eng. C. Bn.
Robert Miller 29th Div
Ray Nance 29th Div
Doc Parker 6th NBB
Mug Pawless 146th Eng C. Bn.
John Pawley USMC
John Perry 5th Rangers
Steven Pikta 146th Eng C. Bn.
Tom Poe USS Charles Carroll
John Polniak 29th Div
Ed Regan 29th Div
Dan Relihan 29th Div
Dean Rockwell LCT-535
Don Van Roosen 29th Div
Wesley Ross 146th Eng C. Bn.
Sidney Salamon 2nd Rangers
Julius Shoulars 7th NBB
George Siracusano USS President Warfield
George Smith 112th Eng. C. Bn.
John Sullivan 29th Div
Frank Thompson 7th NBB
Howard Vander Beek LCC-60
Albert Velleco 29th Div
Wally Weyant 1st Div
Doc Weidner 1st Div
Jack Womer 29th Rangers
Russell Woodhill 5th Rangers

Also involved in the production of all color reconstructions for this book were the following French and Belgian reenactors and collectors: A.S. Batens, Régis Macquart, Philippe Ferbert, Alain Marchal, André Ivanof, Philippe Bellengier, Philippe Lebreuilly, André Rakoto, Jean-Pierre Rigot, Jean-Michel Besson, Sébastien Tessier, Erick Lacou, Paul Bennardo, Gilles Goria, Fabrice Letribot, Stéphane Topsent, Daniel Cabrol, Olivier Conte, L. Tromski, Yves Tannière, Olivier Bourdeaux, Gilles Demarets, Jean-Jacques Panpalonne, Bruno Alberti, Laurent Pradier and Laurent Rougé; as well as Christophe Deschodt (Musée de la Seconde Guerre Mondiale, Ambleteuse), Pierre Besnard (Le Poilu shop, Paris), Patrick Lesieur, Jean Bouchery and Frédéric Finel (Overlord shop, Paris).

A number of other people were instrumental in helping me get this book done. Among them are: Steve West and the 29th Historical Association, Carl Isley Jr., Jean-Yves Nasse, Ken Davey, Kim Jeter, Dave Powers, and Marcel Leveel, Jonathan Lewis, Rory Aylward, Richard Dzialo (Preserve History), Bob Adams (B&L Collectables), Steve Caroly of the CB Journal. The staff at militaria.com, Jon Strymish, Bob Phillips and the entire crew at the New England Mobile Book Fair: the best bookstore in New England.

Joe Balkoski, author of one of the best books on Omaha Beach (Beyond the beachhead), was of enormous help with the details of that landing.

I also need to thank my family, who put up with the book writing process. I especially need to thank my editor Philippe Charbonnier for bringing order out of chaos.

If anyone wishes to provide further information on any of these units, or point out where I may have gone astray, please feel free to contact me at: P.O. Box 2925, Framingham, MA. 01703, USA.

Jonathan Gawne

SA au capital de 1 200 000 F
5, avenue de la République
F-75541 Paris Cédex 11
France
Telephone : 01 40 21 18 20
Fax : 01 47 00 51 11
e-mail: milmag@histecoll.com

This book has been designed, typed, laid-out and processed by Histoire & Collections, entirely on integrated computer equipment.
Supervision and lay-out : Philippe Charbonnier.
Computer graphics by Christophe Camilotte and Morgan Gillard, color photography by J. Gawne and P. Charbonnier, cover design by Patrick Lesieur, U.S. National Archives pictures, reenacted picture at top of cover by A.S. Batens.
Printed in Spain, European Union, by Elkar,
10 December 1999